Rome and
the Enemy

The publisher gratefully acknowledges the generous contribution to this book provided by the General Endowment Fund of the Associates of the University of California Press.

Rome and the Enemy

Imperial Strategy in the Principate

Susan P. Mattern

UNIVERSITY OF CALIFORNIA PRESS

Berkeley / Los Angeles / London

University of California Press
Berkeley and Los Angeles, California

University of California Press, Ltd.
London, England

© 1999 by
The Regents of the University of California

Library of Congress Cataloging-in-Publication Data

Mattern, Susan P.
    Rome and the enemy : imperial strategy in the principate /
by Susan P. Mattern.
        p.   cm.
    Includes bibliographical references and index.
    ISBN 0-520-21166-9 (alk. paper)
        1. Rome—History—Empire, 30 B.C.–284 A.D.—Historiography.
    2. Rome—History, Military—30 B.C.–476 A.D. 3. Rome—Military
    policy. 4. Rome—Foreign relations—30 B.C.–284 A.D. I. Title.
    DG271.M18   1999
    937'.07—DC21   98-40630
                                                                CIP

Manufactured in the United States of America

9 8 7 6 5 4 3 2 1

The paper used in this publication meets the minimum requirements
of ANSI/NISO Z39.48-1992 (R 1997) (*Permanence of Paper*). ⊗

*To my parents, Nancy and Peter,
and my sisters, Emily and Elizabeth*

Contents

LIST OF MAPS AND ILLUSTRATIONS   IX

PREFACE   XI

NOTE ON ABBREVIATIONS   XV

ROMAN EMPERORS, 31 B.C.–A.D. 238   XVII

CHAPTER 1   Introduction: The Decision-Making Elite   1

CHAPTER 2   The Image of the World   24

CHAPTER 3   Strategy   81

CHAPTER 4   Income and Expenditure   123

CHAPTER 5   Values   162

EPILOGUE   Carthage Must Be Destroyed   211

REFERENCES   223

INDEX   245

Maps and Illustrations

MAP OF THE ROMAN EMPIRE
IN THE SECOND CENTURY A.D.   XX

FIGURE 1   The *Peutinger Table;* routes east of the Caspian   42

FIGURE 2   The world according to Strabo   45

FIGURE 3   *Mappamundi* from a manuscript of Lucan   48

FIGURE 4   The world according to Agrippa   50

FIGURE 5   The world according to Ptolemy   62

Preface

It is the understandable tendency of the modern student of Roman history to seek there some sort of lesson or practical example. After all, the Romans achieved immense success in certain areas—war, empire building. How did they accomplish these things, we ask? And it is perhaps our uniquely modern tendency to seek the answer to this question not in Roman valor or fortune, as the ancients did, but in the Roman mind; to attribute their success to some superior insight or expertise, some science of war or administration. We would like to see expert strategists tracing defensible borders and buffer zones on the well-plotted topography of Europe and Asia; evaluating the political and military strengths and weaknesses of their enemies; collecting, tracking, and allocating financial resources to meet their strategic goals.

The Roman mind is, in fact, precisely what this study seeks to explore. It asks the question, What were the reasons behind the Roman leadership's most important decisions about foreign war and peace? It has been argued in recent years that the image of the Romans as expert military strategists *in the modern sense* is illusory, and in general that conclusion is supported in this work. But what, then, were the motivations governing Roman foreign relations? What were the rules of the game at which they were so successful, and what ultimately determined the limits of that success?

The chronological boundaries of this study are roughly the battle of Actium, in 31 B.C., and the fall of Severus Alexander in 235. In choosing them, I do not mean to suggest that the conclusions of this study are

not applicable to other time periods; in fact, some of the most characteristic aspects of Roman foreign relations were also the most traditional
and enduring. Rather, these limits are convenient because the system set
up by Augustus—a certain arrangement of provinces and armies, and
the taxation system that paid for them—remained substantially unchanged throughout the centuries under discussion here, and the literary evidence required is especially abundant. After 235, however, the literary sources almost completely disappear and the Augustan system
itself largely ceased to function. The loss of literary sources is important
because it is on this evidence that my discussion mainly relies; the reasons behind this choice of source material are outlined in the first chapter, which seeks to define and to describe the people who made Rome's
foreign-relations decisions. For the most part these were members of
the Roman senatorial aristocracy; and, since their class produced much
of what remains of Greek and Latin literature, that literature can be used
as a source of information on how they thought about foreign-relations
issues. The chapters that follow discuss four aspects of this question.
Roman conceptions of geography, military strategy, and economics are
examined in turn; but a great deal of Roman thinking on the subject of
warfare and empire is expressed in value terminology, which is the subject of the final chapter.

   This study suggests that international relations, for the Romans, were
not so much a complex geopolitical chess game as a competition for
status, with much violent demonstration of superior prowess, aggressive
posturing, and terrorization of the opponent. The Romans behaved on
an international level like Homeric heroes, Mafia gangsters, or partici-
pants in any society where status and security depend on one's perceived
ability to inflict violence. Image or national "honor" emerges as the
most important policy goal. In this sense Roman strategy was coherent
and consistent over a remarkable period of time; and in a world where
the technology and information necessary for more modern and familiar types of military strategy were lacking, it was quite effective. The
value attached to honor, which was maintained by conquest, terror, and
retaliation, explains the repeated, often unsuccessful attempts at expanding the empire, and the seemingly disproportionate investment of
force in retaining territories of questionable strategic or economic value
such as Britain and Mesopotamia. On the other hand, Roman concerns
about the strength and geographic distribution of the army, and the
financial cost of war, conquest, and occupation, emerge as the main factors limiting the empire's growth. The tension between these differ-

ent concerns ultimately helped to determine the shape of the Roman empire.

This book is intended not only for students of Roman history but for nonspecialists as well, to provide a survey of many key features of Roman decision making over a long period of time. Thus it necessarily includes some material that has been discussed already by others, in more technical works; and it is necessarily incomplete, too, as it would be impossible to incorporate all of the vast and sophisticated scholarship that has been produced on all of the subjects discussed here. In particular, I have not attempted to review or synthesize the insights offered by the very extensive body of work on Roman frontier archaeology. The premise of this book is rather to let the Romans speak for themselves through their literature. Also, works published after 1996 could not, for the most part, be included in the bibliography.

It is a pleasure to acknowledge the many scholars and friends who have contributed their time and energy to this book, and who are mainly responsible for whatever merits it may have. My greatest debt of gratitude is to Professor Ramsay MacMullen, for his insight, advice, and encouragement on this project over several years, and for all, besides this, that he has taught me. The book's editors, Mary Lamprech and Kate Toll, provided invaluable advice and detailed commentary on several sections, as well as tireless attention to the endless complexities of production. Professor Arthur Eckstein and Professor Carlin Barton generously gave their time to read the manuscript, and improved it greatly with their suggestions. I would also like to thank Professors Thomas Arnold, William Harris, Donald Kagan, and Gordon Williams, who read and commented on the entire text at an earlier stage; and Professor Heinrich von Staden and Brian Fuchs for their limitless patience with my queries about Greek texts and for their help, friendship, and encouragement. My translations owe much to the Loeb versions in most cases.

Finally, I could not have written this book without the faith and support, through some difficult times, of my family, to whom it is dedicated.

Lewisburg, Pennsylvania
August 1997

Note on Abbreviations

Abbreviations for ancient sources and reference works follow the third edition of the *Oxford Classical Dictionary*.

Roman Emperors, 31 B.C.–A.D. 238

EMPEROR	YEARS OF REIGN
Augustus	31 B.C.–A.D. 14
Tiberius	A.D. 14–37
Gaius (Caligula)	37–41
Claudius	41–54
Nero	54–68
Galba	68–69 (a)
Otho	69
Vitellius	69
Vespasian	69–79
Titus	79–81
Domitian	81–96
Nerva	96–98
Trajan	98–117
Hadrian	117–138
Antoninus Pius	138–161
Marcus Aurelius	161–180
Lucius Verus	161–169 (b)
Commodus	176–192 (b)
Pertinax	193 (a)
Didius Julianus	193
Septimius Severus	193–211
Pescennius Niger	193–194
Clodius Albinus	193–197

Caracalla	198–217 (b)
Geta	209–211 (b)
Macrinus	217–218
Elagabalus	218–222
Severus Alexander	222–235
Maximinus Thrax	235–238

Notes

(a) The years 69 and 193–197 were years of civil conflict with two or more "rival" emperors.

(b) Marcus Aurelius and Lucius Verus ruled simultaneously as co-emperors; so did Marcus Aurelius and Commodus, Septimius Severus and Caracalla, and Septimius Severus and Geta.

Map of the Roman empire in the second century A.D.

LAZYGES

DACIA
● Sarmizegethusa

MOESIA
(UPPER)   MOESIA (LOWER)
Danube

THRACIA

MACEDONIA

● Actium

ACHAEA

Tanais (Don)

Sea of Azov
(Palus Maeotis)

BOSPORUS

*Black Sea
(Euxine)*

BITHYNIA-PONTUS

ALANI

*Caspian
Sea*

IBERI

ALBANI

ARMENIA
● Artaxata

GALATIA
Ancyra ●   CAPPADOCIA

ASIA

CILICIA

Samosata ●
● Carrhae   Nisibis ●
● Hatra

Antioch ●   *Euphrates*   *Tigris*

SYRIA   ● Ctesiphon

rranean Sea

Cyrene ●

JUDAEA
● Jerusalem

PARTHIA

CYRENAICA

Alexandria ●

ARABIA

AEGYPTUS

Nile

Introduction:
The Decision-Making Elite

When Marcus Aurelius died in A.D. 180, his son, the new emperor Commodus, had to decide what to do about the war on the Danube frontier. The circumstances surrounding the decision are recorded in detail only by the unreliable Herodian;[1] however, the purpose here is not to evaluate the ultimate accuracy of Herodian's account, but to determine whether Commodus' decision seems plausible in light of other ancient sources—and, as we shall see, it does. Commodus talks over the options with the "friends" who had accompanied his father on the expedition. They urge him not to abandon the war:

To leave the war unfinished, besides being dishonorable (ἀπρεπές), is also dangerous (ἐπισφαλές). For thus we will give confidence to the barbarians, who will accuse us not of a desire to return to our country but of flight and fear. But it would be splendid for you, after mastering all of them and bounding the empire on the north with the ocean, to return home triumphing and leading bound barbarian kings and satraps as prisoners. (1.6.5)

But Commodus is eventually swayed by other arguments: the relative comfort of Rome compared to the discomforts and legendary bad

---

1. See also Cass. Dio 72[73].1–2. The best commentary on Herodian's text is that of Whittaker in the Loeb edition (1969–1970).

1

weather of the Danube frontier, and the fear that a pretender might take advantage of his absence from the capital to seize power (1.6.1–3).

It is natural to view an account like this with some skepticism; in fact, for example, Commodus seems to have continued Marcus' war for a few months before making his notorious choice to withdraw.[2] Nevertheless, the tremendous value of the testimony of literary sources for the reasoning and motivations behind the type of decision Herodian describes should not be underestimated. For these decisions were not made by experts trained in economics, political science, or military theory, nor did those making the decisions even, very often, have a great deal of specialized experience to aid them. Roman foreign policy was conducted by wealthy but otherwise relatively ordinary men. In fact, the class of people who made Rome's foreign-relations decisions in the period under discussion here, from the first century B.C. to the third century A.D., is largely indistinguishable from the class that composed what remains of Greek and Latin literature. For example, the philosopher Seneca was one of the emperor Nero's most trusted advisers; his nephew Lucan, also a member of the imperial entourage, wrote a surviving epic on the civil war between Caesar and Pompey; Pliny the Elder, author of the extant *Natural History* and lost historical works, was an *amicus*, or "friend," of the emperor Vespasian and visited him every day. The Latin historian Tacitus and his friend Pliny the Younger, whose letters survive along with a panegyric to the emperor Trajan, both governed provinces; the latter helped judge cases as a member of Trajan's council. Tacitus also had a close relationship with his father-in-law, the famous governor of Britain and the subject of his biography *Agricola*, with whom he discussed questions of strategy. Arrian, the author of an important history of Alexander the Great, works on tactics, and two geographical treatises, governed the province of Cappadocia and repelled an invasion of the Alani. Fronto's correspondence with the emperors Marcus Aurelius and Lucius Verus, whom he tutored, survives. Cassius Dio, the author of a largely extant history of Rome in Greek, was a "friend" of three emperors (Severus, Caracalla, and Severus Alexander), and governor of several provinces, including the crucial military province of Upper Pannonia on the upper Danube.[3] We do not know whether any of these individuals was consulted about any specific foreign-affairs decision, but

2. See Alföldy 1971 and Whittaker's commentary (1969–1970) ad loc.

3. On Seneca as adviser to Nero, see Griffin 1976, 76–103; on Pliny the Elder, Plin. *Ep.* 3.5.7–9; Pliny the Younger helping Trajan judge cases, ibid., 4.22, 6.22, 6.31, with Sherwin-White 1968 ad locc.; Tacitus and Agricola, Tac. *Agr.* 24; on Arrian's military exploits, see Bosworth 1977; on his life and works generally, Stadter 1980. Fronto's role as friend of the

they and others of similar education, status, and background were the most likely candidates for the emperor to call on: their views are important. Others, like the Augustan poet Horace and the geographer Strabo, were not part of the circle directly involved in decisions, but they had friends who were. Conversely, many emperors, commanders, and provincial governors were authors: Marcus Aurelius wrote philosophy, and Claudius wrote history and geography; the prince Germanicus translated Aratus' poem on astronomy into Latin; and Cornelius Gallus, the militaristic prefect of Egypt under Augustus, was most famous for his love elegies.[4] This cultural tradition was inherited from the Republic and persisted well beyond the time period discussed here. During his Gallic campaigns Caesar had written a treatise called *On Analogy,* and Quintus Cicero, serving as legate under him, composed four tragedies;[5] in the fourth century, the historian Ammianus would accompany the emperor Julian on campaign against the Persians. The Roman aristocracy was educated mainly in literature and rhetoric, and valued these pursuits highly as an important part of their cultural and class identity, as I shall argue later in this chapter. A division between literature and policy that might seem natural enough to a modern observer might not have seemed obvious to them. That is, it may be tempting for the modern reader to assume that Roman aristocrats must have thought differently, and articulated different concerns, when they were conferring about a foreign-relations issue than when they were composing a history or an epic poem. But much of the evidence that we shall see suggests—although it cannot prove—the opposite conclusion. The question I would like to ask in this work is, Supposing we take the Romans at their word, what are the views that emerge from Roman literature on questions of war and peace, and can they in fact help us understand Roman actions?

The status of Herodian, the author of the statement with which this chapter began, is unknown. It is not clear whether he belonged to the senatorial aristocracy and whether he had any way of knowing what was in fact said to Commodus by his advisers, though he does claim to be a contemporary of the events he describes.[6] Nevertheless, there are sev-

---

Antonine emperors is the subject of Champlin 1980, chap. 7. On Cassius Dio's career, see Millar 1964, 16–27.

4. On the literary efforts and attitudes of emperors, see the interesting work of Bardon 1940; Augustus, for example, wrote a tragedy entitled *Ajax* (ibid., p. 15; Suet. *Aug.* 85); on Gallus, see especially Crowther 1983.

5. Fronto, *Ep.* (Loeb) 2:29; Cic., *Q fr.* 3.5.7.

6. On Herodian's life and status, see Whittaker 1969–1970, 1:ix–xxiv. Whittaker argues that Herodian may have been an equestrian procurator and, as such, would have had senatorial patrons and access to their information and views.

eral significant features of the conversation as he imagines it. There is concern, first of all, about what is "dishonorable"; and, apparently closely related to this, a strong necessity not to appear afraid in front of barbarians; and the idea that a lack of aggressive action will undermine security by producing a certain state of mind ("confidence") in the enemy. There is also a desire for the glory of conquest; a special significance to achieving the northern "ocean" as frontier; and relish at the thought of leading barbarian kings (and, confusingly, satraps)[7] in a humiliating triumph. All of these, I shall argue, are very typical Roman concerns. Also, Herodian cannot imagine an aggressive, expansionist campaign waged by anyone other than the emperor. If Commodus wants to enlarge his reputation by conquering barbarians and annexing territory, he has to do it himself and not through a subordinate.

Commodus and his advisers do not, in Herodian's version of these events, discuss the relative merits of the Danube River as a frontier. They do not look at maps, and they seem, in their optimism about reaching what they call the "ocean," profoundly to underestimate the distance to the Baltic coast. They do not specifically discuss the cost of the war, the revenues available, or the potential economic benefit of withdrawal. Herodian attributes Commodus' ultimate decision to a defect in his character: his laziness. On this last point he is not alone; his more reliable contemporary Cassius Dio takes the same view (72[73].1.2). Perhaps, we might think, a better description of the process of making a foreign-relations decision, by a more competent historian than Herodian, would reveal a very different set of concerns. But in fact no such descriptions exist for the period we are discussing here.

This study will attempt to discover whether Herodian's scenario, for example, accurately reflects the most important factors in Roman decisions about war and peace in the period from Augustus to Severus Alexander. The importance of the subject needs no defense. The decision to invade Dacia, conquer Britain, or withdraw from newly acquired provinces beyond the Euphrates could affect a hundred thousand lives directly and had cultural consequences that persist to this day. But while the subject is important, it is also one that resists exact definition. What is "Roman," for example, and what is "foreign"? Though the empire came to have certain fixed psychological boundaries, nevertheless there were always tribute-paying tribes and "client-kings" of ambiguous sta-

7. Herodian's choice of the word *satrap* to refer to the barbarian chieftains of Marcus' Danube campaigns seems odd, though the word may have had a rather general meaning at the time. See the entry for this term in Liddell and Scott's *Greek-English Lexicon*, especially Philostratus *VS* 1.524, with Bowersock 1969, 52, where it refers to a Roman procurator.

tus beyond its borders. Conversely, the Romans thought of provincial revolts like those in Dalmatia and Pannonia in A.D. 6, or in Judaea in A.D. 69, as foreign wars.[8] Thus we must be prepared, in our discussion, for some divergence between ancient and modern notions of "foreign relations."

The time boundaries, too, are problematic. The period we are considering here begins with the reign of the first emperor, Augustus, usually described as beginning with his defeat of Antony at Actium in 31 B.C., and ends with the reign of Severus Alexander, whose death in A.D. 235 marked the fall of the Severan dynasty. After this, the empire entered a period of crisis during which evidence of the type used in this study—literature produced by the aristocracy, and especially historiography—either was not produced or does not survive. But until then, the system established by Augustus—often called the "Principate" (for Augustus styled himself "princeps" or "first citizen"), or the "empire," because of the title *imperator,* which he and his successors assumed—remained relatively stable, though Rome gradually added territory to its empire and the size of the army also, gradually, increased. However, the ideas we shall encounter regarding the proper conduct of foreign relations in this period do not differ sharply from those of the long period of constitutional oligarchy that preceded Augustus' reign, called the Republic, or from those of the so-called Dominate that emerged in the fourth century A.D. It is therefore inevitable that examples from outside the stated chronological boundaries of this study will emerge here and there in support of some of my arguments; but it would not be practical to undertake a systematic survey of all the evidence from these other periods, and I do not claim to do so, though I have tried especially to touch on the Republican background to many of the ideas and institutions of the Principate.

The ultimate responsibility for the conduct of foreign affairs in the imperial period lay with a very few people. In the Republic, the senate traditionally held this central role;[9] but in the Principate, its place was

8. On the Dalmatian war as *bellum externum,* see Suet. *Aug.* 20, *Tib.* 16; see Rosenberger 1992, 66–67 and passim, on the different terminology of civil and foreign wars. The propaganda campaign with which the Jewish victory was advertised indicates a foreign war; see below, chap. 5, p. 193.

9. A detailed study of the role of the senate vs. the individual general in foreign-relations decisions in the Republic is available in Eckstein 1987. He argues that while the senate retained the tradition of ultimate responsibility, in fact much of foreign policy was necessarily determined by generals in the field. On the transition to the Principate and the senate's role in foreign relations under the empire, see Talbert 1984, 411–425. The senate retained a formal role, especially in hearing embassies. See id. 1988 for an instance from

gradually usurped by the emperor and his circle of advisers. These advisers included one or both of the praetorian prefects—commanders of the elite troops stationed in Rome—who were always in close attendance on the emperor,[10] plus a number of people usually called his "friends" (*amici*), some of whom would accompany him on a trip or campaign as "companions" (*comites*). As a group they were sometimes called his "council." Also influential might be the secretary *ab epistulis* (of letters), often (though not always) a Greek intellectual, who sometimes traveled with the emperor; and in general the presence of a number of Greek doctors, sophists, or other intellectuals in the imperial court should be assumed for all periods.[11] The emperor relied on these men (not women, of course)[12] to advise him on administrative matters and judicial decisions as well as foreign relations.[13] But the latter function was an important one, as the ancient sources indicate in the few cases where they describe such decisions actually being made. The best example is a scene from the beginning of Nero's reign; one of the first decisions the new emperor, like Commodus, had to face involved a major foreign crisis, this time in the east. Rome's nominee to the Armenian throne had been expelled by the Parthians, who were pillaging the country. Tacitus describes the anxiety felt by some over Nero's potential performance in this situation:

Therefore in a city eager for gossip, they were questioning how a *princeps* hardly seventeen years old could handle this danger or repel it; and what refuge there was in one who was ruled by a woman, and whether battles, and

---

Commodus' reign where peace with a hostile tribe is apparently concluded before the senate.

10. On the role of the praetorian prefects see Millar 1977, 122–131, and Halfmann 1986, 103–105.

11. On the *ab epistulis* on imperial journeys, see Halfmann 1986, 106; cf. 108–109 on doctors. On this subject, see also Bowersock 1969, chap. 4; on the secretaries *ab epistulis,* ibid., 50–56. The issue of the criteria for choosing the *ab epistulis* is, like all questions of this sort, controversial; see further N. Lewis 1981 and A. R. Birley 1992, 21–25, 41–54.

12. Though see a reference in Millar 1977, 120, to a passage from the *Acta Alexandrinorum* where Claudius hears a case between an embassy from Alexandria and King Agrippa of Judaea accompanied by twenty *assessores,* sixteen consulars, and some Roman matrons (*Acta Isidori* ii.7–8 = Musurillo 1954, 19).

13. On the emperor's friends and advisers generally, see Crook 1955, 21–30 and passim; Millar 1977, 110–122; and Halfmann 1986, 92–103; on the issue of who was responsible for foreign-affairs decisions, Millar 1982, 4–7. On the role of the *amici* in judging cases and receiving embassies, see also Millar 1977, 119–122. The most famous council is the one called by Augustus to hear the claimants to Herod's throne, in which his grandson Gaius was allowed, for the first time, to participate (Crook, op. cit., 32–33; Joseph. *BJ* 2.25, *AJ* 17.229). For a list of attested *comites* of the emperor, see Halfmann 1986, 245–253.

attacks on cities, and the rest that war involves could be handled by school-teachers. Others, however, contended that things had come out better than if Claudius, weak with old age and inaction, had been called to the labors of war, ready to obey the orders of slaves; but Burrus and Seneca were known for their experience in many matters. . . .[14]

While Tacitus' representation of the public mood may reflect his own biases rather than reality, nevertheless this passage includes some interesting assumptions. The historian assumes that the decision about Armenia will be made personally by the emperor in close consultation with advisers. The character and social position of these advisers is important to him: Claudius is reviled for consulting freedmen, and the idea that a woman, Nero's mother, might have some influence here is repellent. It is especially interesting to note that Seneca took part in this and presumably other important foreign-affairs decisions, because a large body of his work survives and can be examined. It is also interesting that Tacitus describes Seneca and Burrus as exceptionally qualified to advise Nero in this case, though it is probable that neither had substantial military experience or specialized knowledge about Armenia or Parthia.[15]

Later in his reign, facing another crisis in the same area, Nero again consults with advisers—this time described as "the most prominent men in the state (*primores civitatis*)"—about whether to embark on "dangerous war or disgraceful peace."[16] Other examples emerge here and there. Maecenas, Augustus' friend, may have advised him on foreign issues;[17] Hadrian's "friends" dissuade him from abandoning Dacia.[18] Severus Alexander also confers with his "friends" upon hearing the bad news of Ardashir's invasion (Herodian 6.2.3). Later, facing invasions in Germany, our source writes that "both Alexander and the friends who were with him feared even for Italy itself" (6.7.4).

The council of friends was by now a traditional element of Roman

---

14. *Ann.* 13.6: *Igitur in urbe sermonum avida, quem ad modum princeps vix septem-decim annos egressus suscipere eam molem aut propulsare posset, quod subsidium in eo, qui a femina regeretur, num proelia quoque et obpugnationes urbium et cetera belli per magistros administrari possent, anquirebant. Contra alii melius evenisse disserunt, quam si invalidus senecta et ignavia Claudius militiae ad labores vocaretur, servilibus iussis obtemperaturus. Burrum tamen et Senecam multarum rerum experientia cognitos. . . .*

15. The evidence for Burrus' career is collected by Pflaum (1960–1961, 1:30–31). His military experience before becoming praetorian prefect seems to have been limited to one term as military tribune, though Tacitus credits him with "an outstanding military reputation" (*egregia militaris fama*) in *Ann.* 12.42.

16. Tac. *Ann.* 15.25. "Nor did they hesitate to choose war."

17. Hor. *Carm.* 3.8.17–25 and 3.29.25–28; and see Crook 1955, 31.

18. Eutropius 8.6.2; see Crook 1955, 65; and cf. Lepper 1948, 14.

political life. The government of the Republic had only a small official bureaucracy, and much decision making was done by aristocrats in consultation with a council formed partly of their friends, whether they were acting as head of the family, governor of a province, or commander of an army.[19] Thus the council was not an "official" body, and there were no strict rules about its composition. Deferring to the senate's traditional role in foreign policy, Augustus had established a rotating advisory group including the consuls and fifteen senators chosen by lot (Cass. Dio 53.21.4, Suet. *Aug.* 35.3–4); remnants of this system survived early in the reign of Tiberius, whose council was composed of "old friends and household members," plus twenty of the "foremost in the city" (Suet. *Tib.* 55). By now, the emperor could choose whomever he liked.[20] Young rulers, or potential successors entrusted with weighty missions, were of course especially dependent on the advisers chosen for them. Gaius was only nineteen years old when his grandfather Augustus sent him to the eastern front in 2 B.C.; the worried emperor provided him with trustworthy counselors to help with whatever decisions might arise (Cass. Dio 55.10.18). In A.D. 14 Tiberius sent some of his own advisers with Drusus to Pannonia; these were, again, "the foremost of the city" (*primores civitatis*) and included the later-notorious Sejanus (Tac. *Ann.* 1.24). Vespasian's "friends" advised the young Domitian against an unnecessary German expedition (Suet. *Dom.* 2.1). Nero, Commodus, and Severus Alexander, all very young at their accession, were also especially dependent on their advisers.[21]

Throughout the imperial period the emperor was, at least in theory, the ultimate authority responsible for all foreign-relations decisions. Embassies were usually sent to him rather than to the senate or the

19. Cf. Crook 1955, 4–8; Gelzer 1968, 101–103. E.g., Flamininus settles matters in Greece "either by himself or with his own friends" (Polyb. 18.34.3); Augustus took part in Tarius' *consilium* about the fate of his son (Sen. *Clem.* 1.15.3–4). On war councils, see also Szidat 1970, 17.

20. On Augustus' formal rotation system and Tiberius' modifications, see Crook 1955, chap. 2; on the essential informality of the council in later periods, see ibid., 104–106. Crook cannot find a consistent official designation, in Latin or Greek, for what is now usually called the *consilium principis*.

21. On Nero, see Tac. *Ann.* 13.6, quoted above; in the case of Commodus, the dying Marcus entrusted him to his own advisers, who had accompanied him to the front (Herodian 1.4; Cass. Dio 72[73].1.2), and Commodus is said to have ruled well as long as he listened to them (Herodian 1.8.1); Severus Alexander's advisers were apparently chosen by his mother (Herodian 6.1.1–2; and see Halfmann 1986, 97 n. 346, for further references); on the point generally, see Halfmann 1986, 96–97, arguing that in the early empire the *comites* of young princes were perhaps more likely to be men of greater experience and high rank.

nearest governor, for example.[22] Thus the king of Thrace writes directly to Tiberius, who responds through the governor of Moesia (Tac. *Ann.* 2.65–66). The Dacian king Decebalus negotiates with Domitian directly, though Domitian responds by appointing a special commander against him (Cass. Dio 67.6.5). Claudius, responding to a plea from the king of the Suebi, directs the governor of Pannonia to station troops on the Danube frontier (Tac. *Ann.* 12.29); and he is supposed to have sent Aulus Plautius to Britain because a native chieftain had convinced him to come to his aid (Cass. Dio 60.19.1). Thus, much foreign policy was carried out by the emperor indirectly, through communications to governors or through special commanders. The degree to which the governors of provinces, especially imperial legates who commanded troops, could act autonomously is difficult to determine but may have been greater earlier in the Principate.[23] Early in the reign of Augustus, imperial legates seem to have retained much of the power of decision—and potential to achieve glory—that characterized the senatorial class during the Republic, though from the very beginning it was clear that this created a political threat. Thus while Licinius Crassus was granted a triumph in 29 B.C. for his reduction of Thrace, he was denied other honors: the title of *imperator*, which was traditionally voted to a victorious general by acclamation of the army; and the *spolia opima*, the dedication of the armor of an enemy leader slain in single combat by a Roman general, an honor that was extremely rare.[24] Cornelius Gallus' campaigns in Ethiopia, and the loud publicity he gave them, eventually led to his downfall.[25] And in 19 B.C. Cornelius Balbus, proconsul of Africa, became the last commander ever to celebrate a triumph who was not an em-

22. See n. 9 above, and further Millar 1988, 348–352, citing, e.g., Augustus' boasts in *RGDA* 35. A major exception is from the reign of Claudius, where Parthian envoys appear before the senate (Tac. *Ann.* 12.10), but they are answered by a speech from Claudius. For some other exceptions, see Talbert 1984, 428; Millar 1982, 4. In the famous speech composed by Cassius Dio (52.31.1), Maecenas recommends that foreign embassies be introduced to the senate.

23. For more detailed discussion of the degree of autonomy and potential for glory available to the governors of public and imperial provinces, see Millar 1982, 7–15, including most of the examples that follow; see also Campbell 1984, 348–362. Austin and Rankov (1995, chap. 7) argue that governors must have retained a significant degree of autonomy; Potter (1996) argues for explicit instructions from emperors to governors and special commanders.

24. Cass. Dio 51.24.4; Syme 1939, 308 n. 2. On the title of *imperator*, see below, chap. 5, n. 115.

25. See Cass. Dio 53.23.5–7 on Gallus' boasting, exile, and suicide; *ILS* 8995 for his ostentatious record of achievements; and *PIR* II, C1369. See also Suet. *Aug.* 66.1–2 and Syme 1939, 309–310.

peror or a member of the imperial family.[26] Nevertheless, provincial governors still acted autonomously to some degree, as in the case of Petronius, another prefect of Egypt. He carried out extensive retaliatory operations against the queen of Meroë in Ethiopia, capturing and burning cities, refusing embassies, enslaving natives, and leaving a garrison at Premnis. Later, the garrison was attacked and Petronius marched to defend it; the queen sent ambassadors to make peace, and Petronius this time sent them on to Augustus. They replied, however, that "they did not know who Caesar was or where they were supposed to go to him," so Petronius provided them with guides (Strab. 17.1.54). Here apparently the prefect conducted his campaigns independently until the time came to negotiate peace. The role of the emperor was critical, but remote.

Under Augustus, Aelius Catus transplanted into Thrace 50,000 Getae from across the Danube (Strab. 7.3.10). Similarly, a famous inscription on the tomb of Ti. Plautius Silvanus, governor of Moesia under Nero,[27] records that he brought over more than 100,000 "Transdanuviani" and reduced them to paying tribute; he repressed a Sarmatian threat; negotiated with foreign tribes and received hostages from some of them; and, as he is particularly proud to note, "deterred even the king of the Scythians from the siege of the Chersonese that is beyond the Borysthenes [i.e., the Crimean Peninsula]." How much of this was done on his own initiative and how much under instructions from the emperor is a question about which we can only speculate.[28] We know that Tiberius gave specific orders to Vitellius on his negotiations with the Parthians (Joseph. AJ 18.96; 101–104); Corbulo also was given specific guidelines when he set out for the east, and at one point he refused to invade Armenia because "he did not have those instructions from the emperor" (Tac. Ann. 15.17).[29] In A.D. 72 Caesennius Paetus, the governor of Syria, wrote to Vespasian accusing the king of Commagene of conspiracy with the Parthians and asking permission to invade; and a law still on the books prescribed death for waging an unauthorized war.[30]

26. Campbell 1984, 358–359; see Pliny HN 5.36 on Balbus' triumph, also noteworthy because he was not born a Roman citizen.

27. ILS 986, using Dessau's suggested emendations in n. 11. For a discussion of this well-known inscription, see Conole and Milns 1983.

28. See Millar 1982, 7–8. Note also ILS 985.

29. "Instructions" here is mandata, the Latin word used to indicate the instructions given to governors on their appointment (ἐντολαί); these seem to have covered all aspects of administration and to have contained some elements that remained unchanged from reign to reign. See Millar 1977, 314–317; id. 1982, 8–9; Potter 1996.

30. Joseph. BJ 7.220–225 and Campbell 1984, 348–349; Dig. 48.4.3 and Talbert 1984, 429 with n. 36.

Yet it is unclear whether such permission was always in fact required, at least early in the imperial period. Tacitus appears in several passages to assume that the provincial governors themselves bore the responsibility for a decision to invade. Thus under Tiberius the governor of Moesia sends a detachment of troops to deal with a situation in Thrace and accompanies them himself on the campaign (*Ann.* 3.39). When the Frisians refuse to pay tribute, the governor of Lower Germany summons reinforcements from Upper Germany and attacks them; Tacitus writes that this happened "when [the news] was known to Lucius Apronius, propraetor of Lower Germany"—not after he had asked the emperor's permission (*Ann.* 4.73). Similarly, Suetonius Paulinus invaded the island of Mona for his own reasons: because he wished to emulate Corbulo's success in Armenia; again, he is given sole credit for this decision (Tac. *Ann.* 14.29). Tacitus ascribes aggressive and glorious, or weak and defensive, foreign policy in Britain to the character of its governors—not of the emperors.[31]

Certainly practical considerations of distance and travel time meant that much would need to be left to the governor's discretion.[32] Arrian's famous confrontation with the Alani, who had encroached on his province of Cappadocia on their way back from a raid on Armenia, could not have waited for authorization from Hadrian. And yet this campaign was not necessarily a limited defensive maneuver but may have taken Arrian well into enemy territory and possibly resulted in a rearrangement of the border between the kingdoms of Iberia and Albania in the Caucasus Mountains.[33] Tacitus provides a clearer illustration of the tension between imperial authority and the need to make decisions quickly, on the

31. E.g., *Agr.* 14: "Aulus Plautius was the first of the consular governors in charge [of Britain], and then Ostorius Scapula, both exceptional in war; and the nearest part of Britain was reduced little by little to the form of a province, and a veteran colony was founded besides. . . . Then Didius Gallus maintained what his predecessors had acquired, only putting out a few forts in the regions beyond, through which he sought the glory of having expanded his office. Didius Veranius took over, and he died within a year. Then Suetonius Paulinus enjoyed successful undertakings for two years, subjecting tribes and consolidating them with garrisons. . . ." On Britain, see also *Ann.* 14.29, and cf. 13.53: "Until now the situation in Germany had been quiet, due to the temperament of the generals; for the triumphal ornaments had become so debased that they hoped for honor rather from having continued the peace."

32. On this point, see Millar 1982, 9–11; cf. Austin and Rankov 1995, 123–125. On travel time and communications speed, see chap. 3 below, p. 99.

33. On this campaign, see Bosworth 1977. The evidence is mainly Cass. Dio 69.15, and of course Arrian's own Ἔκταξις κατὰ Ἀλανῶν—which, however, focuses entirely on battle tactics and gives no historical context. Bosworth (op. cit., 229–230) notes that a fourth-century oration by Themistius (*Orat.* 34.8) credits Arrian with establishing the boundaries between the two kingdoms.

spot, when the governor of Syria learns that Rome's nominee to the throne of Armenia has been deposed and killed. He calls a council of his own friends to decide what action to take; they determine to do nothing at first, but nevertheless the governor, Quadratus, sends an embassy with a stiffly worded message to the invaders, "lest he appear to condone the crime and Caesar should order something different" (*Ann.* 12.48). Here, Quadratus intends to write to the emperor about the situation but cannot wait for his reply to make an important decision. Thus the emperor's authority placed limits—albeit vague ones—on what a governor could do. When Tiberius dies, Vitellius must return from a campaign against Nabataea because he is no longer empowered to conduct the war.[34] In another example, this time under Claudius, Corbulo negotiates with the Frisians, provokes hostilities with the Chauci, and appears to be in the process of occupying enemy territory by the time he receives a letter from Claudius ordering him to withdraw behind the Rhine.[35] In the eastern war under Nero, neither Corbulo nor Paetus has the authority to make a binding peace treaty with the Parthians;[36] in fact, from Republican times all treaties made by military commanders in the field had to be ratified by the senate, which occasionally, though rarely, refused to do so.[37] Thus while significant decisions could be made by imperial legates, the most significant and far-reaching decisions had to be made, or at least approved, by the emperor.

When Trajan undertook the conquest of Dacia it was still noteworthy that he did it himself.[38] His predecessors were often content to entrust major campaigns to commanders like Vitellius or Corbulo, or to go just near enough to the front and stay just long enough to acquire a military reputation. In a famous passage, Fronto describes Antoninus Pius' role in the British war as one of remote supervision: "Although he himself remained on the Palatine in the city [of Rome] and had dele-

---

34. Joseph. *AJ* 18.124; Millar 1982, 8–9. In *AJ* 18.115 Tiberius orders Vitellius to declare war after receiving a letter from Herod the tetrarch that his army had been attacked and destroyed by the Nabataean king Aretas.

35. Tac. *Ann.* 11.19; Cass. Dio 61.30.4–5.

36. Tac. *Ann.* 15.14 for Paetus' notorious truce, and Vologeses' sending an embassy to Nero; in 15.16 Paetus promises that the Romans will stay out of Armenia *donec referrentur litterae Neronis, an pace adnueret* (until Nero's response should arrive, about whether he approved the peace); the emperor rejects the peace in 15.25; see Cass. Dio 62.22.3 on Corbulo's treaty.

37. Eckstein 1987, xiii.

38. Cass. Dio 68.10.4: "καὶ ὁ Τραιανὸς δι᾽ ἑαυτοῦ καὶ αὖθις, ἀλλ᾽ οὐ δι᾽ ἑτέρων στρατηγῶν, τὸν πρὸς ἐκεῖνον πόλεμον ἐποιήσατο" (and Trajan once again waged the war on him [Decebalus] himself, and not through other commanders).

gated the authority to wage the war (*gerendi eius mandasset auspicium*), still like one guiding the rudder of a warship, he earned the glory of the whole navigation and voyage."[39] But by the end of our period the authority to command an army on a major campaign may have become more concentrated in the emperor himself.[40] Thus Marcus Aurelius conducted the complicated negotiations with various trans-Danuvian German and Sarmatian tribes personally and not by letter, leading campaigns and negotiating peace terms on the spot (Cass. Dio 71[72].3–11). When Marcus died, Commodus' decision to return to Rome meant that the campaign beyond the Danube had to be abandoned. By now any important campaign seems to have required at least the proximity of an emperor (or a co-emperor or chosen successor).[41] When the aggressive Persian monarch Ardashir invaded Roman territory, Severus Alexander had to choose between leading an expedition himself and trying to solve the crisis through diplomacy (Herodian 6.2–3). While the emperor was at Antioch, the news arrived that German tribes had invaded the Rhine provinces and that his presence was required (6.7.2–3), whereupon he marched the three thousand miles to the northern frontier. The campaign could not be delegated, even though Alexander knew it would be some six months before he could take command of it.[42] Still, it seems that minor campaigns, which would require only a governor's provincial army, would be handled by the governor; this seems to be the implication of an obscure passage from Cassius Dio (71[72].33.1): "When matters in Scythia again required him [Marcus], he gave Crispina as a wife to his son earlier than he wanted to on account of it; for the Quintilii were unable to end the war, although there were two of them and they had a great deal of intelligence, courage, and experience, and for this reason it was necessary for the emperors themselves to set out on campaign."[43] But the governors, in normal circumstances, should have been able to handle the situation. And even now it was still possible for a legate to undertake an invasion without the emperor's knowledge; in a passage from Lucian's satirical *Alexander,* which refers to events in the

39. Fr. 2 (Loeb 2:251); cf. Millar 1982, 12.

40. Ibid., 11–15. See also Millar 1988, 374–375; Austin and Rankov 1995, 205–212.

41. Thus Cass. Dio 71.1.3 tells us that it was in response to the Parthian crisis that Marcus married his daughter to Lucius Verus, who was then dispatched to the east. The actual conduct of the war was entrusted to Avidius Cassius, however (ibid., 71.2.2), with disastrous results, for Cassius led a revolt against the emperors (71[72].17.22–26).

42. Millar 1982, 13.

43. Marcus probably married off the young Commodus in order to enhance his authority with the army, as Augustus does with his grandson Gaius in Cass. Dio 55.10.18.

reign of Marcus, the pseudoprophet persuades the governor of Cappadocia to invade Armenia. The campaign results in disaster when the
legate is killed and a legion destroyed.[44]

The reasons for this concentration of power in the emperor's hands
will be examined in a later chapter. For now it is enough for us to ob-
serve that especially toward the end of the period we are discussing, ultimate responsibility for foreign-relations decisions lay with the emperor
and his circle of friends. To some limited extent the governors of provinces were in a position to determine policy. These were for the most
part men of very high rank. At the pinnacle of Roman society was the
small, elite class of senators, a largely hereditary group that supplied all
Rome's provincial governors and high-ranking military officers, as well as
its emperors. Governors of the armed, "imperial" provinces were called
legates; the emperor retained ultimate power or *imperium* over these
provinces—a device for controlling the glory and status attached to military victory. In any case, these legates, depending on the province involved, would be senators who had held the office of praetor or the
highest office, that of consul—which conferred extra status on the senator within his community. A larger order, lower in prestige and generally in wealth, of *equites,* or "knights," held military commissions and a
variety of civil-service posts in the imperial government; the prefect of
Egypt, a province too critical to be entrusted to someone of sufficient
prestige to threaten the emperor, was also a knight. Both the senate
and the equestrian order had property qualifications, and movement
between the two orders was not unusual. The emperor's friends and advisers normally came from these groups.[45] It is common, as we have seen,
for our sources to describe the emperor's council as composed of "the
best" or "most prominent" citizens,[46] and the pressure to choose advisers from society's upper echelons is clear.[47]

We might wonder to what degree the education and training of a

44. Lucian *Alex.* 27; Fronto *Principia historiae* 16 (Loeb 2:215); Cass. Dio 71.2.1;
Angeli Bertinelli 1976, 25–26; Birley 1987, 123–124.

45. See Halfmann 1986, 94–101, on the rank of those attested as the emperor's *comites;*
after the Julio-Claudians these are always *equites* or senators (usually senators).

46. See Tac. *Ann.* 1.24, where young Drusus' companions on his journey to Pannonia
are described as *primores civitatis;* 15.25, cited above, on Nero's advisers (again, *primores
civitatis*); Cass. Dio 72 [73].1.2, where Commodus' advisers are οἱ κράτιστοι τῶν βουλευτῶν, the most powerful men in the senate; SHA *Marcus* 22.3, where Marcus confers *sem-
per cum optimatibus,* always with the best men.

47. See Millar 1977, 59–60, pointing out that the period of influential freedmen was
a very short one and contrary to the values of the society; on their influence, see ibid., 69–
83; cf. Tacitus' comment in *Ann.* 13.6, quoted above—by no means the only criticism of
Claudius on this point. See also Isaac 1992, 386–387.

member of the Roman aristocracy prepared him to make the crucial decisions about war and peace that we will be examining.[48] Traditionally, in the system that Augustus inherited from the Republic, the Roman command structure was class-based. As mentioned earlier, the officer class came from the narrow aristocracy of senators and equestrians. The great armies of the Republic were commanded by senators who had attained the rank of consul, the pinnacle of their society. Their training in military science came mainly from experience: until the later second century B.C., aspiring senators were required to serve in ten campaigns before they could hold political office.[49] Intellectual education was brought to Rome by the Greeks and began to take hold in the Roman aristocracy sometime in the second century B.C.; thus it is the Greek Polybius who advocates a formal training for generals in tactics, astronomy, geometry, and history.[50] And in fact some basic education in astronomy and geometry—which Polybius suggests would be useful for calculating, for example, the lengths of days and nights or the height of a city wall— was normal for a Roman aristocrat of the late Republic or the Principate. Aratus' verse composition on astronomy, several times translated into Latin, was especially popular.[51] But by the late Republic the law requiring military service for office was long defunct; and Roman education as described by Seneca the Elder or Quintilian was designed mainly to produce orators. The emphasis was overwhelmingly on literature and rhetoric;[52] one did not take courses, for example, on "modern Parthia" or military theory. Details of grammar and rhetorical style were considered appropriate subjects for the attention of the empire's most responsible individuals; this is attested in the letters of Pliny the Younger, the musings of Aulus Gellius, and the correspondence of Fronto with Lucius Verus and Marcus Aurelius.[53] Of Marcus, Cassius Dio writes that "he

48. On this question in general, see MacMullen 1976, 49–58.

49. See Harris 1979, 10–16.

50. 9.12–20; 11.8. Polybius also wrote a treatise on tactics; see 9.20, with Walbank 1957–1979, vol. 2, ad loc.

51. On Aratus, see recently A. M. Lewis 1992; cf. Walbank 1957–1979, vol. 2, at 9.15.7–11; on Republican education, see Marrou 1956, 229–254; and note the discussion of Harris 1979, 14–15. Cato the Elder's education of his son is described by Plut. *Cat. Mai.* 20, and see Bonner 1977, 10–11. Cicero's ideal education included, besides rhetoric, astronomy (of which geography was a subcategory), geometry, and music (ibid., 77–79). On Hellenization, see Rawson 1985, chap. 11, and recently Gruen 1993.

52. On what was taught in Roman secondary schools (by the *grammaticus*), see Bonner 1977, chap. 14; and Marrou 1956, 274–283.

53. Aulus Gellius' own rank and status are unknown, but his observations of others are revealing; cf. 19.13.1, with MacMullen 1976, 51 n. 8 and 49–52. Fronto, *Ep.* (Loeb) 2:29, addressed to Marcus after the disaster of Severianus in Armenia, protests that if Caesar

was greatly aided by his education, having been trained in rhetoric and in the arguments of philosophy; in rhetoric his teachers were Cornelius Fronto and Claudius Herodes, and, in philosophy, Junius Rusticus and Apollonius of Nicomedia" (71[72].35.1). Here one of the empire's most experienced statesmen describes training in eloquence and, probably for its moral emphasis, philosophy as the ideal education for a chief of state.

This emphasis on rank, and on the literary education that distinguished gentlemen from ordinary people, is certainly not unique to the Romans; but it is important not to project modern ideas about qualifications and competence onto a society that thought differently. To some degree any senator, simply by virtue of his birth and rank, was considered qualified and indeed entitled to lead; he required only an education in how to make his ideas persuasive. Of the twenty young aristocrats who started their political careers each year as *vigintiviri,* the entry-level office, virtually all would hold praetorian office; half would become consuls.[54] The "senatorial" provinces, including the proconsular provinces of Africa and Asia, were assigned to qualified senators *by lot.*[55]

The same was not true of the commanders of Rome's great armies, the imperial legates of consular rank. Their careers have been much scrutinized with a view to establishing how they were chosen from among the senatorial elite. Some have traced patterns of promotion as far back as their position among the more privileged offices of the vigintivirate—when they were only eighteen years old. This probably means that ancestry and patronage—connections in high places, and especially with the emperor—played an important role.[56] Specialization in their careers—in particular, military specialization—is hard to

---

could write his *De analogia* while conquering Gaul ("among the flying arrows discussing the proper declensions of nouns, and the aspirations of words and their properties amid horns and trumpets"), Marcus could surely find time "not only to read poems and histories and the precepts of philosophers, but even . . . to resolve syllogisms."

54. By the end of the first century there were eighteen praetorships available each year, thus virtually no attrition up to that point (Eck 1974, 180–181; A. R. Birley 1981, 15; Talbert 1984, 19–20). On the number of consuls, see especially Alföldy 1977, 11–21; and A. R. Birley 1981, 24–25.

55. This was the case in theory, though Millar (1977, 309) notes some instances of imperial interference.

56. Certain positions in the vigintivirate, especially the *triumviri monetales,* were more prestigious than others; senators of exceptionally noble birth usually held them, and a disproportionate percentage of consular legates may have started their careers in these posts. For the argument, see especially E. Birley 1954, 201–205; and A. R. Birley 1981, 4–8. The traditional view of E. Birley and Syme (see below) that at this point the decision about a senator's future career was somehow based on aptitude or ability is surely not tenable; nor was experience relevant at this stage; patronage seems an inviting alternative (cf. the suggestion of A. R. Birley, op. cit., 5, and his comment, p. 7).

prove.[57] Most senators would have had some military experience in their careers; a year, perhaps more, as military tribune was usual and vaguely perceived as valuable training.[58] A large proportion—more than half—of all who had been praetors would command a legion, with a term of perhaps two or three years;[59] but this was not always a prerequisite for the command of a military province.[60] In fact, most imperial governors of consular rank had experience in a combination of civil and military

57. The polemical way in which the debate over the system of promotion for senators is usually framed masks, as often, the fact that substantial common ground now exists. A view long associated with Syme (see A. R. Birley 1992, 14 n. 53, for full bibliography) and E. Birley (1954) argued for a class of *viri militares* or military specialists whose careers were characterized by a rapid advancement to the consulship and a military emphasis in their praetorian careers, notably command of a legion and of an armed praetorian province. The main outlines of this view were endorsed by Eck in his very influential article (1974), but Eck's scheme also has much in common with the rather different argument of Alföldy (1977; summarized in English in 1976). The latter has consistently advocated a thesis that fast promotion to the consulship depended mainly on birth, and draws a division between imperial and senatorial careers, rather than civil and military ones, that emphasizes the importance of loyalty and a close relationship to the emperor in promotion (1977, 34–37, on the typology of senatorial careers; 95–125, on the criteria for advancement; 54–60, on the importance of loyalty and a close relationship with the emperor). Alföldy argues that at the level of consular legate—that is, commander of large armies—birth ceases to be a factor and "new men" with longer careers are overrepresented, perhaps because of their substantial experience, thus coming to the opposite conclusion of Syme and E. Birley; on this point, see also Eck 1974, 217–218; this argument is, however, difficult to prove statistically, except for the well-known rarity of patricians in these very important posts.

The main challenge to the views of Syme and E. Birley has come from Campbell (1975), who seeks mainly to attack the notion of military specialization in the empire's high command. He points out that the phrase *vir militaris* used in this sense is a modern construction (ibid., 11–12) and finds only a small number of senators whose careers conform to the pattern specified by Syme and E. Birley. A. R. Birley (1981, 4–35; 1992, 14–15, 31–40) defends some of their views, notably about the "fast track" to the consulship, but does little to advance the case for specialization and seems himself willing partially to concede this point (1981, n. 19; but cf. ibid., 33). Finally, Lendon (1997, 185–191) argues that the chief criterion for appointment to any office was aristocratic "prestige," which depended mainly on such factors as birth, wealth, moral virtue, and friendship with other prestigious individuals. A similar debate exists regarding the equestrian civil service, which I shall not enter into here; the main challenge to traditional views of specialization has come from Brunt 1975 and 1983.

58. On the military tribunate, see Campbell 1975, 18–19, citing, e.g., Suet. *Aug.* 38.2 and Pliny *Ep.* 8.14.4–5. On the length of service, some debate exists; Birley (1981, 9 n. 19) defends a longer term of two or three years; Eck (1974, n. 70) thinks three years is too long; Campbell (1975, 18) argues that one year is possible.

59. On legionary legates, see, e.g., Eck 1974, 190; A. R. Birley 1981, 17–20. Tenure of more than one of these posts is attested but apparently unusual.

60. See Campbell 1975, 19–20, for examples; cf. Eck 1974, 176 with n. 76. E. Birley (1954, 208) also notes examples of consular legates who had never commanded troops and points out that Antoninus Pius, for example, had never held a military post before becoming emperor.

posts; and after all, their duties included both spheres. A few might have very little experience of any kind. The idea of specialization seems to have been alien to the Roman aristocracy, where some competence in a variety of fields was expected—including, of course, literary ones.[61]

It has been argued, in this context, that the many treatises on tactics produced during our period—five have survived—were meant to be used as textbooks by senators thrust into positions of command with no formal training and, sometimes, with little practical experience.[62] The literary element persists here too. In conformity with the archaizing trend of the Second Sophistic, Arrian wrote his tactical treatises under the pseudonym Xenophon, referring to the historian of the fourth century B.C.,[63] and Polyaenus' treatise addressed to the emperors Marcus Aurelius and Lucius Verus draws nearly all of its examples from classical and Hellenistic Greek history.[64] The *Stratagems* of Frontinus, an experienced commander and governor of Britain, mixes relatively recent sources like Caesar with the more ancient, traditional material found in Livy, Herodotus, and Thucydides.[65] His section titled "Exploring the Plans of Enemies," for instance, includes no examples later than the second century B.C. and one mythical example.

Nor did the Romans develop the idea of geographical specialization —that is, of creating a high-level expertise in a specific area of the empire or the world. This has been persuasively argued for the Republic, and geographical patterns of promotion are equally difficult to detect for the Principate; the traditional ideals and values of the Republic did not change on this point.[66] There is only one known senator who served

---

61. A. R. Birley (1992) provides a list of eighty-seven consular governors whose careers are fully known; this is an updated and slightly altered version of Campbell's list (1975) (Birley strikes six names because they were patricians and thus not expected to hold offices at the praetorian level, leaving a total of eighty-one, but I include the patricians since this aspect of their status is not relevant here). Of the eighty-seven senators, ten held only civil posts, nineteen held only military posts, fifty-four held both civil and military posts, and four (all, presumably, patricians) had no experience at the praetorian level at all; eight held only one praetorian (civil or military) position. On literary competence see, e.g., A. R. Birley, op. cit., 12, 25–26; and below.

62. Campbell 1987.

63. On Arrian's *Tactica* and *Ectaxis* see Stadter 1980, 41–49; he argues that Xenophon was a given name of Arrian's and not a pseudonym (ibid., 2–3).

64. Krentz and Wheeler 1994, 1:xiv–xv; Campbell 1987, 15–16.

65. Herodotus in Frontinus, *Str.* 1.3.6, 1.5.4, 1.5.25, etc.; Xenophon, 1.4.10, 1.8.12, 1.11.10, etc.; Thucydides, 1.1.10, 1.3.9, etc.; Campbell 1987, 14–15.

66. On the Republic see Gruen 1984, 1:203–249. For the Principate, E. Birley (1957) and some others (e.g., Sherk 1971) tentatively identified patterns of promotion whereby legates of certain praetorian military provinces would go on to govern certain other consular provinces (e.g., first Lower Pannonia, then Upper Pannonia). Eck 1974, 215 n. 296;

as military tribune, legionary legate, and governor of the same province
—the famous case of Agricola, the father-in-law of Tacitus. It is possible
that emperors actually sought to avoid this type of specialization, for
good political reasons; an army might grow too loyal to a long-familiar
commander.[67] If so, it would not be the first instance in the discussion
so far where issues of political prestige took precedence over efficiency;
recall Severus Alexander's march from the Euphrates to the Rhine. The
idea of geographic specialization emerges, apparently, only once: Cassius Dio, looking back two centuries to the reign of Tiberius, writes that
the emperor "made many, and especially those who had governed them
in the past, party to his decisions" when he received embassies.[68] But
in situations of international crisis, the emperor Nero, as we have seen,
consults the *primores civitatis*, and Commodus seeks the advice of οἱ
κράτιστοι τῶν βουλευτῶν—"the most prominent men in the senate"—
not those most knowledgeable about Armenia or the northern frontier.
There is a possible exception: the council of Marcus Aurelius in the late
160s was formed largely of former governors of the Danube provinces.[69]

The exact criteria used to select those who governed provinces and
commanded armies are thus difficult to determine. Since imperial legates
could only be senators, the emperor was necessarily choosing from a
very small pool of talent. A connection to the emperor, who controlled
all appointments, and continual displays of loyalty to him were naturally
critical at all stages.[70] The idea that officials should be selected according
to merit of some kind, as distinct from birth or patronage connections,
is attested.[71] But this idea did not necessarily include expert knowledge
or specialized experience. The author of a treatise on tactics, writing
in the first century A.D., has the following advice on how to choose a
general:

Not according to birth, as in the case of priests, nor according to wealth, as
gymnasiarchs, but one who is intelligent, self-controlled, sober, frugal, used
to hardship, thoughtful, indifferent to money, neither young nor old, and

---

Campbell 1975, 21–22; and A. R. Birley 1981, 29–30, all treat this argument with skepticism.
Philo *Leg.* 245 considers it a rare piece of good luck that the heroic procurator of Judaea,
Petronius, had in the course of his career acquired "some glimmerings" (ἐναύσματα) of
knowledge about Jewish religion.

67. Cf. A. R. Birley 1992, 9.

68. 57.17.9; Crook 1955, 37.

69. See Campbell 1975, 22; Austin and Rankov 1995, 206–207.

70. See Millar 1977, 300–313; and Saller 1982, 42–46, on imperial control of senatorial appointments and the role of patronage. Alföldy 1977, 54–60, emphasizes the importance of loyalty and a close relationship with the emperor.

71. Saller (1982, 94–111) discusses the Roman idea of merit in promotion.

if possible also the father of children and eloquent, and with a good reputation. (Onasander 1.1)

The emphasis is on moral qualities and eloquence rather than specialized training and experience, and this is typical of Roman concerns.[72] Tiberius is praised for his wise policy of distributing offices based on "the nobility of ancestors, the brilliance of military deeds, and illustrious civil abilities."[73] The first qualification, noble ancestry, is given equal weight with skill and achievement. When Pliny writes to the governor of Pannonia asking for an equestrian military post for a friend, he mentions in his recommendation first his friend's lineage, second his friendship with Pliny, third his skill in rhetoric and literary accomplishment (*Ep.* 2.13); in another letter making a similar request he describes his candidate as, first of all, aristocratic and wealthy (*natus splendide abundat facultatibus*), and furthermore "a most fair judge, a most brave advocate, and a most faithful friend" (7.22).[74] Social rank, literary accomplishment, and loyalty emerge as three critical factors in the choice of Rome's most powerful officials.[75] Roman foreign-relations decisions were made not by "experts," but rather by a small elite group that was expected to engage in a wide range of official and semiofficial duties and an equal variety of literary pursuits. Pliny the Elder, while completing a full equestrian career and serving as "friend" to the emperor Vespasian, still also contributed 102 erudite volumes to Latin literature—an accomplishment for which he was very much admired (Pliny *Ep.* 3.5).

This study attempts to reconstruct the point of view of this elite class that made Roman foreign-policy decisions: the focus is on the center rather than the periphery, and on the psychological rather than the material. But this is not the only possible approach to the issue of Roman imperialism in the Principate, which has been the subject of several recent studies offering syntheses of the vast and sophisticated scholarship in the field of frontier archaeology.[76] The very nature and purpose of Ro

72. See ibid., 95–98, 101–103, on the prominent moral aspect of merit in ancient sources. On morality as an element of aristocratic prestige, see Lendon 1997, 40–42.

73. *nobilitatem maiorum, claritudinem militiae, inlustris domi artes spectando* (Tac. *Ann.* 4.6).

74. On this point see E. Birley 1957, 105–106 with n. 24. On Pliny's commendations, see also Saller 1982, 106–110, arguing that their vague nature and emphasis on moral qualities, and on qualities such as deference and loyalty, make them relatively meaningless outside the context of a traditional system where ties of friendship and patronage are the organizing principles behind the bureaucracy.

75. See n. 57 above.

76. See especially Isaac 1992 and Whittaker 1994, discussed below. The debate up to this point is summarized in Whittaker 1996.

man frontiers have become the subjects of critical reassessment. While it was once usual to imagine the Roman frontier as a carefully planned and rationally constructed system of defense,[77] this view has been challenged in a recent work by Benjamin Isaac, first published in 1988.[78] Isaac argues that Roman goals in the eastern provinces were never defensive, but that the function of the military infrastructure in that region aimed primarily at aggression against Parthia and control of the local population. Another work, that of C. R. Whittaker (1994), seeks to replace the idea of military frontier lines with "frontier zones" of mainly social and economic significance. All Roman frontiers individually are also undergoing reanalysis and reinterpretation. This, however, I must leave to those more qualified. The premise of the present work is that the surviving literary evidence also provides valid insights into the thinking or strategy behind Roman foreign relations, and that this literary evidence, like the material evidence, should benefit from reexamination.

The sense that emerges from much of recent scholarship on Roman frontier archaeology is one of fragmentation. Scholarship has tended to emphasize, instead of a long-term military strategy, the discontinuities and disjunctions of place and time that seem to preclude generalization: frontier structures now reflect local circumstances rather than a coherent empire-wide plan. The Romans, it is argued, did not have the tools or the information to formulate a geopolitical strategy in the modern sense. Frontiers were not chosen for strategic reasons but congealed as a result of failure or nonmilitary factors.[79]

This study supports some of the ideas just described. But a further question then arises: If no coherent strategy or plan that is immediately recognizable *to us* emerges from a study of Roman frontiers, how then do we explain the success, or even the existence, of the empire? Are we perhaps seeking Roman strategy in the wrong places, and possibly using terms (*aggression, defense*) that are inadequate to describe it?

The Roman view of the geographical world, for example, as it emerges from abundant literary evidence, seems at first glance schematic—that is, simplistic; too simplistic a framework for a complex geopolitical strategy. When we turn to the Romans' image of peoples outside the empire, we also find that they had no specific understanding of foreign social or political institutions. But though Roman perceptions of the world seem to lack a certain level of complexity from the modern point

77. A view usually associated with Luttwak 1976; more recently, see Ferrill 1991 and Wheeler 1993. In defense of imperial "grand strategy" see also Potter 1996.

78. Cited here in the second edition: Isaac 1992.

79. See, e.g., Mann 1974 and 1979, Millar 1982, Isaac 1992, Whittaker 1994.

of view, they were based on a long and intricate literary tradition. This tradition reflected a certain set of values and sense of cultural identity. And it is here—in questions of values and image or identity—that we should seek what we would call today foreign policy.

The division of a subject into manageable chapters is never an easy task, and in the present work it is especially problematic. The categories of military strategy and economics seem straightforward and necessary enough to a modern reader; further, manpower and money placed certain "real" constraints on Roman policy and did form a fundamental part of Roman thinking. Legions could be shuttled and reassigned only at a risk; war was expensive, and methods of raising money were limited. But in each case we find that Roman thought on what seem to be the most practical questions involves issues of status or morality—thus the emphasis on terror and vengeance in Roman military strategy, or the powerful symbolism of dominance and submission, honor and deference that was attached to the collection of tribute. It is especially here, in the realm of the moral and psychological, that we find complexity in Roman thought and policy.

The categories of "strategy" and "income and expenditure" then, are a convenience; they cannot really be separated from the category of "values" (which forms the final chapter of this book), where we ultimately find the explanations of Roman behavior. Most of all, this was a system of responses based on a concern for the empire's status or "honor." What mattered most was how the empire, and to some degree the emperor, were perceived by foreigners and subjects. Symbolic deference from the enemy was a policy goal; arrogance and insult, described in exactly those words, were just and necessary causes for war. Terror and vengeance were instruments for maintaining the empire's image. Roman strategy was thus partly moral and psychological in nature. If this strategy is not easy to trace on a map, that does not necessarily mean it was incoherent, "irrational," or ineffective. The system I have briefly outlined could dictate specific responses to specific situations, which remained consistent over a long period of time. And the Romans, unlike some modern nations, knew when they had won or lost a war.

While the Romans emerge from this study as relatively aggressive in their foreign policy, I would also like to suggest that "aggression" and "defense"—though the latter forms a convenient subheading for the third chapter, on strategy—are ultimately inadequate to describe Roman foreign relations. Rarely was the drive to expand the empire *in itself* an impetus for war; money in the form of plunder, and personal glory

for the emperor or military commander, were also secondary considerations, although all three of these things were considered to be good
results (not good *causes*) of a successful war, and were occasionally the
"real" causes as well. But the most compelling pattern of behavior is one
of insult and revenge, revolt and retaliation, which involved the image
or status of the Roman state as a whole rather than that of individual
emperors and generals. The Romans succeeded in part because they believed in this system.

---| CHAPTER 2 |---

The Image of the World

1. Introduction

It is difficult to imagine how one would approach the study of Roman history without maps. Today's maps are based on exhaustive land surveys and, more recently, satellite photographs; superimposed on this surface are the results of many decades of research on the locations of ancient cities, forts, and frontiers. There are, as a rule, no vast tracts labeled "terra incognita" or "here the dog-headed creatures live." But in these respects modern maps are of limited use if we truly wish to understand the thinking behind Roman foreign relations, for nothing of the kind existed in the Roman world.[1]

1. On Roman geographical conceptions and their relationship to foreign relations, substantial bibliography exists. Brunt 1963, 175; Moynihan 1986; and Nicolet 1991 (first published in French in 1988) all focus on the reign of Augustus; see also the important review by Purcell (1990a) of Nicolet's work. More generally, see Millar 1982, 15–20; Talbert 1987; Purcell 1990; Isaac 1992, 401–408; Whittaker 1994, 12–18; and especially Brodersen 1995 (this chapter was completed before I had the opportunity to read his important work). Cf. also MacMullen 1976, 52–54. On the later empire, see the recent work of Lee 1993. For the *cenocephali*, see the *Tabula Peutingeriana*, section IX.5. For Ptolemy's famous "γῆ ἄγνωστος," or terra incognita, cf. Romm 1992, 43. On modern maps and atlases of the ancient world, see Talbert 1992, stressing the inadequacy of these efforts; but anyone who has taught or taken an ancient-history course knows how much these tools, no matter how flawed, shape the modern scholar's understanding of the subject.

Today's flat political maps that make the earth look like a colored checkerboard are obviously not the only way, nor are they necessarily the "best" or most "realistic" way, to represent the world. But our perception based on such maps influences how we think about the relationship between nations. What about the Roman point of view? It is important to try to see the world as Rome's leaders saw it. Much of the information that the postindustrial age takes for granted—political, economic, or topographical, for example—was not available to the Romans, although to some degree they were able to acquire concrete data about the world around them, such as distances along a certain route. This material was largely gathered by the army, which is the subject of the next part of this chapter. But it was very difficult, under the conditions prevailing in antiquity, to acquire such information. Much of what the Romans knew or believed about the world had another character— that of literary tradition. This is true especially for the genre of ethnography, which recorded Roman perceptions about the world's peoples. Yet the idea of the barbarian is by no means simple or, in its own way, unsophisticated. It is important not only to examine the limitations on the information available to the Romans, but also to reconstruct in a positive way the traditions that formed, literally, their worldview.

The typical education of a member of the senatorial class focused, as noted in chapter 1, mainly on rhetoric. Geography was a minor subject, touched on lightly; in a well-known passage, one third-century panegyrist suggests that schoolchildren should be taken to see a map of the world painted on a portico, the better to admire the glory of the Roman empire. It is possible that a good example of what might be taught by a *grammaticus* (secondary-school teacher) survives in the brief verse geography of Dionysius Periegetes. It was probably composed in the second century, and by the fourth century had become popular enough to acquire a Latin translation and scholia; in fact, the author writes that the purpose of his poem is "to relate to you the appearance of the land . . . whereby you will appear respectable and more impressive, explaining the details to an ignorant person" (170–173).[2] It was not unusual to find geographic and ethnographic digressions in historical works, such

2. Geography was considered a subcategory of astronomy and is included in the astronomical treatises of Manilius, Geminus, and Cleomedes. Astronomy traditionally belonged to the liberal arts and was considered fundamental by Cicero (Bonner 1977, 77–79); but Marrou (1956, 281–282) argues that the sciences were in fact largely neglected by the Romans. On Dionysius see recently Jacob 1990, with a French translation of the text; a date in the reign of Hadrian is indicated by an acrostic in the poem. The Greek text is published in Karl Müller 1882. On its pedagogical purpose, see ibid., xv; Aujac 1987a, 171–

as Caesar's commentaries on his Gallic campaigns, or Tacitus' biography of his father-in-law, the governor of Britain. There was thus a perceived relationship between geography and war. Strabo, writing in Greek in the reign of Augustus and Tiberius, expresses the hope that his treatise may help generals to avoid recent mistakes in Parthia and Germany, where ignorance of the land allowed the Romans to be tricked and outmaneuvered by barbarians accustomed to fighting in deserts and swamps; or more legendary errors such as that of Agamemnon, who sacked the wrong city (1.1.16–17). Someone like Strabo or Pliny the Elder, who threw himself into the task, would use not only earlier geographical sources but the latest reports from the army, merchants, or embassies (see below); others, like the Latin geographer Pomponius Mela, would rely on older, more traditional sources, including Homer and Herodotus. Thus Arrian, governor of Cappadocia under Hadrian and author of historical and tactical works in Greek, uses no source later than the third century B.C. for his treatise on India.[3] Traditional views of the world and its peoples persisted even after new information became, theoretically, available. There is thus some tension in Roman geography, and in ethnography as well, between a drive to acquire new information and a respect for what was, by now, a long and complex literary tradition about the world and its peoples.

2. The Army

The Romans inhabited a world without modern land-surveying techniques, without aerial or satellite photography, and without the compass. The bird's-eye view was not available to them; the only reliable way to acquire information about an area was to march through it, ideally with an army. Thus ancient sources give us the impression that detailed geographical knowledge of a region could normally result only from direct military intervention in the area; such knowledge was gathered on campaign. Strabo writes that tribes beyond the Elbe River in Germany are unknown because the Romans never advanced that far (7.2.4). In the exhaustively researched geographical books of his *Natural History,* Pliny the Elder also implies that one cannot expect to know

---

172; Dilke 1987a, 255; Jacob, op. cit., 11–14. For Eumenius' suggestion about the map, see Mynors 1964, IX(IV).20.2.

3. On Mela's sources see Silberman 1988, xxx–xliii; Mela does mention Roman expeditions in Germany and the recent campaigns of Claudius. On Arrian's sources, see Brunt 1976–1983, 2:444–453.

much about places where the Roman army has never been.[4] Pomponius Mela, apologizing for his ignorance about the island of Britain, expects better information soon: "behold, having been closed so long, the greatest of emperors [sc., Claudius] opens it, victor over tribes not only unconquered before him, but in truth even unknown" (3.49). Tacitus writes that the empty rhetoric of earlier authorities about the island was replaced by hard fact only when it was "fully conquered" (*Agr.* 10).[5] It is to war that the ancient sources attribute their information about the north coast of Germany, the Arabian peninsula, and Armenia and the Caucasus region, as well as the Mount Atlas region and other parts of the interior of Africa.[6] But evidence is scanty, which makes it difficult to generalize about the sort of material that was acquired on campaign and the detail and consistency with which it was collected. This is because, after Caesar, none of the commentaries, memoirs, or dispatches in which geographical information was usually reported have survived. Important works that probably made use of these sources, such as Pliny the Elder's history of the German wars and all seventeen books of Arrian's *Parthica*, have also been lost. Nevertheless, from what remains it is possible to form an impression of the nature of the material.

The most common sort of information that could be gathered on campaign was the itinerary. When Trajan invaded Dacia, he took along,

4. In 4.102, on Britain: "Pytheas and Isidorus report that it means in circumference 4,875 [sc., Roman miles] and almost thirty years ago Roman arms extended the knowledge of it, not beyond the vicinity of the Caledonian forest." In 5.51: "The Nile arises from uncertain sources, since it runs through burning wastelands for an immense span of distance; and it is explored by unarmed rumor only, without the wars that have discovered all other lands." In 4.98, Agrippa records that Germany, Raetia, and Noricum together have a length of 636 miles and a width of 248 miles, "though the width of Raetia alone is almost greater than that; granted that it was conquered around the time of his [Agrippa's] death, for Germany was not thoroughly known for many years after that, and even then not all of it."

5. See also ibid., 33.3, where Agricola tells his troops that "we do not grasp the boundary of Britain by legend and rumor but we hold it with camps and arms; Britain has been discovered and subjected."

6. On Germany, see Pliny *HN* 4.97, Tac. *Germ.* 1, and below; on Arabia, Pliny *HN* 6.160–161 and Strab. 2.5.12, both crediting the expedition of Aelius Gallus; on Armenia and the Caucasus, Pliny *HN* 6.23 writes that he has more accurate information about the interior of Asia from Corbulo's expedition; the area was also known to the Romans from the campaigns of Pompey, which were recorded by the historian Theophanes, who accompanied him (Strab. 11.5.1), and from Antony's expedition, of which an account was written by his friend Dellius, who was there (Strab. 11.13.3); on Africa, Suetonius Paulinus explored the Mount Atlas region (Pliny *HN* 5.14–15); Petronius explored Ethiopia (ibid., 6.181; cf. Strab. 17.1.54), and Balbus the territory south of Cyrenaica (see below). On the role of the army in acquiring geographical information, including most of the expeditions mentioned here and below, see Sherk 1974; Nicolet 1991, chap. 4, "Explorations and Expeditions"; and Austin and Rankov 1995, 112–115 and passim.

among other technical experts, a surveyor named Balbus, whose duties seem to have included measuring the distances between stops along the route.[7] A schematic rendering of this itinerary may appear on Trajan's column.[8] The *Antonine Itinerary*, a list of place-names and distances along routes throughout the empire dating to the third century A.D., may have originated as a plan for Caracalla's march to the east and related movements of troops.[9] The *Historia Augusta* records that Severus Alexander not only followed an itinerary when he set out for the eastern front but published it beforehand, so that he could be located at any time (*Alex. Sev.* 45); and in the fourth century certainly, the author of a military handbook asserts the importance of itineraries on campaign, whether lists of places and distances, or what he calls *itineraria picta*, drawings showing routes and distances, mountains and rivers.[10] There is also evidence that some commanders collected this sort of information when they ventured into unknown territory. The records from Petronius' campaigns in Ethiopia under Augustus indicated that the farthest point he reached was 870 miles from the city of Syene.[11] The campaigns of Nero's general Corbulo in Armenia produced what Pliny describes as *situs depicti*, "places drawn," and another expedition under Nero drew a *forma Aethiopiae*, a picture of Ethiopia, which may have been similar to Vegetius' "drawn itineraries." [12] The *Geography* of Ptolemy, written

7. Sherk 1974, 541–542, including the text of Balbus' letter describing his duties as preserved in the *Corpus agrimensorum*, n. 27. The existence of military surveyors in the legions, praetorians, and even auxiliaries is well attested; their duties seem to have involved planning and laying out camps, military colonies, and land allocated to soldiers, as well as constructing roads (ibid., 546–558).

8. Koeppel 1980.

9. Van Berchem 1937, 166–181; cf. id. 1973; Rivet and Smith (1979, 151–153) accept his conclusions. See Reed 1978 for a somewhat different interpretation, arguing that the *Itinerary* reflects specific imperial journeys and routes for military supplies. The *Antonine Itinerary* is published in Cuntz 1929.

10. Vegetius 3.6 recommends that a conscientious general have detailed itineraries, "drawn" if possible, on hand for all regions in which the war will be fought: "first he should have thoroughly written out as fully as possible itineraries of all the regions in which the war is being waged, so that he may learn thoroughly the intervals between places, not only regarding the number of miles but even the quality of the roads, and inspect carefully the shortcuts, bypaths, mountains, and rivers, faithfully described; indeed the more prudent generals were fortified by having obtained itineraries of the provinces to which necessity used to take them, which were not only annotated but even drawn." On itineraries generally, see Kubitschek 1916; Dilke 1985, chap. 8; id. 1987c, 234–242; Brodersen 1995, 165–190. On the later empire, see Lee 1993, 85–87.

11. For Petronius' expedition, see *HN* 6.181–182; Desanges 1978, 307–321.

12. On Corbulo's maps, see Pliny *HN* 6.40: "The error of many must be corrected at this point, even of those who were recently on campaign in Armenia with Corbulo. For they call 'Caspian' the gates of Iberia, which I have indicated are called 'Caucasian,' and the

sometime in the mid–second century A.D., may have used itineraries produced by the campaigns of Agricola as a source for place-names in Scotland.[13] Information like this—the distances between towns—was important to a commander who had to find food and water for his troops and fodder for the cavalry and the animals in the baggage train: while an army might be supplied "as far as the boundaries of the barbarians" via the empire's system of roads and taxes (see below, chap. 4), once in enemy territory it necessarily relied on foraging and pillaging.[14] Corbulo's army, on campaign in the deserts of Armenia, suffered from lack of water and food until it reached cultivated land, and Severus' campaigns in Mesopotamia encountered similar problems.[15] The fact that Severus had difficulties with supplies in this region even after Trajan's Parthian campaigns should warn us that information, once gathered, was not necessarily available or useful to subsequent commanders.

Military expeditions might also contribute to geographical knowledge in a more general sense. Tiberius' and Drusus' campaigns in central Europe discovered the source of the Danube River,[16] and campaigns in Germany under Augustus advanced Roman knowledge about the Cimbric peninsula, or modern Denmark, and islands of the Baltic Sea.[17] Corbulo sent diagrams of the Caucasus region to Rome, as noted above, and also offered an opinion on the source of the Euphrates (but disagreed on this point with Licinius Mucianus, who accompanied him on the campaign).[18] During the course of his conquests in Britain, Agricola sent an expedition to prove that it was an island (and not, presumably, the undiscovered continent that some imagined it to be) by circumnavigating it, and in the process "discovered" the Orkney Islands.[19] Cor-

---

drawings of regions (*situs depicti*) that were sent from there have this name inscribed on them." For the *Aethiopiae forma*, see Pliny *HN* 12.18–19; cf. Austin and Rankov 1995, 115.

13. Rivet 1977, especially pp. 54, 58.

14. See the influential study of Engels (1978) on the difficulties of carrying supplies over long distances; on the Roman army, see Breeze 1987–1988, 19–23; Roth 1990, 243–267. *Usque ad fines barbarorum* (SHA *Alex. Sev.* 45, quoted in chap. 4 below).

15. Corbulo, Tac. *Ann.* 14.24; Severus, Cass. Dio 75.2.1–2; cf. SHA *Sev.* 16.1–2, where soldiers must live on the local roots and grasses around Ctesiphon. On these examples see Adams 1976, 225–227, 235–236; and 217–267 on the question of supplies in general. For more on army supply, see below, chap. 4, sec. 2.1.

16. Strab. 7.1.5; see Dion 1977, 242–245, on this expedition and its contribution.

17. On the complicated question of which expeditions in the region discovered what, see Nicolet 1991, 87, with n. 17.

18. For Corbulo and Mucianus on the source of the Euphrates, see Pliny *HN* 5.83; on these sources in general, see Sallmann 1971, 44–47.

19. Tac. *Agr.* 10.4; Cass. Dio 39.50.4; however, the Orkneys are already known to Mela (3.54) and Pliny (*HN* 4.103). On the expedition under Agricola, see Ogilvie and Richmond 1967, 31–32.

bulo also made a scientific note of the hour at which a solar eclipse was observed in Armenia, probably in order to establish the longitude of his position; Caesar before him had carefully measured the lengths of the days in Britain in order to ascertain its latitude, and so, later, did Septimius Severus.[20]

Certainly a careful record of tribes and cities conquered, as well as local mountains and rivers—including as many previously unheard-of names as possible—was necessary for anyone who hoped to celebrate a triumph, and Pliny the Elder lists the *Acta triumphorum*, or triumphal records, as a source in the indices of his geographical books. The most striking example is the case of Cornelius Balbus, who celebrated a triumph over the Garamantes of northern Africa in 19 B.C.; Pliny lists thirty towns (*oppida*), tribes (*nationes*), rivers, and mountains whose "names and representations" were carried in the procession (*HN* 5.37).[21] The details of the region's topography and terrain that Pliny reports (5.35–36) probably resulted from the same expedition. Balbus was the first Roman general to penetrate so far into the interior of Africa. It is possible that he recorded the mileage of his route, and that this information lay behind a correction of the map attributed to Agrippa by Pliny (in *HN* 6.209), making Africa much wider than was previously thought.[22]

Military intervention could also produce ethnographic, political, or economic information in some cases. The records from the future Augustus' assault on the Getae reported that their country was divided into five parts and that the Dacians could field an army of forty thousand (Strab. 7.3.11–12). When Aelius Gallus returned from his disastrous expedition to Arabia Felix in 25–24 B.C., he brought back—besides a list of "towns not mentioned by authors who wrote before," which he had destroyed—information on the customs of the tribes of the Arabian

20. On the eclipse, see *HN* 2.180; for measuring the lengths of days, Caes. *B Gall.* 5.13; Cass. Dio 76[77].13.3.

21. The *titulus* of Mount Gyrus announced the interesting fact that gemstones were produced there. Petronius provided a list of towns captured in Ethiopia (Pliny *HN* 6.181), as did Aelius Gallus in Arabia (ibid., 6.160–161). Triumphs seem always to have included *tituli* and/or representations of tribes, cities, and major geographical features, which would have to be kept track of; e.g., Ovid *Ars Am.* 1.210–229, Tac. *Ann.* 2.41, etc.; for the full list of references on this point, see Ehlers 1939, 502–503, and Brodersen 1995, 118–126. The *tituli* for the Jewish triumph of Titus are clearly depicted in the south relief panel from Titus' arch, showing the procession of the spoils (see, e.g., Künzl 1988, 22, with illust. 8).

22. On his expedition, see Desanges 1978, 189–195. For the theory that Balbus is the source for Agrippa's figure ("Agrippa made [the width of Africa] 910 miles at the Cyrenaic part, including the desert up to the Garamantes, as far as was known"), see ibid., 193–195.

peninsula. He also reported on the resources of each tribe, and that the Sabaeans were the wealthiest of them all, producing gold and the immensely lucrative perfumes for which Arabia was famous.[23] However, this particular fact or legend is recorded by another author a century earlier, and the literary tradition, rather than autopsy, may be Gallus' source.[24] His overall contribution to Roman geography was disappointing; Strabo explains that because of the extreme difficulties Gallus encountered in the Arabian campaign, he did little to advance knowledge about the area (16.4.24). Pliny, who must have had access to the general's reports, describes the Arabian peninsula as being about the size and shape of Italy.[25] It is especially in this respect—the spatial representation of the world—that Roman perceptions differed radically from what is available to modern readers; I shall return to this point below.

Two African expeditions of the later first century A.D. led to a major revision of the map by some experts. Marinus, a geographer of the first century A.D. whose work is known only through the critical comments of Ptolemy in his *Geography,* recorded that one Septimius Flaccus "after setting out on campaign from Libya arrived at Ethiopia from the [land of the] Garamantes in three months, journeying to the south." Later, Julius Maternus, again setting out from Garama, had come in four months to a place called Agisymba, "a land of the Ethiopians where rhinoceroses congregate" (*Geog.* 1.8.5).[26] While both Flaccus and Maternus recorded the distance between Garama and the coastal city of Leptis Magna as 5,400 stades,[27] they apparently did not keep such records of the rest of their march or attempt astronomical measurements like Caesar's or Corbulo's. Marinus based his calculations of Africa's width solely on the length of time that Maternus' journey took. He initially located Agisymba 24,680 stades south of the equator but, alarmed at this figure, reduced it arbitrarily to 12,000 stades. Ptolemy, arguing that rhinoceroses could not exist more than 8,200 stades south of the equa-

23. Strab. 16.4.24; Mela 1.61; Pliny *HN* 5.65, 6.160–161, 12.53–84. Strabo was a personal friend of Gallus, and accompanied him to Ethiopia (2.5.12).

24. Diodorus 3.46–47, probably based on Agatharchides; see Klaus Müller 1972–1980, 1:281–283.

25. *HN* 6.143–144.

26. See Aujac 1993, 113–117. On the expeditions of Flaccus and Maternus, see Desanges 1978, 189–213, arguing that Maternus was a civilian merchant seeking to procure the exotic animals reported by Flaccus.

27. On the length of a stade, a perennial problem, see Engels 1985; by Pliny's time the ratio of 1 Roman mile to 8 stades had become canonical (*HN* 2.85), which yields the ratio of 1 English mile to 8.7 stades.

tor because they were not found more than 8,200 stades north of it, reduced the distance still further. It was beginning to become clear that
Africa was much wider than had once been thought. But the data to
form a convincing two-dimensional image of the continent were not
there.[28]

In some cases, the accuracy and practical applicability of the geographical information gathered on campaign may have been limited by
the form in which it was presented. It seems that most of this information was recorded and preserved in the form of dispatches to the senate,
together with the commentaries or memoirs of the emperor or military
commander if he produced any. All of these were subject to manipulation by their authors with a view to self-glorification. In the case of dispatches, the evidence suggests that their main function was not to report regularly on the progress of the war but to announce victories.
These letters were sometimes grandiloquent in style and blatantly self-
serving.[29] Tacitus singles out Agricola for praise because he did not affix
laurels to the report of his suppression of the Ordovices (*Agr.* 18.6) and
did not exaggerate his deeds in his dispatches (ibid., 39.1). But this is
clearly considered unusual. It is true that Lucian, complaining of the
quality of recent histories of Lucius Verus' eastern campaigns, writes that
historians sometimes report exaggerated casualties that conflict with figures recorded "in the letters of the generals" (*Hist. conscr.* 20); he thus
implies that military dispatches could be, on this point, a check on the
accuracy of historiography. On the other hand, a long letter survives by
his contemporary Fronto in praise of the rhetorical style (*eloquentia*) of
the same emperor's latest letter to the senate, in which he announced

28. On the expeditions of Flaccus and Maternus, see Desanges 1978, 197–213. On the
measurement from Leptis Magna to Garama, see Ptol. *Geog.* 1.10.2; Ptolemy's estimate of
8,200 stades, 1.10.1; rhinoceroses (plus elephants and black people), 1.9.9; Marinus' distances to Agisymba, 1.8; cf. Thomson 1948, 266. A translation of the more substantial narrative parts of Ptolemy's *Geography* may be found in Aujac 1993.

29. On announcing victories, see, e.g., Tac. *Ann.* 3.47, where Tiberius informs the
senate of the war with Sacrovir only after it has been won; though Tacitus remarks on Tiberius' self-restraint: "he neither detracted from the truth nor added to it." Also Suet.
Gaius 44.2; Cass. Dio 68.29.1–2 (Trajan), 71[72].10.5 (Marcus); SHA *Sev.* 9.1–3; Cass. Dio
77[78].22.3 (Caracalla). See also Herodian 3.9.12: after the sack of Ctesiphon, Severus
"wrote to the senate and the people, extolling his accomplishments, and having his battles
and victories set up in public displays." Letters announcing victories had laurels affixed to
them (Pliny *HN* 15.133; Cass. Dio 62.19.1, etc.). The task of conveying the news of a victory was a prestigious one (Alföldy and Halfmann 1979; Cass. Dio 60.21.5, with Halfmann
1986, 99). On imperial dispatches and their tone, see Campbell 1984, 148–149; also Talbert 1984, 230, 427–428; on commentaries, letters, and memoirs as containing geographical information, Sherk 1974, 537–543, and Austin and Rankov 1995, 118.

certain victories in the eastern war: the emphasis here is on what appears to be the very high rhetorical content of the dispatch (*Ad Verum imp.* ii.1, Loeb 2:129–151). The temptation to exaggerate the distances progressed, to convert villages into cities, and perhaps even to invent nonexistent peoples must have been overwhelming.[30] Trajan wrote to the senate during his Parthian expedition that he had progressed farther than Alexander, and Caracalla boasted in his letters that he had subjected the entire east.[31] Both claims, of course, were wildly exaggerated.

Of the commentaries and memoirs produced by generals on campaign, none has left enough trace for us to be able to determine its tone.[32] Appian, however, complains that he can get little information about Pannonian history from Augustus' commentaries on his campaigns there, and that he still does not know how some Illyrian tribes came under Roman rule, because the emperor "did not write about others' accomplishments, but of his own, how he forced those who had revolted to pay tribute again, and how he subjected others who had been free from the beginning, and how he conquered all those who live in the heights of the Alps, barbaric and warlike tribes who used to plunder neighboring Italy" (*Ill.* 14–15). In all of these sources—imperial dispatches, commentaries, and memoirs—there was thus an important ideological agenda that went beyond the mere recording of fact. Appian recognizes a tension here and is frustrated by it; Lucian's comment on the accuracy of casualty figures, cited above, reflects the same point of view; but such comments are relatively rare. In general I would argue that we do not see a sharp distinction in the Roman mind between rhetoric and "fact." The genre of history was and is rhetorical. So, apparently, was the genre of the senatorial dispatch. So was the genre of war commentary, as Appian suggests, and as any reader of Caesar's two masterpieces must acknowledge; in fact, it was in Caesar's commentaries on the Gallic war that the problematic concept of "Germany" was invented (see below).

The focus of discussion so far has been on information gathered on

---

30. This is well attested in the Republic; cf. Versnel 1970, 304 n. 2, and a remark in Strab. 3.4.13: Polybius says Tiberius Gracchus destroyed three hundred cities in Celtiberia, but Posidonius criticized this number as exaggerated, for "he called the towers cities just like in the triumphal parades."

31. On Trajan, see Cass. Dio 68.29.2; on Caracalla, Herodian 4.11.8.

32. Titus and Vespasian wrote commentaries on the Jewish war, which Josephus used; Trajan wrote commentaries on the Dacian wars, of which only one sentence remains; Balbus, Corbulo, Septimius Severus, and possibly Hadrian wrote memoirs. See Campbell 1984, 151–155; Sherk 1974, 539–540.

campaign—but what about where the army had never been? How much geographical and topographical reconnaissance was possible for the Romans, and how much did they attempt? On the tactical and "operational" levels—during the course of a particular campaign, for example—scouts, spies, and the like are well attested.[33] Of long-term advance reconnaissance only three examples survive. The first is from the reign of Augustus, who in 2 B.C. sent his grandson Gaius on an expedition to the east. Before he left, Augustus had two reports prepared, according to Pliny (he is discussing the city of Charax, on the Persian Gulf):

> It has not escaped me that this is the place where Dionysius was born, the most recent author of a geography of the world (*situs orbis terrarum*), whom the divine Augustus sent ahead to report on everything in the east, when his older son [i.e., Gaius, his adopted son] was about to go to Armenia to the Parthian and Arabian campaigns (*ad Parthicas Arabicasque res*); . . . at this point nevertheless I would rather follow Roman arms and King Juba, and the volumes he wrote to the same Gaius Caesar concerning that same Arabian expedition. (*HN* 6.141)

It is possible that a part of one of these reports survives in the form of the *Parthian Stations* of Isidorus of Charax, if "Dionysius" here is in fact, as seems likely, a mistake for "Isidorus," and if, as seems less likely, the work that survives today is a fragment of that report.[34] The report, called *Stathmoi Parthikoi* in its original language, gives distances—in *schoeni*, a Persian measurement—between stops across the Parthian empire along a route from Zeugma to Alexandropolis in Arachosia. It is detailed for the route down the Euphrates, where Isidorus provides measurements for short distances between towns, sometimes also naming their founders, and whether they are fortified, and a few other items. The text becomes increasingly less informative as it progresses east; for

---

33. E.g., Tac. *Ann.* 13.5 (*exploratores* inform Corbulo about the movement of the enemy's army); Trajan's army included scouts (πρόσκοποι; Cass. Dio 68.23.2). Deserters might reveal an army's plans, as in Tac. *Ann.* 2.12 and Cass. Dio 68.14.5. See Austin and Rankov 1995, chap. 3; Breeze 1987–1988, 14–15.

34. No Dionysius of Charax is mentioned in Pliny's indices or known today, though an Isidorus of Charax appears among the list of sources for book 2. For the arguments on this point, see Weissbach 1916, 2065–2066; more recently Sallmann 1971, 50–52; and Tarn 1984, 54–55. The identification of this Isidorus of Charax with the author of the *Parthian Stations,* which contains no certain references later that 26 B.C., can be found in Karl Müller 1882, 1:lxxxi–lxxxv, as well as in the edition, with English translation and commentary, of Schoff (1914, 17). One Isidorus of Charax wrote a *Journey around Parthia,* cited by Athenaeus on pearl fishing in the Persian Gulf (3.93), which was much more elaborate than the jejune treatise that survives. It is possible that the *Journey around Parthia* was the work composed for Augustus' grandson, and that the *Parthian Stations* is a fragment of it.

the farthest-off regions, Isidorus offers only the name of the region, the length of the route through it, and the number of stations (σταθμοί) to be found there. His identification of Alexandropolis as the eastern border of the Parthian empire is problematic and probably anachronistic.[35] One theory holds that Isidorus' report is based on a survey conducted by Mithridates II around 100 B.C.; if so, he may have been looking at an official Parthian document, but this is pure conjecture.[36] Another source frequently cited for information on the east by authors of the imperial period is the survey conducted by Alexander the Great on his campaign. He brought with him two surveyors, or *bematistae*, Dagnetus and Baeton, who measured his march and published the results in a work called *Stations of Alexander's March*, mentioned by Pliny the Elder and later by Athenaeus. One Amyntas also published a *Stations of Asia*, apparently based on the same information.[37]

Other potential sources of information on the Parthian empire were the merchants who plied the overland trade routes to India and China, though to what degree they were used (or useful) is unclear. Although there is no direct evidence after Caesar that merchants were consulted for purposes of military reconnaissance, the geographical sources refer to them often; Marinus and Tacitus both ascribe their information about Ireland to merchants, though Marinus is dismissive (Ptol. *Geog.* 1.11.8; Tac. *Agr.* 24.2). In his discussion of amber, Pliny reports that a knight sent on a special expedition to procure this commodity in Nero's reign recorded the distance from Carnuntum, in Pannonia, to the Baltic coast as six hundred miles.[38] But usually traders are cited in discussions about the sea route from the Red Sea to the Persian Gulf or to India; the direct route to India had been exploited since the discovery of the monsoon in the late second century B.C.[39] Merchants also sailed from the

35. On the political history of Parthia, see Debevoise 1938; Colledge 1967; Bivar 1983; Wolski 1993.

36. For this argument see, Tarn 1984, 54–55.

37. Pliny *HN* 6.61, cf. 6.45; Strab. 15.1.11, 15.2.8. On these sources see Pearson 1954–1955, 440–443; Brunt 1976–1983, 2:487–489; also Engels 1978, app. 5, table 8, on the measurements of the *bematistae* (as recorded in Strabo and Pliny) vs. actual distances. The measurements are very accurate.

38. *HN* 37.45; Kolendo 1981.

39. See Strab. 2.5.12 on merchants as sources for Arabia and India, together with Aelius Gallus' expedition; 15.1.4 on the limitations of their information about India. Pliny cites *mercatores* or *negotiatores* as sources for several points east: *HN* 6.101 on the sea route to India; 6.88 for a vague reference to the trade with China; 6.139–140 on the town of Charax, together with King Juba and "envoys of the Arabs;" 6.146 for some political history of Charax; 6.149 on ports of the Persian Gulf; 6.173 on the coast of Ethiopia. On the

Red Sea south along the African coast as far as Rhapta and, by Ptolemy's time, beyond;[40] the anonymous *Periplus Maris Erythraei,* or "Voyage around the Red Sea," written in the mid–first century by a trader familiar with the route to Rhapta and at least the western coast of India, is an example of what this type of source might have to offer.[41] It is noteworthy, however, that while Strabo, Pliny, and Ptolemy refer to these merchants as important sources, the second-century author Arrian, reporting that Alexander's expedition had considered but not attempted the circumnavigation of the Arabian peninsula, does not know that such a voyage is possible (*Ind.* 43).

By Marinus' time Roman merchants had been all the way to China; and a Chinese source records the presence there of a delegation from Marcus Aurelius in 166 A.D.[42] But Marinus and Ptolemy can report only that the journey took seven months from the Stone Tower (an unidentified point in modern Afghanistan), so that, even after reducing Marinus' estimate of the journey's distance by an arbitrary one-half for stops and deviations in the route, Ptolemy still greatly overestimates the length of Asia.[43] Merchants were untrustworthy sources. Caesar complained that the *mercatores* he questioned about Britain knew only about the part that faced Gaul, and "therefore although he called merchants to him from everywhere, he was unable to discover the magnitude of the island, nor which nations inhabited it nor how many, nor what style of war they had nor what customs they used, nor which harbors were suitable for a great number of large ships" (*B Gall.* 4.20). In the imperial period, Strabo complains that the merchants who have been to the Ganges are "private citizens and useless for the history of the places" (15.1.4), and Marinus adds that "they do not care about investigating the truth, since they are busy with trade; and often they exaggerate distances a great deal in boasting." Thus he rejects the merchant Philemon's information about the length of Ireland (Ptol. *Geog.* 1.11.8). The author of the *Periplus Maris Erythraei* is able to provide fairly accurate distances in stades between ports in the Red Sea, the south coast of Arabia, and part of the west coast of India; and vaguer distances in night-

---

history of the trade with India there is a long bibliography; Casson 1989 is very useful, and see Sidebotham 1986, 8–9, on the discovery of the monsoon.

40. Pliny *HN* 6.173; Ptol. *Geog.* 1.17.6.

41. For a recent edition of the *Periplus* with an English translation and a thorough introduction and commentary, see Casson 1989; on the date of the work, pp. 6–7.

42. Ptol. *Geog.* 1.11.4–1.12; on the Chinese account, see Casson 1989, 27; Ferguson 1978, 594; the Chinese view of Rome is summarized in Raschke 1978, 854.

43. See Aujac 1993, 120–124.

and-day "runs" for other parts of the routes he describes, though for some parts he provides no distances at all.[44] Besides the products produced and imported by each station, and some general coastal topography (rivers, harbors, peninsulas, islands, shoals), he also notes the rulers of each region, where possible, and sometimes the capital city. But this is normally the extent of the political and historical information that he offers. His description of the island of Taprobane (Sri Lanka) as oriented east-west and stretching almost to Africa (chap. 61) illustrates one of the limitations of the type of information available in a *periplus:* it is essentially one-dimensional, describing only a line. The leap from the one-dimensional itinerary or *periplus* to the two-dimensional map is not an easy one; this will be further illustrated below.

One example of long-range military exploration survives from the imperial period. Pliny writes that Nero, "among his other wars also contemplating Ethiopia," sent praetorian soldiers under a tribune to explore that region and that they reached the famous city of Meroë. Nero also sent "scouts" to the Caucasus region at the same time, in preparation for a projected campaign there, but about this we are less well informed.[45] Besides reporting that most of the region was a wasteland, the expedition measured the distance between stops from Syene to Meroë and concluded that the total distance was 975 miles. It also noted that "the plants around Meroë were at last somewhat greener; and some forest had appeared, and the tracks of rhinoceroses and elephants," and that this island was ruled by a woman, Candace—which was the name or title of all the Meroitic queens (Pliny *HN* 6.184–186). The expedition also drew some type of diagram of the region (*Aethiopiae forma*), perhaps similar to Corbulo's.[46]

This is the only sure case, after Caesar, of a mission sent out to explore in advance of military action. The only other example of long-

44. On the distances in the *Periplus* and their accuracy, see Casson 1989, app. 2; he concludes that where the author gives distances in stades or runs, his figures are good to within about 20 percent for shorter distances, though longer distances can be overestimated by as much as 50 percent. Casson points out that mariners of this period had no way of measuring distance at sea except to multiply the length of the journey in days by some fixed number of stades.

45. Pliny *HN* 6.181; cf. Sen. *Q Nat.* 6.8.3: "the two centurions whom Nero Caesar, an ardent lover of all the virtues, but especially of truth, sent to investigate the source of the Nile"; Cass. Dio 63[62].8.1: "Nero did not sail against him [Vologeses], although he was angry at him, nor against the Ethiopians nor the Caspian Gates, either, as he planned. For among other things he sent scouts (κατάσκοποι) to both places. . . ." See Kolendo 1981, chap. 3.

46. See Sherk 1974, 559–560; Pliny *HN* 12.19.

term military reconnaissance is the *Periplus of the Euxine Sea* (now the Black Sea), a Greek version of a Latin dispatch from Arrian, then governor of Cappadocia, to the emperor Hadrian. Arrian himself did not sail past what he describes as the limits of the Roman empire at Sebastopolis on the eastern coast, but writes that he will include information about the north coast as far as the Crimea, because Cotys, the king of that land, has just died, and Hadrian might have plans for the region.[47] The information he provides includes sailing distances between stops along the coast, the locations of harbors, and the names of cities and of kings; he also offers an estimate of nine thousand stades for the circumference of the Palus Maeotis, or Sea of Azov, where his source must be the same as Strabo's (*Periplus* 29; Strab. 7.4.5). He makes no general comment on the shape of the Euxine, though other sources describe it as similar to a "Scythian bow," since the Crimean peninsula makes a dent in the arc of the northern coast. The first part of the work describes the southern shore of the Euxine, and it is interesting that Arrian judges it necessary to provide such basic information about the coastline of provinces long incorporated into the empire.

Ancient sources, as noted above, assume that it is only after military intervention that one can expect detailed information about a geographical region. This was perhaps partly because advance reconnaissance in far-off, usually hostile areas must have posed fundamental practical problems.[48] The Romans had to be willing, and were willing, to lead armies into completely unknown territory. Thus Aelius Gallus knew so little about Arabia that on account of poor guidance, a march that could have taken sixty days took six months (Strab. 16.4.24). His experience was similar to that of his Republican predecessors Crassus and Antony, who met with disaster in Parthia when their ignorance about the region's geography left them vulnerable to treacherous guides: thus Strabo's remark on the importance of geographical study, noted earlier.[49]

Certain kinds of information were not available at all, or were very problematic. This is especially true of facts about the size, shape, orientation, and relative position of territories and land masses, though the Romans did attempt to learn and describe these things and also, in some cases, to correct perceived errors as new information became available. Such errors, striking to the modern historian and often noted, could be

---

47. 17.2–3; on the *Periplus,* see the commentary of Silberman 1995.
48. Cf. Caes. *B Gall.* 4.21 on the mission of Volusenus.
49. On Crassus, see Plut. *Crass.* 21–22, Florus 1.46.6–7; on Antony, Strab. 11.13.4. This problem is also noted by Isaac (1992, 403).

prodigious, even for places where the Romans had campaigned extensively. Thus Posidonius underestimated the distance from the Caspian
to the Euxine by half despite his close friendship with Pompey, who campaigned there.[50] Agrippa seriously miscalculated the size of the province
of Baetica in Spain, though he had led armies into the northern part
of the peninsula (Pliny *HN* 3.16–17); Appian made the dimensions of
Spain an incredible 10,000 by 10,000 stades or about 1,150 English miles
square (*Hisp.* 1.1). Though Ptolemy seems to incorporate Agricola's information about Scotland, its orientation on his map is rotated by seventy degrees.[51]

The problem was partly with the itinerary or *periplus* form of much
of the information available to the Romans. Scholars drawing on modern theories of spatial cognition have emphasized the difference between
the one-dimensional "odological" view of the world that seems to prevail in antiquity and a two-dimensional cartographic one.[52] Itineraries
were useful for logistical purposes. A military commander with access to
the *Antonine Itinerary,* for example, would have known the distance
in miles or Gallic leagues between each stop on a particular route, could
have added them together to predict the length of a march between specific points (total distances for each separate route were also published
in the itinerary), and could have organized supplies in this way. Distances
along the empire's roads were known, measured, and marked with mile
stones,[53] though it is important not to overestimate the availability or
accuracy of this information even for provinces long incorporated into
the empire. Despite Pliny's exhaustive research, his distances in North
Africa contain prodigious errors.[54] Besides the *Antonine Itinerary,* several other documents recording distances internal to the empire survive.[55] The most spectacular example is the *Tabula Peutingeriana,* because it is not just a list, but a road map of the world that displays stops
and distances in graphic form. It survives today as eleven sheets of parchment roll dating to the twelfth century, which can be joined together
to form a single document 34 centimeters in width and 6.75 meters
long. The first section of the map disappeared sometime prior to the
creation of the copy that survives, so that most of Britain, Spain, and the

50. Strab. 11.1.5–6; cf. Isaac 1992, 403–4.
51. Rivet (1977, 51–62) plots the data from Ptolemy's Scotland on the modern map.
52. Janni 1984; Bekker-Nielsen 1988.
53. On milestones, see Chevallier 1976, 39–47. About four thousand milestones survive, and their inscriptions are being collected in *CIL,* vol. 17.
54. Rebuffat 1967.
55. Kubitschek 1916; Dilke 1985, 112–129.

westernmost part of Africa are missing.[56] Roads are represented by lines, stops by jags in the lines, and distances between stops are inscribed as on modern road maps. Spas and villages are represented as symbols; the Mediterranean is a snaky green line through the middle. The length of the *Peutinger Table* is more than twenty times its width, probably because it was originally drawn on a papyrus roll. Thus it illustrates the limitations of "odological" information very well: it is not possible to tell the direction of a route on this map or to gain a two-dimensional sense of the shape of any region, though the entire known world is represented. Itineraries, then, provided information of a useful but limited type. And even the information they offered was usually available only where the army had been before. Distances within the empire, as mentioned above, were known and measured; but those without, by and large, were not. Thus the *Antonine Itinerary* stops short at the Rhine, the Danube, and Hadrian's Wall, and only a few points east of the Euphrates are named.[57] The *Peutinger Table* can record only the names of tribes across the Danube and the Rhine, although four routes in Trajan's province of Dacia, which was abandoned in the third century, are preserved.[58] The four routes from Ecbatana eastward require only one of the table's twelve segments (see fig. 1); two routes stretch all the way to eastern India, but these portions of the itinerary are problematic. The last points where multiple routes converge are Artaxata in Armenia and Ctesiphon, the Parthian capital in southern Mesopotamia; the Roman army had reached these cities more than once.[59]

The critical role of the army in expanding geographical knowledge meant that the Romans perceived themselves as conquering unknown lands, and they were proud of this.[60] Thus Claudius is "victor over tribes not only unconquered before him, but in truth even unknown" (Mela 3.49). Only sporadic, tenuous, and dangerous exploratory missions were sent out to the lands beyond the empire; the rumors and reports of

56. Several facsimile editions of the *Peutinger Table* have been published: Miller 1916, Weber 1976, and Levi and Levi 1978. Place-names with commentary are published in Miller 1916a. For discussion, see Levi and Levi 1967, 17–23; Dilke 1985, 113–117.

57. The routes of the *Antonine Itinerary* are plotted on the modern map in Cuntz 1929; on the *Antonine Itinerary* in Britain, see Rivet and Smith 1979, 150–184. In fact, some of the place-names were located slightly to the north of Hadrian's wall, contrary to the indications of the *Itinerary* itself (Rivet and Smith, op. cit., 155, 158).

58. Miller 1916a, 539–555.

59. Ibid., 751–752, for the routes in Mesopotamia and Armenia plotted on a modern map; 781–802 on the routes through Parthia and India.

60. E.g., Vell. Pat. 2.106.1 on Tiberius; Pliny *HN* 6.160–161 on Gallus, quoted above.

merchants or prisoners could flesh out this picture only a little. The *oikoumene*—the inhabited world—remained wild, mysterious, and unknown until the Roman army subjected, measured, and built roads through it. Cassius Dio reports that Claudius' troops mutinied before the expedition to Britain, terrified of setting foot on what they thought might be the edge of a whole new world (60.19.2). But for the most part the Romans were undaunted. Geopolitical explanations of Roman international behavior that require a two- or three-dimensional understanding of foreign territory are inappropriate. We find ourselves referring to psychological concepts like the pride and glory of far-flung conquest, or the fear of the unknown.

Modern policy makers would not dream of conducting foreign relations or planning a war, much less undertaking one, without accurate scaled maps. Roman thought processes must have been different if this type of information did not exist for them in the same way that it does today. But even if the world beyond Rome's borders remained uncharted to a degree that rendered two-dimensional maps useless for military purposes, and even if they were not used for those purposes, it is nevertheless true that the Romans came to the field with a general, traditional image of what they thought the world looked like. The next section of this chapter investigates the nature of their general conceptions about the world's size and shape.

3. Geography

Maps in the sense of two-dimensional, scaled representations of the world, as distinct from itineraries, were obviously not the familiar objects in antiquity that they are today.[61] There was no Greek word that meant, specifically, "map,"[62] and there appears to have been

61. See Janni 1984, 15–78, "Gli antichi e loro carte," and most recently Brodersen 1995. On the debate over Roman "map consciousness," see also Bekker-Nielsen 1988; Purcell 1990; and Talbert 1991—all arguing that ancient conceptions of space must have been fundamentally different from modern ones; for a different perspective, see recently Nicolet 1991. On the history of scholarship, see Brodersen 1995, 14–28. Dilke (1985) is usually perceived as taking the optimistic view of Roman cartographic sensibilities. In a review of this work, Talbert (1987) points to the contrast between the relative scarcity of cartographic thinking in Roman antiquity and the more highly developed "map consciousness" of China. On Strabo, see Aujac 1966; on Ptolemy, on which the bibliography from earlier in this century is massive, see recently ead. 1993.

62. Janni 1984, 23–24.

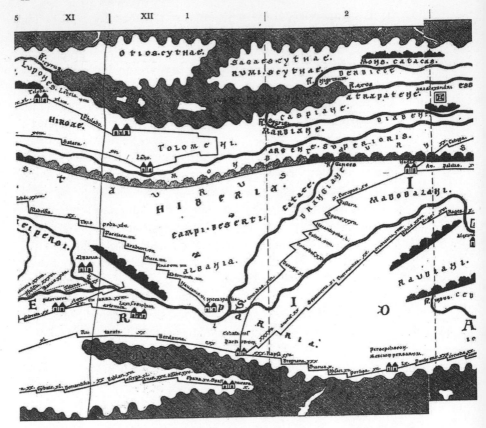

Fig. 1. The *Peutinger Table,* showing routes east of the Caspian. From the facsimile edition of K. Miller, *Die Peutingerische Tafel* (Stuttgart: Strecker und Schröder, 1916; reprint, Stuttgart: Brockhaus/Antiquarium, 1962).

none in Latin either; different expressions indicating pictorial representations of the world survive (we have seen *forma, situs depicti, itinerarium pictum*), but in most cases it is difficult to determine exactly what we are supposed to imagine. Vitruvius, in his treatise *On Architecture,* composed in the first century B.C., writes that the sources of rivers "are drawn or described [i.e., located verbally] on the inhabited world in chorographies."[63] Domitian executed one man for carrying around a

---

63. 8.2.6: *Haec autem sic fieri testimonio possunt esse capita fluminum, quae orbe terrarum chorographiis picta itemque scripta plurima maximaque inveniuntur egressa ad septentrionem.* . . . Brodersen (1995, 26–27) argues that Vitruvius is describing a text only.

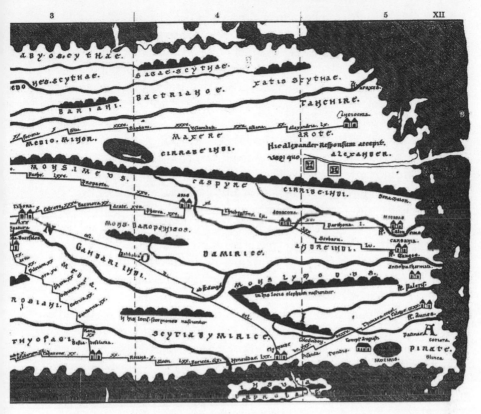

"world drawn on a parchment" (*depictus orbis terrae in membrana*).[61]
Should we imagine scaled maps here, or, as seems more likely, schematic
images?

The practical tools available to generals were mainly the itineraries
compiled by the army; travelers could use the *periploi* composed by merchants, where these existed. Scaled maps probably were not used or perceived as useful for military or strategic purposes. While the argument
from silence is always suspect for antiquity, it is striking that no author
of any tactical treatise and no historian of antiquity including Caesar
mentions maps in a military context or even, virtually, at all.[65] Never-

64. Suet. *Dom.* 10.3; cf. Cass. Dio 67.12.4, where his offense is that he "had the inhabited world depicted on the walls of his room" (ὅτι τὴν οἰκουμένην ἐν τοῖς τοῦ
κοιτῶνος τοίχοις εἶχεν ἐγγεγραμμένην). On this, see Arnaud 1983. For other references,
see Brodersen 1995, 101–109.
65. Janni 1984, 23–32; Brodersen 1995, 78–81, on the "practical use" of maps.

theless, it is clear that a mental image, however broad and vague, of the world was available to educated Romans—first, through verbal descriptions in geographical texts. Geographers offered their opinion on the shape of what they called "the inhabited world" (*oikoumene*) in Greek or *orbis terrarum* in Latin. They all agreed that it was oblong and approximately oval, shaped like a cloak, or a sling.[66] Some could supply measurements as well. Strabo, for example, writes in the second book of his geographical treatise that the inhabited world is about 70,000 stades (or 8,046 English miles) long from east to west, and about half as wide, from north to south. The Nile marks the halfway point. The world is divided into the continents of Europe, Asia, and Africa by the Mediterranean, the Tanais (Don) River (supposed to flow directly north from the Palus Maeotis), and the Nile. Asia is neatly bisected by the Taurus Mountains, which Strabo pictures running across the whole continent from east to west in a straight line. Both Europe and Africa become narrower toward the west, so that Africa especially comes to a point. The inhabited world is located entirely in the northern hemisphere, in the "temperate" zone between two uninhabitable (cold and hot) extremes. How far to the north or south the temperate zone extended was a matter of debate. Strabo considered Ireland, which he pictured to the north of Britain, practically uninhabitable.[67] The world was surrounded entirely by the outer sea that both Greek and Latin writers called the ocean.[68] Strabo would not, of course, have to describe the world this way if his text was accompanied by drawings; it was not. But the second book of his work unquestionably conveys a reasonably coherent, and very simple, mental image of what the world looks like; such an image could have been sketched, at least roughly, with results perhaps similar to the modern "reconstruction" in figure 2.

Although Strabo's work seems to have been unknown to Latin writers and is not cited in the very comprehensive bibliography of Pliny's *Natural History,* nevertheless the same basic image of the world pervades the literature of the imperial period. We find it, for example, in

66. For Strabo's "chlamys," see 2.5.6; 2.5.9, etc. For Posidonius' sling, see Fr. 200 = Edelstein and Kidd 1988, 180, with the commentary of Kidd (1988–1989), 2.ii:716–717; also in Dionysius Periegetes, vv. 5–7.

67. Strab. 2.5.6–9, 14–15; see 2.5.26 for the boundaries between the continents; and on the five-zone theory, see 2.3.1 and 2.5.3. Dion (1977, 255–260) argues that Strabo's grim portrayal of the poverty of Britain and the utter barbarity of Ireland and his rejection of the legend of Thule—traditionally the northernmost point in the *oikoumene* since the explorations of Pytheas in the fourth century B.C.—reflect the need to minimize the failures of Caesar and Augustus in this area.

68. On ancient conceptions of the "ocean," see Romm 1992, 20–26.

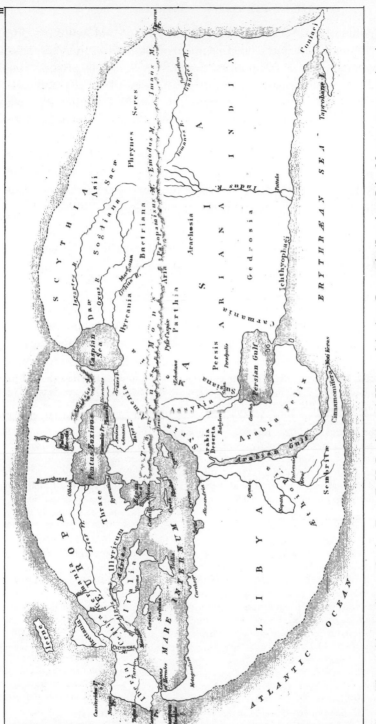

Fig. 2. The world according to Strabo. From E. H. Bunbury, *A History of Ancient Geography* (London: John Murray, 1879; reprint, Amsterdam: J. C. Gieben, 1979).

Pomponius Mela, Seneca, Lucan, Pliny the Elder, and Aelius Aristides, as well as in the brief but influential poem of Dionysius Periegetes. Traces also emerge in the *Periplus Maris Erythraei*.[69] It was, by Strabo's time, already long traditional. The origins of this view of the elliptical *oikoumene* lay in the work of Eratosthenes, in the third century B.C., who wrote a geography using the latest information from Alexander's campaigns and other recent explorations.[70]

A verbal description is not the same as a physical image. References to such images are relatively rare, and some complaints about the perceived inadequacies of the existing pictorial representations survive. Geminus, writing about 70 B.C., writes that

the length of the inhabited world is at least twice its width. For this reason those who draw geographies proportionally draw them on oblong tablets (οἱ κατὰ λόγον γράφοντες τὰς γεωγραφίας ἐν πίναξι γράφουσι παραμήκεσιν), so that the length is twice the width. Those drawing round [geographies] have strayed far from the truth (16.1.3–4).

The round maps Geminus describes may have been common in antiquity; he is not the first to criticize them.[71] They were possibly simi-

69. In Mela 1.4–1.8 the world has five zones; its length is greater than the width; it is surrounded by the ocean, which has four gulfs (Mediterranean, Red Sea, Persian Gulf, and Caspian); and the Nile and Tanais divide the continents. Seneca (*Marc.* 18.6) writes of the "ocean, belt of the land, dividing the continuity of peoples with its triple gulfs" (i.e., the Mediterranean, the Red Sea, and the Caspian); in Lucan 9.411–420, Europe and Libya together make one-half the world, while Asia is the other half; the boundaries are the Tanais and the Nile. Pliny (*HN* 2.242–243) also describes an oblong world (he offers length estimates of 8,568 and 9,818 and 8,995 Roman miles, and a width estimate of 5,462), and his circumnavigation stories (ibid., 167–170) also support the idea of a Caspian gulf and a navigable northern ocean. Dionysius Periegetes (vv. 5–7) describes the world as not entirely circular, but narrowing at the ends like a sling; he describes the traditional boundaries of the continents, though he adds that the isthmus between the Caspian and the Euxine, and the Arabian isthmus, are alternative boundaries. Aelius Aristides (*Orat.* 36.87) describes four gulfs, and the traditional boundaries between continents. The author of the *Periplus Maris Erythraei* believes that the coast of Africa trends east after Rhapta to the Atlantic (chap. 18, and see the commentary of Casson 1989 ad loc.). The five-zone theory may be found, e.g., in Virgil *Georg.* 1.231–258; Ovid *Met.* 1.45–51; Mela 1.4; Pliny, *HN* 2.172 passim. The heat of the torrid zone made Hanno's circumnavigation impossible (Arr. *Ind.* 43.11–12); and Arrian had the same theory about the Arabian peninsula. But some believed the torrid zones might be habitable (e.g., Eratosthenes, Polybius, and Posidonius; see Nicolet 1991, 65–66). On this traditional perception of the *oikoumene*, see recently Brodersen 1995, 82–109.

70. Nicolet provides a recent discussion of Eratosthenes' work and the history of geography in the Roman period up to the Augustan age (1991, 60–74). Also on Eratosthenes, see Aujac 1966, 49–60, and ead. 1987, 153–157.

71. The first on record is Hdt. 4.36; on this, see Romm 1992, 32–41.

lar to the very schematic drawings found in medieval manuscripts of Lucan, Sallust, and Isidore of Seville, which depict the world as a circle divided into three parts by a T formed by the traditional water boundaries of the continents (cf. fig. 3); or they may have resembled the "zonal" round maps that accompanied texts of Macrobius' *Commentary on the Dream of Scipio,* which showed the traditional five climatic zones.[72] It is likely that these round maps were the more common visual representation of the world; but Geminus also seems to imply that there were "those drawing geographies proportionally," thus more accurately representing in two dimensions what was *believed* to be the physical shape of the habitable world. Ptolemy complains that most maps give Europe a disproportionally large space to accommodate all the place names, while Africa is made too narrow and Asia too short.[73] Plutarch similarly tells us that

in maps (γεωγραφίαις) . . . the historians squeeze into the outermost edges of their drawing tablets the parts that escape their knowledge, writing in explanations to the effect that "the regions beyond are waterless sands full of wild beasts," or "murky swamps," or "Scythian frost," or "frozen sea" (*Thes.* 1.1).

Both he and Ptolemy are criticizing what they perceive to be a failure of ancient cartography: a failure to draw an accurate two-dimensional image of the world. Such scaled maps, then, as we have suggested, were rare; but both Plutarch and Ptolemy not only seem to have an idea, like Geminus, of how the world "ought" to look; they also are interested in the possibility of a cartography that would convey not just routes or place-names or schematized images of the traditional three continents, but a scaled, two-dimensional impression of the physical shape of the world. And Ptolemy himself wrote detailed directions on how to produce such a map.

Thus there were efforts to create scaled maps, especially by Greek experts in the science of geography. Cartographic projection already had a long history, and by Ptolemy's time it had reached a high level of sophistication.[74] Eratosthenes had divided the world into four sections by a central meridian (through Rhodes and Alexandria) and a central parallel (through Gades and Athens all the way to India); he apparently

---

72. Destombes 1964, secs. 10–12, 29–31 on Sallust; 13–16, 32–34 on Lucan. On *mappaemundi,* see Woodward 1987.

73. *Geog.* 8.2–3. See Levi and Levi 1981, 140–141.

74. This point is made by Nicolet (1991, 71).

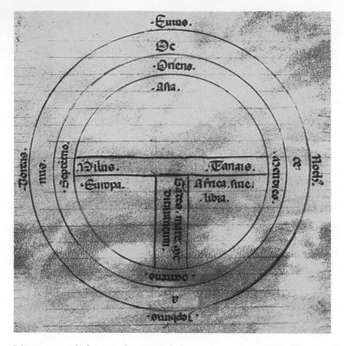

Fig. 3. *Mappamundi* from a fourteenth-century manuscript of Lucan. Paris: Bibliothèque Nationale, ms. Lat. 8045.

drew other parallels as well. He also used a device he called *sphragides,* or easily drawn geometrical shapes, to produce a rough idea of the two-dimensional shape of the world's regions and their relationship to each other.[75] Strabo also described a cylindrical projection system with meridians and parallels (2.5.10), which Marinus advocated as well. Ptolemy rejected this system, since it distorted the northern regions in the way familiar from some modern maps. He proposed a conical projection, where all the meridians converge to a point at the top, and a more difficult "modified conical projection" as the best ways of representing the world on a plane surface.[76] It is doubtful whether any of the geographers mentioned, including Ptolemy, actually drew maps to illustrate their texts.[77] But a world map could have been drawn from Ptolemy's

75. Strab. 2.1.1, 2.1.22–23; Aujac 1987, 156–157.

76. On Marinus' projection system, see Dilke 1987, 179; on Ptolemy's system, ibid., 184–189; Ptolemy's criticism of Marinus' system, *Geog.* 1.20.

77. On the history of the atlases found in medieval and renaissance manuscripts of Ptolemy—whether the prototypes were drawn by Ptolemy himself and accompanied his manuscript, were drawn later in the second century by the mysterious "Agathodaemon,"

instructions at any time; just as a world map could have been produced from the texts of Eratosthenes, Strabo, or Marinus. Ptolemy especially was an expert of a type that, as we have seen, we would not be likely to find among Roman decision makers, but Strabo, on the other hand, was part of that circle.

Perhaps the most important map for the purposes of this study is the famous "map of Agrippa." Apparently this was an image of the world painted on the Porticus Vipsania, a building funded by Augustus' close friend Agrippa in the Campus Martius, and completed after his death by Augustus. It divided the world into twenty-four regions, and may have been accompanied by a commentary, which was also published separately.[78] The commentary offered length and breadth measurements for each of the twenty-four sections.[79] One reconstruction, based on these measurements as they are preserved in Pliny's *Natural History* and elsewhere, gives the result seen in figure 4. But the evidence is very scanty.[80] Pliny refers to Agrippa's *orbis terrarum urbi spectandus*, the "world to be looked at by the city" (*HN* 3.17), and several times cites the commentaries, thus preserving Agrippa's measurements as just mentioned. But this is all we know. It is unclear, for example, whether the map was drawn to scale according to a projection system or not.[81] It has even been argued that Agrippa's famous work was a text only and that no map existed.[82]

But regardless of the actual appearance or even existence of Agrippa's

or were done at some later point in time—see recently Dilke 1987b, 268–275, and Aujac 1993, 165–178. The most accurate are those of the recension A tradition, which contains twenty-six regional maps and the world map, and of which the earliest example is the Codex Urbinas Graecus 82, produced probably in the late thirteenth century. Karl Müller's edition of Ptolemy's text (1883–1901)—which, however, breaks off at book V when Müller died—is accompanied by a volume of thirty-six regional maps that he apparently reconstructed from the text, with results similar to those of the recension A tradition (they are paired with modern maps drawn to the same scale for purposes of comparison). I refer to Müller's reconstructions in the discussion below.

78. On the map of Agrippa and the commentaries, on which much long-standing academic debate exists, see Tierney 1963; Sallmann 1971, 91–107, 207–211; Dilke 1985, chap. 3; Nicolet 1991, chap. 5. Attempted reconstructions based on the measurements preserved in Pliny's *Natural History* and elsewhere may be found in Moynihan 1986, 162, and Sallmann 1971, 208–209.

79. By "length" (*longitudo*) Agrippa, like other ancient authorities, normally means distance between longitudes or east-west, and by "width" (*latitudo*) he means distance north-south. See Tierney 1963, 162–163; Sallmann 1971, 208 n. 35.

80. Ancient references are collected and analyzed in Brodersen 1995, 273–284.

81. See Nicolet 1991, chap. 4, for the optimistic view; *contra*, see, e.g., Bowersock 1983, 164–171. The bibliography on this issue is extensive; see Sallmann 1971, 102 n. 38.

82. Brodersen 1995, 268–285.

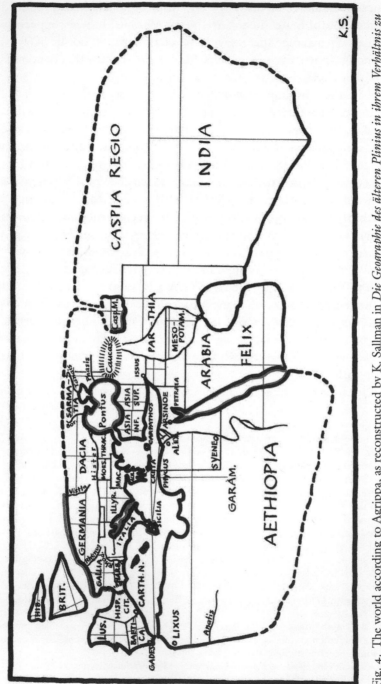

K.S.

Fig. 4. The world according to Agrippa, as reconstructed by K. Sallman in *Die Geographie des älteren Plinius in ihrem Verhältnis zu Varro* (Berlin: Walter de Gruyter, 1971)

map, the measurements that have been preserved confirm the impressions discussed above about how educated Romans imagined the world and about the mental picture they brought to their wars and conquests. It is clear from what information remains that the traditional image of the oblong world survives here. Like his contemporaries, Agrippa pictured Africa as narrow and the regions north of the "Taurus Mountains" as negligible in extent, so that the whole inhabited world becomes a schematic and compact, if largely unexplored, entity. Tales of circumnavigation were not uncommon. Pliny writes that Gaius Caesar found in the Red Sea the wrecks of Spanish ships that had apparently sailed around Africa (*HN* 2.168); he also expresses the belief that the expedition of Hanno the Carthaginian, an explorer of the fifth century B.C., had reached the "borders of Arabia" (2.169). Mela records that Indians had reached Germany by circumnavigating the northern ocean (3.45), and Pliny repeats this story (*HN* 2.170; both citing Cornelius Nepos); Pliny also writes that Patrocles, the famous Seleucid explorer, sailed from India all around the eastern and northern oceans to the Caspian Sea, which was imagined to be a gulf of the ocean (*HN* 2.167, 6.58).

Because of this schematic image of the world's shape, the Romans tended to picture the north coast of Europe as flat, and this notion remained very persistent. Caesar himself, the conqueror of Gaul, confidently proclaimed that "all of Gaul inclines toward the north" (*B Gall.* 4.20.1). In Strabo we discover a highly theoretical Europe where the coast of Gaul, as in Caesar, faces north; the Pyrenees run north-south (in reality they run almost due east-west) and the Rhine runs parallel to them, so that Gaul has a square shape; and the south coast of Britain stretches out parallel to the Gallic coast *for its entire length from the Rhine to the Pyrenees.*[83] The flat northern coast was also a feature of Agrippa's geography; he made the Gauls, excluding Narbonese Gaul, 420 Roman miles in length (east-west) and only 318 miles in width (north-south; Pliny *HN* 4.105). Agrippa also recorded that the area covered by Germany, Raetia, and Noricum together was 686 miles long and only 248 miles wide; but Pliny dismisses these figures, with the explanation that at Agrippa's death Raetia was only recently conquered and Germany still unexplored (4.98). On Ptolemy's map the flattened

---

83. Dion 1977, 250–254, including a collection of the references from Strabo; on Britain, see Strab. 4.5.1. Mela 3.1.2 also claims that the entire coast of Europe and Asia all the way to the "Scythian promontory" faces north; cf. Silberman (1988, ad loc.), who also discusses the passages from Strabo.

northern coast of Gaul and Spain is still evident, and the Pyrenees run northwest-southeast.[84]

The persistent image of a flat northern Europe may partly explain the Greco-Roman vision of the orientation of Britain and its relationship to Spain. Britain in fact remained one of the most obscure and problematic features of the Roman geographical imagination throughout the imperial period. In the late fourth century B.C., Pytheas had described an island 4,875 miles in circumference. This influential image of the gigantic Britain reemerges at least through the first century A.D.[85] Caesar's description, dating from the 50s B.C., remained one of the most accurate:

The island is triangular in nature, with one side opposite Gaul. One corner of this side, which is at Kent . . . faces east, and the lower corner faces south. This side extends about five hundred [Roman] miles. Another side inclines toward Spain and the west, in which region is Ireland, about half the size, it is estimated, of Britain, but the crossing is of the same length as it is from Gaul to Britain. . . . The length of this side, in the opinion of the people there, is seven hundred miles. The third side faces north, and no land lies opposite this part; but the corner of this side points more or less to Germany. This side is judged to be eight hundred miles in length. Thus the whole island is two thousand miles in circumference (*B Gall.* 5.13).

Here Caesar is strikingly correct about Britain's proportions, though its orientation is difficult to picture. The assertion that "Another side inclines toward Spain and the west" is startling to the modern reader. But the image of a flat Gaul brings Britain closer to Spain; Appian, for example, wrote that it was only one-half day's sail away (*Hisp.* 1). As noted above, Strabo pictured Britain's south coast stretching all the way to Spain; Pliny and Tacitus describe Britain as facing Germany, Gaul, and Spain (Pliny *HN* 4.102, Tac. *Agr.* 10.3). Cassius Dio writes that the island "stretches along the rest of Gaul and almost all of Spain" (39.50.2), thus, like Strabo, making its longest side parallel to the northern European coast; and this image of its orientation is also evident in Ptolemy,

84. See fig. 6 (Gaul) in Karl Müller 1883–1901, vol. 3, for the orientation of the Pyrenees and the flattening of Gaul; also Janni 1984, 99–102; and the outlines of Britain and Gaul as plotted by Dion (1977, 281).

85. Diod. Sic. 5.21.4; Pliny writes that Isidorus adopted Pytheas' figure for the circumference of Britain (*HN* 4.102); Appian writes that the island is "larger than the largest continent" (*Gall.* 5); Josephus in Herod Agrippa's speech to the Jews writes that Britain is the same size as the οἰκουμένη (*BJ* 2.378); on this idea of Britain as "another world," see Romm 1992, 140–141.

who twists Scotland so that Britain lies roughly parallel to Europe, this time along the coast of Germany.[86]

All of these authors are interested in describing Britain's orientation so as to convey a two-dimensional mental impression of its relationship to the continent of Europe. By the time Dio wrote, the southern part of the island had been a Roman province for almost two centuries. But for whatever reason, whether it was the limitations on the type of information that the Romans were able to gather, or respect for the authority of venerated texts, the image of Britain as lying parallel to Europe endured. We might put it this way: Roman geography had an important practical element, especially in the itineraries and *periploi* produced by the army or merchants and which could contain very accurate records of distances. It also had a theoretical element, a Greek theory of the world's climatology, symmetry, and proportions that persisted throughout antiquity. But it also had what we might call a more literary and traditional, even "poetic" or romantic, element. That is, the cloak-shaped world was by now more than just a theory; it was a tradition. The tales of its famous explorers had a legendary character, such as the story of Patrocles, who sailed the eastern ocean all the way around to the Caspian "gulf," or that of Pytheas, who sighted Thule, the northernmost part of the world, through a terrifying confusion of sea and sky. Germanicus' voyage on the North Sea was the subject of epic poetry.[87] All of these aspects of Roman geography were part of the cultural baggage of every aristocrat, and they affected Roman decisions, sometimes in startlingly practical ways. Thus Agricola contemplated an invasion of Ireland, hoping that "Ireland, located halfway between Britain and Spain (*medio inter Britanniam atque Hispaniam*), and convenient also to the Gallic Sea, would unite the strongest region of the empire to great mutual advantage" (Tac. *Agr.* 24). Roman decisions were based on their ideas of the world's geography, not ours. Their picture of the world and the nature of their understanding of it were in some ways very limited, even about areas they were very familiar with. Agricola, after all, governed Britain for seven years. Strategic argumentation of the type that

86. On Ptolemy's turning of Scotland, see Rivet 1977, 47–51, and Rivet and Smith 1979, 111–114; they hypothesize that this error is due, on the one hand, to traditional conceptions about the shape and position of Britain, and on the other, to Ptolemy's belief that the inhabited world could not extend beyond the latitude reported for Thule, joined with the fact that he made the circumference of the earth too small. Janni (1984, 112–114) argues that such errors of orientation are characteristic of "odological" cognition.

87. Strab. 3.4.1; Sen. *Suas.* 1.15; Braccesi 1991, 27–64; Romm 1992, 140–149.

he offered about Ireland was, not surprisingly in view of these limitations, rare.

The tendency to truncate and flatten the northern regions continues
as one progresses east. Roman ships had sailed only as far as the "promontory of the Cimbri," modern Denmark. The Romans did not know
the nature of Scandinavia (which Pliny describes as a large island in the
ocean, *HN* 4.96) or of the enormous territory that is now Russia. Even
Europe north of the Danube tends to be flattened and compressed.
Strabo writes that the river divides eastern Europe approximately in half
(7.1.1), and Agrippa recorded that "this whole tract from the Ister to
the [northern] ocean is 1,200 miles in length and *396 miles in width* to
the river Vistula from the deserts of Sarmatia" (*HN* 4.81). The territory
farther east, in the region north of the Black Sea and around the Caspian Sea and beyond, was unexplored. It was populated with Amazons,
Hyperboreans, and the mythical Rhipaean Mountains. A tendency existed—for example, in Ptolemy's work—to exaggerate the size of the
Palus Maeotis, making it stretch far to the north; to place the ocean not
very far beyond that; and to perceive the entire region north of the
Black Sea as eternally snowy, impossibly cold, barely habitable.[88] The

88. On the Caucasus, see Braund 1994, chap. 1, mainly focusing on myths about the
region (such as the Golden Fleece); on Ptolemy, especially Berthelot 1930, 209–220, and
the reconstructions of Karl Müller 1883–1901, vol. 3, fig. 16 (Sarmatia Europaea, Chersonesus Taurica), showing a vague, flat Baltic coast and a much-exaggerated Palus Maeotis approaching the coast. See also ibid., fig. 31, and Ptolemy *Geog.* 5.9.19 for the Amazons.
Pliny supplies estimates for the circumference of the Black Sea ranging from 2,119 to 2,540
Roman miles (*HN* 4.77). In comparison, the circumference of the Palus Maeotis is estimated at 1,406 or 1,125 (Roman) miles (*HN* 4.78); the 1,125 is Strabo's 9,000 stades, which
Arrian also reports (*Peripl. M. Eux.* 29). Strabo makes the distance from the Cimmerian
Bosporus (Straits of Kertsch) to the mouth of the Tanais 2,200 stades (11.2.2), and Pliny
makes it 275 miles (*HN* 4.78). The Hyperboreans and Amazons appear in Mela 1.12 and
3.36, and are said in Plut. *Pomp.* 35.3–4 to have fought against Pompey in Iberia; on them,
see also Strab. 11.5.1. Pliny is skeptical about the Hyperboreans (*HN* 4.88). Strabo does
not believe in the Hyperboreans or the Rhipaean mountains and says the Tanais flows
from an unknown source (7.3.1, 11.2.2), but for Agrippa the Rhipaeans are the source of
that river (Pliny *HN* 4.78), as they are for Lucan (3.272–273), and they appear on Ptolemy's map; the Rhipaean mountains are also mentioned by Mela (1.117): "and beyond that
lies the shore, which faces the ocean." The distance to this ocean from the Palus Maeotis
was thought to be small: see fig. 2 for a reconstruction of Agrippa's views based on Pliny
(*HN* 4.91), though Pliny adds: "I consider measurements in this part of the world uncertain." Lucan (3.277–278) and the author of the *Periplus Maris Erythraei* (64) believed that
the Palus Maeotis was actually attached to the ocean. On the terrible weather of the region, see Strab. 3.1.2 on Iberia, 11.2.2 on the Tanais region; Mela (2.1) writes that the area
is so cold, with continually falling snow, that those who go there cannot see what is there;
also Sen. *Q Nat.* 4B.5.2; Dionysius Periegetes vv. 665–679; cf. Lucan 2.639–41. The same
grim view prevailed regarding the Rhine/Danube region; e.g., Sen. *Prov.* 4.14–15; Tac.
Germ. 2; Herodian 1.6.1; Cass. Dio 49.36.2 (Pannonia). Ovid's description of Tomis also

Caspian was thought to be attached to the northern ocean, and Agrippa wrote that "the Caspian Sea and the peoples around it, and with them Armenia, bounded on the east by the Chinese Ocean, on the west by the Caucasus Mountains and on the south by the Taurus Mountains, and on the north by the Scythian Ocean, extend as far as is known 480 miles in length and 290 miles in width."[89]

Thus Roman geographical conceptions were guided by a traditional and schematic view of the shape of the inhabited world. Their concrete perceptions faded out beyond the boundaries of the empire, to be replaced by a partly theoretical, partly mythologized image of an elliptical land mass and a primeval ocean. Huge tracts of Europe and Asia did not exist for them; others were considered wild and barely habitable. The same tendencies are evident in the Roman perception of Africa.

The continent of Africa was traditionally described as a triangle or trapezoid, widest at Egypt and coming to a point in Mauretania or modern Morocco.[90] Strabo, Dionysius Periegetes, and King Juba himself of Mauretania all imagined Africa's shape in this way. Thus the image of this continent, like that of northern Europe and Asia, reflected the pattern of Roman contact and familiarity, with Egypt taking up the most space because it was better known. Exploratory missions by land and sea were sometimes attempted, more often here than in other areas of the world.[91] By Augustus' reign two famous and daring missions had sailed down the western coast: these were the journeys of Hanno the Carthaginian in the fifth century B.C. and of the historian Polybius in the second century B.C.[92] Perhaps based on Polybius, Agrippa and Pliny made Mauretania wider than Strabo probably imagined, a little less than 500 miles.[93] Pliny also knew of the campaigns of Suetonius Paulinus, who

conforms to the image of an unchanging, continually snowy climate, though he, of course, lived there; Brodersen 1995, 102–103.

89. *HN* 6.37; the Caspian Sea was "proved" to be a gulf of the ocean by Patrocles, and this conception remained standard (though not accepted by Ptolemy): Dion 1977, 216–22?; Romm 1992, 42–43; Pliny *HN* 6.58. Strabo makes the distance from the innermost recess of the Caspian to the northern ocean only 6,000 stades, less than 700 English miles (2.1.17, cf. 11.11.7). Note that the *Peutinger Table* (segment XII.1; see fig. 1 above) also has the Caspian attached to the ocean.

90. Strab. 2.5.33 (trapezoid) and 17.3.1 (triangle); Dionysius Periegetes vv. 10–11 (triangle) and 174–175 (trapezoid); Pliny *HN* 6.175 on Juba.

91. Desanges 1978.

92. On Hanno and Polybius, see Pliny *HN* 5.8–10, with Desanges 1980 ad loc. A version of Hanno's commentary survives; on this text and Hanno's journey, with extensive bibliography, see Desanges 1978, 39–85. Like most *periploi*, Hanno's gives no clear indication of the direction of the coastline.

93. Pliny *HN* 5.21, with the commentary of Desanges (1980, 109–111).

had explored beyond Mount Atlas in the reign of Claudius. As mentioned above, the campaigns of Balbus were possibly responsible for an increased estimate of the width of Cyrenaica, 910 miles. All this suggests that the Romans did have an interest in establishing and correcting a two-dimensional "cartographic" image of Africa. But their perception of this continent was still very much shaped by the traditional schematic view of the *oikoumene,* which dictated an elliptical land mass with more east-west length than north-south width, and by a tradition of the uninhabitability of far-off latitudes to the north or south. Strabo placed the uninhabitable torrid zone only 3,000 stades south of Meroë in Egypt (17.3.1); Pliny says that a distance of 625 miles from Meroë to the ocean is "practically agreed among authorities" (*HN* 6.196).

But concerning Asia south of the "Taurus," the story is different. Asia was, for the Romans, a vast and almost endless land. It is true that they did not know the size and extent of China and believed that the easternmost land was India.[94] But as far as India, Asia had been explored and documented by Alexander the Great in antiquity's most glorious and spectacular tale of conquest. Long before the Romans, Alexander had linked geographical exploration with imperialism. He had, as noted above, taken along experts to measure the length of his march. On the way back, he had sent Nearchus and Onesicritus to explore the coastline from the Indus River to the Persian Gulf, and they are still cited frequently by sources from the Roman period. Under the Seleucids, Alexander's successors in the east, Deimachus and Megasthenes had lived in India and published descriptions of it, and their reports on the land's enormous population and immense number of towns and tribes were well known.[95] Manilius, in his long poem on astronomy of the first century A.D., wrote that India was *notitia maior,* too big to be known (4.674); Pliny records that "the companions of Alexander the Great wrote that in that tract of India that he conquered there were 5,000

94. On Roman conceptions of China, see, e.g., Ferguson 1978, 582–585.

95. Ancient discussions on the sources for India include Pliny *HN* 6.58: "[India] has been revealed not only by the arms of Alexander the Great and the kings who succeeded him, for Seleucus and Antiochus and their prefect of the fleet Patrocles sailed all the way around even into the Hyrcanian and Caspian Sea, but also by other Greek authorities, who stayed with the Indian kings, like Megasthenes and Dionysius, who was sent by Philadelphus for this purpose, and also reported on the strength of the tribes." See also Strabo, who considered that "all those who have written about India have been liars for the most part" (2.1.9), especially Deimachus and Megasthenes. On these sources and Strabo's skepticism, see Romm 1992, 94–109; on Nearchus and Onesicritus, also Pearson 1960, chaps. 4–5; and Pédech 1984. On conceptions of India, especially in Pliny and Strabo, see also Dihle 1964 and 1980, cited below.

towns . . . and 9 tribes, and that India is a third part of the whole world" (*HN* 6.59; cf. Strab. 15.1.33 for the same statistics). Seneca, he says, has written a treatise on India naming sixty rivers and 118 tribes.[96] Pliny goes on to list the immense military forces available to various kings, some of whom could field armies in excess of one hundred thousand infantry (6.60–63). Agrippa, he writes, had made India's breadth 3,300 miles (6.57). About the size of India, however, there was some controversy. Strabo imagines it as a rectangle, with a tail about 3,000 stades long stretching out to the southeast; he sides with Eratosthenes, who made India 16,000 stades (or about 1,816 English miles) long from the Indus to the eastern ocean, against those who made it longer (15.1.11–12, cf. 2.1.4). Arrian, too, rejected the testimony of Onesicritus and Ctesias, who claimed that India was one-third of the world (*Ind.* 3.6). But both Strabo and Arrian emphasize its enormous population.[97]

Even though more recent information about India was available from overseas merchants, and though embassies from there had been received by Augustus and Trajan,[98] Roman authors tend to rely on early Hellenistic sources here, and their images of India retain a strong mythical element.[99] Megasthenes and Deimachus had reported strange stories about gold-digging ants (also found in Herodotus), umbrella-footed people, and people with no mouths.[100] The luxury trade gave India, like Arabia, a reputation as a land of immense wealth. Its rivers were of legendary proportions.[101] The size of the island of Taprobane (Sri Lanka)

96. These figures are derived from Megasthenes (Arr. *Ind.* 5.2, 7.1).

97. Strab. 2.5.32; Arr. *Ind.* 10.2.

98. On Trajan, see Cass. Dio 68.15.1. Augustus boasts about more than one embassy from India in *RGDA* 31. These seem to have been a subject of fascination for Romans; according to Strabo (15.1.73), Nicolaus of Damascus had met one of the embassies at Antioch and recorded "that the letter was in Greek written on leather, and showed that Porus was the one who wrote it, ruler of six hundred kings, but all the same he deemed it a very great thing to be a friend of Caesar." The gifts included a man without arms, whom Strabo saw himself; numerous very large snakes; a giant tortoise; a giant partridge; and "the man who burned himself up at Athens." Lucan writes that the Indians drink juice from the sugarcane, dye their hair, wear cotton with gems, and burn themselves alive (3.237–241). Florus records that the Indians live directly beneath the sun, that the embassy to Augustus brought elephants, gems, and pearls, and that the journey took four years (2.34.62); the embassy is also mentioned by Suetonius (*Aug.* 21.3), Horace (*Carm. saec.* 55–56), and Cass. Dio 54.9.8–10, again emphasizing the suicide.

99. See Dihle 1964, 17–20, and id. 1980. On Arrian, see above, n. 3.

100. See especially Pliny *HN* 7.21–30 and Strab. 15.1.57 for strange people; on the gold-digging ants, see Strab. 15.1.44, Mela 3.62, Pliny *HN* 11.111, Hdt. 3.102. Strabo is skeptical of these stories in 2.1.9 and 15.1.57.

101. On the immensity of the Ganges, see Pliny *HN* 6.65; on the Indus, Lucan 3.235–236; on the Indus and the Ganges, Strab. 15.1.35 and Arr. *Ind.* 3.9, 4.2–3.

was also legendary; Pliny records Eratosthenes' estimate of seven thousand stades or more than eight hundred English miles in length. An embassy from this island to the emperor Claudius told him, among other things, that the moon was visible there only from the eighth to the sixteenth of the month, and that the island was ten thousand stades long (Pliny *HN* 6.84–88).[102]

But how did the Romans imagine their great rival, the eastern empire of Parthia? As an organized political entity, potential sources about it were diverse. King Phraates' four sons, for example, had spent decades in Rome as hostages; and embassies back and forth seem to have been routine.[103] One citizen of Charax was the author of Greek works on geography known to Pliny and a report for Augustus' grandson. Strabo writes that the Parthian empire has contributed greatly to Roman geographical knowledge of the east; he may be thinking especially of his source Apollodorus of Artemita (a Greek city east of the Tigris), who wrote a history of Parthia up to the year 87 B.C. Other Parthian authorities were known to the Romans, including the source used by Trogus (if this was different from Strabo's source) and the source of Plutarch's account of Crassus' expedition.[104] It is unfortunate for this discussion that little of what the Romans recorded about Parthia survives. In his geography Strabo says that he will not describe Parthian institutions because he has examined them extensively in his (now lost) histories (11.9.3); Arrian's *Parthica* in seventeen volumes has, as we have noted, disappeared; Cassius Dio refrains from a detailed discussion because "many have written about their race and customs" (40.15.1).

Of what remains, Pliny's account is the most detailed, but very jejune. He names Corbulo among his sources as well as "kings sent from there as suppliants or the children of kings as hostages" (*HN* 6.23). He reports that Parthia is divided into eighteen kingdoms "around two . . . seas, the Red Sea to the south, and the Hyrcanian [= Caspian] Sea in the north"; eleven of these provinces are defined as "upper," and they "begin at the border of Armenia and the Caspian shores and extend to the Scythians" (6.112). His most detailed information is about Mesopotamia, just as in Isidorus' *Parthian Stations,* although Pliny does not

102. On the tradition of the gigantic Taprobane, see also *Periplus Maris Erythraei* 61, cited above; and Berthelot 1930, 357–362.

103. A document from Dura records an embassy from Parthia on its way to the emperor as though this were a routine occurrence (Millar 1988, 370). On this document, perhaps dating to 207, see Chaumont 1987.

104. Strab. 2.5.12; on Apollodorus of Artemita and other Parthian authors known to the Romans, including Isidorus, see Tarn 1984, 44–55.

seem to have used him as a source here. Of Parthia (proper), Media, Hyrcania, and other kingdoms toward the east, he names the lands that surround them and some major cities and mountains.

The Parthian empire, according to Pliny, measures 944 miles in width (*HN* 6.126). Agrippa had reported that

Media and Parthia and Persia, bounded on the east by the Indus, on the west by the Tigris, on the north by the Caucasian Taurus, and on the south by the Red Sea, extend in length 1,320 miles, and in width 840, and besides that Mesopotamia alone, bounded by the Tigris on the east, the Euphrates on the west, the Taurus on the north, and the Persian Gulf on the south, has a length of 800 miles, a width of 360. (Ibid., 6.137)

The first item, which must have been one of Agrippa's twenty-four "regions," is especially interesting because the source is one of Augustus' most trusted generals and advisers; and also because it is from one of the few "cartographic" works that is known from antiquity. It is important to note that the geography of Parthia reflected here is traditional, even romanticized. The idea that the Indus River formed the eastern boundary of Parthian or Persian territories, which did not in fact extend nearly so far east, must reflect Agrippa's debt to the Hellenistic age and the campaigns of Alexander, when the Indus was believed to form the western boundary of India: Alexander, famously, crossed it.[105] Similarly, by the "Caucasian Taurus" Agrippa may mean the Hindu Kush mountains; since Alexander's expedition, the name Caucasus, and the legendary location of Prometheus' prison, had been transferred to this range also.[106]

We might also note that the world as described by Pliny, for example, was, not surprisingly, a Eurocentric one. The Parthian empire's 944 miles does not seem formidable when we read that Italy, for him, was over 1,000 miles long (*HN* 3.43). Europe was 8,714 miles long, compared with Asia's 6,375 miles.[107] Also in Agrippa's work and on Ptolemy's map, the Parthian empire is diminished by an exaggerated Mediterranean.[108] Julius Caesar had apparently intended to conquer it. He had

105. On the Indus as the boundary of India, see Brunt 1976–1983, 1:544–547; Strab. 15.1.10; Arr. *Anab.* 5.4.3, 5.6.3, *Ind.* 2.5.

106. Strab. 15.1.8; Arr. *Anab.* 5.3.1–4, citing Eratosthenes.

107. 6.208–210. He goes on to say that "it is clear that Europe is larger than Asia by a little less than half the size of Asia, and twice plus one-sixth as large as Africa."

108. Agrippa's Mediterranean was 3,440 miles long (Pliny *HN* 6.207). Ptolemy's Mediterranean is still exaggerated by several hundred miles, as illustrated in the reconstruction of Karl Müller (1883–1901, vol. 3, fig. 27). See also Thomson 1948, 337–338.

planned to begin by conquering Dacia and then to circle around from the north, an idea that reflects the traditional view of the *oikoumene* and especially of a truncated or nonexistent northern Europe and Asia.[109] It was, probably, an ecumenical scheme. Under Augustus, an expedition penetrated deep into Ethiopia in what may have been an attempt to reach Meroë, traditionally the last important city before the ocean. Augustus had thought twice of crossing to Britain.[110] He had planned, before Actium, to return to the Danube and cross over to Dacia.[111] Under his auspices Germany was conquered to the Elbe and a fleet sailed along the northern shore of the ocean, perhaps in an effort to circumnavigate it.[112] He had been content with a diplomatic victory in Parthia in 20 B.C., when the standards lost by Crassus and Antony were returned. Yet in 2 B.C. he sent his grandson to the eastern front, armed with descriptions of Parthia (including perhaps the itinerary that survives, reaching that empire's eastern borders and beyond) and of Arabia. Nero sent an exploratory mission to Meroë and was, on his death, preparing a war against the Iberians in the Caucasus region.[113] He, too, may have desired to reach the nearby ocean. The world in the imagination of the Julio-Claudians was a relatively small world—and, on the other hand, an unexplored and romanticized world. Its outer limit was alien and unknown, but within reach; and that limit on every side was the ocean. Conquest to the ocean was, then, an exceptional source of glory and pride.[114]

Trajan's conquest of the new province of Dacia comes to mind in this context, because of its strange appearance on the modern map. Its frontier took an odd form that extended the empire's border by 370 miles. One scholar observes that "in fact, on the map the new province pre-

109. Suet. *Caes.* 44.3. Or perhaps the other way around, as in Plut. *Caes.* 58.3: "He prepared and intended to campaign against the Parthians, and when he had subdued them, and come around the Black Sea through Hyrcania along the Caspian Sea and the Caucasus, to invade Scythia, and having attacked the lands around Germany and Germany itself to return to Italy through Gaul, and to complete the circle of his empire, bordered on every side by the ocean." The traditional schematic view of the *oikoumene* is evident in this passage. See also Vell. Pat. 2.59.4; Suet. *Aug.* 8.2; App. *Ill.* 13 and *B Civ.* 2.110; Gelzer 1968, 322; Brunt 1978, 178.
110. Cass. Dio 49.38.2, 53.22.5, 53.25.2; for further references, see Gruen 1996, n. 219.
111. App. *Ill.* 22–23; cf. Strab. 7.3.13.
112. On the navigations of Germanicus and his father, Drusus, and their purpose, see Nicolet 1991, 87. Cf. *RGDA* 26, Pliny *HN* 2.167, Tac. *Germ.* 34.2–3; on the mythic aura surrounding these expeditions, Romm 1992, 141–148; a fragment of an epic poem about Germanicus' voyage survives (ibid., 141–142; it is preserved in Sen. *Suas.* 1.15).
113. On Nero's plans, see Griffin 1984, 228–229; Braund 1986.
114. See below, chap. 5, n.31.

sents a classic profile of vulnerability."[115] But it is not clear that Trajan and his advisers thought of strategy in terms of two-dimensional geography at all; or if they did, the vulnerable salient evident to modern cartography was not necessarily what they imagined. For example, Ptolemy's work, composed at some time several decades after the conquest, shows the Carpathian Mountains running east to west in a straight line[116]—a distortion in orientation typical, as noted above, of the type of information available to the Romans from mainly military sources. Dacia, on Ptolemy's map, looks very different and more "rational" than on a modern one. But the most likely frontier imagined by Trajan when he invaded this territory was the ocean itself. It is likely that he shared the prevalent view of a flattened northern Europe; Agrippa had, after all, placed the ocean only 396 miles from the Danube River. The total conquest of eastern Europe must have seemed an attainable goal. Marcus allegedly planned to create new provinces of Sarmatia and Marcomannia (SHA Marc. 27.10), which were possibly supposed to reach, again, the ocean;[117] this was also Maximinus' goal, according to Herodian (7.2.9). Similar conclusions seem appropriate about Nero's prospective Caspian campaign;[118] because of the mainly mythological nature of Roman conceptions about the area, it seems probable that the emperor was motivated by notions of reaching the northern ocean and the exciting prospect of exploring and conquering exotic, unknown territory, which was also supposed to be rich in gold.[119]

The world described by Ptolemy, following Marinus, is very different from the traditional *oikoumene* or *orbis terrarum* of Strabo or Pliny (see fig. 5). Rather than accept the idea of a symmetrical land mass surrounded by the ocean, Ptolemy extended unknown territory into a vast "γῆ ἄγνωστος," unknown land or terra incognita, which had also been the approach of Herodotus nearly six hundred years previously.[120] Southern Asia is longer in his work than Strabo or Pliny had imagined, and even the "known" part of Africa extends below the equator. But few Roman policy makers were experts in geography. Ptolemy's work, which was so fundamental to Renaissance cartography, had only a slight impact on later Roman geography and remained obscure until the fourteenth

115. The figure is that of Szilágyi (1954, 205, with n. 516); adopted, with the comment quoted, by Luttwak (1976, 100).

116. See Karl Müller 1883–1901, vol. 3, fig. 18.

117. Cf. Cass. Dio 71[72].33.4 and Herodian 1.6.5.

118. As, e.g., Bosworth 1977, 226.

119. On myths about the Caucasus region and how these might have affected Nero's plans, see Braund 1986.

120. Hdt. 4.36–45.

Fig. 5. The world according to Ptolemy. From E. H. Bunbury, *A History of Ancient Geography* (London: John Murray, 1879; reprint, Amsterdam: J. C. Gieben, 1979).

Terra Incognita

Scythia

Stone
Tower

CASPIUM
MARE

A   S   I   A

Ganges

Indus   India

Taprobane

I N D I C U S   O C E A N U S

Terra Incognita

century.[121] The third-century work of Solinus is based entirely on (the more entertaining parts of) Mela and Pliny. Sources from the fourth century and later (Ammianus, Jordanes, Marcian of Heraclea) refer to Ptolemy, but the image of the world's shape in that period remains unchanged. Thus, the work of Dionysius Periegetes remained very popular and was translated twice, and in the sixth century it was still being recommended as a teaching aid.[122] Macrobius and Martianus Capella still describe a world similar to Eratosthenes'.[123] Nevertheless, in two cases—the lengthening of Asia and the widening of Africa—Ptolemy's conclusions are based on information that was probably known to the Roman court. Merchants had reached China, and a delegation from Marcus Aurelius had been there. And two expeditions in Africa had gone much farther than anyone had conceived possible.

Especially in Africa, a number of campaigns and explorations under the Julio-Claudians and through the reign of Domitian are attested: we have mentioned the campaigns of Cornelius Gallus and Petronius into Ethiopia, of Balbus to the land of the Garamantes, and of Suetonius Paulinus beyond Mount Atlas in Mauretania. Nero sent an exploratory mission to Ethiopia; under Domitian, Flaccus and Maternus ventured on lengthy explorations of the interior. The Romans persisted in northern Africa, although they knew or imagined the territory as rough, waterless, and infested with a terrifying variety of poisonous snakes and scorpions.[124] All of these explorers probably expected to reach the

121. On the influence of Ptolemy, see Dilke 1985, 154–166; cf. Brodersen 1995, 73–74. Ptolemy in fact reached the height of his popularity in the Age of Discovery with well-known results: he underestimated the world's circumference and also exaggerated Asia, so that the known world extended nearly halfway across this smaller globe, thus encouraging Columbus to believe that America was in fact India (= China), and to persist in his quest for spices, gold, and the Great Khan. On the geography of the later empire, see Lee 1993, 81–90.

122. By Cassiodorus, in the *Institutiones divinarum et saecularum litterarum;* this is pointed out by Dilke (1987a, 255, with n. 118); and see n. 2 above.

123. For Macrobius' geography, see *Commentary on the Dream of Scipio* 5–9 (= Stahl 1952, 200–216), especially 9.5–8. Like some other classical geographers, he believes in another inhabited world in the southern hemisphere, unreachable because the torrid zone cannot be crossed. For Martianus' geography, see 6.611–625 for general views and 626–702 on individual regions. Note that in 6.703 he reproduces Agrippa's figure of 910 miles for the depth of Africa (cp. Pliny *HN* 6.209) and in 6.619 both the Caspian Sea and the Palus Maeotis are attached to the ocean.

124. On Ethiopia, see Pliny *HN* 6.181. On North Africa, Sen. *Q Nat.* 3.6; Africa's topography is compared to the skin of a leopard, spotted with oases, in Strab. 2.5.33 and Dionysius Periegetes v. 181; Mela (1.21) writes that Africa is full of sterile sands and dry earth, and "infested by numerous and evil sorts of animals"; Manilius 4.662–670, Lucan 9.619–733, and App. *Praef.* 4 also emphasize the animals.

ocean. Everything in geographical theory told them that they should be close. But Flaccus and Maternus marched for months and there was still no end in sight. Thereafter we hear no more of ventures into the depths of Africa. The general schematic image of the continent remained uncorrected into the fourth century; but the experiences of the Roman army in Africa may have discouraged further efforts at exploration and conquest.

The Roman elite's view of the geography of the world always remained a literary one. Pomponius Mela's *Geography* and the verse handbook of Dionysius Periegetes almost certainly represent the ideas of the "average" senator more accurately than the exhaustively researched and more up-to-date works of Strabo, Pliny, or Ptolemy.[125] Even Strabo devotes the entire first book of his work to a discussion of the geography of Homer, while authorities like Pliny and Arrian do not necessarily privilege recent information over Hellenistic sources[126]—which may be striking to the modern reader,[127] but antiquity did not share today's pronounced tendency to value the new over the old in scholarship, at least not to the same extent. Partly because of the weight of literary tradition, ideas that are dismissed or corrected in one source may persist in another, later source: thus Mela's description of the island of Britain seems to owe more to Eratosthenes than to the campaigns of Caesar; and the latter were already, by his time, nearly a century old.[128] The vague and problematic geography of Tacitus, much commented on,[129] is partly the result of a certain conception of the genre of historiography: it was considered inappropriate to clutter what should be an elegant style with difficult place-names and other excessive detail (Lucian, *Hist. conscr.* 19). But this in itself reflects a worldview that considers moral and social issues more worthy of record than geographical "fact," even in a genre with a high military and foreign-relations content. Tacitus' account of Corbulo's campaigns in Armenia is extremely informative about Roman views of honor and discipline, as I shall argue in the final chapter. If the location of Tigranocerta remains uncertain to this day,[130] it is because it seemed less important to the historian—and thus is less important for us, if we wish to understand how he and his

---

125. See Brodersen 1995, 73–74, 82–100.
126. Dihle 1964, 17–20, and id. 1980.
127. Cf. Isaac 1992, 405.
128. Mela 3.50, with Silberman 1988 ad loc., n. 11.
129. E.g., Walser 1951, 23–28; Syme 1958, 1:392–396.
130. Bivar 1983, 45–46.

friends, colleagues, and contemporaries thought about foreign-relations problems.

4. Intelligence and Ethnology

As Roman geography had a strong literary and traditional element, so did the Romans' perception of the world's inhabitants— the outsiders they called "barbarians." Here too a tension emerges between a drive to collect the more practical information that today is called "intelligence"[131] and a strong tendency to perceive the barbarian in traditional and stereotypical ways. This is especially true in the case of Parthia. The Parthian empire was the only other highly organized political system known to the Romans, and more than one ancient author describes the Parthians as "rivals" of the Romans, their empire as "another world."[132] After the disastrous battle of Carrhae in 53 B.C., an explosion of specialist literature (none of which survives) attests an interest in explaining the disaster and "knowing the enemy."[133] Most of the emphasis was focused on weapons: Crassus was defeated in part because he did not know how to counter the Parthian archers and cataphracts (heavy-armed cavalry). Thus much of the ethnography that survives is devoted to descriptions of Parthian weapons and tactics.[134] The Romans

131. Strategic intelligence in the late empire is explored in detail by Lee (1993, chap. 4); for the classical period, see Austin and Rankov 1995.

132. Manilius 4.674–675: "and the Parthians, a sort of other world"; Strab. 11.9.2: "and now they rule over so much land and so many peoples, that in a way they have become rivals (ἀντίπαλοι) of the Romans in the size of their empire"; Lucan 8.290–307: "The Euphrates separates a huge world with its waters, and the Caspian Gates divide off immense recesses; and a different axis turns Assyrian nights and days. . . . The fates that move the Medes are too similar to our own fates"; Trogus (Justin) 41.1.1: "the Parthians, who now rule the east, having as it were divided the world with the Romans"; Cass. Dio 40.14.3: "they finally advanced so much in glory and power that they then made war even on the Romans, and ever since have always been considered rivals (ἀντίπαλοι)." Greek and Latin sources on Parthia are discussed recently by Wolski (1993, 12–15).

133. Gabba 1966, 53–57, citing the lost works of Julius Polyaenus of Sardis on Ventidius' campaigns, Q. Dellius on Antony's campaign, the digressions on the Parthians that were included in the histories of Strabo and Nicolaus of Damascus, and the lost work of Timagenes.

134. In Trogus (Justin) 41.2, the army is composed mainly of slaves; they fight with missiles rather than hand to hand and often counterfeit flight on horseback; men and horses are protected by plate armor; in Cass. Dio 40.14.4–15.6, Parthians use no shields, rely mainly on cavalry and a small infantry of archers, cannot fight in the winter because the air is bad for bowstrings, are nearly invincible on their own territory but rarely suc-

seem to have adapted to Parthian fighting styles and altered the composition of their own forces to some degree in response.[135] But on the level of "grand" strategy—not the question of how many *alae* of cavalry to send to the front, but of whether to undertake the war at all—it is more important to determine whether the Romans were able to discover or predict their rivals' long-term military plans, or acquire an understanding of their social and political institutions. Can we find here, as well, traditional and literary elements to their understanding of the world?

During his Gallic campaigns, Caesar was able to obtain and check valuable information about the plans, history, and numbers of his enemies from pro-Roman Gauls.[136] No comparable text exists from the imperial period, but some evidence suggests that the emperor was indeed able to learn about the political situation in neighboring lands. One commander receives reports that the Thracians are "fortifying places and about to make war" (Cass. Dio 51.25.4). Corbulo has information that Vologeses, the Parthian king, is occupied with a revolt in Hyrcania (Tac. *Ann.* 13.37), and later the same commander receives "reliable news" about Vologeses' military buildup and planned invasion (ibid., 15.3). Caecina Paetus, governor of Syria, sends reports—perhaps false—to Vespasian accusing Antiochus of Commagene of conspiracy to revolt (Joseph. *BJ* 7.219–220). Trajan learns that Decebalus is breaking the treaty of 102 and annexing territory of the Iazyges (Cass. Dio 68.10.3). Marcus Aurelius learns that the Quadi intend to migrate to the land of the Semnones (71[72].20.2); Caracalla writes to the senate that a quarrel within the Parthian ruling family will weaken their state (77[78].12.3).

In these cases we are not told how the Romans received their information, but other examples are more revealing. In A.D. 15 Germanicus attacked the Chatti because he believed that they had been weakened by a factional split between Arminius, who had led the revolt against Quintilius Varus in A.D. 9, and Segestes. In this case the informant was probably the pro-Roman Segestes himself, who had warned Varus about the impending revolt and remained hostile to Arminius after the disaster (Tac. *Ann.* 1.55). In A.D. 35 Tiberius received a secret embassy from

---

ceed outside it, and are incapable of protracted warfare (on which point cf. Tac. *Ann.* 11.10.4 and below); Plut. *Crass.* 24–25 describes Parthian weapons at length; cf. Gabba 1966, 54.

135. Gabba 1966; Coulston 1986.

136. E.g., *B Gall.* 2.2, 2.4; Austin and Rankov 1995, 22–24, 97–102.

Parthia seeking a king from among the hostages in Rome; the ambassadors must first have explained the situation outlined by Tacitus:

He [Artabanus, king of Parthia] had imposed Arsaces, the oldest of his sons, on it [Armenia] since its king Artaxias had died. . . . At the same time he boasted, with arrogant language and threats, of the old boundaries of the Persians and Macedonians, and that he was going to invade the lands possessed first by Cyrus and afterward by Alexander. (*Ann.* 6.31)

In A.D. 47 Pharasmanes, king of Iberia and brother of Rome's temporarily deposed nominee to the Armenian throne, informed the Romans that "the Parthians were in conflict and the rule of the empire was in doubt"; this was their chance to reinstate Mithridates in Armenia (*Ann.* 11.8).

In all these instances those seeking intervention from the Romans made sure they knew about the situation, and no doubt presented the case in the light most favorable to themselves.[137] It is possible that Artabanus' boast, cited above, was invented as a way of mobilizing Roman intervention on his rivals' behalf. Other examples indicate that the Romans otherwise had limited means of gathering information about day-to-day political events, especially in a systematic and regular way. From the Republic, the letters of Cicero offer a fascinating record of his struggle, as governor of Cilicia, to keep informed about a Parthian invasion of Syria in which he becomes involved. He arrives at his province with no knowledge of the situation and only with some delay is able to discover the location of his own troops. Even as his campaign progresses, doubts emerge about who exactly has invaded Syria and then, later, whether the enemy has withdrawn.[138] In the Principate this situation may have changed as the governor's office developed a massive military staff and bureaucracy.[139] Especially in the later second century, special units of *exploratores* are attested epigraphically; exactly what their duties were and how far they patrolled in enemy territory is uncertain.[140] Examples from Tacitus indicate how difficult it could be to obtain information even on important military developments. In one complicated instance, King Pharasmanes of Iberia, goaded by his son, attacks and occupies Armenia, deposing its pro-Roman king, Mithridates. The

137. On diplomatic channels for intelligence, see Austin and Rankov 1995, 120–123.
138. Ibid., 102–107.
139. Ibid., 149–155.
140. Ibid., 189–195; the authors argue for an improved intelligence situation after 160, but some of the evidence, such as the role of *beneficarii* or of the secretary *ab epistulis Latinis,* seems speculative.

Roman garrison there was under the command of an auxiliary prefect and a centurion. Pharasmanes bribes the prefect; but the centurion, taking a firmer stance, decides that "if he could not deter Pharasmanes from the war, he would inform Ummidius Quadratus, the governor of Syria, about the situation in Armenia" (*Ann.* 12.45); that is, the governor would not otherwise know. Quadratus in fact learns what is going on only after Mithridates is dead and his kingdom lost (*Ann.* 12.45–48). Later, the emperor Nero, receiving conflicting reports about the Armenian war from his general Paetus and an embassy from King Vologeses, asked the centurion who escorted the embassy "what was the situation in Armenia" (*quo in statu Armenia esset*); the centurion replied that "all the Romans had left" (*Ann.* 15.25). In another passage Tacitus records that the critical news leading to Corbulo's Armenian expedition—that the Parthians had expelled the king of Armenia and were pillaging the country—was brought to Rome by "rumors."[141] Sometimes we are told that an emperor first became aware of a major invasion on receiving a message from the provincial governor, who writes after his province has been attacked.[142] These invasions were not predicted, prevented by "first strikes," or met at the frontier.[143] Such preventive action was an inappropriate strategy for the Romans. Instead, they relied on punitive or retaliatory campaigns that might be waged at any time after the crisis occurred. We will return to point this in the next chapter.

The Roman emperor was constantly receiving embassies from all over the world. They often sought his intervention in their homeland's politics and often received it. In this way the emperor and his council could stay in touch with affairs happening far away and act on them. However, embassies seeking Roman help might well present their case in a biased way. The Romans had no real way to obtain political and military information on foreign territories systematically and objectively. Merchants could be questioned, but they were unreliable; the information of prisoners and refugees became outdated quickly.[144] Permanent legations or ambassadors to foreign lands were unknown in the ancient world. Gar-

---

141. *Ann.* 13.6: *Fine anni turbidis rumoribus prorupisse rursum Parthos et rapi Armeniam adlatum est, pulso Radamisto. . . .* Lee 1993, 149–165, describes how military information of this type could be transmitted by casual or "informal" channels.

142. Herodian 6.2.1, implying also that Severus Alexander learned of the Persian revolution only in 230, several years after it had taken place; see also ibid., 3.14.1 (a revolt in Britain) and 6.7.2 (the Rhine/Danube frontier).

143. Lee 1993, chap. 4, argues that in the later empire such invasions were usually predicted, but that this knowledge usually was not or could not be acted on.

144. Cf. Austin and Rankov 1995, 135–136.

risons might be placed in client kingdoms, but not necessarily.[145] In these respects Rome's neighbors were at an advantage, for many of their leaders had served in Rome's auxiliaries or lived in Rome as hostages or had received their education there.[146]

On the other hand, a substantial body of literature produced in the imperial period describes the culture and customs of peoples outside the empire. This is the genre of ethnography, which was invented by the Greeks in the fifth century B.C.; they also invented the term *barbarian*, to denote non-Greeks.[147] We might consider at this point the image of the Parthians and other "barbarians" that emerges from this tradition. In what ways did the Romans understand foreign political and social institutions? The modern world affords many examples of nations or ethnic groups, especially with long-standing hostile relationships, who perceive one another in terms of cultural stereotypes that resist change. I will argue that for the Romans this was largely true even of the decision-making elite; that their decisions were based more on a traditional and stereotyped view of foreign peoples than on systematic intelligence about their political, social, and cultural institutions. The Greeks and Romans began a long tradition of western perceptions of the alien or "barbarian." The relationship between these perceptions and later imperialist efforts such as the Crusades, the conquest of the New World, or nineteenth-century European imperialism is obvious even to a non-specialist like myself, and was important in the ancient world as well.

Unfortunately, the ethnography of Parthia has, as noted above, largely disappeared; in the works that survive, Strabo and Cassius Dio explicitly say that they knew much more than they recorded. Herodian knew and reported the interesting fact that the Parthians had no standing army—that it had to be called up when the occasion arose (3.1.2). Other Roman ideas about Parthian military capabilities have the character of legend or stereotype. For example, it was widely believed that the Parthians were invincible on their own territory but incapable of waging long campaigns outside it, and that their army was composed mainly of slaves.[148] The Parthians were supposed to be a warlike people.

145. Millar 1988, 368–369; Braund 1984, 94.

146. Braund 1984, 9–21.

147. On Roman ethnography, see Klaus Müller 1972–1980, vol. 2; Dauge 1981. Lund 1990 offers a recent and sophisticated analysis. Cf. also Sherwin-White 1967 and Balsdon 1979. On early Greek portrayals of the barbarian, see Hall 1989.

148. Invincibility: Cass. Dio 40.15.6; cf. Lucan 8.368–371, Trogus (Justin) 41.2, Tac. *Ann.* 1.11.4. Slaves: Trogus (Justin) 41.2.5–6; Plut. *Crass.* 21.6; discussed in Gabba 1966, 59–62; Wolski 1983; id. 1993, 102–104.

They were descendants of the barbarous, nomadic Scythians.[149] Thus Tacitus contrasts the soft lifestyle of King Vonones, who was raised in Rome, with that of his challenger Artabanus, whom the Parthians prefer because he was raised among the Scythian Dahae (*Ann.* 2.2–3). Vonones disdains hunting, horses, and banqueting. Trogus also comments on the Parthian love of hunting and horses, writing that the Parthians conduct all business on horseback (41.3.2–3). He has something to say about their costume: they wear loose, flowing clothes (41.2.4). These were an object of derision for the Romans, as we see in Lucan's poem (8.367–368). Both Lucan and Trogus write that the Parthians are polygamous (Trogus [Justin] 40.3.1; Lucan 8.397–401). This, we discover, is typical of all foreigners; the Germans are "almost the only barbarians content with a single wife" (Tac. *Germ.* 18.1).[150]

Trogus has more to say about Parthian character: they are not to be trusted. "The character of the race is arrogant, seditious, untrustworthy, and shameless."[151] This is also typical of other barbarians[152]—not only of easterners, as in Horace (*Carm.* 4.15.1), Polyaenus (7 *praef.*), and Tacitus (*Ann.* 12.46.1), but of northern barbarians as well. Velleius Paterculus tells us that the Germans "are in their extreme ferocity also extremely cunning, a race born for lying" (2.118.1). Polybius had described the Celts in the same way.[153] Pliny writes of the drunkenness of Parthians (*HN* 14.144, 148), which also was a common barbarian trait, typical of Scythians, Gauls, and Germans;[154] and this particular stereotype was already current in the fifth century B.C.[155]

Thus what begins to emerge is a more generalized stereotype of the alien or barbarian.[156] The most prominent barbarians in the Roman

---

149. On the Scythian origin of Arsaces and the resemblance of Parthians to Scythians, see Paratore 1966, 526–527, citing, e.g., Hor. *Carm.* 4.14.41–43, Strab. 11.9.2, Mela 3.33, Trogus (Justin) 41.1, Lucan 8.295–302.

150. The sexual promiscuity of barbarians was an important theme in ancient ethnography. See van der Vliet 1984, 65, citing Strab. 4.5.4 on the Irish, 7.3.7 on Scythians, and 11.11.8 on the Siginni, a Caucasian tribe; see also Caes. *B Gall.* 5.14 on Britons, Diod. Sic. 3.14.2 on "ichthyophagoi," Cass. Dio 76[77].12 (quoted below) on Scottish tribes, and the recent discussion of Lund (1990, 66–67).

151. *Ingenia genti tumida, seditiosa, fraudulenta, procacia* (41.3).

152. Cf. Wheeler 1993, 33 n. 100; Alföldi 1952, 10.

153. See Eckstein 1995, 122.

154. On the drunkenness of Germans, see Tac. *Germ.* 22–23, *Ann.* 11.16; of Parthians, Pliny *HN* 14.144, 148; of Gauls, Polyb. 2.19.4, Diod. Sic. 5.26.3; of Scythians, Cass. Dio 51.24.2.

155. Hall 1989, 133–134 (of Thracians).

156. For a general discussion of the genesis, development, and character of the Roman idea of the barbarian, see Lund 1990.

imagination were the northern tribes of Britons, Gauls, Sarmatians, and especially Germans, who all conform to a specific, very stable typology. They are generally described as nomadic. They build no permanent structures; they eat mainly meat, sometimes raw, and drink milk, rather than consuming the bread and wine cultivated by "civilized" societies. They also lack other important Greco-Roman cultural institutions such as monogamous marriage, anthropomorphic religion, money, and law; are very warlike; and live by plundering. They may wear skins or leaves or, sometimes, no clothes at all. Because of the harsh climate of all regions approaching the "frigid zone," they are inured to cold and hunger but vulnerable to heat and thirst. Strabo writes of the Germans, for example, that "it is common to all [the peoples] in this land that they migrate easily, because of the extreme simplicity of their way of life, and because they do not farm, or store things up, but live in small huts that have only a temporary structure, and most of their food comes from animals, like the nomads" (7.1.3).[157] Another geographer, this time writing in Latin, reports that the Germans are ferocious, warlike, and enduring of hardship and especially cold; that they wear only leaves despite the harsh climate, prefer to lay waste territory rather than cultivate it, know no law except the law of force, and eat raw meat (Mela 3.25–28). Seneca also tells us that the Germans are nomadic and build no houses, eat mainly the meat of wild animals, wear no clothes, and are extremely warlike and aggressive.[158] Cassius Dio describes the tribes of Scotland in a similar way:

They live in wild and waterless mountains and desert, marshy plains, having no walls, cities, or agriculture. . . . They live in tents, naked and barefoot, having the women in common, and raising all the children in common. They practice democracy for the most part, and they love to plunder. . . . They are able to bear hunger, cold, and all kinds of hardship, for they go down into the swamps and endure there for many days, having only their heads out of the water. (76[77].12)

Again, parts of this perception of the barbarian had a long history. In a famous argument, one scholar has traced the image of the lawless, meat-eating, aggressive nomad from ancient Mesopotamia to the

---

157. On Strabo's barbarians, see Thollard 1987, especially 6–12; van der Vliet 1984.
158. *Prov.* 4.14–15, *Ira* 1.11.3. More Germans of this type can be found in Joseph. *AJ* 19.120 and Plut. *Marius* 11; cf. Caesar *B Gall.* 6.21–24 and Tacitus' *Germania,* discussed below. For a modern study of the Roman view of Germans, see Lund 1990, 60–75.

present day.[159] The first surviving Greek ethnographic writing dates to the fifth century B.C.; it was at the same time, in the aftermath of the Persian wars, that the concept of the barbarian was "invented."[160] Thus Herodotus' history of the Persian war contains long digressions on barbarian peoples, including, for example, the nomadic Massagetae (1.216). Like barbarians of the Roman era, they share women in common; they also worship only the sun, and eat mainly meat and fish, and sometimes even people. The most famous of Herodotus' nomadic barbarians are the ferocious, bloodthirsty Scythians, to whom he devotes much of his fourth book.[161]

Another type of barbarian also emerges from his work: the luxurious, cowardly easterner, represented especially by Persia.[162] The Persians' character defects were partly the result of their political institutions; Herodotus and other fifth-century authors portray them as enslaved to a despotic tyrant, while the Greeks are proud of the "liberty" associated with their own civic institutions of the *polis*.[163] The author of the Hippocratic treatise *Airs, Waters, Places*, for example, agrees: Asians are likely to be more cowardly and less warlike than Europeans, because of their political structure, but also because of the temperate climate (chap. 16). Similar rhetoric survives in the Roman period. Thus Mela, Seneca, and Florus all agree that it is the harsh climate that renders northern barbarians so ferocious.[164] Tacitus, a critic of his own society and especially the quasi-monarchic Principate, writes: "Not even the Parthians have reproached us more often [than the Germans]; German liberty is harsher than the tyranny (*regnum*) of Arsaces [the Parthian ruling house]" (*Germ.* 37.7). The stereotype of the effete easterner also persisted; this version of the Parthians can also be found in the epic of Lucan:

All the peoples of the north and anyone born in the frosts are invincible in war and lovers of death; but as one goes toward the eastern lands and the warm part of the world, the people are softened by the gentle sky.

159. Shaw 1982, 29–35; id. 1982a.
160. Hall 1989.
161. On Herodotus' Scythians, see Hartog 1988.
162. On the stereotype of easterners, see Wheeler 1996.
163. E.g., the famous speech of Demaratus (Hdt. 7.101–104). See Hall 1989 on the emergence of this stereotype, a topic that is much more complex than this brief description suggests.
164. Mela 3.33; Sen. *Ira* 2.15.5; Florus 1.37.2; see also Lund 1990, 36–55, on north/east polarities; cf. Wheeler 1996, 241–242.

There you will see loose clothes and flowing garments even on men. (8.363–368)

Cowardly Arabians, Ethiopians, and Moors are also on record.[165]

Thus the Greeks brought their conceptions of the barbarian to Rome. Polybius in the second century B.C. had described Celts that were very similar on the one hand to the Thracians of Athenian tragedy, and on the other to the stereotype, described above, of the northern barbarian from a period centuries later: they are nomadic, fierce, cruel, treacherous, disorganized in battle, drunken, greedy for plunder, lacking in discipline.[166] In a passage strikingly similar to the later stereotype of, especially, the Germans, he writes that they "inhabited unwalled villages, without knowledge of the other arts of civilization; for because they slept on straw (or leaves; στιβαδοκοιτεῖν), and ate meat, and moreover practiced nothing besides warfare and agriculture, they had simple lives, and no other science or craft at all was known to them" (2.17.9–10).[167] Polybius drastically minimizes the sophistication of Gallic culture, though his account may be based on firsthand observation.[168] Caesar's characterization of the Gauls, which is also of course an eyewitness account, differs from Polybius' description of the Celts; especially, Caesar's Gauls are no longer nomadic. But it is impossible to know, and probably not productive to ask, how much of his account is based on his own observations of Gallic culture, and how much reflects what he thought he knew about barbarians based on a long literary and cultural tradition. His discussion of the Druids and their horrific human sacrifices describes a cultural reality—one already known to the Romans, but also one that was perceived as typical of barbarians in general.[169] Elsewhere the stereotype of the barbarian as greedy for plunder, aggressive but lacking stamina, fickle, and treacherous emerges where it is convenient and is echoed in Strabo.[170]

165. E.g., Manilius 4.654; Strab. 16.4.23–24, 17.1.53; and Cass. Dio 78[79].27.1, where he attributes Macrinus' disgraceful treaty with the Parthians to his "natural cowardice, for he was a Moor (Μαῦρος) and terribly timid."

166. Eckstein 1995, 122–124; for these characteristics of barbarians in tragedy, see Hall 1989, especially 122–126, 133–138.

167. I adopt Walbank's translation of τῆς λοιπῆς κατασκευῆς ἄμοιροι (1957–1979, 1:184).

168. See ibid. at 2.17.10 and pp. 172–173.

169. B Gall. 6.16. Human sacrifice was an important ideological marker of barbarism and is associated with other barbarians as well; see Rives 1995, 67–70. Posidonius had included human sacrifice in his account of the Celts, and Caesar probably drew on this material (ibid., n. 22).

170. Strab. 4.4.2. On Caesar's Gauls, see Rambaud 1966, 324–333; Sherwin-White 1967, 18–29; Klaus Müller 1972–1980, 2:68 ff.; and recently Bell 1995 and Walser 1995.

Caesar may have been motivated to "civilize" his Gauls to some degree by his desire to justify his wars in their defense against the terrifying Germans.[171] It is especially in his description of the Germans that Caesar seems to reflect a traditional ideology, part stereotype and part projection of Roman values and cultural norms. His Germans inhabit, or originally inhabited, the territory across the Rhine River, which he thus perceives as a cultural boundary of some significance, constantly using it as a reference point for the division between Germany and Gaul.[172] They are nomadic pastoralists who live on meat and milk; worship only the sun, moon, and fire; remain chaste until the age of twenty; own no property; and do not value money. They are also warlike and aggressive in the highest degree (*B Gall.* 6.21–23).

The Germans go on to hold a prominent place in the Roman imagination. Examples from later centuries of the same stereotype appearing in Caesar's account have been discussed above. The only surviving exclusively ethnographic treatise from Roman antiquity is, in fact, Tacitus' treatise on Germany. It is thoroughly researched and contains much that Caesar does not record, including details about clothing and hairstyle that agree with representations on ancient monuments.[173] Tacitus' Germans also build houses and farm land, unlike Caesar's pastoralists. But this treatise, too, is pervaded by the familiar stereotype of the northern barbarian: the Germans have "large bodies, strong only in the first assault; they have not the same endurance of labor and work, and are conditioned to tolerate thirst and heat only a little; but they have been accustomed by the climate and the soil to bear cold and hunger" (4.3). They are also drunken like Scythians or Gauls,[174] and prefer to plunder rather than farm (*Germ.* 14.4). Thus the literary stereotype of the barbarian pervades and colors the work very extensively. On several issues archaeological evidence challenges Tacitus' account and suggests that he, like Caesar, perceives the Germans in Greco-Roman terms, often projecting the ideas and values of his own society onto the primitive

171. Rambaud 1966, 324–333.

172. See Lund 1990, 82–100, on Caesar's Germany and his construction of the Rhine boundary, which is complex but very significant. The Rhine forms a reference point not only for his image of the cultural division between Germans and Celts, but also for his own conquests; see his symbolic crossing in 4.16–19 (also cf. 5.9), and several passages where either he drives German tribes back behind the Rhine or Germans cross the Rhine to invade Gaul (1.1, 2, 27, 28, 31, 33, 35, 43–44, 53, 54; 3.11; 4.1, 3, 4, 14, 16; 5.27, 29, 55; 6.35, 41, 42).

173. Cf. Anderson 1938, 105–109, 179–180. On the relationship of the *Moorleichen* (bog bodies) of northern Germany and Denmark to the punishment of criminals described in *Germ.* 12, see Lund 1988, 146–147.

174. See n. 154 above.

outsider: thus his Germans are cremated and buried only with weapons and horses, they make no images of gods, and the interior tribes do not value precious metals and use livestock for currency. Independent evidence suggests that none of these statements was a "true" representation of *German* culture; however, they all provide excellent though indirect evidence for *Roman* values and cultural identity, which shaped how the Romans perceived the foreigner to a very high degree. Again, the task of separating the "real" Germans from Tacitus' construction of them would be futile. Rather than creating an independent and objective understanding of his subject, his work helped to create and perpetuate a certain cultural stereotype of the enemy, which also reinforced the Romans' sense of their own identity and values.[175]

Julius Caesar, it has been argued, invented Germany.[176] His perception of this area of the world reflects his political and imperial agenda, and traditional concepts of the barbarian; these are impossible to separate from whatever objective "reality" might be represented, although his commentaries are the best surviving example of the type of firsthand military chronicle that formed the basis for much of ancient historiography. Archaeology finds no cultural division on the Rhine; linguistic analysis suggests that most of the names of tribes Caesar identifies as German were Celtic, mixed Celtic and German, or neither. The Germany imagined by Caesar, Strabo, and Tacitus and displayed confidently on Agrippa's map may never have existed as a cultural, linguistic, or political entity at all.[177] But to the Romans it existed; and so did the clear, stable image of the "barbarian" in their minds. They carried with them an ideology of the foreigner with the authority of literary tradition. This ideology affected how they perceived their neighbors even after firsthand observation, a phenomenon not unknown to modern anthropology. Two examples especially illustrate the profound influence of Roman ethnic stereotypes.

175. On the character of ancient ethnography, see Lund 1990, 19–35; on *Germania,* id. 1988 and 1991; for a full annotated bibliography on *Germania,* id. 1991a. On burials, see *Germ.* 27.1; on images, 9.3, with Lund 1988 ad locc. On German use of coins and precious metals, see Lund 1991, 1884–1887, with bibliography.

176. Wells 1972, 14–32; Sallmann 1987, 123–126; Lund 1990, 82–100; cf. Walser 1956, making the same argument from a more literary perspective.

177. See Todd 1987, 11–13, on Caesar's account and its problems; ibid., 8, on the names of tribes. Wells (1972, 14–32) argues that in fact a "Germany" of roughly Caesar's description was created by the Romans themselves when building on the Rhine frontier created a sharper distinction between the provincial culture on the west bank and the barbarian culture on the east bank; but Whittaker (1994, 74–78) argues that the Rhine was never a cultural boundary (his discussion includes substantial bibliography on this difficult issue). See also Lund 1991, 1954–1968.

The first is Pliny the Elder's account of the Chauci, who inhabited the tidal mudflats of what is now the Netherlands. Pliny served in Germany under the famous general Corbulo and here is explicitly describing something he saw himself:

There, wretched race, they occupy high mounds or platforms (*tribunalia*) built with their hands according to their experience of the highest tide, and they put houses on top of them, . . . and they hunt the fish who flee with the sea around their huts. It does not befall them to have flocks, to be nourished with milk, like their neighbors, nor even to fight with wild animals, since every shrub is far removed. They make ropes of sedge and marsh reeds in order to spread nets for the fish; they gather mud with their hands and dry it more in the wind than in the sun, and with earth they warm their food and their own entrails, frozen by the north wind. They have no drink except from rainwater stored up in trenches at the entrance of their houses. (*HN* 16.3–4)

Archaeology has in fact discovered traces of the platforms that Pliny describes.[178] But this description of the Chauci is an excellent example of how the filtering agents of tradition, ideology, and Roman moral outlook create a cultural construction from an observed reality. The Chauci's diet of fish and rainwater makes them even more marginal than the "ordinary" meat- and milk-eating barbarians with whom they are compared. They lack not only agriculture but basic technology: twice Pliny insists that they do things "with their hands." The climate, at the limits of the habitable world, is described as unimaginably cold, though Pliny must have experienced summer in Germany; similarly, Ovid had described the climate of Tomis on the Black Sea, where he was exiled, as relentlessly bleak.[179]

Later, Cassius Dio offers the following image of the Pannonians, which is especially interesting because of his experience in the area:

[T]hey are the most wretched of men. . . . They cultivate neither olives nor wine, except a very little and very bad at that, because they live most of their lives in the harshest winter . . . but they are considered the bravest men of whom we know. For they are very spirited (θυμικώτατοι) and murderous (φονικώτατοι). . . . This I know, not just because I heard it or read about it, but I learned it also from experience *when I governed them.* (49.36.2–3)

---

178. For references see Sallmann 1987, arguing that imperialist ideology is more prominent than fact in this description; Pliny wants to see a particularly wretched and barbarous people here. On the mudflats, cp. Manilius 4.794–795 and Lucan 1.409–411.

179. Brodersen 1995, 102–103.

Here again we have a harsh climate, a warlike, aggressive nature, and a people almost without agriculture and especially without the olive and vine that characterized "civilization" for the Greeks and Romans. Sometimes barbarians are perceived as possessing pristine virtues that belonged to the Romans of old; at other times they embody vices, such as lack of discipline, that are opposed to Roman virtues. Their reputation for cruelty and atrocity also persisted and emerges, not surprisingly, especially in war narratives such as the story of Arminius' revolt (Tac. *Ann.* 1.61; Florus 2.30.37) or the torture scene from Trajan's column (scene XLV) or accounts of the revolt of Vercingetorix (Caes. *B Gall.* 7.4.10) or of Boudicca (Cass. Dio 62.7). The barbarian was, like the *oikoumene* itself, a cultural construction.

Those who study ancient literature are right to point out that the genre of ethnography—even when it appears, as it almost always did in the Roman period, as a digression in a historical narrative—was much more tolerant of the exaggerated, marvelous, or unlikely than the genre of history.[180] But for our purposes, what matters is that whatever the Romans knew or believed about the customs of foreign peoples was preserved in this form. Aelius Gallus invaded Arabia Felix based on a long and romanticized tradition about that land:

There was also the age-old rumor that they were rich (τὸ πολυχρημάτους ἀκούειν ἐκ παντὸς χρόνου), selling aromatics and the most expensive gemstones for silver and gold, and spending none of the profits among foreigners. For he [the emperor, Augustus] hoped either to deal with rich friends or to rule over rich enemies. (Strab. 16.4.22)

This information comes from the geographer Strabo, a friend and companion of Gallus[181] who was in as good a position as anyone to know what was in the commander's mind. The legend behind the invasion of Arabia has rightly been compared with the El Dorado myth that led to the conquest of South America.[182] It is not certain that the riches Gallus expected to find actually existed. The author of the *Periplus Maris Erythraei,* writing in the first century A.D., records that "[Eudaimon Arabia] was called 'eudaimon' (blessed)—for once it was a city—because, when no one yet came from India to Egypt and no one dared cross over from Egypt to places beyond, but came only this far, they re-

---

180. Note the remarks of Lee (1993, 101).

181. Strab. 2.5.12

182. Braund 1986, 43. For Arabia's reputation of wealth, and especially for incense, perfumes, and pearls, see, e.g., Manilius 4.654–657, Mela 1.61, Statius *Silv.* 2.1.61, Dionysius Periegetes vv. 933–939; on pearls, especially Lucan 6.676–677, Pliny *HN* 12.84.

ceived the shipments of both" (chap. 26). In his time, since the establishment of a direct sea trade with India, Arabia Felix was no longer a city but merely a "κώμη," village. At roughly the same time, Pliny writes that Arabia Felix received its epithet because of the incense trade (*HN* 12.51). He repeats the tradition that "the Arabians are, as a whole, the richest peoples in the world, since the greatest wealth of the Romans and Parthians remains with them; for they sell what they take from the sea [sc., pearls] and their forests [sc., incense], without buying anything in return" (*HN* 6.162). He could have replaced his traditional image of the land with recent information from merchants such as the author of the *Periplus,* and so could Augustus or Gallus; but it was the legend that was guiding Roman actions.

And this was true in a general sense about the Roman decision-making elite. Consider the occasion of Nero's accession, as Tacitus describes it: disturbing news arrives from the east; will the young prince be able to handle the situation? Relying on his advisers, he makes what is perceived as a prudent decision (*Ann.* 13.6). One of these advisers, indeed one of the most trusted, produced a substantial body of literature, much of which survives.

Seneca was a philosopher, a tragedian, and an educator. An examination of his work produces no evidence of a nonliterary, nontraditional approach to geography or ethnography; on the contrary, he is a rich source for the stereotypical ethnic barbarian.[183] His treatise on India has been lost; but the statistics it contained, as recorded by Pliny, are from Megasthenes, a source sharply criticized by Strabo for his mythologized, wonder-telling approach to ethnography.[184] There may be reasons—constraints of genre, for example—that prevent Seneca from revealing a less traditional, more practical and "expert" approach to the questions discussed in this chapter. But the evidence does not constrain us to

183. The *De ira* and *De providentia,* as noted above, both contain digressions on the barbarians of the north: the Germans are warlike and inured to suffering, they fight without armor and do not live in houses (*Ira* 1.11.3); the "Germans and whatever peoples around the Danube attack us" suffer terrible weather and sterile soil, have no houses or only structures of straw and leaves, and eat wild beasts (*Prov.* 14.14–15). The tragedies often focus particularly on the barbarity of the inhabitants of the northern Pontic region: e.g., *Hercules furens* 533–546 (nomadic Scythians, frozen northern ocean, long-haired Sarmatians, Amazons); also *Troades* 8–13; *Hippolytus* 165–170, 906–907; *Hercules Oetaeus* 1251; *Thyestes* 629–632. Other stereotypes include incense-laden Arabia and sunburnt India (*Hercules furens* 909–911, *Hippolytus* 67, *Hercules Oetaeus* 336–337, etc.); several passages offer lists of rivers including the Tanais, Nile, Tigris, Rhine, Tagus, Danube, Hydaspes, Baetis, etc. (*Hercules furens* 1323–1326, *Medea* 723–726, *Hippolytus* 58–59, *Hercules Oetaeus* 623–630).

184. See above, n. 95.

make this assumption; on the contrary, the Roman elite was educated primarily in rhetoric, literature, and philosophy by people precisely like Seneca. The argument from silence is always suspect. But, on the other hand, it will not do to ignore the substantial body of evidence for Roman thinking that does exist in favor of an image of the Romans that might seem more rational to a modern audience, but for which evidence is lacking.

There is, in fact, no great difference between the poetic description of the world and its peoples that appears in Seneca's tragedies—or in Lucan's epic, or Statius' *Silvae,* for example—and the one that emerges from historical, philosophical, or ethnographic works. In both geography and ethnology the Romans had concrete and practical information of a type suitable for short-term, tactical thinking—itineraries, catalogs of weapons. But on a broader scale their knowledge and understanding of the world around them was different in character; they pictured a schematic, oval-shaped world, framed by zones of bitter frost and scorching heat, surrounded by the ancient, impassable ocean, and inhabited at its edges by primitive, exotic, sometimes mythical peoples. These conceptions must form the background for any further discussion of the mentality behind Roman imperialism.

---| CHAPTER 3 |---

Strategy

1. The Limitations of the Imperial Army

Strategy is a word with a long history—meaning, originally, something like "generalship." Traditionally, military historians
recognized a simple division between tactics and strategy—one having
to do with battles, the other with wars. Modern historians have added
a level of "operations" between strategy and tactics, which is not so
important for this study. And another level emerges on top: a level of
"grand strategy" of potentially much more general scope, including
nonmilitary aspects. One military historian has recently suggested that
"the crux of grand strategy lies . . . in *policy,* that is, in the capacity of the
nation's leaders to bring together all of the elements, both military and
nonmilitary, for the preservation and enhancement of the nation's long-
term (that is, in wartime *and* in peacetime) best interests."[1] By this very
broad definition, "grand strategy" is, in a way, the subject of this book
—though whether we choose to define as "policy" the set of ideas, assumptions, and values that governed the Romans' actions and reactions

---

1. Kennedy 1991, 5. Kennedy seeks especially to expand the notion of grand strategy
to include the spheres of economics, diplomacy, and national morale. For further discussion of terms, see Wheeler 1993, pt. 1, 21–22.

in the international sphere I leave to the reader, ultimately, to decide. In any case, this chapter will discuss the specifically military aspects of this "grand strategy."

I choose the word as the title of this chapter because it is so evocative—conjuring, to a naive audience like myself, an image of men in uniforms sticking pins into a vast, multicolored map. The pins might represent troops or equipment, forts or other military structures, perhaps supply lines. We know already that one element of this image is inappropriate to our model of Roman decision making: the map. What about the other aspects of the image—the troops, for example? Can our sources give us some indication about what determined where and how they were deployed, and what the Romans hoped to accomplish with their military resources? We must begin with a survey of the Roman army.

It has often been remarked that under the Principate, Rome managed to secure, defend, and even expand its empire with a relatively small military force. Augustus kept twenty-eight legions under arms but lost three in Varus' German disaster in A.D. 9, and they were not replaced. The size of the legionary army grew only gradually as later emperors raised new legions, while others were destroyed or disbanded, so that by the end of our period there were thirty-three legions in existence.[2] Exactly how many soldiers that represented is difficult to say. On paper, a legion contained about 6,000 or 5,280 men.[3] But they were not always up to strength; for in crisis situations special levies had to be conducted, even when no new legions were formed, presumably to replenish the ranks of the existing units.[4] As for auxiliary units, it was Tacitus' impression that

2. This is the traditional scheme; Ritterling 1924–1925 is still the basic reference for the legions under the Principate. For the arguments on the number of Augustus' legions in A.D. 6, see ibid., 1215–1217. The total of thirty-three legions is assured by an inscription at Rome (*ILS* 2288) from the reign of Severus, listing twenty-eight legions in geographical order, with the new legions raised by Marcus and Severus added at the end.

3. See G. R. Watson 1969, 13 n. 7, for the major sources, including Hyginus (*De munitionibus castrorum*), who gives 480 men for cohorts II to X, the first cohort being double strength, for a total of 5,280 men. This conflicts with other sources who assume 6,000 men to a legion, including Vegetius (1.17). Brunt 1971, 687–688, shows that legions in the late Republic were commonly believed to comprise either 5,000 or 5,200 or 6,000 men.

4. MacMullen 1980, 452–454. See also Alston 1995, 44–46, calculating that the "average" legion may have contained 4,600 to 4,800 men; he also notes "big" recruitment years associated with crises. Once again Brunt (1971, 688–693) is relevant, though he is considering the late Republic. His evidence indicates that legions were often severely under-enrolled and that the average legion in the civil wars may have numbered about 4,000. On emergency recruitment, see Mann 1983, 52. Literary references include Tac. *Ann.* 13.7, where Nero orders the deployment of the "troops raised in the nearby provinces for the

they were approximately equal in strength to the legions (*Ann.* 4.5). In fact, under Antoninus Pius one scholar counts more than that: 338 quingenary cohorts, each about 500 strong on paper; and 48 milliary cohorts, numbering twice that, with an estimated paper strength of about 224,000. Whether the auxiliary units were also underenrolled is more difficult to say. There seems to have been some flexibility regarding the size of these units, and some contained more soldiers than they were supposed to, others less.[5] The legions at that time numbered twenty-eight, for a paper strength of about 140,000 or 168,000, depending on the size of a legion; adding the praetorians and other troops stationed in Rome, plus perhaps 30,000 for the fleet, this amounts to a paper strength of 405,500 or 433,500 for the entire army.[6] We should probably allow for underenrolled units, imagining an actual figure of, perhaps, 400,000.[7] By the end of our period the number of legions had increased to thirty-three, and probably the auxiliary units increased at least proportionally; thus a round estimate of 425,000, and probably not more than 450,000, seems plausible for the army in the Severan period. This of course is a very small percentage of the empire's population. This small, fixed size of the army, I shall argue, was a key factor in Roman strategy; it is important to realize that the Romans did not conquer and hold their empire by means of sheer, overwhelming force. It is worthwhile, in this context, to investigate what determined the size of Rome's military force.

Augustus discharged a large number of troops during his reign, eventually settling for twenty-eight legions permanently under arms. He may have believed that this was the largest force that could reasonably be recruited and maintained; that is, manpower constraints played a role

---

replenishment of the legions of the east"; also 13.35, where Corbulo discharges veterans and "sought replacements (*supplementum*); and drafts (*dilectus*) were held throughout Galatia and Cappadocia"; also 16.13: "drafts were held throughout Narbonese Gaul and Africa and Asia, to replenish the legions of Illyricum, from which those tired out by old age or sickness were being discharged"; cf. Fronto *Principia historiae* 10 (= Loeb 2:207), where Lucius' eastern campaign requires a levy. Cf. Brunt 1974, 101.

5. Thomas and Davies (1977) report a quingenary cohort under Caracalla containing 457 men after "permanent losses" have been deducted (with "temporary losses"—soldiers temporarily posted elsewhere—the cohort could not have numbered more than 331). However, Alston (1995, 22–23) assembles five figures for the enrollment of quingenary auxiliary units attested on papyri; all but one are higher than 500, and two are substantially higher.

6. See Holder 1980, 217–240, for the list. The figures are from A. R. Birley 1981a, 39–43, which is based on Holder's study.

7. Cf. MacMullen 1980, 451–454, with corrections in id. 1984, 571–572, proposing a figure of 375,000.

in determining the size of the army. It is true that the civil wars of 49–31 B.C. involved enormous numbers of troops; the battle of Philippi, where Octavian (the future emperor Augustus) defeated Brutus' army in 42 B.C., was fought with no less than thirty-eight legions; at the time sixty-six legions were in existence, which probably represented about 216,000 to 270,000 Italians plus 48,000 to 60,000 provincials. It is estimated that at this point 25 percent of the Italian youth was under arms.[8] At Actium eleven years later, Octavian fought with at least sixteen legions and had control over a total of twenty-eight or perhaps more than that, while Antony controlled probably twenty-three legions, though those were seriously underenrolled.[9] But these were extraordinary circumstances. The armies of the civil war were levied with considerable force, although the terms of service were much more generous than what eventually developed under the empire.[10]

The army of the late Republic still operated along the lines of a traditional system whereby all Roman citizens were obliged to serve in the legions for a certain number of campaigns, said by Polybius, a historian of the second century B.C., to be fixed at sixteen. In fact, this system had become impractical as Rome's empire grew, and soldiers could no longer return to Italy in the off season to tend their fields. Soldiers serving in Spain, at that time the main province requiring a permanent overseas standing army, had to be relieved after six years or so. In fact, most citizens seem to have served less than ten years in the army, but even that would be ruinous to a farmer forced to neglect his crops. Conscription was employed, especially during the civil wars.[11] Beginning with Marius in the late second century B.C., discharged veterans were sometimes rewarded with grants of land. Such rewards became a powerful tool for securing the loyalty of an army, and by the civil wars of the late Republic they were a right demanded by all veterans.[12]

When Augustus settled two great waves of veterans in 30 and 14 B.C., he avoided the wildly unpopular confiscations of 41, but at a price: it was expensive. Cassius Dio writes that the veterans discharged after the defeat of Antony and Cleopatra at Actium were paid from the spoils of

8. Brunt 1971, 480–488, 510–512.

9. Ibid., 498–505; Keppie 1983, 27–28.

10. On this point see Brunt 1971, 408; id. 1974, 94–95.

11. See Brunt 1971, 399–402, on the average length of service under the Republic and the length (and unpopularity) of service in Spain; 391–415 on conscription under the Republic; and p. 636 nos. III.8 and III.9 for references to the (especially harsh) levies of Pompey and Caesar in 49.

12. Mann 1983, 1–8; Keppie 1983, 39–40.

Egypt.[13] The financial element was probably decisive in determining the size of the army, and will be discussed in the next chapter. For now we should note that by the end of Augustus' reign, the army had a different character. Soldiers served first for sixteen, then for twenty years before discharge; by the end of the first century this term had lengthened to twenty-five years.[14] They were posted virtually permanently in provinces on the periphery of the empire; and in return they received modest pay and *praemia*, rewards of land or money on retirement. Already under Augustus, the conditions began to be unattractive to Italians and the western legions were increasingly composed of recruits from Spain, Africa, and the Danube region, who would often be posted to their home provinces;[15] only service in the praetorian guard, which involved a shorter term, better pay, and posting in Italy, continued to attract Italian recruits.

It is no doubt true that if Roman emperors had employed systematic conscription they could have produced a much larger army. In fact, the draft was sometimes used, especially in emergencies or when ambitious campaigns were being planned;[16] but for the most part Rome seems to

13. 51.4.8. On the settlement of veterans by Octavian/Augustus, see Keppie 1983, 58–86; for bibliography, ibid., 49 n. 1.

14. Brunt 1971, 332; sixteen years for legionaries and twelve for praetorians was established in 13 B.C. (Cass. Dio 54.25.6); in A.D. 5 this was raised to sixteen and twenty years, respectively (Cass. Dio 55.23.1); in fact, many soldiers were detained longer, and the term of service seems to have stabilized at twenty-five to twenty-six years sometime in the first century (Forni 1953, 37–38).

15. Forni 1953, chap. 5; Mann 1983, 54–55; see also MacMullen 1988, 53–55, with fig. 13. From an early date the legions in the east were composed mainly of *peregrini* who were granted citizenship on recruitment; in the west the soldiers were usually Roman citizens but not all Italians, and the proportion of Italians becomes smaller until finally there are virtually none (Mann, op. cit., 49, 54–55). However, there seems to have been a policy of recruiting all new legions in Italy (Mann 1963).

16. Brunt 1974, and see also Mann 1983, 49–50; these scholars take different views, but both agree that Rome relied largely on volunteers but employed conscription, too, especially in the provinces, though only infrequently in Italy; Brunt argues that this was common and Mann that it was irregular. Both point out that the word *dilectus* (or *delectus*) is apparently ambiguous and can refer either to voluntary recruitment or compulsion (a convincing array of references to *dilectus* as forced levy is compiled in Brunt 1971, app. 20). Brunt (1974, 107–112) argues that the literary evidence for conscription dies out in the Severan period, perhaps because of better pay, more reliance on local recruitment, and Severus' famous edict allowing soldiers to marry; but cf. MacMullen 1980, 453 n. 6, arguing that conscription continued in the third century. In Tac. *Ann.* 4.4 (A.D. 23), Tiberius sends Drusus on a tour of the provinces and remarks that "there was a shortage of voluntary recruits, and even when the number was sufficient, they did not act with that same virtue and self-control, because for the most part only the poor and vagrant joined the army voluntarily." Gaius prepared for his German campaign with "legions and auxiliaries called forth from all regions, and drafts (*dilectus*) carried out everywhere very harshly"

have relied on voluntary recruitment.[17] One reason for this reliance on volunteers is clear: conscription under the terms of service that prevailed in the Principate meant forcibly removing someone from his home and family, possibly to a very distant land, virtually forever.[18] Even if the soldier was posted in his own province, he had only about a 50 or 60 percent chance of surviving his term of enlistment to receive his reward upon discharge;[19] and in the meantime, pay was modest, at least until Severus (see below, chap. 4). One can imagine the odium that the draft must have produced, and this probably explains why emperors were especially reluctant to resort to it in Italy.[20] New legions, however, were always raised in Italy for reasons that are unclear but may include traditionalism; thus any increase in the empire's legionary forces would involve, at least initially, an unpopular draft of Italians.[21] And whereas we can assume a greater willingness to conscript auxiliaries, this also created problems if pursued too zealously; Tacitus' accounts of the Thracian revolt of A.D. 26, Boudicca's rebellion in Britain, and the revolt of Civilis in Gaul all emphasize the levy as one of Rome's most oppressive demands.[22]

Whatever the reason, there seem to have been some limits on the number of soldiers that could be enrolled; Augustus was twice reduced to drafting freedmen, after the disasters of A.D. 6 and A.D. 9, and Varus'

(Suet. *Gaius* 43). On conscription in preparation for campaigns, see also n. 4 above. Cf. Vell. Pat. 2.130.2, of Tiberius: "with what calm does he provide for that thing of such constant and intense fear for men, the *supplementum,* without the consternation of the draft (*delectus*)." See below for emergency conscriptions in the crises of A.D. 6, 9, and 69.

17. Forni 1953, 30, notes that the legions would have required only 5,000 to 6,000 new recruits per year, a number that should have been sustainable by voluntary recruitment.

18. Cf. Civilis' speech in Tac. *Hist.* 4.14: the levy separates children from parents and brother from brother "like death" (*velut supremum*); the situation was no different for legionaries.

19. Mann 1983, 59; Alston 1995, 44–46.

20. See Brunt 1974, 94–100, on conscription in Italy; Mann 1983, 50.

21. Brunt 1974, 97–98; on traditionalism or "blind conservatism," see Mann 1963, 488.

22. For these examples, see Brunt 1974, 106–108; Webster 1985, 144–145; and Isaac 1992, 59. On the conscription of auxiliaries generally, see Saddington 1982, 140–141. The passages mentioned are Tac. *Ann.* 4.46 on the Thracians, *Agr.* 15.3 on Boudicca, and *Hist.* 4.14 on Civilis. In the case of the Thracians, it was once again service far from one's native country, and being forced to serve under Roman officers (they had previously been allowed native commanders), that was objectionable. Civilis' revolt is provoked directly by a levy of troops for Vitellius' civil war, "which, by nature burdensome in itself," is exacerbated by the corrupt behavior of the officials in charge. Another relevant incident is recorded in *Agr.* 28, where a cohort of Usipi from the Lower Rhine hijack three warships and attempt to force them to sail back to Germany. Instead they sail around Scotland and become one of only two expeditions to circumnavigate Britain.

lost legions were not replaced.[23] The events of the crisis year A.D. 69—
the "Year of Four Emperors"—also suggest that it may not have been
easy to raise new troops, even when the stakes were high. The collective
efforts of all major contenders for the throne resulted in only four new
legions (two were later demobilized by Vespasian). Of these, two were
recruited from the fleet, as one of Nero's new legions had been—an indication that manpower may have been in short supply.[24] Otho's troops
at the battle of Bedriacum included two thousand gladiators, and Vitellius also resorted to levies of gladiators, slaves, and the urban plebs.[25] In
167 the plague that struck Marcus Aurelius' army, together with emergencies on the Danube frontier, supposedly forced the emperor to resort to similar measures, including a draft of gladiators and an auction
of his personal possessions.[26]

This same emperor, when forced to make peace with the ferocious
Iazyges, included a clause requiring them to furnish eight thousand cavalry to the Roman army.[27] Similarly, Commodus' peace with the Marcomanni and the Quadi stipulated that they supply troops.[28] Increasingly after this, Rome came to rely on special cavalry units drawn from
the most ferocious barbarian tribes on the fringes of the empire.[29] Still,
these troops are not really so different from the special levies of Batavians or Thracians in the early Principate, both considered especially fierce
and both allowed, at first, to serve under native commanders. This could
be further evidence that, for whatever reason, it was not easy to increase
the size of the army from the Italian or provincial population. The apparent problem of desertion would indicate the same thing. Cassius Dio
claims that most of the Dacian king Decebalus' army was composed of

23. Brunt 1974, 95–96, with n. 33; Mann 1983, 49. A famous passage from Suetonius'
life of Augustus (23.2) describes the emperor bashing his head against a door post, shout-
ing, "Quintilius Varus, give back my legions!"

24. On legions raised during A.D. 69, see Ritterling 1924–1925, 1265–1266; Mann
1963, 484; Saddington 1982, 179.

25. Ibid., 114, 118; on Otho's gladiators, see Tac. *Hist.* 2.11; on Vitellius, ibid., 3.57–58,
and Suet. *Vit.* 15.1–2.

26. SHA *Marcus* 21.6–9; Daniels 1991, 50 (arguing that this was the reason for the
final Antonine withdrawal from Scotland); A. R. Birley 1987, 159–160. On this and other
evidence of manpower difficulties, see Smith 1972.

27. Cass. Dio 71[72].16.2; these cavalry were immediately transferred to Britain, perhaps because the Iazyges were notoriously untrustworthy. The Flavian generals refused to
use them in the civil war of A.D. 69 (Tac. *Hist* 3.5).

28. Cass. Dio 72[73].2.3: "thirteen thousand soldiers from the Quadi and less from
the Marcomanni, and in return for these he removed their obligation to supply men each
year."

29. M. P. Speidel 1975, especially on the Mauri.

deserters; Trajan obliged him to return them. The treaty of Commodus, mentioned above, contained similar clauses; and the same historian considers desertion and lack of discipline the main difficulties facing Rome in its impending conflict with Persia in the 220s A.D.[30]

Wars in foreign territory, especially those resulting in conquest, obviously required high concentrations of troops. To some degree these could be supplied by raising new legions. In fact, when the number of legions was increased, it was always for a projected expansionist campaign, except during the civil wars of 69.[31] But this, as we have seen, meant forcible conscription. If we accept that there were fairly strict limits on the size of the army that could be recruited or paid for, it becomes obvious that any campaign into enemy territory required extensive shuffling of legions and auxiliaries. This inevitably drained them out of regions where they were needed, sometimes with disastrous consequences. The critical year A.D. 6 provides the first illustration of the Roman army's limitations. Germany had been pacified, it was thought, as far as the Elbe River, and Tiberius was across the Danube, trying to conquer the Marcomanni. This war was apparently fought with twelve legions, including the entire armies of Illyricum (under Tiberius) and of Raetia and the Rhine (under Saturninus).[32] Illyricum erupted in what is usually perceived as the worst revolt in Rome's history. The legate of the army of Moesia managed to rescue the city of Sirmium, but in his absence his province was raided by Dacians and Sarmatians, forcing him to return. Tiberius was forced to conclude a hasty truce with Maroboduus, king of the Marcomanni, so that he could return with his army; and troops had to be transferred from elsewhere, so that at one point

30. On Decebalus, see Cass. Dio 68.9.5–6; Trajan's treaty requires him "to give up the deserters (αὐτομόλους) . . . and not to receive any deserters nor to use any soldier from the Roman empire (for the majority and the best [of the soldiers] there he had procured by persuading them over)." On Commodus, see 72[73].2.2; on the Persian problem, 80.4. A thorough study of this issue, unfortunately, cannot be attempted here, but it would be a worthwhile project.

31. Mann 1963; and see id. 1983, 63, with n. 577, arguing that Marcus' two new legions were not raised in the emergency of the barbarian invasion but for a preplanned campaign across the Danube frontier; similarly XV and XXII Primigenia were raised either for Caligula's German campaign or Claudius' invasion of Britain; I Italica was raised for Nero's projected exploits in the Caucasus; Domitian raised I Minervia for his war against the Chatti; II Traiana and XXX Ulpia Victrix were raised, probably, for Trajan's second Dacian war; and eventually Severus raised I, II and III Parthica for his war with the Parthians (Mann 1963).

32. Ritterling 1924–1925, 1232–1236; on twelve legions, see Tac. Ann. 2.46; this may not be accurate (cf. Syme 1933, 23–24), but contradictory evidence is lacking.

no less than ten legions were involved in suppressing the revolt.[33] Augustus resorted to a levy of freedmen in a desperate effort to replace the lost men, as we have noted. This was the Principate's first lesson in how far imperialism could go without increasing the size of the army.

Up to this point, there is little evidence of the defensive, conservative policy attributed to Augustus by later ancient sources and some modern scholars.[34] Rather, the early years of Augustus' reign seem to radiate an almost euphoric expansionism, with ambitious campaigns into what were perceived as the remotest corners of the world—Ethiopia, Arabia Felix, and the interior of Africa; Europe was conquered to the Danube, the last remaining corner of Spain was subdued and annexed, and there was talk of invasions into Britain and Dacia.[35] From 15 B.C. until A.D. 6, armies were committed to the pacification of the Alps and to campaigns across the Rhine.[36] Then, as we have seen, the emperor sent Tiberius

33. The main sources for the Pannonian revolt are Cass. Dio 55.29–34, 56.12–17; and Vell. Pat. 2.110–114. On this episode, see Wells 1972, 237–238; and Mócsy 1974, 37–39. On the peace treaty, see Tac. Ann. 2.46, Cass. Dio 55.28.7; on the cause of the revolt, ibid., 55.29.1; on the rescue of Sirmium, 55.29.3; and on the invasion of Moesia, 55.30.4. "The most serious of foreign wars after the Punic wars" (Suet. Tib. 16.1). For the troops involved in the war, see Ritterling 1924–1925, 1233–1236; and Syme 1933, 25–28; five legions were transferred from overseas (Vell. Pat. 2.112.4); these probably included the Macedonian army under Caecina; they joined the army of Illyricum, recalled from Bohemia, for a total of ten legions plus seventy cohorts, ten alae, and more than ten thousand veterans, plus Thracian cavalry (ibid., 2.113.1). Suet. Tib. 16, however, claims that fifteen legions took part in the war; this is dismissed by Syme (1933, 27–28).

34. For Cassius Dio's analysis of Augustus' foreign policy, see 54.9.1 (under the year 20 B.C.): "He did not think it worthwhile to add anything to the former [subject territory, τὸ ὑπήκοον] or to acquire more of the latter [allies], but thought it right to be content with exactly those that already existed." See also 56.33.5–6 (Augustus' advice to Tiberius, discussed below) and 56.41.7. For Suetonius' assessment, see Aug. 21.2: "Nor did he make war on any tribe without just and necessary causes, and he was so far from the desire to increase the empire or his military reputation by any means at hand that he forced the leaders of some barbarians to swear in the temple of Mars the Avenger that they would honor the promises and peace that they were seeking." Wells (1972, 9–10) is right to point out that Suetonius here is emphasizing Augustus' reluctance to pursue "unjustified" wars and to extend the empire "by any means at hand" (quoquo modo).

35. On the campaigns of Cornelius Gallus and Petronius in Ethiopia, of Aelius Gallus in Arabia, and of Balbus in North Africa, see chap. 2 above. On Britain, see Cass. Dio 49.38.2, 53.22.5, 53.25.2. On Dacia, App. Ill. 22–23; cf. Strab. 7.3.13. On the Danube frontier under Augustus, see Mócsy 1974, 32–37; it is proclaimed the boundary of the empire in RGDA 30.

36. On all aspects of the German wars under Augustus, see Wells 1972 and more recently Wolters 1990, 134–228; a gap in the evidence exists between 6 B.C. and A.D. 4, but there was still significant activity in the area during this time (Wells, op. cit., 158). On the German frontier in the Augustan period, including an excellent map, see Schönberger 1969, 144–151. On the trans-Danuvian campaign, Wells, op. cit., 159–161; Mócsy 1974, 37.

across the Danube into Bohemia. It had been Caesar's plan, as several sources attest, to conquer what remained of the world, especially the Dacians and the Parthians.[37] Most of them agree that he intended to start with the subjection of Dacia; for this he sent sixteen legions and ten thousand cavalry across the Adriatic shortly before his death (App. *BC* 2.110), troops that ultimately became involved in the civil wars that followed. There is much to suggest, as we have seen, that Augustus intended to carry out this scheme, and notably to complete the conquest of Europe,[38] at least until the two great crises of A.D. 6 and 9 arose.

For the Pannonian revolt was not the only setback to Augustus' plans; three years later another disaster ended his ambitions in Germany, when Arminius, chief of the Cherusci, rebelled and annihilated the Roman garrison. In response, Augustus sent six legions to reinforce the Rhine under the command of Tiberius, who first took measures for the defense of Gaul and then began the series of campaigns in Germany that later continued, after Augustus' death, under Germanicus.[39] Whether he aimed at reconquest, or revenge in some other form, we do not know. In any case, freedmen were once more drafted into the army—but Varus' three legions could not be replaced, and were not. It may have become clear to the emperor at the end of his life that the Roman army had reached the upper limits of what it could do. Well-known passages from Tacitus, Suetonius, and Cassius Dio tell us that the documents the emperor left behind at his death included a list of the troops under arms and the revenues and expenses of the empire, as well as some advice to the effect that it should be restricted to its present boundaries.[40] If the

37. Suet. *Jul.* 44, *Aug.* 8.2; Vell. Pat. 2.49.4; App. *Ill.* 13, *BC* 2.110; Plut. *Caes.* 58; Brunt 1978, 178.

38. The theory of the "Elbe frontier policy," which was based largely on a passage from Strabo, who writes that Augustus forbade his generals to proceed beyond the Elbe (7.1.4), has been out of favor in recent years. Cassius Dio tells us that Drusus planned to cross over in 9 B.C, without success (55.1.3), and that Domitius Ahenobarbus campaigned beyond the river with somewhat better results (55.10a.2). The first major criticism of the "Elbe frontier policy" is Wells 1972, 5–6; cf. also the discussion of Austin and Rankov 1995, 125–127.

39. Vell. Pat. 2.120; Wells (1972, 237–245) argues that Augustus abandoned the goal of conquering Germany after Varus' defeat; Lehmann (1991) argues that this happened only under Tiberius, with the recall of Germanicus in A.D. 16–17.

40. Cass. Dio (56.33.2–6) writes that Augustus left behind a total of four documents: the instructions for his funeral; his list of accomplishments; a record of "things having to do with the armies and the public revenues and expenses, and the amount of money in the treasury"; and a number of "instructions and commands" for his successor, including the advice "to be satisfied with the what they had at present and by no means to want to expand the empire further." Augustus' reason, according to Cassius Dio, was that "it [i.e., the empire] would be hard to guard (δυσφύλακτος), and as a result they would risk

last item is genuine,[41] it would indicate that he had come to some basic conclusions about the relationship between the size of the army, its cost, and the size of the empire. Tiberius, in any case, added no new territory to the empire under his reign, except for the peaceful annexation of Cappadocia and Commagene in Asia Minor (the latter was restored by his successor Gaius); both Tacitus and Suetonius perceive his policy as weak and defensive, relying on diplomacy rather than force whenever possible.[42]

The army of the empire, then, was not especially large, and warfare on two fronts posed a dangerous problem. It is therefore at first surprising that emperors after Tiberius continued to wage wars of conquest. But unquestionably they did—though not all of them succeeded, and some of these campaigns are poorly attested.[43] These efforts, as mentioned above, required large concentrations of troops. Gaius assembled a gigantic force for his German expedition, and it is perhaps in his reign, rather than Claudius', that two new legions were recruited.[44] In any case, Claudius took advantage of these new legions for his conquest of

---

losing even what they had." Cassius Dio adds his own view of Augustus' policy—namely, that "in fact he himself always observed this policy not only in word but in deed. For though it was in his power to acquire much barbarian territory, he chose not to." The passage from Tacitus is *Ann.* 1.11, where Tiberius orders the reading of a document recording "the public resources (*opes*), the number of citizens and allies under arms, the number of fleets, kingdoms, provinces, direct and indirect revenues (*tributa aut vectigalia*), necessary expenses and special distributions (*necessitates et largitiones*). All of which Augustus had written out in his own hand, and had added the advice that the empire ought to be kept within its boundaries (*consilium coercendi intra terminos imperii*)." Tacitus attributes this advice to *metus* (fear) or *invidia* (jealousy); unlike Cassius Dio, he does not approve. Suetonius (*Aug.* 101.4) writes that the emperor left three documents, the first three named by Dio, but does not mention the "advice."

41. Ober (1982) doubts the authenticity of the document or codicil containing the "advice," especially on the grounds that Suetonius does not mention it (see previous note); he argues that this tradition may have been invented by Tiberius to justify his own nonexpansionist policy.

42. Suet. *Tib.* 37.4: "He suppressed enemy threats through legates, undertaking no more expeditions; and even this he did hesitantly and of necessity." See ibid., 41, on the neglect of the empire's defense during Tiberius' retirement on Capri; Tacitus in several places attributes to this emperor a deliberate policy of relying on diplomacy rather than coercion to solve foreign-affairs problems, e.g., *Ann.* 2.26.3, 4.32.2, 6.32.1; cf. Syme 1958, 1:438.

43. See Isaac 1992, 388–392, and Whittaker 1994, chap. 2, for many of the examples that follow.

44. According to Cassius Dio 59.22.1, Gaius assembled a force of 200,000 or 250,000; cf. Suet. *Gaius* 43; for references to the massive number of troops assembled for this campaign, see Ritterling 1924–1925, 1245; and ibid., 1244–1246, for arguments that the new legions were raised for this campaign and not for Claudius' British expedition; on this cf. Mann 1963, 483.

Britain.[45] A substantial war was waged in Armenia under Nero,[46] and at the end of his reign he was planning a major offensive in the Caucasus, which involved, according to Suetonius, a new legion composed of Italians all over six feet tall, which he called the "phalanx of Alexander the Great."[47]

The literary sources for Domitian's expeditions in Germany and the Danube region are extremely inadequate; they agree, however, that the wars were ultimately unsuccessful. For his campaign against the Chatti at the beginning of his reign, he raised a new legion (the I Minervia) and constructed 120 miles of roads into enemy territory; he apparently conducted the campaign with the four legions from Upper Germany plus the XXI Rapax from Lower Germany, and vexillations (detachments) from nine others, including the four British legions.[48] Both Tacitus and Cassius Dio are contemptuous about how little was achieved,[49] but it is not unreasonable to imagine that Domitian hoped to succeed where Augustus had failed; certainly his propaganda announced: "Germany captured."[50] Domitian also waged a war across the Danube following the defeat of the legates Oppius Sabinus and Cornelius Fuscus. His ultimate aims are unclear; but Cassius Dio tells us that he repeatedly refused peace offers from the Dacians and killed envoys from the Marcomanni and the Quadi, whom he had attacked when they refused to help him against the Dacians. But a defeat by the Marcomanni eventually forced him to grant notoriously generous terms to Decebalus, the Dacian king.[51] Again, he was willing to devote a considerable military force to the task.[52] In the meantime, Agricola's campaigns probably

45. Frere 1987, 48, on the troops for Claudius' invasion.

46. See Angeli Bertinelli 1979, 54–55; Corbulo captured Artaxata and Tigranocerta, and Paetus is said to have favored annexation until his notorious disaster forced Nero to come to terms (Tac. *Ann.* 15.6).

47. Suet. *Nero* 19.2. Braund 1986 emphasizes mythological conceptions about the Caucasus region that may have fueled Nero's ambitions. The new legion was the I Italica.

48. On this war, see Strobel 1987a; B. Jones 1992, 128–131; on the force assembled, ibid., 130; Ritterling 1924–1925, 1276; and Schönberger 1969, 158–159; on roads, Frontinus *Str.* 1.3.10.

49. Cass. Dio 67.4.1; Tac. *Germ.* 37.6, where the Germans are "triumphed over rather than defeated."

50. E.g., Schönberger 1969, 158; *contra,* arguing that Domitian did not aim at extensive conquests, see Strobel 1987a.

51. Cass. Dio 67.6–7 on these events and the final peace with Decebalus. The Romans agreed to give not only money to Decebalus but, in an interesting clause, valuable artisans (δημιουργούς). For criticism of the peace, see Pliny *Pan.* 12.2; Cass. Dio 67.7. See further chap. 5, sec. 2, below.

52. On Domitian's Danube campaigns, see Wilkes 1983, 268–270; B. Jones 1992, 138–139, 141–143, 150–152; and Strobel 1989. On troops for the first *expeditio imperatoris* (fol-

aimed at the total conquest of Britain, and a daring expedition circum-navigated the island and caught sight of Thule, the legendary northern-most limit of the world. But the transfer of troops from there for Do-mitian's second Danube campaign meant a withdrawal from Scotland: *perdomita Britannia et statim omissa,* "Britain was completely con-quered and immediately lost."[53]

This was not the end of Roman ambitions in the Danube region; Tra-jan's conquest of Dacia is especially noteworthy because he assembled what was perhaps the greatest concentration of military force in the im-perial period. By the end of the second Dacian war the number of le-gionaries and auxiliaries along the middle and lower Danube may have approached two hundred thousand, or about half the Roman army;[54] his eastern expedition, however, was to employ a comparable force.[55] Marcus' Danube campaigns are almost as poorly attested as Domitian's, but even if we ignore the evidence of the notoriously unreliable *Histo-ria Augusta,* which alleges that he intended to create two new provinces along the upper Danube, it is beyond doubt that Roman troops were occupying territory across the river until withdrawn by Commodus, at his accession. Cassius Dio writes that Marcus "would have conquered all of that territory" (71[72].33.4), perhaps to the ocean.[56]

---

lowing the defeat of Oppius Sabinus), see ibid., 44–46; troops were apparently trans-ferred to Moesia from Pannonia, Germany, Dalmatia, and possibly Syria and Cappadocia.

53. Tac. *Hist.* 1.2. On troops for the second expedition, see Strobel 1989, 57–58; on Domitian's aims in Scotland, the circumnavigation of Britain, and the withdrawal of troops, see id. 1987.

54. Strobel 1984, 80–154; for a summary, see 153–154. The number of legions on the middle and lower Danube rose to fourteen from the total of nine under Domitian. By 101 there were eleven legions or, at full strength, 66,000 legionaries at the front; by 105 there were fourteen legions, twenty-nine *alae* (of which twenty-four are attested as taking part in the war) and seventy-eight cohorts (of which sixty-eight are attested as taking part in the war).

55. Lepper (1948, 173–178) counts eleven legions in the east for the campaigns, plus unknown numbers of vexillations and auxiliaries; Angeli Bertinelli (1976, 11–12) counts eleven to thirteen legions plus vexillations and auxiliaries.

56. SHA *Marcus* 27.10. On Marcus' aims and the garrison, see A. R. Birley 1979, 483–494, and cf. Isaac 1992, 390–391. *Contra,* arguing that Marcus did not seek to annex new territory, see mainly Alföldy 1971. The main evidence for this garrison is Cass. Dio 71[72].20, on the Quadi and Marcomanni: "the twenty thousand troops in forts for each of them would not allow them to herd or farm or do anything else without fear, but kept taking in deserters from them and prisoners of their own, while they [the Roman soldiers] themselves were suffering no hardship at all since they had baths and all necessary things in abundance, so that the Quadi, unable to bear the fortresses, tried to emigrate as a whole people to the Semnones." This sounds like an army of occupation during the difficult "consolidation" stage described by Isaac (1992, 56–60). Commodus withdraws the gar-rison (Cass. Dio 72[73].2.4). An argument that part of the Parthian empire was annexed

In the east, Trajan briefly annexed Armenia and probably all of Mesopotamia, but Hadrian withdrew the garrisons.[57] Septimius Severus, the
emperor responsible for the largest increase in the size of the Roman
army, raised three new legions (the I, II, and III Parthica), annexed
northern Mesopotamia, and was engaged in the conquest of Scotland
when he died. For this war he assembled a massive force, huge sums of
money, and great quantities of supplies.[58] The garrison there was withdrawn by Caracalla on his father's death; this emperor, however, waged
wars with the German Allemanni and, in conformity with his famous
obsession with Alexander the Great, with the Parthians; it was in the
latter campaign that he fell off his horse and died. These efforts, like
Domitian's war with the Chatti, drew criticism as being unnecessary;[59]
but at the end of our period, Maximinus Thrax apparently led the army
collected by Severus Alexander on a glorious expedition of conquest in
Germany.[60]

When deciding upon a war of conquest, with the aim of acquiring
new territory, the first and most obvious consideration for an emperor

after Verus' campaigns also exists, discussed by A. R. Birley (1979, 480–481) and Angeli
Bertinelli (1976, 30–31), taking opposite views.

57. On Trajan's conquest and the creation of the provinces, see Lepper 1948; Angeli
Bertinelli 1976, 5–22, with extensive bibliography, n. 15; also Potter 1991; Millar 1993,
100–104.

58. On the expansionist nature of Severus' foreign policy generally, see A. R. Birley
1974; also D. Kennedy 1980, especially 885–886, arguing that this policy required not only
new legions but more extensive use of vexillations from areas where whole legions might
not be required. On Severus' British expedition, see A. R. Birley 1988, 170–187; on the
preparations, including the building of huge storerooms, 173; on the gigantic camps of this
period that have been found in Scotland, 180–181; Severus is said to have lost fifty thousand men in the effort (Cass. Dio 76[77].13.2). Dio states in 76[77].13.1 that he intended
to conquer the entire island. Caracalla withdraws the garrison (Cass. Dio 77[78].1.1; Herodian 3.15.6; A. R. Birley, op. cit., 188).

59. On Domitian's war with the Chatti as unnecessary, see Suet. *Dom.* 6.1 (*expeditiones partim sponte suscepti, partim necessario; sponte in Chattos . . .*); on Caracalla's German expedition, Cass. Dio 77[78].13.3–5; contrasted with his "necessary" wars
(77[78].13.1); the Acts of the Arval Brethren for the year 213 record that the emperor "is
about to enter the [sc., land] of the barbarians through the boundary of Raetia for the
purpose of extirpating enemies" (*ILS* 451); on this war, see Schönberger 1969, 173; on the
massive buildup of troops for this expedition, Ritterling 1924–1925, 1317–1319. On Alexander, see Cass. Dio 77[78].7–8; Caracalla's pretext for the Parthian war was first that Vologeses refused to return two refugees (Cass. Dio 77[78].19.1–2), then that the king had
refused his offer to marry his daughter (ibid., 78[79].1.1).

60. Unfortunately, we have only Herodian's evidence plus SHA *Max.* 11.7–9 and *Alex.
Sev.* 61.8; however, Herodian claims that Maximinus "threatened—and he would have
done it—to destroy and subject all the barbarian tribes of Germany as far as the ocean"
(7.2.9); see Schönberger 1969, 175, for rebuilding along the frontier under Maximinus;
Ritterling 1924–1925, 1333–1334, on troops for the expedition.

was that a large force would have to be assembled, and inevitably transferred from elsewhere. This could have severe negative consequences. The best-documented example of what might be involved in assembling a force for an invasion is from the reign of Nero, where Tacitus' detailed account of the campaigns of Corbulo in Armenia survives.[61] Corbulo's original command involved two of Syria's four legions and one-half of its auxiliaries (*Ann.* 13.8), until a third legion was transferred from Germany. In 62 he sent two legions against Tiridates, the Armenian king, plus a third transferred from Moesia, and kept the remaining three legions with him in Syria (15.6); but after Paetus' humiliating defeat he took the field himself with four legions, including one transferred from Pannonia, plus all the auxiliaries from his province (15.25–26). This reduction in the number of his troops was not insignificant to the governor of Moesia, who boasts of a military success against the Sarmatians "though he sent a large part of his army to the expedition in Armenia" (*ILS* 986). Nero's projected Caspian campaign included a new legion, the I Italica; also a military buildup in Alexandria, perhaps for a concurrent expedition to Ethiopia, involving vexillations from Africa and the Rhine; plus transfers of troops from "Germany and Britain and Illyricum," including the famous XIV Gemina, which had defeated Boudicca.[62] The laborious transfer of soldiers from places as remote as Britain was probably made necessary by the Jewish revolt, which was tying up the available forces in the east.[63]

Nero's troops were never used for the grandiose Caspian expedition he had planned. He had to recall them to manage the revolt of Vindex in Gaul (Tac. *Hist.* 1.6). The civil conflict of 69, which followed immediately afterward, illustrates the potential consequences of shuffling large

61. On the forces used by Corbulo, see Keppie 1986, 415–416; Millar 1993, 66–68.

62. On Nero's projected invasion, see Pliny *HN* 6.40; on the transfer of troops, Tac. *Hist.* 1.6, describing the situation that greeted Galba on his arrival at Rome: "Since a Spanish legion had been brought in, and the one that Nero had conscripted from the fleet remained, the city was filled with an unaccustomed army; and added to this were many units (*numeri*) from Germany, Britain, and Illyricum, picked troops that had been sent ahead to the Caspian Gates and the war that he was preparing against the Albani, and which Nero had likewise recalled when the revolt of Vindex had to be suppressed." (The legion enrolled from the fleet was the I Adiutrix, raised apparently to deal with Vindex's revolt and not identical with the I Italica, which was raised for the Caucasian campaign; see Mann 1963, 483–484.) Suetonius (*Ner.* 19.2) writes that the I Italica was composed entirely of Italians six feet tall and was called the "phalanx of Alexander the Great"; Cassius Dio (63[62].8.1–2) states that Nero also considered an Ethiopian expedition. For modern discussions of the Caucasian project, see, e.g., Bosworth 1977, 225–226; Keppie 1986, 418–419; Braund 1986.

63. Keppie 1986, 419.

numbers of legions and auxiliary units around the empire. Tacitus explains the problem in a speech attributed to Suetonius Paulinus, who argues that Vitellius cannot possibly reinforce the army he has sent to confront Otho because the provinces under his control cannot spare them; he would risk revolt or invasion.[64] In fact, if Tacitus is reliable on this point, Vitellius withdrew no less than seventy thousand troops from the two Germanys for his march to Italy (*Hist.* 1.61). Otho countered with four legions withdrawn from Dalmatia and Pannonia, an unspecified number of auxiliaries, five praetorian cohorts, the cavalry vexillation from the first legion, and, as noted above, two thousand gladiators.[65] The Rhoxolani took the opportunity to invade Moesia, but were repelled by the governor with a single legion.[66] When Vespasian decided to enter the contest for the throne, he was fighting the Jewish war with three legions; in preparation, he reached agreements with the kings of Armenia and Parthia, to forestall potential invasions in case a massive withdrawal of troops from the east were required.[67] While his subordinate Mucianus advanced with a small force, generals loyal to Vespasian fought the battle of Cremona, and then plundered the city, with five legions and auxiliaries totaling about forty thousand troops, including, apparently, Moesia's entire army. Before withdrawing the troops from Moesia, they had made deals similar to Vespasian's with the Iazyges and the Suebi; the latter contributed cavalry to their cause.[68] But it was the Dacians who invaded Moesia and were about to attack the legionary camps when Mucianus, who happened to be passing by with his army, saved the situation (Tac. *Hist.* 3.46). Later in the same year, the Sarmatians invaded Moesia, defeated the Roman troops, killed the governor, and overran the countryside until Vespasian, on hearing the news, ap-

---

64. *Hist.* 2.32: "The Gallic provinces are restless, and it would do no good to desert the bank of the Rhine with such hostile tribes ready to invade; the British army is detained by the enemy and the sea; the Spanish provinces have no such abundance of troops. . . ."

65. Tac. *Hist.* 2.11; on the legionary troops in the civil war, see H. M. D. Parker 1958, 140–145; Ritterling 1924–1925, 1265–1266. On Vitellius' troops, Syme 1958, 1:162 (Syme is skeptical of the figure of seventy thousand, which would represent virtually the entire garrison of both Germanys). See ibid., 2:680–682, on Otho's army at Bedriacum; it is impossible to tell from Tacitus' account how many troops actually showed up at the battle. See also Saddington 1982, 107.

66. Tac. *Hist.* 1.79: "while attention was turned to the civil war, no thought was given to external affairs. Emboldened by this, the Rhoxolani, a Sarmatian tribe, who had destroyed two cohorts the previous winter, invaded Moesia with high hopes, nine thousand cavalry in strength. . . ."

67. Tac. *Hist.* 2.81–82, with Dabrowa 1981, 188–189.

68. On the withdrawal of the Moesian army, and deals being made with the Suebi and Iazyges, see Tac. *Hist.* 3.5; on the number of troops at Cremona, ibid., 3.21, 3.33.

pointed Rubrius Gallus to drive them back and reinforce the frontier.[69] The withdrawal of the Rhine army also had consequences, when the disgraceful behavior of the magistrates conducting a draft of Batavians for Vitellius provoked the devastating revolt of Civilis; in the speech Tacitus wrote for him in the *Histories,* the rebel argued that "Rome's circumstances had never been more wretched, and that there was nothing in the winter camps but booty and old men; let them only lift their eyes and not tremble at the empty names of legions."[70]

Partly because of the dangers of concentrating troops on a single front, attempts at conquest could be unsuccessful, even disastrous. When Suetonius Paulinus, as governor of Britain under Nero, attempted to conquer the island of Mona, the Iceni rebelled under Boudicca.[71] Domitian's ambitious campaigns in the Danube region required reinforcements from Britain, and the evacuation of much of the territory conquered by Agricola, including the deliberate destruction of a legionary fortress that was not yet complete.[72] Similar troubles attended other campaigns. In Marcus' reign, three legions plus vexillations from others were transferred from the Rhine and Danube for Lucius' eastern war of 162–166.[73] If the *Historia Augusta* is reliable on this point, trouble in the northern regions began almost immediately, but the governors of those provinces managed to put off war while their armies were depleted.[74] It was in 166 or early 167, with the legions still in the east, that the first invasion took place; according to Cassius Dio the invaders numbered six thousand Langobardi.[75] Marcus retaliated—in fact, he had already raised two new legions, a sign that he was planning a major offensive even before the invasion[76]—but the plague that the troops

69. On these events, see Mócsy 1974, 41–42; Wilkes 1983, 261–263; see Tac. *Hist.* 3.46 for the Dacian attack; Joseph. *BJ* 7.89–95 on the Sarmatian invasion.

70. *Hist.* 4.14. See ibid., 4.15, where the depleted troops are too feeble to ward off Civilis' attack; and 4.22, where a double legionary camp is defended by only five thousand troops.

71. Tac. *Ann.* 14.30, *Agr.* 14.3–15.1; Cass. Dio 62.7.1.

72. Hanson and Maxwell 1983, 43–44; Hanson 1987, 151–152; Strobel 1987. The fortress was at Inchtuthil. Cf. Tac. *Hist.* 1.2: *perdomita Britannia et statim omissa,* "Britain was completely conquered and immediately lost."

73. On the troops for Verus' campaigns, see Mitford 1980, 1204; A. R. Birley 1987, 123.

74. SHA *Marcus* 12.13: "While the Parthian war was being waged, the war with the Marcomanni began, which for a long time was delayed by the cunning of those who were there, so that the Marcomannian war could be fought after the eastern war was finished" (*dum Parthicum bellum geritur, natum est Marcomannicum, quod diu eorum, qui aderant, arte suspensum est, ut finito iam orientali bello Marcomannicum agi posset*); see A. R. Birley 1987, 249.

75. 71[72].3.1a; see A. R. Birley 1987, 249.

76. Mann 1983, 63.

had brought back from the east appears to have prevented any effective military action, and probably in 170, Italy itself was invaded. Marcus responded with campaigns across the Danube, possibly with the intention of conquering Europe to the ocean.[77] Certainly he planned the complete extermination of the Iazyges, but the revolt of Avidius Cassius in Syria forced him to grant terms.[78] In the meantime, the withdrawal of troops from Britain for the Danube campaign required yet another evacuation of Scotland.[79] Under Severus, a governor of Britain was required to buy peace from the Caledonians in Scotland, since the army was occupied elsewhere—probably in the civil war, for Severus' rival Albinus seems to have withdrawn large numbers of troops from the province, perhaps all of them.[80] Meanwhile, the Parthians captured the newly conquered territory of Mesopotamia, requiring a second expedition that included the sack of Ctesiphon, the capital (Cass. Dio 75[76].9.1, 4).

But perhaps the most graphic example of the Roman army's limitations comes at the very end of our period, with Severus Alexander and the Persian crisis. The emperor twice sought a diplomatic solution to the problem, much to Herodian's disgust, before deciding on an expedition into enemy territory (6.2.3, 6.4.4). At some location in the Danube region he collected a large force, probably drawn from the northern provinces; detachments from legions on the Rhine and Upper Moesia are attested.[81] In addition, special levies were held, and a new legion (IV Italica) may have been created.[82] A three-pronged invasion ended in disaster when one of the contingents was completely destroyed in battle and another badly depleted because of the difficulty of the terrain (Herodian 6.5). But Alexander was still in Antioch planning a second campaign when news reached him of serious invasions on the Rhine frontier, perhaps a result of the depleted garrisons there, which required the army from the east (ibid., 6.7.1–3). Alexander undertook a march of three thousand miles. Again, he sought a diplomatic solution, offering generous terms to the Germans including money payments (6.7.9); in

77. On Marcus' aims, see n. 56 above.

78. Cass. Dio 71[72].13.1; 71[72].16–17, with Instinsky 1972; on Cassius' revolt, see Millar 1993, 115–118.

79. Daniels 1991.

80. Frere 1987, 155–156; A. R. Birley 1988, 124; Cass. Dio 75[76].5.1. Cassius Dio records that the battle of Lugdunum was fought with 150,000 troops (75[76].6.1), probably meaning that number altogether and not on each side, as the passage was understood to mean until the discussion of Graham (1978).

81. 6.4.3, with Whittaker's commentary (1969–1970) ad loc.

82. SHA Max. 5.5 claims that Severus Alexander created a new legion; on this, see Mann 1963, 486.

response, his army mutinied. Maximinus Thrax, his short-lived successor, had a much more aggressive plan.

The events of Alexander's reign illustrate another strategic problem for the Roman army: not only was it small, but travel speed in antiquity was slow. It has been pointed out that the configuration of the empire —a hollow oblong—could hardly be less advantageous logistically.[83] Sea transport could be much faster than marching overland, but it was also riskier and could not be undertaken in the winter; and it was impractical for long distances, requiring large transport ships that would also have to carry food and fresh water for the passengers—a considerable burden if the travel time was long.[84] A few short routes, such as Brundisium Dyrrachium across the Ionian Sea, were commonly used and could take weeks off of the journey; by land, a large force could probably march only about fifteen miles per day.[85] Severus Alexander's march from Antioch to the Rhine probably proceeded entirely by land and would require over six months.[86] Delays of this type were not much of a problem in a preplanned campaign, but a large-scale crisis could not receive an instant response, especially if part of the army was off on campaign somewhere else. To the amount of time required to transfer troops, to arrange supply routes—and to send out a commander, if necessary—we should add the time it took for the emperor to find out about the crisis, which probably could be substantial.[87]

83. Luttwak 1976, 81.

84. On this point, see Amit 1965, 218.

85. See Luttwak 1976, 80–84, on this problem; on the speed of troops see also the discussion in Engels 1978, app. 5, table 7, noting that an army's march rates are closely related to the length of the column. Alexander the Great's army of 48,000 plus animals and camp followers achieved an average of 13 English miles per day, and a maximum of 19.5; but light detachments could cover over 40 miles per day. Vegetius puts the speed of the Roman soldier at 20 to 24 Roman miles per day (1.9; cf. Amit 1965, 219–220), which would be possible for a small force.

86. Amit (1965, 216–220) calculates that the journey from Rome to Antioch was 4,000 km (c. 2,500 miles) by Roman roads, a journey of 125 days at 20 miles per day or over 160 days at the perhaps more realistic rate of 15 miles per day; the journey from Antioch to the Rhine was around 5,000 km, or about 3,125 miles—that is, over 200 days at 15 miles per day; and if some troops accompanied Alexander on his detour to Rome to celebrate his triumph, this added 800 km (if they also proceeded entirely by land).

87. On communications speeds in the empire, see Duncan-Jones 1990, 7–29. This study is based on the length of time required for the news of an emperor's death to be announced in Egypt (when papyri would stop being dated by that emperor). The median elapsed time before the *first* Egyptian acknowledgment of an emperor's death is fifty-two days (ibid., 8–9). Even the "counter-seasonal fast times" (fast times outside of the usual sailing season), which should reflect a special effort to get the message through quickly, hover around thirty days. Any communication involving sea travel, as the Rome–Egypt route, could suffer huge vagaries on account of weather and other factors; Duncan-Jones

It is important to emphasize that places, once conquered, could still be lost. Exactly this had happened with Germany in A.D. 9. Any emperor or general considering the subjection of new territory had to bear in mind that this territory would need a garrison, possibly a very substantial (and costly) one, and possibly for a very long time, to prevent revolt. An early and vivid example of the investment that might be required can be found in Augustus' conquest of northwestern Spain; except for this part, all of the Iberian peninsula was already under Roman control. But the war required seven legions and was notoriously difficult. In 27 B.C. the emperor personally led an assault on the Cantabri.[88] Once conquered, they revolted no less than four times despite brutally repressive measures. The first revolt forced Augustus to cancel his projected invasion of Britain for the second time (Cass. Dio 53.25.2). Ultimately he is said to have resorted to relocating the Cantabri from the mountains to the plains.[89] To retain this small patch of territory, Spain required an initial garrison of (probably) four or five legions, reduced to three by the end of Augustus' reign; thus between one-tenth and one-fifth of the empire's legionary army was stationed in a province that had no frontier at all.[90]

---

discusses the anecdotal evidence on pp. 25–29, including the famous story of Petronius, procurator of Judaea, who received his death sentence from the emperor Gaius twenty-seven days after the news that Gaius was dead. However, some very fast times are recorded for urgent messages carried by land. The average speed of the Roman imperial post was probably about 50 miles per day (Ramsay 1925), or around 48 days for Rome–Antioch; however, important messages could be carried (by messengers in *vehicula* using relays of horses) at a rates of around 160 miles per day (ibid., 63–67), and news of barbarian invasions would qualify as important; cf. Juv. 4.147–149: "as though about to say something about the Chatti or the savage Sugambri; as though an urgent letter had arrived from the far-flung parts of the world on speedy wing."

88. On the Cantabrian wars, a notoriously obscure chapter in Roman history, see Syme 1970; Le Roux 1982, 58–68; Keay 1988, 44–46. Augustus is said to have faced an army of 100,000. On heavy losses, see Cass. Dio 54.11.5; Florus 2.33.56–57.

89. See Cass. Dio 53.29 on the first revolt in 24 B.C.; the Romans laid waste enemy territory, burned some forts, and cut off the hands of the prisoners. On the second revolt, see 54.5.1; on the third revolt, 54.11. Agrippa himself took command of this expedition, and "killed nearly all of the enemy of military age, and disarmed the rest, and he made them come down from their forts to the plains." On this last, see also Florus 2.33.59–60. On the fourth revolt (16 B.C.), see Cass. Dio 54.20.3.

90. There is no question that Spain's garrison was three legions by the time Strabo wrote his outline of the Spanish forces (3.4.20); Tacitus also lists three legions in Spain in his description of the deployment of the army under Tiberius; but on the number of legions in the initial garrison (from, say, 16 B.C. to A.D. 9) there is some disagreement. Szilágyi (1954, 131–132) follows Ritterling, placing five legions in Spain until Varus' disaster; Syme (1933, 22–23) argues for four; and Le Roux (1982, 84–85) argues for three after 13 B.C. or so.

The role of the Roman army as an army of occupation, as opposed to a defensive force, has begun to receive scholarly emphasis.[91] In fact, in their descriptions of the deployment of the Roman legionary army, Josephus and Tacitus write as though its primary, if not only, function were to suppress revolt.[92] It has been pointed out that under Augustus and Tiberius, three legions were stationed in Spain and two in Dalmatia, though neither of these were frontier provinces;[93] these garrisons were reduced to one and zero legions, respectively, probably when the provinces were considered adequately pacified; though Tacitus also describes the units in Dalmatia as a forward defense against invasion of Italy (*Ann.* 4.5). The tiny province of Mauretania Tingitana required a garrison of about ten thousand to maintain the empire's hold over its rebellious inhabitants; and the purpose of the garrison of Egypt, which required two legions, was probably entirely to control the local population.[94] Revolts, sometimes very serious, were not uncommon, especially early in the imperial period, for newly acquired territory was naturally more likely to rebel—though an Avidius Cassius or a false Nero could also start major uprisings in provinces long incorporated into the empire.[95] Augustus faced revolts in Cantabria and two dangerous rebellions in Pannonia, and Tiberius' reign saw the revolt of Thrace and the prolonged war with Tacfarinas in Africa, as well as the revolt of Sacrovir, who is supposed to have collected an army of 40,000 (Tac. *Ann.* 3.40–46), neither the first nor the last revolt in Gaul under the Principate; Britain proved very difficult to hold, as we shall see; Domitian actually annihilated the Nasamones when they rebelled and defeated the governor of Numidia (Cass. Dio 67.4.6); even Pontus rebelled shortly after it became a province (Tac. *Hist.* 3.47). The Jews revolted three times, despite brutally repressive measures; this province of course is a special case,

91. See Le Roux 1982, and especially Isaac 1992, chaps. 2–3.

92. *BJ* 2.366–383; *Ann.* 4.5; cf. Cass. Dio 53.13.1, where Augustus takes command of the imperial (armed) provinces for ten years, promising to return them to the senate earlier if he can pacify them sooner.

93. Luttwak 1976, 17–18.

94. On Mauretania Tingitana, see Shaw 1986, 67–69; on Egypt, Joseph. *BJ* 2.385–386. Britain always had a very large army and a very short frontier, as noted below. Conversely, a province with a very long—and hostile—frontier (Dacia) seems to have required only one legion after Hadrian.

95. The list that follows is by no means complete. Pekáry (1987) collects a chronological list of references for the period from Augustus to A.D. 161, exploding the myth that this was a peaceful period of history. On revolt, see also Isaac 1992, chap. 2; Dyson 1971; id. 1975; Bowersock 1987. On false Neros, see Pekáry, op. cit., under the years 69, 79–81, and 88–89; on Avidius Cassius, Millar 1993, 115–118.

but it is noteworthy that the tiny territory of Judaea required a garrison of about 10,000 troops (a legion and about 5,000 auxiliaries) after 70, which was more or less doubled in Trajan's or Hadrian's reign.[96] The first revolt required a total of over 50,000 troops to suppress, and to oppose them Josephus claims implausibly to have collected an army of over 100,000 from Galilee alone.[97] In the suppression of the Bar-Kochba revolt of 135, at least four legions took part and Hadrian probably took command in person.[98] These are well-known events, but countless others escaped literary notice or are mentioned by our sources only in passing.[99]

The case of Britain is one of the best-documented examples of what might be involved in the conquest and occupation of new territory under the Principate. Strabo thought it could probably be held by a garrison of a single legion (2.5.8), and that even that would be too costly; his estimate was to prove very optimistic. The invading force led by Aulus Plautius in 43 consisted of four legions, three transferred from the Rhine (where two were replaced by recently recruited legions) and one from Pannonia plus auxiliaries for a total of about 40,000 troops.[100] From this time forward Britain would always occupy what seems like a disproportionately large percentage of the empire's available forces, and yet despite at least two attempts the Romans never subdued the entire island. From the beginning, a war with Caratacus and the Silures in Wales occupied the first legates of the province; and it is unclear whether they had been subdued by 60, when the new governor, Suetonius Paulinus, set off to conquer the island of Mona (Anglesey). In that year the revolt of Boudicca broke out.[101] According to Cassius Dio she led an army of 230,000 and in the destruction of Colchester, London, and Verulamium killed a total of 80,000 Romans and allies (62.8.2, 61.1.1). Even if the figures are exaggerated, they show that the rebellion was serious enough to acquire truly legendary proportions. Paulinus supposedly defeated her with a mere 10,000 troops, those he had brought back from Mona.

---

96. Isaac 1992, 105–107; Millar 1993, 107–108; Eck (1984) argues for the earlier date.

97. *BJ* 2.576; on the Roman troops in the Jewish revolt, see Millar 1993, 71–73, 75; Titus at the siege of Jerusalem apparently commanded four legions, with detachments from two others, twenty cohorts, eight *alae*, forces from three client-kings, and an Arab contingent. Note that to install the statue of himself in the temple of Jerusalem, Gaius sent a force of no less than either two legions (*AJ* 18.262) or three (*BJ* 2.185–186).

98. Millar 1993, 107; cf. Rosenberger 1992, 97.

99. See Pekáry 1987, with his comments, p. 146; cf. Woolf 1993, 187–188.

100. Frere 1987, 48.

101. The main sources on Boudicca's rebellion are Tac. *Ann.* 14.29–39, *Agr.* 15–16; Cass. Dio 62.1–12. See Frere 1987, 70–73.

The episode should serve as a reminder that the original provincial army of 40,000, even though it probably represented more than one-tenth of the empire's total army, was still a relatively small force.

Throughout the imperial period Britain continued to require a large army; Agricola's forces may have numbered 47,800 auxiliaries *plus four legions*.[102] Under Hadrian this was reduced to three legions and about 36,000 auxiliaries, still a very substantial percentage of the empire's total force, and in the Antonine period northern Britain alone was held by over 30,000 auxiliaries. The Romans never succeeded in the total conquest of the island; Scotland could not be held successfully after Domitian withdrew troops for his Danube campaigns, and the Antonine wall was occupied twice, briefly, and then abandoned. Toward the end of our period Severus made a final attempt to subdue the rest of Britain, but Caracalla withdrew the garrison.[103]

It is perhaps worth emphasizing here that despite some modern perceptions to the contrary, the history of Rome's expansion is not a story of effortless, brilliant successes.[104] Most places had to be conquered not just once, but more than once, sometimes several times; and the Romans seem to have known and expected this. Thus it was perhaps the need to garrison new territory against revolt that explains why new legions were usually raised before wars of conquest.[105] Trajan raised two new legions for the Dacian wars—probably for the second war of 105–106, which resulted in occupation.[106] Marcus also raised two legions, and in Cassius Dio his conquests across the Danube are held by a garrison of, probably, 40,000 men;[107] and of Severus' three new legions, two were used to hold Mesopotamia.[108] The disaster of A.D. 9 is a vivid example of what could happen if the garrison of a new province was insufficient or mismanaged. Even so, Trajan was willing to undertake very extensive conquests with

102. On the strength of Britain's garrison, see Holder 1982, 15–18; Breeze 1984, 264–268; Frere 1987, 143–147.

103. On Domitian's withdrawal of troops, see Strobel 1987; on the Antonine conquest, Hanson and Maxwell 1983, chap. 4; on Severus' war, A. R. Birley 1988, 170–188. Nero is said to have contemplated abandoning this costly province (Suet. *Ner.* 18).

104. The persistent idea that the tactical superiority of Rome's army made conquest almost effortless (e.g., Ferrill 1991) or that attempts at revolt from the empire were uncommon is a misconception.

105. Mann 1963, 483–484; id. 1983, 63; Pflaum 1950, 107–109.

106. Strobel 1984, 97–98.

107. On this garrison, see n. 56 above. It seems unclear from Cassius Dio's text whether 40,000 troops (i.e., 20,000 for each of the two tribes) or 20,000 (20,000 troops for both tribes together) is meant: "δύο μυριάδες ἑκατέροις στρατιωτῶν ἐν τείχεσιν ὄντες." The reading of 40,000 is perhaps the more natural.

108. See D. Kennedy 1987.

only two new legions, and this may be part of the reason why his eastern acquisitions could not be held.[109] Shortly before his death, the new
provinces of Armenia, Mesopotamia, and Assyria revolted and defeated
or massacred their garrisons; Trajan sent legates to suppress the rebellion, with some success, but crowned Parthamaspates king of the Parthians (instead, presumably, of creating another province), "fearing that
the Parthians would revolt also."[110] Cassius Dio writes that "he used
to say that he had progressed farther even than [Alexander], and wrote
this to the senate, but he was unable even to preserve what he had acquired" (68.29.1). Hadrian abandoned the new provinces, and one tradition claimed that he abandoned Dacia too—so writes Marcus Cornelius Fronto, friend and tutor of emperors, a passage that illustrates
further the limitations on the geographical information available to, or
used by, the Roman elite (*Principia historiae* 10 [Loeb 2:207]).

The idea that to expand the empire might take more force than the
Romans could safely or easily concentrate in one place may seem obvious; but it does reflect one of their own most important concerns. In
the literary sources we often encounter the idea that, in attempting further conquests, the Romans might lose what they possess already.[111]
Both Strabo and Agricola speculate about the force it might take to acquire and garrison Britain or Ireland (Strab. 2.5.8; Tac. *Agr.* 24.3). It
is also likely that emperors and especially governors knew how many
troops were stationed in each province and approximately where they
were. Augustus, as we have seen, left behind a document cataloguing
the empire's legions and auxiliaries. Tacitus is able to offer a list of the
legions stationed in each province in the time of Tiberius; Appian promises that the last book of his *Roman History* will record "the size of their

109. Pflaum (1950, 107–109) argues that all Trajan's predecessors had raised new forces
before annexing territory, but that while Trajan raised two legions for the Dacian war, he
did not raise any for the Parthian war. He further argues that this was the reason that the
new territory could not be held.

110. On the revolt of the new provinces, see Cass. Dio 68.29.4; on legates, and the
crowning of Parthamaspates, 68.30.1–3; in 68.33.1, Trajan is preparing a fresh expedition
at the time of his death. On Trajan's Parthian war, the establishment of new provinces,
and their evacuation, see Lepper 1948; Angeli Bertinelli 1976, 7–25, with extensive bibliography; ead. 1979, 72–76; Potter 1991.

111. Strabo gives this reason for Augustus' prohibition of conquests beyond the Elbe
(7.1.4); Appian writes that "altogether, since they hold by good judgment the best parts
of land and sea, they prefer to preserve them rather than to extend their rule boundlessly
to barbarian tribes that are poor and unprofitable" (*Praef.* 7); cf. Tac. *Ann.* 12.32 (on Ostorius, governor of Britain), and *Agr.* 14.3 on Suetonius Paulinus' decision to invade Mona.
See also Dio's criticism of Trajan (68.29.1) and Augustus' advice to Tiberius (56.33.5).

army and the tribute that they collect from each province, and what they spend on naval garrisons, and other things of that sort"; and a Latin inscription of Severus' reign lists the legions in geographical order (though new legions have been added at the end).[112] Censuses of citizens and provincials were carried out for tax purposes and their results collected at Rome; they may also have been used to recruit the army.[113] The wealth of detail available in Roman military records rivals that of the empire's tax documents; we have the remains of rosters, duty lists, guard lists, lists of officers and soldiers in order of seniority, casualty lists, absentee lists, and strength reports.[114] At the provincial level, a substantial military bureaucracy helped to generate and track all this information.[115]

It is not clear how much of it was available in a digestible form to the governor or, especially, at Rome. To the degree that important decisions were made by the emperor, they were probably made on the basis of the more general information contained, for example, in Augustus' testament. Few exact figures on Rome's army have entered the historical tradition, which may be significant. The paper strength of a legion remains a subject of controversy to this day. Also, though literary sources sometimes tell us how many and which legions were involved in a war or stationed in a province, it is often a different matter to determine where they were stationed; this information must sometimes be reconstructed from epigraphic or archaeological evidence. And it is probably significant that the ancient literary sources supply very little information at all on Rome's auxiliary units, so that it is difficult to determine how many were stationed in a province or what their distribution was without extensive use of aerial photography, archaeological research, and papyrological and epigraphical analysis. Velleius Paterculus, Tacitus, and Josephus sometimes provide us with detailed, credible, and apparently accurate information on the Roman troops assembled for various campaigns. They are also capable of providing figures that evoke universal disbelief. This is especially true of casualty figures: Tacitus asserts that 70,000 Romans and allies were slain in the revolt of Boudicca (*Ann.*

112. Tac. *Ann.* 4.4–5; App. *Praef.* 15; cf. MacMullen 1976, 61–62; the inscription is *ILS* 2288.

113. On the census under the empire, see Nicolet 1991, 130–139; Augustus records the results of three citizen censuses in the *RGDA;* also, Tacitus reports the results of a census by Claudius (*Ann.* 11.25; the figure is 5,984,072); similarly, Pliny can give the total population for three districts in Spain (*HN* 3.28). In a famous passage, Josephus also records that the population of Egypt is 7,500,000 excluding Alexandria (*BJ* 2.385).

114. Collected and published in Fink 1971.

115. Austin and Rankov 1995, 149–161.

14.33); in Cassius Dio, this number is 80,000 (62.1.1) and Boudicca's army numbers 230,000 (62.8.2); Suetonius Paulinus killed 80,000 of them with only 400 Roman casualties (Tac. *Ann.* 14.37). Josephus writes that in the Jewish war 40,000 rebels were killed at the fall of Jotapata;[116] and Severus is said to have lost 50,000 men in his British war (Cass. Dio 76[77].13.2). But Cassius Dio may have been working from Severus' memoirs, and Josephus, of course, was there.

One ancient comment on casualty figures in historiography survives. Lucian writes (*Hist. conscr.* 20) that historians tend to report exaggerated casualties that differ from the figures given "in the letters of the generals," presumably in senatorial dispatches. Thus he expresses an opinion on the desirability, for whatever reason, of accurate casualty figures in historiography, as well as the perception that these figures are not in fact accurate and the idea that a check on these figures might be available in the form of senatorial dispatches. About the accuracy of these dispatches, again, we can only speculate; but it seems dangerous to assume, as Lucian apparently does, that they were not subject to ideological distortions of their own—through the emperor's desire for self-glorification.[117] It is understandable that historians might inflate the size of an enemy's army and the number of casualties inflicted, to capture the reader's interest or to enhance a patriotic subtext.[118] For different reasons, perhaps because of the prominence of the idea of revenge in Roman warfare (see chap. 5 below), casualties might be exaggerated also by the side that suffered them. On this issue, as on questions of ethnography, the profound moral and ideological slant of historiography is clear. Again we are warned that even in an area as practical and mundane as troop deployments, Roman thinking has another dimension.

Campaigns in foreign territory and the conquest of new lands were risky and difficult enterprises. In at least one case, the Romans backed away from the military option in foreign policy—that is, the case of Parthia under the early Julio-Claudians. Evidence indicates that Augustus and his immediate successors may have feared a full-scale confrontation with Parthia. Two attempts to conquer it in the late Republic had resulted in disaster, and the ghost of Crassus in particular still haunts

---

116. Joseph. *BJ* 3.337. Smallwood (1976, 308 n. 59) writes that the last figure is "impossible for a town the size of Jotapata."

117. See chap. 2 above, p. 33.

118. Cf. Brunt 1971, 694–697, on the inaccuracy of casualty figures in the Republic. These are often substantially inflated even by the side that suffered them, but especially when the enemy is involved.

the literature of the first and second centuries.[119] The Parthians acquired a reputation for being invincible on their own territory—an idea that persists in Cassius Dio, though by his day Ctesiphon had been sacked three times.[120] The Parthian empire was perceived as "another world," a "rival" to the Roman empire.[121] Augustus certainly settled for a "diplomatic victory" over Parthia in 20 B.C., when he secured the return of the military standards lost in the disastrous expeditions of Crassus and Antony. It is possible that in fact the emperor was following Caesar's plan, waiting to complete the subjection of Europe, which of course never happened.[122] The original aims of Gaius' expedition in 2 B.C. may have been more ambitious, but if this is true, the expedition failed, and certainly an accord was reached with the king Phraataces in A.D. 2.[123] Tiberius and Claudius are said to take actions expressly to avoid provoking war with Parthia.[124] It may have been Trajan's war that convinced the Romans that Parthia was not as invincible as they had thought. Campaigns into Parthian territory became more common after this.[125]

119. On Crassus and Antony, see, e.g., Fronto *Principia historiae* 3 (Loeb 2:203): "Of all men only the Parthians have maintained a reputation hardly ever to be despised, as enemies of the Roman people; this is demonstrated well enough not only by the disaster of Crassus and the shameful flight of Antonius; but even under the leadership of the bravest of emperors, Trajan, a legate was killed with his army, and the retreat of the princeps, withdrawing to his triumph, was by no means secure or bloodless." In Tac. *Ann.* 2.2, the Parthians remember *illam gloriam trucidantium Crassum, exturbantium Antonium* ("the glory of those who cut down Crassus and drove out Antony"). See Timpe 1962, especially 128–129.

120. Cass. Dio 40.15.4; cf. Lucan 8.368–371.

121. See above, chap. 2, n. 132.

122. On this possibility, see Brunt 1990, 456; Augustus' Parthian policy is traditionally the most cogent argument that he favored a defensive foreign policy. For a brief but enlightening discussion, see Gruen 1990, 396–399; also Barzanò 1985, 212–214. On Augustus and the Parthians, see also Sherwin-White 1984, 322–341 (arguing that Augustus feared the loss of face that would result from a disaster on the scale of Crassus' or Antony's), and Campbell 1993, 220–228.

123. On Gaius' mission, see Romer 1979; it included an expedition to Arabia, attested in Pliny (*HN* 6.141, 160; Romer, op. cit., 204–208). On his departure Ovid anticipates a Parthian triumph (*Ars amat.* 1.117–228); and if the conjecture in chap. 2 above about the *Parthian Stations* of Isidorus is true, he was prepared for the possibility of a full-scale invasion. Gaius' meeting with the Parthian king on an island in the Euphrates is described by Velleius Paterculus (2.101), who was an eyewitness.

124. Tiberius evacuates Vonones from Armenia instead of offering armed support (Tac. *Ann.* 2.4: "if he were defended by our forces, a war with the Parthians would have to be taken up"). On this, see also Joseph. *AJ* 18.49–51; Claudius recalls Helvidius Priscus to Syria from Armenia *ne initium belli adversus Parthos existeret*, "lest a cause of war with the Parthians should arise" (Tac. *Ann.* 12.49.2; cf. Chaumont 1976, 81).

125. On the new phase of Roman-Parthian relations beginning with Trajan, see Angeli Bertinelli 1979, 72–73; and Frézouls 1981, 195–196. On Severus' sack of Ctesiphon, see

Trajan was not the last to reach Ctesiphon; it was sacked by Lucius Verus and Septimius Severus, and Caracalla invaded Parthia twice. Rome never seriously attempted to annex the Parthian empire, or at least not much of it; but this may have been because of the potential difficulty of occupying it. It is also noteworthy that Augustus, Tiberius, and Claudius were all criticized for their approach toward relations with Parthia or toward foreign policy generally.[126] The argument from fear of an enemy's superior strength, while it may have influenced some Roman decisions, was not necessarily one that conformed to Roman ideas of correct foreign policy.

There were some strict limits on what could be achieved in expanding the empire, and these limits had to do with the force available. Retaining conquered territory also normally entailed a tremendous commitment of troops and money. Nevertheless, expansion was attempted, sometimes with success; still more often, campaigns were waged far into hostile territory. At first we may be tempted to conclude only that the value attached by the Romans to conquest and domination caused them to make more or less "irrational" decisions to expand the empire with a limited force. I shall argue that the reality is more complex. In the first place, it has been noted that some expansionist campaigns—those of Domitian and Caracalla—drew criticism as "unnecessary"; that is, some campaigns seemed irrational *to the Romans,* while others presumably did not. We are left to conclude that in some cases there was a purpose to military aggressiveness beyond just a drive toward glorious conquest (although this was also an important motive); the tenacity with which Romans held new territory was a related phenomenon. In both cases, I shall argue, it is the image of Rome that was the primary issue. Rome's success, its very safety, ultimately depended less on the force that it could wield, which was not necessarily large or overwhelming, than on the image of the force it could wield and on its apparent willingness to use that force at whatever cost.[127] This is the concept of national honor, to be discussed more fully in chapter 5 below. Revolving around this idea of image or honor, Roman policy worked largely on the psy-

Cass. Dio 75[76].9.4; Caracalla's invasions, ibid., 77[78].19, 78[79].1. On Verus, Angeli Bertinelli 1976, 25–31; Mitford 1980, 1203–1206; A. R. Birley 1987, 123–126, 128–132; he sacks Ctesiphon and Seleucia and invades Media (Cass. Dio 71.2.3); also builds a new Armenian capital and crowns Sohaemus, an Arsacid but also a Roman senator, king of Armenia (ibid., 71.3.1).

126. On Augustus, see below, chap. 5, p. 174; Tiberius, see *Ann.* 6.31 and Cass. Dio 59.27.2–3. On Claudius, cf. *Ann.* 11.20, where he proves weak on the issue of Germany, and ibid., 13.6, quoted in chap. 1.

127. A point made by Luttwak (1976, 195–200).

chological (as opposed to the strictly military or economic) plane. This psychological element of Roman strategy becomes especially evident when we turn to a discussion of the defense of the empire.

2. Defense

The defense of the provinces, or of other territories over which the empire claimed dominion, of its "allies" or dependent monarchs, was part of the Roman army's job. Raiding Roman territory was unacceptable. This brings us to the difficult question of the origin and nature of the empire's frontiers, since until recently they were usually interpreted as the empire's primary means of self-defense.[128] A vast scholarship on frontier archaeology has revealed much about troop deployments, roads, and military structures in the frontier provinces throughout the imperial period. The interpretation of this evidence has changed drastically over the years, reflecting a changing view of Roman imperialism generally.

It was once the tendency of modern historians to see in these remains "frontier systems," which they sometimes classified by periods; that is, the Julio-Claudian period had one system and one set of goals; in the Flavian period another system and another set of goals evolved; and so forth.[129] It was, and to some extent still is, also common to perceive the establishment of permanent, defensible frontiers and speedy frontier communications as an essential goal of Roman foreign policy. Thus the idea that Augustus espoused an "Elbe frontier policy," or statements such as "Frontier security . . . was Rome's immediate preoccupation" in Cornelius Gallus' campaigns; that Marcus' campaigns against the Marcomanni sought to "neutralize the northern threat, not least because the mountain frontier thereby attained would be superior to the river line"; that the purpose of Domitian's war against the Chatti was to "strengthen the Rhine defenses . . . giving Rome better control of the tribal movements to the east of the Rhine and providing a quicker route between Mainz and the Danube."[130]

The evidence of the literary sources, and how they perceived the nature of Rome's frontiers and the problem of the empire's defense, is not uniform or straightforward, but it is strikingly different from

128. On the nature of Roman frontiers, see recently Whittaker 1994.
129. E.g., Luttwak 1976.
130. Statements quoted from Kirwan 1978, 19; A. R. Birley 1987, 254; and B. Jones 1992, 131.

the highly rationalizing, geographically oriented argumentation cited above. Everyone knew that the empire had borders, and any educated person would tell you that they were the rivers Rhine and the Danube in the north; the Euphrates in the east; the desert in Syria, Arabia, and Africa; and the ocean everywhere else. The Romans tended to associate these boundaries with the first emperor, Augustus.[131] After Severus, the Tigris became the new boundary in the east; and Britain's walls were recognized in the same way.[132] No source from our period except the geographical expert Ptolemy even attempts to describe the boundaries of Dacia.[133]

In some ways the river boundaries functioned as political borders. Thus Gaius, Augustus' grandson, meets with the king of Parthia on an island in the Euphrates, and so does Tiberius' legate Vitellius.[134] Claudius orders Corbulo, apparently in the process of annexing the Chauci, to withdraw his troops back behind the Rhine (Tac. *Ann.* 11.19). A famous inscription (*ILS* 986) describing the career of Ti. Plautius Silvanus, governor of Moesia, also illustrates that the Danube was perceived as a significant political border: "Transdanuviani" are relocated to the Roman side of the river, and "hostile kings" are brought to its bank to do obeisance to Rome. And when barbarians invade, historians describe them as breaching the "wall that divided them from the Roman army" or crossing a river to Roman territory.[135]

How do the literary sources perceive the role of the frontiers in the defense of the empire? Some of them describe a ring of forts or troops

131. On rivers, see Millar 1982, 19–20, with n. 128 for some references, especially Joseph. *BJ* 2.363 and App. *Praef.* 4; Florus 2.34; Sen. *Q Nat.* 6.7.1, *De brevitate vitae* 4.5; Philo *Leg.* 11. On the Rhine and Danube, see Lucan 2.49–52, Tac. *Germ.* 1, Herodian 6.7.6; on the Rhine, Strab. 4.3.5; the Danube, *RGDA* 30; etc. On the Euphrates, see Wheeler 1991, 505, for references; Herodian 4.10.2 (Caracalla's letter to the king of Parthia); see also Fronto *Principia historiae* 4 (Loeb 2:201; the "hostile rivers"). On Augustus, Sen. *De brevitate vitae* 4–5, Florus 2.34.61, Tac. *Ann.* 1.9; cf. Herodian 2.11.4–5.

132. On the Tigris, see Herodian 6.2.1; on the wall, ibid., 3.14.10, with Whittaker (1969–1970) ad loc.; Cass. Dio 72[73].8.2, quoted below; and *It. Ant.* 463.3–464.1: "Iter Britanniarum . . . a limite, id est a vallo . . . ," on which see Rivet and Smith 1979, 155.

133. Ptolemy *Geog.* 3.8.1–4. Cf. Jordanes *Get.* 74 and Gudea 1979, 65, for a few other late references. Ptolemy's Carpathians run due east-west (Bogdan Cataniciu 1990, 225, with illustration, p. 228).

134. On Gaius, see Vell. Pat. 2.101; on Vitellius, Joseph. *AJ* 18.101–102. On the Euphrates as a legal or political boundary, see K. H. Ziegler 1964 passim, e.g., 54–55 on Gaius; Wheeler 1991, 506–507; Millar 1993, 33; and Whittaker 1994, 51–53. Philostratus (*VA* 1.37) relates a fictitious but interesting story, where a legate of Syria and the king of Parthia dispute control of some villages on the Euphrates.

135. See Cass. Dio 72[73].8.2 on a British invasion under Commodus; which wall is meant, however, is unclear. On rivers, see, e.g., Joseph. *BJ* 7.90, Herodian 6.2.1; see Isaac 1988, 128–132, on the meaning of *limes* as "boundary."

surrounding the empire, whose purpose is to ward off barbarian invasions. Appian writes that the Romans "fortify the empire around in a
circle with great armies, and they guard so much land and sea as if it
were an estate" (*Praef.* 7); and we find similar descriptions also in Aelius
Aristides (*Or.* 26.82–84) and in Herodian.[136] However, the function of
Roman frontiers as defensive systems has long been perceived as a problematic issue.

In the first place, it has been observed that the structures on the empire's borders were many and various—strings of forts along the Rhine,
Danube, and Euphrates; artificial barriers like Hadrian's wall, the pali-
sade of Upper Germany/Raetia, the ditch and wall of the *fossatum Africae.* They also arose at different times and may have fulfilled different
functions; it is thus problematic to argue that they were part of a long-
term, coherent strategy of defense.[137] Thus, for example, the legions of
Germany were stationed along the Rhine from the time of Augustus,
when their purpose was notoriously aggressive; and it is unclear when
troops came to be concentrated along the upper Euphrates.[138] The
Danube was declared the boundary of the Roman empire by Augustus
long before it was ever fortified.[139] The new province of Mesopotamia
had no discernible frontier line in our period,[140] and Britain, we should
remember, ultimately had not one wall but two. And if the Roman emperors did in fact formulate and carry out some plan systematically to

136. Herodian 2.11.5: "From the time when the monarchy came about under Augustus, he relieved the Italians of their labors and stripped them of their arms, and he set garrisons and camps before the empire, and stationed soldiers who were paid according to a
regular salary before the walls of the Roman empire. And he fortified the empire by fenc-
ing it in with the great obstacles of rivers, ditches, or mountains, or with land that is desert
and difficult to cross." Herodian also describes the purpose of the armies on the Rhine
and Danube as protecting the empire from attack (2.9.1) and refers to "the camps along
the banks of the rivers protecting [shielding, προασπίζοντα] the Roman empire" (6.2.5);
Menander Rhetor also emphasizes safety from attack (2.377); and see the speech of Cerialis to the Gauls, where the Roman army is supposed to protect them from the Germans
(Tac. *Hist.* 4.73; cf. Whittaker 1994, 28).

137. This point is made by Mann (1974); cf. Whittaker 1994, 49, contrasting situations
in the east and west.

138. Consensus once placed this under Vespasian; but recently the evidence for the Euphrates frontier has come into serious question (e.g., Mitford 1980, 1180–1186, for the traditional view; challenged by Crow [1986], and see the discussion in Wheeler 1991).

139. *RGDA* 30. On this point, see Mócsy 1974, 48; on the history of the fortification
of the Danube, believed to have begun with Vespasian or Domitian, ibid., 42–52 for the
Julio-Claudians, and 80–89 for the Flavians; see also Wilkes 1983, 264–268, pointing out
(p. 267) that on the lower Danube fortification is not attested until Trajan.

140. See Kennedy and Riley 1990 on all aspects of the Roman desert frontier in the
east; especially p. 237 for conclusions about Roman strategy on the eastern frontier including Mesopotamia after Severus' conquest.

fortify and defend the borders of the empire, this plan was not known or recorded by any surviving historian of antiquity;[141] in hindsight later sources sometimes credit Augustus, as we have seen, with such a strategy, but most frontier structures attested archaeologically postdate his reign by a wide margin.

Recent scholarship has argued that the purpose of Roman frontiers is uncertain in all cases. Even where we see large numbers of troops stationed along a boundary, we cannot immediately conclude that their main purpose was to defend against enemy attack, although this was one of their perceived functions, as noted above. A heavy concentration of troops on a frontier could as easily be an aggressive posture as a defensive one.[142] When Corbulo moved troops to the Euphrates in 61, it was to protect Syria from an anticipated Parthian invasion, and Rubrius Gallus had the same purpose in mind when he moved troops to the Danube after the Sarmatian invasion of 69.[143] But when Nero ordered legions moved "closer to Armenia" in 54, it was to prepare for a major offensive (Tac. *Ann.* 13.7); and when Agricola concentrated his forces on the British coast facing Ireland, it was "in hope rather than because of fear" (Tac. *Agr.* 24.1). Vespasian's reorganization of the Euphrates frontier, which involved the annexation of two new provinces, the combination of Galatia and Cappadocia, and possibly a military presence in the Caucasus, has been variously explained as a response to the threat posed by the barbarous Alani of the northern Caucasus region, or alternatively by the Parthians; or an attempt to secure strategic bases for aggression against Armenia and Parthia.[144]

141. See Mócsy 1978, 8–9, on this point.

142. Cf. Isaac 1992, 41.

143. Tac. *Ann.* 15.3: "he placed the rest of the legions in front of the bank of the Euphrates, he hastily raised and armed a band of provincials, he cut off enemy inroads with guards" (*reliquas legiones pro ripa Euphratis locat, tumultuarium provincialium manum armat, hostilis ingressus praesidiis intercipit*). See Dabrowa 1986, 97–98, arguing that this is the beginning of a defensive system constructed along the upper Euphrates by Vespasian; but on the difficulties of this interpretation, see Crow 1986. On Rubrius Gallus, see Joseph. *BJ* 7.94: he "secured the area with more and better guards, so that it would be completely impossible for the barbarians to cross over [the Ister]."

144. For a summary of Vespasian's innovations, see Mitford 1980, 1180; on defense against the Parthians, see, e.g., Dabrowa 1981 and 1986; this interpretation has some support from Josephus, who writes that Commagene was annexed because its king was accused of plotting with the Parthians, and Samosata, the capital of Commagene, "lies on the Euphrates, so that it would be an easy crossing and a safe reception for the Parthians, if they intended something of this sort" (*BJ* 7.224); Suetonius also claims that it was "because of the frequent attacks of barbarians" (*propter adsiduos barbarorum incursus*) that troops were transferred to Cappadocia (*Vesp.* 8.4). This passage was once used to support the theory that Vespasian's primary motivation was defense against the Alani, until this

As for the forts, walls, and ditches that were constructed on some frontiers, it has long been recognized that none of these structures was very good at preventing dangerous, large-scale invasions, and they do not seem to have been designed to do this.[145] An inscription from Commodus' reign states that the emperor fortified a stretch of the Danube with forts and garrisons "against the clandestine crossings of robbers"; that is, they served to police traffic and control banditry.[146] Movement, including economic movement, across parts of the Rhine and Danube was strictly controlled; thus in Tacitus' *Histories* the Tencteri complain that they are not allowed to trade with the Roman colony at Cologne unless they are unarmed and under guard, and have paid a toll; later, we find Marcus regulating trade with the Quadi, Marcomanni, and Iazyges, and it seems likely that river fortifications played a role here.[147] Hadrian's wall also may have been more suited to the task of controlling movement across the frontier and collecting taxes than actually to defending against invasion, though it is by far our best candidate for a mainly military, defensive construction; it was, however, abandoned under Antoninus Pius, and a new wall was constructed to the north.[148] It has been argued that in the desert regions of Judaea, Arabia, and Numidia after the first century, Rome faced hardly any serious external threat, and that the *fossatum Africae*, for example, served again to control trade and collect import and export taxes, or as a "purely local" defense against banditry and raids.[149] Chains of forts along a river could

---

argument was convincingly defeated by Bosworth (1976). He argues for long-range, aggressive plans against Parthia; this is also the view of Isaac (1992, 34–42).

145. It is often observed that rivers do not make good military frontiers and usually do not function as ethnic or cultural boundaries; see, e.g., Wells 1972, 24; Mann 1974, 513; Breeze and Dobson 1987, 7; Wheeler 1991, 505; and Whittaker 1994 passim, e.g., p. 61. *Contra*, see Austin and Rankov 1995, 173–180. On the *via nova Traiana* in Arabia, sometimes interpreted as a frontier structure, see Isaac 1984, 184–189; on the *fossatum Africae* specifically, see n. 149 below. Luttwak (1976, 61–80) argues that artificial-barrier-type frontiers were mainly useful against "low-intensity" threats.

146. The inscription is *CIL* 3.3385, cited in Isaac 1988, 130–131: *Imp. Caes. M. Aur. Commodus Antoninus Aug.* . . . (etc.; Commodus' titles) *ripam omnem bu[rgis] a solo extructis, item praes[i]diis per loca opportuna ad clandestinos latrunculorum transitus oppositis munivit.* "Emperor Marcus Aurelius Commodus Antoninus Augustus [etc.; Commodus' titles] fortified the whole river bank with forts constructed from the ground [i.e., with new forts], and also with garrisons stationed at advantageous places against the clandestine crossings of robbers."

147. See Kerr 1991; on the Tencteri, see Tac. *Hist.* 4.64; cf. *Germ.* 61, where the Hermunduri are an exception to the usual restrictions; on Marcus and the Danube tribes, Cass. Dio 71[72].11.3, 15, 19.2; see also de Laet 1949, 193–194.

148. Dobson 1986; Breeze and Dobson 1987, 39–43.

149. On nomads in Judaea and Arabia, see Isaac 1984, 173–175; id. 1992, 68–77; see also Graf 1989. For Africa, see Shaw 1982; on the *fossatum* (local defense), 43–46; for the

also ensure the safe and speedy transport not only of trade goods but of military supplies for whatever purpose. Two spectacular projects of Trajan come to mind in this context: his rock-cut road along the Danube River at the Iron Gates of Orsova,[150] and the fortified road constructed through Arabia shortly after it was made a province, the *via nova Traiana*.[151] This road would have facilitated movement between Egypt and the other eastern provinces—in the first place, for the army and military supplies; but also for the luxury trade from the Red Sea, on which Rome collected a 25 percent import tax.[152] Borders between nations today may be heavily policed, even fortified, for reasons that are political, economic, or social, but not military.[153]

Thus the Roman frontiers emerge as complex phenomena, subject to interpretation only with difficulty. Rather than a coherent, mainly defensive system, we see variation, mutation, and ambiguity. A tendency has emerged in modern scholarship to attribute the final shape of the Roman frontiers to unconscious or accidental forces.[154] But before we leave the subject of the frontier structures themselves, one point deserves emphasis. Some of these constructions (though again, not all) had a profound *psychological* impact in addition to whatever they were supposed to accomplish *physically*. The *via nova Traiana* and Hadrian's wall, for example, were vast, sophisticated structures in the middle of what was otherwise relatively primitive and undeveloped countryside. They must have seemed impressive, even terrifying.

---

view that its purpose was mainly economic, Fentress 1979, 112–113, 117; cf. Wells 1991 on this change in the traditional view of desert frontiers. For a defense of the more traditional "nomad menace" view, see S. T. Parker 1991.

150. See Rossi 1971, 32, on the road; ibid., 49, for the inscription (*ILS* 5863). The path was begun under Tiberius (Mócsy 1974, 45–48), but the most spectacular work and the famous inscription belong to the reign of Trajan.

151. The Arabian frontier is the subject of much recent scholarship. After Trajan reduced Arabia he apparently paved and fortified a Nabataean road. The milestones read: "[Trajan's titles], having reduced Arabia to the state of a province, opened and paved a new road from the borders of Syria all the way to the Red Sea" (*redacta in formam provinciae Arabia viam novam a finibus Syriae usque ad mare Rubrum aperuit et stravit; ILS* 5834; see *CIL* vol. 3, pp. 2303–2304). For a summary of the arguments, see S. T. Parker (1991), who defends the traditional view that one of the main purposes of the fortified road was to control the movements of the nomads across it. This view was first seriously questioned by Isaac (1984), who contended that the nomads were not a problem and that the main purpose of the road was the obvious one; see also id. 1992, 118–122. The road itself is the only contender for a frontier structure in Arabia in the Trajanic period.

152. On this aspect of the *via nova Traiana*, see Sidebotham 1986, 72–74.

153. See Dunn 1996 on the U.S-Mexico border; ibid., app. 3, provides a list of U.S. equipment and construction on the border. Recent construction includes fourteen miles of "new 10 foot high solid steel border wall."

154. Mann 1974; Isaac 1992, 387–394; Whittaker 1994, chap. 3.

When we turn from archaeological to literary sources, we find that they virtually do not recognize the idea of defensible frontiers.[155] The exception is a remark by Tacitus that Agricola discovered in the Forth-Clyde isthmus "a border within Britain itself, if the valor of the army and the glory of the Roman name had permitted it" (*Agr.* 23). This isthmus appears on Ptolemy's map, and it is possible that it may have been the goal when Antoninus Pius or his general decided to advance beyond Hadrian's wall.[156] Otherwise we do not find any discussion in ancient sources about which boundaries are preferable from a strategic point of view. The Romans did not, as argued in chapter 2, have the geographical tools to make this type of argument. This point is reinforced further by those Roman innovations on the frontier that seem counterproductive or irrational from a modern "cartographic" perspective—especially the additions of Dacia and Mesopotamia, which look awkward on a modern map; though Severus claimed that the latter province formed a "bulwark for Syria" (Cass. Dio 75.3.2). Britain lay beyond the ocean; the ancient sources themselves suggest that this was the ultimate natural barrier, and the province acquired a mystique of its own, as being beyond the *oikoumene*.[157]

Later, in his oration *On the Peace of Valens,* the fourth-century orator Themistius would write: "What divides the Scythians [i.e., Goths] and the Romans is not a river, nor a swamp, nor a wall—for these one might break through, sail over, or surmount—but fear, which no one has ever surmounted who believed that he was the weaker."[158] I would argue that Rome's real strategy lay in the realm of psychology. The empire was defended not by "scientific frontiers," however we might choose to

155. Whittaker (1994, chap. 3) argues that the Romans formed no concept of scientific frontiers, that no natural frontiers in fact existed, and that frontier zones tended to form in marginal territory for mainly economic reasons.

156. On the Antonine advance, see Hanson and Maxwell 1983, 69–70.

157. Strab. 2.5.8: "Though the Romans could have held Britain, they disdained it, seeing that there was not a single threat from them [the British tribes], for they are not strong enough to cross over and attack us, nor is there any advantage at all to occupying it"; Florus 1.45.2: "the Britons, although separated from the whole world, nevertheless because it pleased [Caesar] to conquer [them]" (*quamvis toto orbe divisi, tamen quia vincere libuit Britanni*); cf. 1.45.16: "as though this world did not suffice, [Caesar] contemplated another" (*quasi hic Romanis orbis non sufficeret, alterum cogitavit [Caesar]*); Joseph. *BJ* 2.378: "You who trust in the walls of Jerusalem, look at the wall of the Britons; for though they are surrounded by the ocean and live on an island no smaller than our inhabited world, the Romans sailed against them and enslaved them, and four legions hold such a great island"; for a similar comment, see Tac. *Agr.* 15.3; and Cass. Dio 60.19.2, where Plautius' soldiers refuse to invade Britain because it lies outside the inhabited world.

158. *Or.* 10.138 D; *Pan. Lat.* vi (vii) 11 is very similar; cf. Isaac 1992, 413. See Haase 1977, 733–734 and passim, on the idea of deterrence through terror.

define such a phrase. For defense the Romans relied mainly, as Themistius suggests, on terror.[159] To illustrate this principle, let us imagine the probable course of events in the case of a crisis, such as a major invasion. If a province's garrison could not manage the crisis, then a response could come only after long delays of months or even years—the length of time required to assemble a large force and send out a commander, or for the emperor to arrive, if he was taking command himself. The Romans were lucky once, as Tacitus points out, when Mucianus and his army happened to be in the neighborhood and prevented the Dacians from storming legionary camps; later in that year they were not so fortunate. Domitian's Dacian wars, Marcus' Parthian and Danube campaigns, Severus' assaults on the tribes of Scotland, Severus Alexander's invasion of Persia, and Maximinus' campaigns in Germany—all were fought after substantial preparation and not as instant responses to a crisis.[160] Severus Alexander appears to have made a detour to Rome to celebrate an eastern triumph before proceeding to the Rhine frontier.[161] Thus the strategic principles in place did not rely on swift action, still less on preventive action, though this was probably preferable if practicable. In the Roman system, reprisals might come at any time, even years, after the attack. All of the campaigns mentioned were also fought on enemy territory; they could include total conquest or other extreme measures. Marcus, as noted above, planned not only to exterminate the Iazyges but, probably, to annex the Quadi and Marcomanni; and Seve-

159. The importance of terror in Roman policy is discussed briefly by Luttwak (1976, 3–4) and Wheeler (1993, 35–36), but its central role has not yet been recognized.

160. In the case of Severus' Scottish campaign there is some question as to whether this was a response to a crisis at all; Herodian mentions a letter from the governor there complaining that the Britons were rebelling (3.14.1), but Dio does not mention this; no archeological evidence has been found in support, and Herodian may be inventing the incident (A. R. Birley 1988, 172). On Domitian's Dacian wars, see Suet. *Dom.* 6; Cass. Dio 67.6–7; Mócsy 1974, 82–84; Wilkes 1983, 270–273; Strobel 1989; B. Jones 1992, 138–139, 141–143. The problem seems to have begun with a Dacian invasion of Moesia in 84–85, in which the governor, Oppius Sabinus, was killed. On Verus' Parthian campaign, see above, n. 125; the governor of Cappadocia had invaded Armenia and lost a legion (Cass. Dio 71.2.1; Fronto *Principia historiae* 16 [Loeb 2:215]; Lucian *Alex.* 27); see Angeli Bertinelli 1976, 25–26, on the outbreak of this war, with full references; Vologeses also defeated the governor of Syria (SHA *Marcus* 8.6). Lucius then took the field, at first offering peace (Fronto *Principia historiae* 14 [Loeb 2.213]), but when refused, he retaliated with an invasion of Mesopotamia and the sack of Ctesiphon and Seleucia; he also relocated the capital of Armenia and crowned a new king (Cass. Dio 71.2–3). It is possible that the annexation of Armenia or Mesopotamia was contemplated at this time but not carried out because of the plague and the Danube invasions (A. R. Birley 1979, 480–482).

161. See Whittaker 1969–1970, n. 3, on Herodian 6.7.5.

rus' British campaign seems to have had exactly similar aims (and results, for Caracalla, like Commodus, withdrew the garrison).[162]

The goals of such expeditions were not normally "defensive." They
were not undertaken, for example, to drive the barbarians out of Roman territory; in many cases the enemy will have left by the time the
army arrived. The aim was to punish, to avenge, and to terrify—that is,
to reassert a certain state of mind in the enemy, or even a certain moral
equilibrium or status relationship between Rome and the barbarian.
This goal could, but did not necessarily, involve the annexation of enemy territory. But diplomacy, as a language communicating domination
and deference, also played an important part in keeping the peace. For
the empire at all times was surrounded by a complex net of alliances and
treaties.[163] As we shall see in a later chapter, these treaties ideally were
sought by the barbarians and the terms were dictated by Rome; they exacted tribute payments, hostages, promises of alliance, sometimes con-
tributions of troops, the return of prisoners and deserters, and an elaborate show of obeisance to Rome, which might include accepting a king
appointed by Rome; the most spectacular examples of this latter practice involved Armenia and Parthia, but it was not limited to the east.
Great importance and prestige are consistently attached to the constant flow of foreign embassies to the capital, seeking friendship and
peace. Augustus boasts of receiving envoys from various exotic peoples
(Cimbri, Semnones, Indians, Scythians, Albani, etc.) in the *Res Gestae*
(26, 31), and so does the famous governor of Moesia, Plautius Silvanus.
Appian claims to have seen personally representatives of minor barbarian tribes at Rome offering to surrender to the emperor, who refuses
them as worthless; he notes that the Romans "give kings to a countless
multitude of other peoples without binding any of them to their rule"
(*Praef.* 7).

It is important to note that the emperor was constantly receiving embassies—many from within the empire, and many from without it—
and listening to their requests. The distinction between foreign relations
and domestic affairs must have been blurred, especially if one could not
easily look at a map to determine whether the Frisii, for example, lived

162. On Marcus' aims, see above, n. 56; on Severus', n. 58.
163. The bibliography on diplomacy between Rome and foreign powers under the
Principate is not as substantial as might be expected. On the mechanics, see Millar 1988
and Talbert 1988; on the case of Mauretania Tingitana, where Rome's negotiations with
local chieftains are attested epigraphically, Shaw 1986. Other studies include Gagé 1959
and Barzanò 1985; K. H. Ziegler 1964, Lemosse 1967, and Cimma 1976 are all very legalistic in approach. See also Braund 1984; and below, chap. 5, sec. 2.

on one side of the Rhine or the other. Indeed, in spite of general talk of the empire's boundaries, the frontier itself has a nebulous quality; it is often difficult to tell whether we should consider a certain tribe or area in or out.[164] Augustus, for example, almost in one breath proclaims the Danube the boundary of the empire and claims to have forced the Dacians on the other side to "obey the commands of the Roman people" (*RGDA* 30). Clearly "client-kingdoms" like Commagene and Cappadocia were considered part of the empire in some way; some of these were eventually annexed and subjected to a Roman governor, but others, like Iberia and Bosporus, never were; Commagene and parts of Palestine were absorbed, released, and reabsorbed. Rome had similar relationships in the west with tribes like the Quadi and the Marcomanni.[165] Domitian crowned Decebalus' envoy (not, to the emperor's eternal discredit, Decebalus himself) as king of the Dacians (Cass. Dio 67.7.3), just as Tiridates had been crowned by Nero. Tribes beyond the frontiers often owe tribute or alliance to Rome and sometimes revolt and have to be reduced to submission, like the Thracians in 26 (Tac. *Ann.* 4.46; their kingdom was not formally annexed until A.D. 46), or the Frisians when they refuse to pay their customary tribute of ox hides (ibid., 4.72–73). Similarly, the "Osroeni and the Adiabeni [were] revolting (ἀποστάντες) and besieging Nisibis" (Cass. Dio 75.1.2), provoking Severus' war of conquest; Nisibis had never been formally annexed, but a Roman garrison apparently remained there after Verus' campaigns.[166] Garrisons could indeed be placed beyond the frontier, often to support a Roman nominee to the throne, as in Armenia;[167] there is even some evidence for a Roman presence in Iberia and Albania, in the Caucasus Mountains, under the Flavians.[168]

An important aspect of Roman strategy was that it did not work, or

164. On this and the points that follow, see the discussion of Roman frontiers in Isaac 1992, 394–401; Millar 1988, 351–352; and Whittaker 1994, chaps. 1–3.

165. On relations with the Quadi and Marcomanni, see especially Pitts 1989; also Mócsy 1974, 40–42, for relations under the Julio-Claudians; under the Flavians and Trajan, ibid., 89; under Antoninus coins announced *rex Quadis datus* (ibid., 49); Tac. *Germ.* 4.2 states that the kings of the Quadi and the Marcomanni owe their authority to Rome.

166. See Isaac 1992, 399–400.

167. See Crow 1986, arguing that no clear frontier line along the upper Euphrates is obvious before the third or fourth century; Tac. *Ann.* 12.45 attests a garrison in Armenia already under Claudius, and garrisons left there by Trajan and Verus are attested epigraphically.

168. On the evidence for Roman garrisons in the Caucasus region, see recently Crow 1986, 80; Isaac 1992, 42–45; and, on garrisons in client-kingdoms generally, Braund 1984, 94; on Roman troops beyond the frontier, see also Isaac 1992, 398–399.

was not believed to work, unless the barbarians were frightened. They were supposed to keep their promises, and the peace with Rome, out of terror of Roman arms, which meant that peace could be insured only by aggression. This idea is well attested not only throughout our period, but long afterward, as we saw in the passage from Themistius cited above; and by Augustus' time it was already long traditional. Polybius, writing in the mid–second century B.C., includes a famous passage on the sack of New Carthage in 209 B.C. by his hero, Scipio Africanus.[169] He describes the horrific sight of human and animal corpses littering a city that the Romans have taken by storm. "It seems to me," he writes, "that they do this for he sake of terror"; the word is κατάπληξις, which describes a mental state of astonishment or panic, from a word meaning literally "to strike down." Caesar, when he crossed the Rhine and invaded Germany, explained that he did this "in order to strike fear into the Germans, to be avenged on the Sugambri, and to free the Ubii from a siege" (B Gall. 4.19). For this he built a bridge, because boats, he felt, would be "neither safe nor in keeping with his own dignity nor that of Rome." Again we see the prominent psychological element in Roman warfare: Caesar uses words like *fear, dignity,* and *revenge* to explain what he is doing. Examples of similar thinking from the historiography of the Principate are numerous: aggression by the Romans achieves fear and compliance from the barbarians; but a "weak" policy results in arrogance and contempt from the enemy, thus in invasion. In the passage with which we began this book, Commodus' advisers make precisely this argument about his Danube war (Herodian 1.5.8). Thus the king of Thrace fears retribution from Augustus if he attacks his brother's lands, but not from the "weak" emperor Tiberius (Tac. *Ann.* 2.64). Artabanus, king of Parthia, plots against Syria because "he had paid no penalty for Armenia" (Cass. Dio 59.27.3). Later, another Parthian monarch requests peace because he fears Trajan, who "proved his threats with deeds" (68.17.2). The strategy of deterrence by terror was not a policy invented by a particular emperor and his council. It was traditional; it was the Roman way.[170]

169. Polyb. 10.15–17; and cf. Ziolkowski 1993 on sacking cities.
170. Some other examples of this idea, but certainly not all, are collected here: in Tac. *Ann.* 4.23–24, Tiberius' withdrawal of troops from Africa emboldens Tacfarinas; conversely, in 4.26 a Roman victory causes the Garamantes to send legates to Rome of their own accord. In *Ann.* 6.31 Artabanus fears Germanicus but becomes arrogant under Tiberius; in 11.20 Claudius' recall of Corbulo results in "contempt from the barbarians, and mockery from the allies" (*contemptio ex barbaris, ludibrium apud socios*). In Cass. Dio 62.10.2, Suetonius Paulinus tells his soldiers that victory will strengthen and extend the

Because of the crucial role of terror in Roman policy, the correct response when barbarians invaded, revolted, or broke treaties was at a minimum counterinvasion, resulting in the extraction of some formal submission to Rome and a humiliating treaty; but it could also include annexation and occasionally genocide. When Decebalus broke his original treaty with Trajan, the emperor annexed his territory;[171] when Vologeses IV defeated a Roman governor in Armenia, Ctesiphon was sacked. Marcus occupied the territory of the Quadi and the Marcomanni, and when the Quadi tried to emigrate he prevented them, to show that his main concern was "not to acquire their land but to exact vengeance from (τιμωρήσασθαι) the people."[172] All of these barbarians presumably considered themselves lucky. When the Bastarnae invaded Thrace and attacked peoples under treaty to the Romans in 29 B.C., Crassus did his best to annihilate them; Cassius Dio notes that they were the more easily defeated because they "wished to save their wives and children" (51.24.4). Germanicus' retaliatory campaigns across the Rhine involved slaughters of the general population: "only the destruction of the race would end the war."[173] When a tribe in Wales revolted and destroyed its garrison, Agricola nearly exterminated them; then, "not unaware that he must follow up on his reputation and that the terror of the remaining enemies would depend on the results of his initial actions," he attacked and conquered the island of Mona.[174] Domitian eradicated the Nasamones when they revolted (Cass. Dio 67.4.6); Arrian threat-

---

empire by terrifying the enemy; later, Decebalus fears Trajan because of his militaristic policies (in contrast to Domitian; ibid., 68.6.1–2 and 68.8.1); see Pliny *Ep.* 2.7.2, where Vestricius Spurinna "established the king of the Bructeri in his kingdom by force and arms, and with the display of war thoroughly subdued (*perdomuit*) this most ferocious people with terror, which is the best sort of victory." In Herodian 2.4.3, barbarians who were about to rebel willingly submit out of fear of Pertinax' military reputation; cf. Cass. Dio 73[74].6.1, where the praetorian prefect demands the return of subsidies paid to barbarians under Commodus, "saying to them, 'Tell those at home that Pertinax is emperor'; for they knew his name very well, because of the things they had suffered when he campaigned with Marcus."

171. See Cass. Dio 68.10.3 on the reasons for Trajan's second war.

172. Cass. Dio 71[72].20.2; probably not meaning, as has been argued (Alföldy 1971, 99–100), that Marcus did not contemplate long occupation of the tribes' territory but only a brief punitive effort. This passage makes sense in the context of an ideology that saw expansion as "unjust" when it was done purely for its own sake but as glorious when it was done in retaliation for a perceived wrong; thus Cassius Dio could be emphasizing that Marcus' aims were not only or primarily to acquire new territory. See further chap. 5 below.

173. On noncombatants, see Tac. *Ann.* 1.51, 56; Germanicus' exclamation, 2.21.

174. *Agr.* 18.3: *caesaque prope universa gente, non ignarus instandum famae ac, prout prima cessissent, terrorem ceteris fore . . .*

ened to wipe out a tribe that refused to pay tribute (*Peripl. M. Eux.* 15); Marcus was bent on the total destruction of the Iazyges (Cass. Dio 71[72].13.1); and when the tribes of Scotland rebelled in 210, Severus ordered his men to invade and "kill everyone they met" (Cass. Dio 76[77].15.1). Although the security of the empire was believed to depend on actions like these, the word *defense* seems inadequate to describe what is going on. *Deterrence* comes closer; even better, perhaps, would be *revenge*.

There was an alternative way to keep the peace in the Roman world, and this was to buy it. The first major example on record is Domitian's notorious agreement with Decebalus, but it is not, of course, the last. Trajan himself seems to have paid subsidies to the ferocious Rhoxolani;[175] Hadrian used a combination of terror, by continuously exercising his troops before the eyes of the barbarians, and money to secure peace without actual fighting (Cass. Dio 69.9). Subsidies play a role in Marcus' negotiations with Danube tribes (ibid. 71[72].11.1, 12.3); a legate of Severus was forced to buy off the Caledonians and Maeatae in Scotland (75[76].5.4); Caracalla is supposed to have persuaded a German tribe to admit defeat with a cash gift (77[78].14.2); and Macrinus procured peace with the Parthians for, allegedly, 200 million sesterces (78[79].27.1). Severus Alexander offered money to the Germans instead of war (Herodian 6.7.9). This alternative, however, invited criticism; the Romans were sensitive to the circumstances and terms of their alliances, to who had asked for peace first, and to who was paying whom.[176] For now we should note that these status concerns seem to have equaled or outweighed strictly military considerations in Rome's diplomatic relations. While we might speculate, for example, that the Romans insisted on appointing Armenia's kings because otherwise the Parthians might be able to station troops dangerously close to Cappadocia, in fact not one strategic argument of this type is ever produced by any ancient source for the immense effort that the Romans made to maintain this tradition; certainly they were willing to fight for it on more than one occasion.

At the conclusion of this discussion, it is important to remember that major decisions about foreign policy rested largely with one man, the emperor (see chap. 1). The sources place immense weight on the personality of the emperor as an important factor in these decisions, and

175. SHA *Had.* 6.8; on subsidies, see Braund 1984, 62; and Wolters 1990–1991, pt. 2, 116–121.

176. See below, chap. 5, sec. 2.

not unreasonably. Any scheme that attributes to the Romans a system of strategic goals stretching out over generations may seem inherently problematic. Yet we have seen that certain ideas about terror, vengeance, and security persisted over not just generations, but centuries. It is here that we should seek the long-term patterns of Roman foreign relations.

These ideas were articulated in the realm of psychology, morality, and status. Thus they will be discussed more thoroughly in chapter 5, "Values." The distinction between strategy and values in the Roman mind in fact did not exist and has been followed here for the convenience of the modern reader. The central aspect of Roman strategy was image. Their army was indeed astonishingly small; frontier construction and troop deployments were inadequate to prevent major invasions. This did not matter in the Roman system as long as the enemy *believed* that he would suffer massive retaliation for a breach of faith and as long as the Romans were both willing and able to enforce this principle at whatever cost. Should the empire's small army, stretched too thin, face more crises than it could successfully avenge, its image would suffer and its empire would founder: this is in fact what happened in the third century.

So a modern scholar might explain the thoughts and actions of the Romans. But the Romans themselves used different words—and in this chapter we have been introduced to the first—namely, *fear.*

CHAPTER 4

Income and Expenditure

1. The Price of Empire

It is reasonable to expect economics to be an important category in the minds of Roman decision makers, since it was something they encountered in their everyday lives in a way that military theory, for example, was not. Even a moderately wealthy senator like Pliny the Younger was used to managing an estate worth millions of sesterces, and perhaps more than a thousand slaves.[1] On the other hand, it is also true that the Roman elite produced no theoretical or technical treatise on any aspect of economic or fiscal activity except agriculture. Before going on to a discussion of economic considerations in Roman foreign relations, we might investigate the nature of the aristocracy's approach to economic decisions on its own estates.

Today the debate over what is usually called the "rationality" of Roman agriculture endures.[2] A recent study of the surviving accounts from

1. On Pliny's finances, see Duncan-Jones 1974, 17–32; his estates were worth perhaps 17 million sesterces; on slaves, ibid., 24–25; and cf. Whittaker 1985, 58–59. Legendary fortunes included Seneca's (Cass. Dio 61.10.3; Tac. *Ann.* 13.42).

2. Now considered traditional are the views of Finley (1985), especially chap. 4, emphasizing the simplicity of Roman economic thought and its subordination to social factors. The study of Ste. Croix on Greek and Roman accounting (1956) argued that the primitivism of Roman accounting methods forbade certain kinds of "rational" behavior, such as calculating the best investment strategies (e.g., comparing the profitability of var-

a large Egyptian estate in the mid–third century describes a sophisticated system of management; it was divided into units called *phrontides*, each under the control of a separate administrator, who sent accounts to a central administration. The estate itself was unified by an internal-transport system so that equipment or produce could be moved between units for consumption or sale, thus saving on production costs.[3] The monthly accounts themselves show many advanced features lacking in other ancient documents: expenditures and receipts are recorded separately and grouped by type, not chronologically, and a running balance was carried over from month to month.[4] One strategy behind this accounting system was to minimize the costs of production.[5] The concern of the estate management for productivity is also obvious and not surprising.

But the demands of a political career left little time for running farms, and Roman senators were absentee landlords who visited their estates occasionally to insure that their managers—who could be slaves or freedmen—were doing an honest and efficient job.[6] The literary sources usually mention only two ways of making money—investing in land or lending at interest—though other opportunities were available and ex-

---

ious crops, or comparing potential returns from commercial vs. agricultural investment); accounts, in his view, were mainly kept to guard against the dishonesty and laziness of estate managers. Macve (1985) argues that primitive accounting methods would not necessarily prevent "sophisticated" economic behavior like taxing monetary income rather than capital or calculating the relative profitability of investments, but concedes that the Romans, for whatever reason, did not do these things. Defenses of the rationality of Roman agriculture can be found in Carandini 1983, criticizing Finley for defining rationality in a narrowly capitalist sense; see also de Neeve 1985, arguing that market-economy considerations played a large part in the perception of land values. Nicolet (1988, especially 117–219) has consistently taken an optimistic view of Roman economic intelligence. A defense of Finley's approach can be found in Whittaker 1985. For some new evidence, see Rathbone 1991, discussed below.

3. Ibid., especially chap. 2 on administration, and pp. 266–278 on the transport system.

4. Ibid., chap. 8, on the accounts. For discussion of the other ancient evidence, see Ste. Croix 1956.

5. Rathbone 1991, 369–386, on the rationale of the accounts.

6. Columella (1 *praef.* 3 and 12) attributes a perceived "decline" in agriculture to the fact that its management is now entrusted to slaves and the aristocracy no longer runs its own estates (I choose this treatise as an example because it falls within the period of this study). On the important police function of a landlord's visits, see ibid., 1.1.18–20; for this reason, it is convenient to have an estate near town. See Rathbone 1991, 84–86, on Appianus (the owner of the estate); he is an absentee landlord, but appears sporadically on the estate, usually to berate the management for some lapse. Note, however, that the estate manager was a landowner in his own right and the unit managers were free men, perhaps rather well off; ibid., 59, 81.

ploited by some.[7] Only one example of a calculation designed to aid an investment decision survives, and it is notorious: Columella's effort to prove that wine-growing is more profitable than lending at 6 percent interest (note, again, the choices).[8] Columella's impression that wine is the most profitable crop is probably based more on the tradition that this is so than on his own calculations.[9]

It is beyond doubt that landlords were interested in the profitability of their estates; and thus for example land being considered for purchase should be in an amenable climate, close to markets, fruitful; it should have roads, water, plenty of tenants, and nice neighbors.[10] But it would be a mistake to assume that Roman economic decisions—or modern ones, for that matter—were purely about money. To realize the importance of moral, social, and political factors one must look no further than the preface to Columella's treatise *De re rustica*, where he argues that agriculture is the best way of making money because it is the most moral, or the letters of Pliny the Younger, who is driven by the demands of patronage to an astonishing variety of methods of simply giving his money away.[11] Even "purely" economic decisions may have had priorities in view that were different from what the complexity of the modern market requires. There was a long tradition that Roman farms ought to be self-sufficient.[12] The Egyptian farm described above, with its internal-transport system, is a good example of what a well-run estate ought to

7. Pliny's revenue came mostly from land, with a small percentage from the interest on loans, and this seems to be typical (Duncan-Jones 1974, 19–21; cf. Pliny *Ep.* 10.54.1–2, where he asks Trajan whether he should force loans of municipal funds on the Bithynians since there is little opportunity to purchase real estate [*praedia*]). *Contra*, see D'Arms 1981, arguing that the senatorial aristocracy engaged in a broad variety of economic activities.

8. Duncan-Jones (1974, 39–48) argues that Columella's calculations are misleading because they leave out important factors such as amortization and building and equipment costs; *contra*, see Carandini (1983, 186–194), who attempts to defend Columella's calculations.

9. Cato *Agr.* 1.7; Pliny (*HN* 14.47–52), in a passage reminiscent of Columella, claims that wine is more profitable than trade with the Far East. Cf. Duncan-Jones 1974, 34–38.

10. See de Neeve 1985 on the factors affecting the value of land, arguing that they reflect an essentially capitalist or market-oriented economy rather than a peasant one. Most of them are listed in Columella 1.3.

11. Pliny endows buildings and foundations, gives cash to friends, makes interest-free loans, and sells an estate below market price; including the provisions of his will, the total in *public* gifts of *known amounts only* comes to 3,966,666 sesterces (Duncan-Jones 1974, 31; on Pliny's private gifts, ibid., 28–29; for the estate sold below market price, to Corellia, Pliny *Ep.* 7.11 and 7.14). On the other hand, Pliny's social position means that inheritance from his friends is a very significant source of income (Duncan-Jones, op. cit., 21–22).

12. Finley 1985, 108–110; Whittaker (1985, 57–65) discusses the implications of the self-sufficiency principle for far-flung estates.

be like if self-sufficiency was perceived as part of the key to profitability. This was a complex system run according to principles that might seem out of place in the modern world but were quite at home in the Roman empire.

We might speculate that the Roman aristocracy ran its empire like it ran its farms. Like a good paterfamilias, the emperor kept accounts, which allowed him to keep track of income and expenses,[13] and ideally to maximize the former and minimize the latter; they may not, however, have allowed very complex calculations, nor would these necessarily be appropriate in a system of limited choices. As in the case with Roman agriculture, it is often difficult to separate political, social, and moral considerations from fiscal ones. In any case, of all the government's expenses, the most significant was certainly the army.[14]

The system created by Augustus involved a permanent standing army, of fixed size, paid for by a permanent flow of revenues. If the size of the army was relatively small and it expanded only gradually, this was possibly because it was the largest force the empire could afford. Indeed, much of the evidence already discussed in chapter 3 supports the idea that Augustus could pay for the twenty-eight legions he kept under arms only with difficulty. Part of the problem seems to have been financing the *praemia,* cash bonuses for veterans on retirement. The large number of soldiers he demobilized early in his reign were paid off, according to Dio, with the booty from Egypt (51.4.8). But further lucrative conquests were not forthcoming. In A.D. 6, Augustus created a special military treasury to pay veterans' bonuses, to be financed by a 5 percent tax on inheritances.[15] The tax, which affected landed citizens, was predictably unpopular; seven years later, amid a general uproar, he threatened to impose a property tax instead.[16] Terms of service for legionaries, originally fixed at sixteen years—the traditional period of liability under the Republic—were raised to twenty and gradually lengthened to twenty-five, perhaps to save money on *praemia.*[17] Large

---

13. SHA *Had.* 20.11, and see below.

14. On the imperial budget in the Principate, see recently Duncan-Jones 1994, chap. 3.

15. On the *aerarium militare,* see Corbier 1977. The literary evidence is Cass. Dio 55.25, Suet. *Aug.* 49.4, and *RGDA* 17.

16. Cass. Dio 56.28. Later Nerva and Trajan would win lengthy praise from Pliny for limiting the effects of the inheritance tax by exempting near relatives (*Pan.* 37–40).

17. See above, chap. 3, pp. 84–85. In Tac. *Ann.* 1.8, Tiberius refuses to abolish the 1 percent sales tax because "the military treasury depended on this revenue; all the same the state was unequal to the burden unless veterans were dismissed in their twentieth year of service"; thus the temporary concessions of the mutiny of A.D. 14 were revoked.

numbers of legionaries were settled in colonies, especially in the provinces, in lieu of cash payment—again, possibly to save money.[18] Auxiliaries, perhaps, got no *praemia* at all.[19]

Pay was fixed at nine hundred sesterces per year for legionaries, and it was not raised until the reign of Domitian. A large percentage of this was deducted for clothing, equipment, and food.[20] Opinions vary as to whether the military salary was high or low—that is, whether the Roman soldier was well provided for in the early Principate.[21] Certainly there was a very serious mutiny of the Pannonian legions on the death of Augustus in A.D. 14. We need not believe every nuance of Tacitus' highly rhetorical account of the mutiny to be convinced that it was mainly about money. The complaints and demands of the soldiers, as they appear in the speech of the rabble-rousing Percennius, touch on several of the points mentioned above and are worth quoting at some length:

18. Forni (1953, 38–41) argued that colonization was a cheap alternative to cash *praemia*. It depends on whether lands were paid for or not, and how much was paid. Corbier (1977, 204–207) questions Forni's conclusion, and certainly early settlements in Italy, if land was paid for at market price, would have been more costly than the cash settlement; veterans may have demanded these terms (cf. Cass. Dio 54.25.5). But most of Augustus' colonies were in the provinces, where land was perhaps cheaper or, possibly, not paid for at all; it may be meaningful that Augustus in *RGDA* 16.1 records that he spent, in 30 B.C. and 14 B.C., 600 million sesterces on lands in Italy and 260 million sesterces on provincial lands (see Brunt 1971, 337, with n. 3). Mann (1983) points out that colonies in newly conquered territory, like Camulodunum, were cost-free since the land was confiscated from the inhabitants (60–61; cf. Tacitus' description of the foundation of Camulodunum [*Ann.* 12.32]). He notes, however, that full advantage was not taken of these opportunities.

19. Brunt (1950, 66–67) argues that auxiliaries must have been paid *praemia*, or traces of their loud complaints would remain. Corbier (1977, 207–208) points out that the most specific source on the subject, Cassius Dio, makes it clear that only citizen troops (πολῖται —i.e., legionaries) qualified for *praemia* (54.25.5–6 and 55.23.1). Alston (1994) argues that auxiliaries were paid equally and generally treated on a parity with legionaries, and thus presumably received *praemia* as well, but evidence is lacking.

20. On pay, see recently M. A. Speidel 1992 and Alston 1994; on deductions, M. A. Speidel, op. cit., 93–94, 97–98; and see Alston, op. cit., 121–122. Tacitus mentions only clothing and equipment (*Ann.* 1.17, quoted below), but it seems clear that food was deducted as well. The deductions seem to be excessive compared to the price of the items (Brunt 1950, 59), but this is, of course, very hard to prove. At some point in the second century deductions ceased, but soldiers may still have been required to purchase their food at this point (M. A. Speidel, op. cit., 97–98).

21. E.g., it is the impression of Brunt (1974, 95) that pay was modest and unappealing to recruits; G. R. Watson (1956, 338–339) and M. A. Speidel (1992, 96–97) point out that all their basic needs were taken care of and some soldiers accumulated savings; Alston (1994, 121–122, and 1995, 103–108) argues that pay rates left only a modest profit after deductions for supplies but that this was enough to attract recruits and, especially in the depressed economic conditions of rural Egypt, to make them substantial citizens on retirement.

Old men, most with bodies mutilated by wounds, were enduring thirty or forty years of service. . . .[22] And if one survived so many disasters with his life, he was then dragged to far-off lands (*diversas in terras*), where under the name of "fields" he received marshy swamps or barren mountain lands. Indeed, military service was inherently difficult, and profitless: body and soul were reckoned at ten asses per day; and from this the cruelty of the centurion was bought off and exemptions from duty were purchased. But blows and wounds, harsh winter, laborious summer, cruel war, or barren peace were eternal. There would be no relief, unless men joined the service under fixed rules, so that they earned a denarius per day, and the sixteenth year of service brought an end to it, and they were not kept under the standards any longer than that, but their *praemium* was paid in cash in the same camp. (*Ann.* 1.17)

It is noteworthy that, whatever coloring Tacitus puts on the mutiny, at least some of the mutineers' basic demands must have seemed reasonable to his readers; sixteen years, for example, was the traditional term of service and the one originally established by Augustus himself. A denarius (four sesterces) per day would have seemed, to an Italian, only a slightly generous "living wage"; it was famously, in Palestine, the wage received by vineyard workers.[23]

It was the emperor's responsibility to balance the budget. Good emperors, like Augustus, kept records of the empire's main revenues and expenses.[24] Later, it would seem that Augustus had invented the imperial budget in the same way he had "invented" Rome's frontiers. The testament he left, which detailed Rome's annual revenues and expenses, was written, according to Tacitus, *sua manu*, in his own hand (*Ann.* 1.11). But Suetonius tells us that to his "summary of the whole empire" he added "the names of the slaves and freedmen from whom the accounts could be exacted" (*Aug.* 101.4). Already we see a special office devoted to keeping track of the imperial budget; this is the secretary *a rationibus*,

22. This is attested in inscriptions (Forni 1953, 38 and app. 2, table II).

23. Alston 1995, 105–108, suggesting an annual "living wage" of three hundred denarii, though Martial, for example, would have considered this unacceptable. But he suggests that especially in Egypt, military pay rates were considered generous. On wages, see also Harl 1996, 275–279; and see Sperber 1974, 101–102, for a wage list from Palestinian sources. Here, daily wages of one to two drachmas, rarely less, are well attested. On vineyard workers, see Matt. 20:2.

24. On the emperor's responsibility, see Pliny *Pan.* 40; it is characteristic of a bad emperor, Nero, that he wastes money and keeps no *ratio impensarum*, "expense account" (Suet. *Ner.* 30.1). In the beginning of his reign, Gaius publishes the *rationes imperii*, "accounts of the empire," which Tiberius had not done (Suet. *Gaius* 16.1). For further references, see MacMullen 1976, 121–122, with n. 76; on imperial records, discussed below, Nicolet 1988, 120–123.

the secretary of accounts. One of these is the subject of a eulogy by the poet Statius, who describes his duties: "Now to him alone was entrusted the records of the sacred treasure, the riches received from all peoples, the revenues from the great world," including the Spanish and Dalmatian mines, the grain harvests of Africa and Egypt, and other resources; he balances these against the major expenses: "how much Roman arms under every sky demand," and how much must be spent on the people (perhaps for *congiaria,* handouts on special occasions), temples, aqueducts, forts, and roads; how much gold to allot to Domitian's famous gilded ceiling, and how much to coin (*Silv.* 3.3.99–105). The historian Appian must have relied on these records for the last book of his *Roman History,* which has unfortunately disappeared, and in which he promised to relate "the size of their army and the tribute that they collect from each province, and what they spend on naval garrisons, and other things of that sort" (*Praef.* 15). It is noteworthy that all of these references seem to indicate the critical importance of military expenses in the budget. Both Suetonius and Appian see a natural link between the size of the empire's army and its revenues; Statius lists the army first among the empire's expenses.

This close relationship between revenues and the army is perceived by other sources;[25] it appears, for example, in the famous speech of Maecenas in Dio's history. He recommends that Augustus keep a standing professional army permanently stationed in the provinces, to be financed by a combination of interest collected on loans from the imperial treasury and taxation. He continues:

Then [it is proper] for you to calculate these [revenues] and everything else that can predictably be added from the mines or from elsewhere, and against them to calculate not only military expenses but all the other things by which the state is well governed, and, besides this, whatever it will be necessary to spend on sudden campaigns or other things of the kind that usually arise on the spur of the moment (52.28.4–5).

It was clearly Dio's impression that the main, though not the only, purpose of taxation was to pay for the army. This impression is shared by, for example, Tacitus and Ulpian, both of whom, like Dio, see a close link between the army and taxes—or more specifically the direct tax on land, *tributum.*[26]

25. For this observation and references, see Crawford 1975, 561 n. 4; MacMullen 1976, 101 n. 18.

26. Tac. *Hist.* 4.74, in the famous speech of Cerialis: "no peace . . . can be had without arms, no arms without pay, no pay without tribute"; Ulp. *Dig.* 50.16.27: "and no

Attempts have been made to estimate the total amount spent, per year, on the army.[27] The answer of course depends on how large we imagine the army to be and how much we believe soldiers were paid in each period. A recent study, using manpower figures somewhat higher than the numbers proposed in chapter 3, suggests that pay for legionaries and auxiliaries plus retirement bonuses for legionaries amounted to about 493 million sesterces under Augustus and perhaps 643 million sesterces under the Antonines, after Domitian had raised legionary base pay. This number would have grown dramatically with further pay increases under Severus and Caracalla, so that the yearly cost of the army and *praemia* for the legionaries under the reign of the latter would have been around 1,127 million sesterces.[28] While these figures assume an army of roughly half a million—probably too large, at least before Severus—nevertheless this may be offset if indeed, as one scholar suggests, auxiliary troops were paid on the same scale as legionaries, and not at the rate of five-sixths used in the calculations summarized here, or at the lower fractions previously imagined—rates that must be deduced entirely from papyrological evidence, for we have no literary references to the pay of auxiliaries at all.[29] It is also possible that figures on the later end of the time line should be revised upward if, as one argument contends, Severus doubled base pay for legionaries to twenty-four hundred sesterces per year, and Caracalla again raised it to thirty-six hundred sesterces—not to twenty-four hundred sesterces, as previously supposed.[30] Furthermore, we must somehow include the fact that Severus seems to

---

doubt tribute is so called because it is a contribution (*intributio*) or because it is given (*tribuatur*) to the soldiers." See A. R. Birley 1981, 39.

27. E.g., Callu (1969, 310–311) estimates 300 million sesterces under Augustus, 900 million under Severus; Hopkins (1980, 124–125) arrives at 445 million sesterces for the army of Augustus for pay and *praemia;* A. R. Birley (1981) estimates 800 million sesterces in pay only for the army of Severus; Campbell (1984, 161–169) estimates 350–380 million sesterces per year until Domitian's pay raise; MacMullen (1984) arrives at 300 million sesterces under Augustus and 576 million under the Antonines; Harl (1996, table 9.2) estimates about 240 million sesterces in A.D. 9 and about 926 million under Caracalla for payroll only; retirement expenses are also calculated (ibid., table 9.3).

28. Duncan-Jones 1994, 33–37, with table 3.3.

29. Alston (1994) argues persuasively that auxiliaries must have been paid at the same rates as legionaries if basic deductions were to be covered with anything left over. Duncan-Jones (1994, 33–37) uses the study of M. A. Speidel (1992), who argued that auxiliaries received five-sixths of legionary pay.

30. M. A. Speidel 1992; see table on p. 88 with notes 8–10. Duncan-Jones (1994, 33 n. 2 and table 3.2) bases his calculations on the more traditional scheme.

have begun the practice of providing soldiers with free food.[31] In 238, Maximinus Thrax doubled pay again (Herodian 6.8.8).

For the sake of argument, let us assume that a figure recorded in Cassius Dio's history (78[79].36.3) is correct, and that Caracalla's pay raises cost the empire 70 million denarii; if the raise was one-third, then the cost in pay of Caracalla's army after the raise was 280 million denarii or 1,120 million sesterces, a figure that is perhaps too low if legionaries (and, presumably, auxiliaries—though again, evidence is lacking) were paid four times more under his reign than under Augustus and the army itself was larger. But precision is, of course, impossible. We should remember, for example, that the figures calculated above are notional in the sense that an indeterminable but high percentage of a soldier's pay was deducted for food and equipment early in the period under discussion;[32] thus a substantial portion, decreasing over time, of the military budget was in kind, not cash. And the issue of donatives, distributions that increased in size and perhaps in frequency as time went on, must still be considered.[33]

So far the discussion has been relatively straightforward. However, at least two serious difficulties arise at this point. First of all, the schedule of military pay raises is puzzling. They are the most important factor in the military budget, since the size of the army increased only gradually. Military pay increased rapidly under Severus and his successors, but before that the only raise had been a relatively moderate one of one-third under Domitian. It is possible to speculate that this pattern reflected the pace of inflation; but it is very difficult to draw conclusions about prices in the Roman empire based on the very scanty and problematic evidence. It seems clear that prices gradually doubled or tripled over the first two centuries A.D., but when exactly they began to rise steeply (before skyrocketing toward the end of the third century) is difficult to say; this was perhaps not until after 238 or so.[34] Before that date there is

31. Develin 1971, 692–695, updating the arguments of van Berchem 1937. The main evidence is Cass. Dio 77[78].28.2.

32. See M. A. Speidel 1992, 93–94, 97–98.

33. On donatives, see below.

34. On inflation, see recently Duncan-Jones 1994, 25–29, with tables 2.1–2.5; the average of attested costs rose by 177 percent from A.D. 100 to 220, but evidence is very patchy. See also id. 1990, 143–155, on wheat prices in Egypt; these roughly doubled between 100 and 200 and then rose steeply sometime before 246. But note that a number of papyri from the Heroninos archive recording prices of wheat show no rise between 250 and 260 (Rathbone 1991, 403, 464–466), though the average (16 drachmas per artaba) is higher than averages for the second century. The study of Lendon (1990) indicates that

no clear relationship between inflation and military pay raises at all, nor do the literary sources perceive one; they describe the third-century increases in political and moral terms.

Second, it is not obvious why Augustus should have had such difficulty financing his army in the first place; nor, if he did, why Caracalla could afford to pay soldiers at four times his rate. Revenues had probably increased in the meantime. But these revenues are extremely difficult to estimate.[35] It has been argued that the empire's national product may have amounted to around 20 billion sesterces.[36] Only a very small percentage of that, levied from the provinces in taxes, should have been enough.[37]

Nevertheless, extracting this small percentage was difficult. Huge amounts of the tribute would go unpaid in any given year; emperors would remit arrears or burn records, as gestures of generosity.[38] The

---

the price of wheat and barley in Egypt rose by a factor of about 2.5 between the reign of Claudius and that of Marcus Aurelius (pp. 109–111, with chart 2 on p. 120). The influential theory of Heichelheim that prices rose sharply in the reign of Commodus as a result of a military pay raise by that emperor and a devaluation of the denarius is no longer tenable; see the study of Pekáry (1959, 446–448). The latter argues for a sharp increase under Severus, but much of the evidence (the cost of the ritual meals of the Arval Brethren, fines for grave robbing) seems very problematic; see the criticism of Crawford (1975, 567). For the date of 238, when the reintroduced *antoninianus* began to drive the denarius out of circulation, see n. 63 below.

35. Frank (1933–1940, 5:4–18) estimated imperial revenues as 450 million sesterces under Augustus and 1,200 to 1,500 million sesterces under Vespasian (ibid., 44–55), based on the scanty literary evidence conveniently summarized by Hopkins (1980, n. 45) and Duncan-Jones (1994, app. 4). Hopkins' own estimate of imperial revenues is 825 million sesterces, but this too seems very arbitrary; cf. MacMullen 1987, 744–745, and id. 1988, 39 n. 142. It seems clear that the government did not collect all the tribute it was supposed to—that is, that revenues were perhaps 5 percent of national product despite much higher advertised rates of tribute (e.g., official rates in Egypt were approximately 25 percent in grain tax alone [Duncan-Jones 1994, 54–55]). This is of course a low rate of taxation by modern standards and even, perhaps, by preindustrial standards; see Goldsmith 1987, 48.

36. Goldsmith 1984; findings are summarized in id. 1987, 35. This estimate is based on a population of 55 million and an average product of 375 sesterces per head.

37. See MacMullen 1987, 744–745.

38. Ibid., 736–739; Brunt 1981, 169–170; Harl 1996, 231–234. On remissions by Trajan, see Pliny *Pan.* 29.4, 40.3; on Hadrian, *ILS* 309, Cass. Dio 69.8.1, SHA *Had.* 7.6, and see Hannestad 1988, 192; coins show the lictor burning records, with the inscription "Reliqua vetera HS novies mill(ies) abolita" [*RIC* Hadrian 590]; on Marcus Aurelius, Cass. Dio 71 [72].32.2: "He canceled the debts of all those who owed anything to the imperial or public treasury for the past forty-six years, not including the sixteen years of Hadrian. And he ordered all the records about them to be burned in the forum." On remissions, see also Duncan-Jones 1994, 59–63 arguing that taxes were reviewed, and often remitted, on a regular schedule.

amount of the debt canceled by the emperor Hadrian was 900 million sesterces.[39] Cities might be granted relief or even immunity if they could produce a very eloquent orator to plead their cause; tribute might be lowered or even canceled at the beginning of an emperor's reign.[40] The popularity to be gained from such gestures was of course immense. But the raising of taxes is much less frequently attested, and only Vespasian is said to have raised the tribute, doubling it in some cases.[41] The bewildering plethora of types of tribute assessed at various rates and in various ways in different provinces, systems often preserved almost unchanged from previous regimes, and the massive documentation they generated, did not facilitate adjustments.[42] New taxes on citizens were sometimes invented, like Augustus' 5 percent inheritance tax, or the innovations of Vespasian, Commodus, or Caracalla.[43] But they provoked the resentment of the most powerful classes.[44] Good emperors (like good landlords) were supposed to balance the budget by cutting expenses; Augustus and Nerva both appointed senatorial commissions to

39. *ILS* 309, and see previous note.

40. MacMullen 1987, 737–738. See, e.g., Cass. Dio 71[72].19.1.

41. Suet. *Vesp.* 16.1, Cass. Dio 66.8.3. Significantly, the two tax increases attested in Egypt (Duncan-Jones 1994, 56) occur precisely in the early years of Vespasian's reign, and in the reign of Severus, which will be discussed below.

42. On diversity in the land tribute, see MacMullen 1976, 132–134; Neesen 1980, 84–98; Brunt 1981, 325–327; Duncan-Jones 1990, 187–198. Evidence from the imperial period is scanty and confused; the notice of Hyginus the land surveyor is important: "For land subject to tax (*agri vectigales*) has many conditions. In some provinces they pay a fixed part of the crop, some paying fifths and others sevenths, others paying money according to the assessment of the land. For certain values are assigned to lands, as for example in Pannonia there are first-rate arable lands and second-rate arable lands, meadows, acorn-bearing woods and regular woods, pasture. The tax on all of these lands is assessed per *iugum* according to its fertility. Unlawful manipulation [*usurpatio*] of the assessment of these [lands] through false declarations must be prevented by diligence in the measurements" (Lachmann, Blume, and Rudorff 1848–1852, 1:205–206; see Duncan-Jones, op. cit., 187–188). The inflexibility of the system is noted by Callu (1969, 189–199) and A. H. M. Jones (1974, 171–172), who credit Diocletian with the invention of the flexible budget by creating the units of *iugum* and *caput*.

43. On Vespasian, see Cass. Dio 66.8.3; on Commodus, ibid., 72[73].16; Herodian 2.4.7; on Caracalla, Cass. Dio 77[78].9; cf. MacMullen 1987, 741.

44. On the *vicesima hereditatum*, see above; the 1 percent sales tax was equally loathed (Tac. *Ann.* 1.78), and Tiberius eventually lowered it to 0.5 percent after annexing Cappadocia. Commodus' tax on the senatorial class, of two *aurei* per year on Roman senators and five denarii for municipal senators, is described in terms of the utmost outrage by Cassius Dio (72[73].16.3), who writes that Commodus spent it all on wild beasts and gladiators. Caracalla's innovations also mainly affected the wealthy, according to the same source; in addition he doubled the inheritance tax and the emancipation tax, this time spending the money on wild beasts, horses, and the soldiers (77[78].9). See Corbier 1988, 263–265.

do just that.[45] Maecenas' advice to Augustus urges taxation as a last resort, and only with apology (Cass. Dio 52.28–29).

Emperors in need of money, for whatever reason, might resort to judicial condemnation and confiscation from the otherwise virtually untaxed senatorial class, or from the provincial aristocracy, a practice that appears to have grown in extent and ingenuity as time progressed, reaching a climax under Severus[46]—despite the fact that nothing was more likely to provoke outrage among the emperor's closest associates and guarantee a bad name in the history books. Many emperors sold their property at auction—one of the few methods of raising money that was actually approved of.[47] Alternately, one could levy special taxes on the provinces, including the "gold crown" tax, traditionally donated on the occasion of a victory. The crown gold collected by Claudius at his British triumph was of legendary and baffling proportions (Pliny *HN* 33.54), and at least one emperor was suspected of declaring triumphs just to collect the tax.[48] One could also resort to levies in kind *extra ordinem*—that is, direct requisition, ideally with state compensation but sometimes compared by the sources to "pillaging"; this method was especially useful for the supply of the army, and under Severus it seems to have become institutionalized as the *annona militaris*.[49] Again, good emperors were not supposed to do this sort of

45. Cass. Dio 55.25.6; Pliny *Pan.* 62.2.

46. Millar 1977, 163–174, on proscription and confiscation; also Duncan-Jones 1994, 5–7; on Severus, ibid., 15–16.

47. E.g., Nerva (Cass. Dio 68.2.2), Marcus (Zonar. 12.1), Pertinax (Cass. Dio 74.5.4), and Macrinus (ibid., 78[79].12.5); see MacMullen 1976a, 24–25, with n. 11; Duncan-Jones 1994, 10.

48. Cass. Dio 77[78].9.2 on Caracalla. On the gold crown, see Callu 1969, 319–320, and Neesen 1980, 142–145; papyri indicate that Elagabalus collected it every month.

49. On extraordinary levies in kind under the Principate, see the discussion of Neesen (1980, 104–116). The question of the nature of Severus' innovations is a difficult one, which I leave to those more competent to address it. Van Berchem (1937) originally argued that Severus, in an age of inflation, invented a new system of payment in kind for the army, combined with new taxes in kind on the provinces. Many of the points of his seminal discussion are still valid, but some elements of the argument are now open to question (cf. van Berchem 1977)—for example, the argument about inflation (see above); it seems unlikely that significant inflation was happening before Severus. The evidence that Severus supplemented soldiers' salaries with payment in grain is not as strong as it once was, though a passage from Cassius Dio seems conclusive (Develin 1971). It seems clear, however, that under Severus and his successors, levies in kind *extra ordinem*—that is, beyond the regular tribute—became much more common and began to accumulate some of the bureaucratic baggage of a regular tax (MacMullen 1976, 130); this way of raising funds had always been especially useful for army supply and especially in wartime (see below); Severus' increasing resort to it should be viewed in this light. See the discussion of Adams (1976, 237–242).

thing;[50] it is Nero or Caligula who exhausts the provinces with extraordinary levies.[51] And provincial levies, depending on where and how they were carried out, could be carried only so far without provoking a barrage of protest, flight from the land, or outright revolt, sometimes very violent.[52]

Perhaps this last point deserves attention. The Romans certainly believed that the tribute was the empire's most onerous and deeply resented burden on provincials. Bato's reply, when asked why the Pannonians had revolted (in A.D. 6), was famous: "you yourselves are responsible, for you send as guardians over your flocks not dogs or shepherds, but wolves" (Cass. Dio 56.16.3; cf. 55.29.11). The speech that Cassius Dio composes for Boudicca emphasizes taxes above all as the cause of her rebellion (62.3.3).[53]

The Frisians, a tribe on the far side of the Rhine accustomed to paying a tribute of ox hides, rebelled when the Roman governor demanded very large ox hides instead of the usual moderate-sized ones; they nailed the soldiers who were collecting the tribute to the gibbet (Tac. *Ann.* 4.72). In the reign of Domitian, the Nasamones, a Numidian tribe, were provoked to revolt "when payments were exacted from them by force." They killed all the tax collectors and defeated the governor of Numidia in battle; the governor, however, succeeded in annihilating the tribe, including "all the noncombatants"; the emperor boasted that he had "forbidden the Nasamones to exist" (Cass. Dio 67.4.6). Arrian seems to threaten similar measures against the Sanni, who have not been keeping up with their payments (*Peripl. M. Eux.* 11): "once they were tributary to the Romans, but now they engage in piracy and do not accurately pay the tribute. But now, God willing, they will accurately pay it, or I will

50. See Pliny's praise of Trajan in *Pan.* 29: "Crops are not seized from vainly protesting allies as though from the enemy, and carried off to rot in granaries . . . nor do they [sc., allies] fail to pay traditional taxes [*vetera tributa*] because they are oppressed by new indictions; the fisc buys what it is proper to buy." See the discussion by Neesen (1980, 106–107). Agricola is also admirable for similar reasons; see Tac. *Agr.* 19.4, where he "made the exaction of grain and tribute easier by the fairness (*aequalitate*) of the obligations."

51. On Nero, see Suet. *Ner.* 38.3; on Gaius (Caligula), Cass. Dio 59.21.

52. On tax resistance generally, see Corbier 1988; on flight, MacMullen 1987, 743; and note Callu 1969, 317–318, for policy measures, beginning with Marcus Aurelius, designed to keep land under cultivation; on revolt, MacMullen, op. cit., 749; and see Brunt 1981, 170–171, for a full list of references; on resistance to the census and tribute in Judaea, see Millar 1993, 47–48. On the idea of tribute as a deeply resented mark of subjection, see also the interesting article of Shaw (1986) on the case of Mauretania Tingitana.

53. See also Tac. *Ann.* 3.40 (the speech of Sacrovir), *Agr.* 30–32 (the speech of Calgacus), and *Hist.* 4.73–74 (Cerialis to the Gauls).

destroy them."[54] There is more involved here than just money; tribute was not simply a way of generating revenue but a mark of subjection—a point we will return to.

Financial options were further limited by the imperial government's dependence on cash—that is, on gold and silver coin and thus ultimately on bullion. It has often been observed that the Roman state had no tradition of deficit spending—no borrowing from the private sector.[55] Surpluses are expressed as quantities of sesterces or denarii in the treasury. Thus Pertinax found only 1 million sesterces on his accession. He was forced to sell statues, horses, and furniture (Cass. Dio 73[74].5.4). Nerva and Marcus Aurelius were reduced to similar measures,[56] though Marcus is supposed to have found a substantial surplus of 2,700 million sesterces in the treasury on his accession (ibid., 73[74].8.3). Gaius found a surplus of 2,300 million sesterces and squandered it all on extravagances (ibid., 59.2). Nero, too, is said to have wasted Rome's revenues on his parties, games, and shows; Vespasian claimed to require 40 billion sesterces as a result—a figure that, as one scholar has pointed out, "resists explanation."[57]

Mystifying calculations, auctions of furniture, revels that consumed the tribute of entire provinces—[58]once again, it becomes clear that we face serious conceptual difficulties in any discussion of the imperial budget. To continue: the reliance on gold and silver coin may partially account for the concern, occasionally expressed in the ancient sources, about the drain of bullion out of the empire, especially to the east via the luxury trade—a concern, however, that is always framed in heavily moralizing terms;[59] properly Rome was in the business of taking precious metals away from barbarians, not giving them back. The income from mines must have been an important, even critical, source of revenue for the government. Pliny the Elder records a figure for the gold production of the mines in Spain: "Some have recorded (*quidam prodiderunt*) that Asturia and Callaecia and Lusitania produce in this way

54. ἀλλὰ νῦν γε διδόντος θεοῦ ἀκριβώσουσιν, ἢ ἐξελοῦμεν αὐτούς.

55. E.g., A. H. M. Jones 1974, 198; Walker 1976–1978, 3:138; Hopkins 1980, 122; on surplus and deficit in the imperial budget generally, see Duncan-Jones 1994, chap. 1.

56. Cass. Dio 68.2.2; Zonar. 12.1; SHA *Marcus* 17.4; cf. MacMullen 1976, 101 n.7.

57. MacMullen 1987, 744; Suet. *Vesp.* 16.3.

58. Caligula spends 10 million sesterces on one banquet, "the tribute of three provinces" (Sen. *Helv.* 10.4; cf. Frank 1933–1940, 5:52).

59. Pliny *HN* 6.102; Tac. *Ann.* 3.53 (Tiberius laments that "for the sake of jewels [for women] our money [*pecuniae nostrae*] is carried off to foreign or hostile peoples"); Dio Chrys. *Or.* 79.5–6. Veyne 1979 argues that the concern was not strictly economic or "mercantilist."

twenty thousand pounds of gold per year"—the equivalent of some 80 million sesterces annually, if it is accurate (*HN* 33.78). But mines become exhausted in time; the only remedy for this is new conquest. War could also, sometimes, provide massive infusions of precious metal in the form of booty. This will be discussed in the second half of this chapter.

On the other hand, gaps between revenue and expenses could be covered by the simple expedient of devaluing the currency, especially the silver currency. It is significant that the overwhelming trend of the silver content of the denarius in the imperial period is downward.[60] The most significant debasements occur precisely where, so far, we should expect them—at the end, beginning under Marcus Aurelius and gaining speed under the Severans, when army pay increased threefold. By the end of Severus' reign, the silver content of the denarius had plummeted to about 55 percent.[61] Caracalla invented an entirely new coin, called the *antoninianus,* which weighed one and a half times the denarius and seems to have been tariffed at two denarii.[62]

Whether these changes were inflationary is difficult to say. It is clear that at least until the reign of Severus and perhaps until the mid–third century the devaluation of the coinage produced no comparable rise in prices. Thus older, purer denarii continued to circulate along with newer, debased coins, in flagrant violation of Gresham's law, until 238.[63]

The situation is even more complicated if we try to calculate and include evidence about total coin production, as Richard Duncan-Jones recently has done.[64] Devaluations often seem to coincide with coin-production peaks, but not always; devaluations might reflect shortages of bullion as well as increases in expenses. Cash revenue from whatever

60. See Walker 1976–1978, 3:140, for graph; cf. ibid., 59, on the great debasement of 194–195; also Duncan-Jones 1994, 223–231, with table 15.6 and fig. 15.6.

61. Walker 1976–1978, 3:59.

62. Ibid., 3:62–64; and see Duncan-Jones 1994, 138–139, on the *antoninianus.*

63. For the example of Egypt, discussing prices and their relation to the devaluation of the Alexandrian silver tetradrachm, see Lendon 1990. On Gresham's law, see Duncan-Jones 1994, 102; however, profitable state withdrawals of purer, older coins, including Trajan's famous recall of 107, did accelerate the "natural" wastage rate (ibid., 198–200). See further Walker 1976–1978, 3:139–140; he contends that the *antoninianus,* reintroduced in 238, quickly drove the denarius out of circulation but concludes that Gresham's law was not in operation before then. Bolin (1958, 60–61) argues that around the year 200 some bronze coinage was driven out of circulation. I am not qualified to judge these matters, but it is clear from Bolin's table on p. 52 that as far as the silver coinage is concerned, significant percentages of coins from the reigns of Nerva, Trajan, and Hadrian continued to circulate under Caracalla and later. On inflation, see n. 34 above.

64. Duncan-Jones 1994, chaps. 8–9. See Howgego 1992 on the limitations of quantitative numismatics.

source might fluctuate wildly from year to year.[65] Some demands on the budget were not fiscal at all; at accession, for example, coin output was typically high, perhaps not only because of increased expenditures but for reasons of public image—the need to flood the market with coins showing the face of the new emperor.[66] In the reign of Marcus, high coin production seems to coincide with a cycle of veteran retirements, confirming the importance of military expenses in the budget.[67]

Some controversy exists about the reasons behind Roman manipulations of the coinage and the nature of Roman thinking about the economy. Most scholars explain devaluations as a more or less straightforward effort to meet expenses with insufficient funds; but an argument also exists for a monetary policy behind certain devaluations, designed to stabilize the gold-to-silver ratio.[68] Related to this is the argument that the Romans developed a theoretical "quantitative" understanding of money in the economy.[69] Roman ideas about price and money are very scantily attested. Some ancient sources do perceive correlations between surpluses or shortages of coin on the one hand and prices and interest rates on the other; concern here is always about land prices and interest rates and how they affect the propertied classes in Italy and in Rome.[70] While it might make sense to a modern observer that long-term inflation required pay raises for the soldiers, it is not obvious that it seemed so to the Roman emperors or that inflation was in fact the reason for the pay raises. Nor is it obvious that Roman emperors expected devaluations to cause inflation (almost no reference to devaluations survives in ancient sources)[71] or that devaluations per se, whether or not

65. Duncan-Jones 1994, 141–143, on the sharp variations in output within reigns.

66. Ibid., 105, 127.

67. Id. 1990, 73–76.

68. A view now especially associated with Lo Cascio (1981), though he is not the first to make this type of argument; see especially Mickwitz 1932, 32–33, on Trajan's debasement. Walker (1976–1978, 3:106–148) argues that devaluations were a response to fiscal needs, and that the occasional attempts to restore the purity of the coinage were mainly moral efforts to win the approval of the senatorial elite.

69. For what follows, see Nicolet 1971.

70. Suet *Aug.* 41.2, *Tib.* 48; Cass. Dio 51.21.5; Tac. *Ann.* 6.17; Nicolet 1971, 1217–1218.

71. Only two passages refer to devaluations under the Principate. The first is to Nero's devaluation of the gold coinage; Pliny correctly notes that his gold coins were lighter than previously, but does not mention Nero's much more significant debasement of the denarius. This comes at the end of a long and interesting passage on the history of coinage (*HN* 33.42–46; see the commentary by Zehnacker [1983, 16–35]; also Nicolet 1984, 122–129; and id. 1988, 160–162). The second reference is from Cassius Dio, who writes that Caracalla paid off the barbarians who came to Rome to extort money from him in "true" gold; "but the money he provided to the Romans was adulterated (κίβδηλον), both the gold and the silver; for the former he made out of lead plated with silver, and the latter he

accompanied by an increase in total coin production, necessarily did so. Very striking, especially in the evidence from legal sources, is the psychological value placed on the image of the emperor that appeared on the coinage, which lent authority to the coin and guaranteed its value.[72] Roman coinage, including the silver coinage, unquestionably had a fiduciary element; thus the belief of the emperors that they could legislate the value of coins.[73] Nevertheless, we can guess that an emperor contemplating a 30 percent reduction in the silver content of the denarius might have anticipated negative consequences for the future. But Severus went through with it anyway.

Thus it is not clear either that inflation accounts for the pay raises of the third century or that the empire could afford these raises. The ancient sources are always critical of military pay raises, for a variety of reasons, including fiscal ones. According to Suetonius and Dio, Domitian was forced to reduce the number of the troops because of his pay raise; thus he "harmed the state greatly, having made its guardians too few, and expensive at that" (Cass. Dio 67.3.5). Suetonius adds that he paid for the increase by proscriptions and confiscations (*Dom.* 12.1–2), and by ruthless exactions from the provinces, including the vigorous prosecution of the special two-drachma tax on Jews.[74] Some provincials, including the Nasamones, revolted, as noted above (Cass. Dio 67.4.6).

Severus swamped Rome with troops, writes Dio, which was disruptive and too expensive. Furthermore, Severus "placed his hopes of safety not in the goodwill of his colleagues, but in their [the army's] strength" (74[75].2.3). Here another problem emerges: on the one hand, the emperor was obliged to buy the loyalty of the army; on the other, the aristocratic classes tended to resent money spent on troops that were after all supposed to be loyal to the emperor personally, not to them.[75] Caracalla was the worst offender. Following his father's famous advice (Cass. Dio 76[77].15.2), he lavished money on the troops—much more, as his ill-fated successor wrote to the city prefect shortly before his death, than the empire could afford (77[78].9.1; 78[79].36.2–3). There was another problem, too: Severus was supposedly the first to corrupt the discipline

---

made out of bronze plated with gold" (77[78].14.3–4). Caracalla did not in fact debase the gold coinage (though he lightened it slightly).

72. Lendon 1990, 112–119.

73. Ibid., 114–117.

74. On the Jewish tax, imposed after the revolt of 66–70, see Joseph. *BJ* 7.218 and Goodman 1987, 232.

75. On money and the loyalty of the army, see in general Kloft 1970, 104–110; Veyne 1976, 609–617; and Campbell 1984, 181–198.

of the army with his pay increase and other privileges (Herodian 3.8.4 – 5). The subject of discipline is an extraordinarily important one in all the sources, and will be discussed in the next chapter.

In any case, Macrinus tried to reverse most of Caracalla's innovations, restoring the inheritance tax and the emancipation tax to their previous rates (Cass. Dio 78[79].12.6), and "most importantly," he tried to reverse Caracalla's military pay raise, at least in the case of new recruits (78[79].12.6, 28.3 – 4) — a measure of which Cassius Dio approves in principle (78[79].29.1); but the army revolted, and Macrinus' reign dissolved in civil war. In a desperate attempt to repair the damage, the emperor offered a donative of twenty thousand sesterces per man (78[79].34.2).

By this time the need or desire to secure the loyalty of the army with money was causing the military budget to skyrocket, perhaps far beyond the state's capacity to pay for it. This process had begun back in the first century. The donatives left by Augustus and Tiberius in their wills — and paid by their successors — were modest, at least by the standards of the late Republic.[76] Claudius, however, was obliged, because of the circumstances of his accession, to pay fifteen thousand sesterces to the praetorians; Suetonius writes that he was "the first of the emperors to procure the loyalty of the army with a bribe."[77] Donatives became crucial issues during times of civil conflict. Galba promised a large donative but did not pay it; Tacitus describes the reaction of the army in tones resonant with moral censure: *laudata olim et militari fama celebrata severitas eius angebat aspernantis veterem disciplinam* . . . , ("his severity, once praised and extolled in his reputation with the army, was irksome to those who rejected old-fashioned discipline").[78] In any case, his parsimony cost Galba his throne (and, ultimately, his life); and the same thing was to happen to Pertinax in 193. As part of a conservative, cost-cutting economic program designed to appeal to the senatorial aristocracy,[79] he offered only a modest donative of twelve thousand sesterces;

76. On donatives and their amounts as attested in literary sources, see Campbell 1984, 165–171; Duncan-Jones 1994, app. 7. Augustus left three hundred sesterces to the legionaries and one thousand sesterces to the praetorians in his will; Tiberius left the same amounts (Suet. *Aug.* 101.2; Tac. *Ann.* 1.8; Suet. *Tib.* 76; Cass. Dio 59.2). Duncan-Jones (op. cit., chap. 8) argues that most coin hoards are in fact buried donatives.

77. *primus Caesarum fidem militis etiam praemio pigneratus* (*Claud.* 10.4).

78. *Hist.* 1.5; the amounts promised were thirty thousand sesterces for praetorians and five thousand for legionaries (Plut. *Galb.* 2).

79. Pertinax advocated fiscal parsimony, forswore confiscations, and auctioned Commodus' possessions (Cass. Dio 73[74].5); he also carried out an extraordinary (and short-lived) coinage reform that returned the denarius to the standard of Vespasian. This reform — and others like it (by Galba, Macrinus, etc.) — is convincingly explained as a moral

he had to sell Commodus' possessions to pay it (Cass. Dio 73[74].1.2–3, 73[74].5.4). In the end he was murdered by his troops. Cassius Dio goes on to describe, with the utmost repugnance, the subsequent "auction of the empire," which was sold by the praetorian guard to Didius Julianus in return for a donative of twenty five thousand sesterces per man (73[74].11).[80]

By now donatives regularly amounted to several times a year's salary. Beginning in 148 it is possible to see coinage devaluations associated with accession dates and important anniversaries—partly no doubt on account of the donatives, as well as the expensive games, shows, and gifts to the plebs required on these occasions, and the need for plenty of coins with the new emperor's face, which has been mentioned.[81] On one well-known occasion, Marcus Aurelius refused the soldiers' request for a donative on the grounds that it would have to be paid "out of the blood of your parents and relatives" (Cass. Dio 71[72].3.3). It is difficult to tell how much of his refusal was motivated by a real financial crisis and inability to pay,[82] and how much by the very firmly held beliefs of the aristocratic class that spending money on the soldiers was the wrong way to procure their loyalty, that it was also the easiest way to corrupt the all-important discipline of the army, and that raising taxes—or raising money by almost any other means—was a sign of avarice, associated with "bad" emperors. It is probably a mistake to try to separate these ideas. A Roman emperor, looking at the imperial budget, would have seen more than just the basic issues of how much cash lay in the trea-

---

appeal to the senatorial class rather than a "deflationary" policy (Walker 1976–1978, 3:127–128).

80. The loyalty of the praetorian guard was even more critical than that of the legionaries, for obvious reasons. Besides being better paid, they received donatives that were much higher, and in some cases only donatives to the praetorians are attested, though lower donatives to the rest of the army may have been granted at the same time; see Campbell 1984, 166–168, on Claudius' donative to the praetorians; Josephus attests that Claudius gave a donative to the provincial army as well (AJ 19.247).

81. See Walker 1976–1978, 3:124–125, on the debasement of 148; this was Antoninus Pius' decennalia and the nine hundredth anniversary of the founding of Rome, both of which were apparently celebrated on a lavish scale. See ibid., 3:125–126, on the debasement of 161, and p. 131 on Caracalla's debasement, shortly after Geta's murder. But Duncan-Jones (1994, 88–89) sees no cluster of coin hoards at the year 148, as would be expected if a donative had been given (see above, n. 76); coin hoards do, however, show a sharp increase in size under Marcus Aurelius, who supposedly gave twenty thousand sesterces to the praetorians and may have given proportionally large donatives to legionaries and auxiliaries as well (Cass. Dio 73[74].8.4).

82. See Pekáry 1959, 448–451, on the conflicting evidence about the fiscal situation in Marcus' reign.

sury, how much more he could safely extort from provincials or confiscate from the senatorial aristocracy, and how much he could devalue the currency that year to cover the deficit. He would also have seen a political imperative on one side—the need to buy the army's loyalty—and moral imperatives on the other, of the kind just described. To the degree that the emperor needed the support of members of his own class, these moral imperatives became political, too. Purely fiscal thinking, we may conclude, was rare. And the imperial budget, at first glance a relatively simple and straightforward system, emerges as a complex entity subject to sometimes extreme pressures—an aristocratic ethos that condemned almost every means of raising money; a provincial populace sometimes willing to risk outright revolt rather than submit to increased taxation; a dependence on raw bullion, of which the supply might fluctuate wildly; incalculable expenditures on conspicuous consumption and public handouts necessary to maintain the image and status of the emperor; and so forth. Within this system emperors innovated, sometimes ingeniously, sometimes—as in the case of the late devaluations of the denarius—with cavalier disregard for what they must have perceived as potentially disastrous consequences. It is on this precarious system that the empire's long-term military capability depended.

This was the situation even in peace. Of course, everything became much more complicated in times of war.

2. War

2.1. THE COSTS OF WAR

It is the not very surprising impression registered in our sources that wars were expensive. They exhausted the treasury; they oppressed the provinces.[83] A passage from Zonaras, probably based on Dio,

---

83. In the Pannonian revolt, according to Cassius Dio (56.16.4), "many men and a great deal of money also were lost; for a large number of legions were maintained for it, and only a little booty was taken." Prices rose during the civil war of 69 because of military expenses (Tac. *Hist.* 1.89); Mesopotamia proved a drain on the state because of the wars necessary to hold it (Cass. Dio 75.3.3); Severus lost much money and all his siege engines during the second siege of Hatra (ibid., 75[76].11.1); and he took on his expedition to Britain "χρήματα πάμπολλα" "a great deal of money" (76[77].11.2). Caracalla used his wars as an excuse for raising taxes (77[78].9.1). Recall also Maecenas' advice to Augustus, to calculate "not only military expenses but all the other things by which the state is well governed, and, besides this, whatever it will be necessary to spend on sudden campaigns or other things of the kind that usually arise on the spur of the moment" (Cass. Dio 52.28.5). See MacMullen 1976, 104; for the idea that wars oppress the provinces, see below.

praising the exemplary behavior of Marcus Aurelius illustrates the strain
that wars were supposed to put on the imperial budget:

Nevertheless, he did not extract money from the provinces because of this,
but once when he was at a loss for money, with wars pressing urgently, he
neither invented any new tax nor could he bear to ask anyone for money,
but he put all the treasures of the imperial residence in the forum, and the
adornments belonging to his wife, and he encouraged anyone who wanted
them to buy them. From this he gathered the money that he gave to the
soldiers. (Zonaras 12.1)

This source's impression that the main increase in expenses during
wartime was pay for the soldiers is, however, almost certainly wrong;
soldiers had to be paid in peacetime too, though some increase would
result from conscription to replenish depleted legions before a campaign. In fact, the main costs of war were in supply and transport, and
they fell most heavily on those provinces near the theater of operations
or through which large bodies of troops would have to march.[84]

Before moving on, it might be helpful to look at an example. Let us
very superficially tally only the most obvious costs of Germanicus' campaigns of A.D. 15 and 16 against the Chatti and Cherusci. The campaign
of 15, which apparently required all eight Rhine legions and ten thousand auxiliaries, involved in the first place the construction of roads and
bridges (Tac. Ann. 1.56); in a reverse the Romans lost numerous horses,
tools, tents, and medical supplies (ibid., 1.65); afterward, "the Gallic
provinces, the Spanish provinces, and Italy contended with each other
to replenish the losses of the army, offering arms, horses, and gold,
whatever was ready at hand for each" (1.71). By the time Germanicus set
out in 16, "the Gauls were exhausted from providing horses"; and weapons were still in short supply (2.5). He decided for logistical reasons
to transport troops and supplies by ship through the North Sea to the
Ems; he sent two officers to conduct a census in Gaul and ordered the
construction of a fleet of one thousand ships (2.6), a string of fortifications across the Rhine, and a bridge across the Ems (2.7–8). The
fleet was wrecked, and besides suffering substantial loss of life the army
was forced to jettison "horses, pack animals, baggage, and even weapons" (2.23).[85]

84. See MacMullen 1984 and id. 1976, 104–108, on the expenses of war; dissertations
on logistics by Adams (1976) and Roth (1990) are also important and will be referred to
below.
85. On the campaigns of Germanicus, A.D. 14–16, see recently Lehmann 1991; on the
census, ibid., n. 29.

It is clear that the main burden of supplying the campaign fell on the Gallic provinces but was not limited to them. Materials and transport would have been requisitioned and ideally (but not necessarily) paid for; whether at market rates or not is another question. It was characteristic of good emperors and administrators that they compensated provincials for what they took from them; thus under Trajan the allies "do not fail to pay traditional taxes because they are oppressed by new indictions [*indictiones*, special irregular taxes]; the fisc buys what it is proper to buy" (*emit fiscus quidquid videtur emere* [Pliny *Pan.* 29.4; he is speaking of the grain supply to Rome]). But even in peacetime such ideals seem to have been flouted regularly.[86]

War was a strain on the regular system of supply to the army, which was complex.[87] The army itself manufactured a huge variety of items from weapons to tiles, and sometimes procured raw materials itself too —by mining, for example.[88] In addition, a large part of the tribute was levied in kind, especially in grain, which perhaps found its way to the troops.[89] Grain was also procured at fixed prices by the system of *frumentum emptum;* and a variety of other items including, probably, pack animals and cavalry horses were also obtained in this way.[90] Beginning with the reign of Augustus, provincials were required to provide carts and animals for the transport of officials and military personnel; from Republican times they probably bore most of the responsibility for maintaining roads. Thus in some ways the empire recalls the large private estate, with its transport system shuttling goods for internal consumption.[91] By the third century the obligation to provide food for the

86. In peacetime at least compensation was apparently routine, and many receipts survive (Breeze 1984, 277–278). But see Mitchell 1976 on pervasive abuse of the transport system.

87. On army supply, see Breeze 1984; Mitchell 1993, 1:250–253; Whittaker 1994, chap. 4. Whittaker argues that military supplies were largely imported, sometimes over long distances, by a system of contractors and subsidies rather than purchased locally on the open market, though that system was used also.

88. MacMullen 1960, 26–29; Breeze 1984, 275–279.

89. Duncan-Jones 1990, 193–194; Mitchell 1993, 1:250–253. On the evidence of the Bar-Kochba papyri for taxation in kind, see Millar 1993, 97–98.

90. See Breeze 1984, 277–278, on requisition with compensation. On animals, see Davies 1969; on horses, a number of papyri from Dura dated from 208 to the mid–third century survive (ibid., 436–439). The rider was always charged 125 denarii for the animal, but this may not reflect the price paid to civilians (ibid., 447–448).

91. On transport, see Mitchell 1976; Isaac 1992, 291–297; on roads, Pekáry 1968, 113–117, and see below; on estates, cf. the article of Whittaker (1985), arguing that fascinating nonmarket economic effects could be produced by the internal dynamics of very large, and sometimes very far-flung, private estates—and by the supply of the Roman army, thus emphasizing the similarities between the two systems.

troops had become institutionalized as the *annona militaris*.[92] This development probably had something to do with the virtually constant state of war at that time; it was one thing to supply a sedentary army stretched out along a frontier—especially a river frontier, where goods could be shipped cheaply and easily—and quite another to provision large concentrations of troops on the move.

The logistics of a campaign could involve years of careful preparation. Corbulo's preparations for the Armenian war stretched out over three years and involved the repair of roads in Cilicia, Bithynia, and Thrace.[93] Trajan's eastern expedition also required major road repairs, which may have begun already in 111 or 112, and his planned invasion is perhaps one of the reasons for the construction of the new *via nova Traiana* through the province of Arabia—which would facilitate the movement of troops and supplies.[94] This is interesting for our purposes since paved roads were in principle expensive to construct or to repair and thus represent a significant notional burden on somebody, even if the expenses were rarely paid by the government in cash. Prices in Italy ranged from twenty to twenty-five sesterces per foot or somewhat more than one hundred thousand sesterces per mile for the repair or paving of existing roads, and the cost of building new roads may have been several times that.[95] Who paid for them, and who provided the labor, is another question. Occasionally the state or the emperor is recorded (on milestones) as the benefactor—most notably in the case of the new road in Italy from Beneventum to Brundisium, which Trajan paid for himself "with his own money" (*sua pecunia*).[96] But for the most part it seems that the obligation to construct or repair roads was a *munus*, or labor tax, levied on the local population.[97] Wartime preparations would thus place a burden on them, even if labor was sometimes provided by the army; milestones dated from 163 to 165, for example, record the repair of a road in Syria, probably for Lucius Verus' Parthian campaign, where the army provided the labor, and expenses were shouldered by the provincial town of Abilene.[98]

92. On the *annona militaris,* see n. 49 above; it appears, for example, in rabbinical literature (Isaac 1992, 285–291; most of his references are from the third century).

93. See Adams 1976, 24–29, on Corbulo; ibid., 11–81, on roads generally.

94. Ibid., 32–34.

95. Pekáry 1968, 93–96; Duncan-Jones 1974, 124–125; cf. Mitchell 1993, 1:126–127.

96. See Pekáry 1968, 97–102, on the emperor's role in financing roads.

97. See ibid., 113–117, for a collection of evidence; the *aerarium* played only a small part in financing road construction and repair (ibid., 102–112). See also Mitchell 1993, 1:127.

98. *CIL* 3.199–201; cited and discussed in Isaac 1992, 294–295. See also Pekáry 1968, 119–121, on labor, including public slaves.

Campaigns required special officers to deal with the supply of the troops—for example, the famous Plotius Grypus, whose career is immortalized in one of Statius' *Silvae:* "Germanicus [sc., Domitian] made you overseer of the supply line that follows [him], and placed you in charge of the stations of all the roads."[99] Or, to take another example, one Valerius Maximus records on his epitaph that he was "chosen by the emperor Marcus Antoninus Augustus [i.e., Marcus Aurelius] and sent to the front for the German expedition, to bring down on the Danube River the provisions that sailed down for the supply of both Pannonian armies."[100] Under Severus the titulature of these officials became fixed: they were *praepositi annonae.*[101]

Their main duties would have been to arrange the supply of food, especially grain, to the army as it marched to the frontier. To this end, a passage from the *Historia Augusta* tells us that Severus Alexander published his military itineraries in advance:

[H]e publicly proclaimed the days of his journeys, so that he posted an edict two months in advance, in which it was written: "on such-and-such day, at such-and-such hour, I will set out from the city; and if the gods are willing, I will stop at the first way station (*mansio*)"; then the way stations in order, then the camping places, then where the food supplies (*annona*) would be received; and so on even up to the boundaries of the barbarians. (*Alex. Sev.* 45)

The Antonine Itinerary may have originated as one of these prepublished routes, designed to facilitate the collection of provisions.[102]

A passage from one of the surviving manuals on land surveying notes that "whenever an army is passing by or some other retinue for whom supplies (*annona*) must be furnished at public expense (*publica*), if wood or straw must be conveyed to them, it is to be inquired which towns (*civitates*) normally furnish services (*munera*) of this sort to which districts."[103] The disturbance created is reflected, for example, in an inscription praising a local benefactor who "supported the army winter-

---

99. *Te Germanicus* [sc., Domitianus] *arbitrium sequenti annonae dedit, omniumque late praefecit stationibus viarum* (*Silv.* 4.9.17–19); on these officials, see Bérard 1984; see also Roth 1990, 283–294.

100. Bérard 1984, 307 no. 5 (= *AE* 1956.124).

101. Bérard 1984, 288.

102. This is the argument of van Berchem (1937, 166–181).

103. *Nam et quotiens militi praetereunti aliive cui comitatui annona publica praestanda est, si ligna aut stramenta deportanda est, quaerendum quae civitates quibus pagis huius modi munera praebere solitae sint* (Siculus Flaccus, in Lachmann et al. 1848–1852, 1:165; see Rostovtzeff 1957, chap. 8 n. 4; Neesen 1980, 189).

ing in the city, and sent along the one that was going to the Parthian war"; in this case the Parthian war is Trajan's, and the city is Ankara.[104] Another inscription, this time from the reign of Hadrian, records the generosity of a Macedonian individual: "When the army of Caesar was passing through, he provided for *annona* 400 *medimnoi* of wheat, 100 *medimnoi* of barley, 60 *medimnoi* of beans, and 60 measures of wine, much more cheaply than the current (i.e., market) price."[105] Numerous similar examples are attested in Greek epigraphy, from the eastern campaigns of Lucius, Severus, Caracalla, or Severus Alexander.[106] Other notices here and there tell of those routinely forced to surrender camels and other pack animals, supplies, and of course food—demands that seem to have increased very much in intensity during the third-century crisis.[107]

The vociferous complaints provoked by these demands seem to be reflected, for example, in edict after edict attempting to restrain abuses in the requisition of services by military and administrative personnel and to enforce the principle that these things should be paid for.[108] It was axiomatic that good emperors paid for the supplies they required, and bad emperors pillaged the provinces in wartime.[109] To the degree that supplies and transport were paid for, rather than levied by indiction or requisition without payment, the expenses of war must have strained the state's cash resources intolerably. Thus the devaluations of the denarius under Nero and Vespasian occur in conjunction with peaks in

104. *IGRom.* 3.173.

105. *AE* 1921.1 (= *SEG* 1.276); cf. Roth 1990, 237. The date is 121/2.

106. See Rostovtzeff 1957, chap. 8, nn. 4 and 6; Mitchell 1983, 139–143; Quass 1993, 164–167.

107. On camels, see Davies 1969, 433–434; note especially the two requisitioned for Caracalla's army in Syria (ibid., 433 [*BGU* 266]); discussed also in Adams 1976, 241. On donkeys etc., cf. Isaac 1992, 292, with n. 151, from the rabbinical literature of the first and second centuries; there were rules about what to do if this happened; also ibid., 292–293, noting that sometimes (but not always) the animals were returned. In *Dig.* 13.7.43 (Scaevola, from the reign of Marcus Aurelius) wine skins are seized for *annona;* see Isaac, op. cit., 292 and 285–291, on the collection of *annona* generally; most of the evidence here comes from the third century. For a collection of papyrological references from the third and fourth centuries, see MacMullen 1963, 185–186.

108. Mitchell 1976, especially 114–115, collecting evidence from the *Digest* and elsewhere; see also id. 1983, 139–145, on the burden of providing for the army; but cf. R. Ziegler 1996, arguing that provincial cities profited from troop movements in the area when soldiers spent their salaries locally.

109. Good: Pliny, *Pan.* 29, quoted above. Bad: Gaius, in Cass. Dio 59.21; also Domitian, implicitly contrasted with Trajan in Pliny *Pan.* 17: "I seem already to see a triumph laden not with spoils of the provinces and gold extorted from allies [i.e., the crown gold?], but with the arms of enemies and the chains of captive kings."

the minting of Syrian tetradrachms, for Corbulo's campaigns and for the Jewish and civil wars.[110] It is not surprising, from this point of view, that several emperors—Hadrian, Commodus, and Caracalla—chose to abandon wars in progress at their accession. Accessions, after all, were a time when it was important to be generous—with donatives for the troops and distributions to the people, expensive games and shows, reductions in taxes.

Two reigns perhaps call for special attention at the end of this part of the discussion. First of all, it would seem that the emperor who spent the most on military factors was Severus. He doubled the pay of the troops; he increased the size of the army by an unprecedented three legions; he fought numerous wars, civil and foreign. To oversimplify greatly, we might say that he paid for all this by a significant devaluation in the currency, and especially for his war expenses by the vigorous expansion and institutionalization of the existing practice of direct requisition for army supply.

On the other hand, the reign of Trajan emerges as an era of more spectacular, ostentatious spending, on everything—but especially in war. We have noted his new road, the *via nova Traiana,* which covered the length of the province of Arabia; the milestones all bore the same, proud inscription: "[Trajan's titles], having reduced Arabia to the state of a province, opened and paved a new road from the borders of Syria all the way to the Red Sea."[111] The road no doubt served a practical function in the Parthian wars, but it seems to go beyond that, too; it seems designed to impress. The same is true of Trajan's famous rock-cut road at the Iron Gates of Orsova on the Danube—a sight still impressive in modern times, though now underwater; and also, of course, accompanied by a suitable inscription.[112] As Cassius Dio notes, that emperor "spent a great deal on war and a great deal on works of peace" (68.7.1).

The same author includes a lengthy, reverent description of the bridge that Trajan built over the Danube, not far downstream from the

---

110. Walker 1976–1978, 3:110–112, 115–117; Duncan-Jones 1994, 113. The great increase in gold output toward the end of Trajan's reign (probably the "Dacian gold," for which see below) was no doubt related to his ambitious eastern campaign (ibid., 129). For literary testimony that wars are expensive, see n. 83 above.

111. *ILS* 5834.

112. See Rossi 1971, 32, on the road; ibid., 49, for the inscription (*ILS* 5863); ibid., 24–25, for pictures. The inscription reads: "Imp. Caesar divi Nervae f. Nerva Traianus Aug. Germ. Pontif. Maximus Trib. Pot. IIII Pater Patriae Cos. III montibus excisi[s] anco[ni]-bus sublat[i]s via[m] f[ecit]."

Iron Gates. The description is all the more striking because the bridge no longer existed in his day; it was destroyed, as he writes in the same passage, by Hadrian. Its architect was the same Apollodorus who probably designed Trajan's forum in Rome; it was probably the longest bridge ever constructed by the Romans:[113]

Trajan built a stone bridge over the Ister, for which I cannot admire him enough (οὐκ ἔχω πῶς ἂν ἀξίως αὐτὸν θαυμάσω); there are other very magnificent works of his, but this is beyond them. For there are twenty piers of squared stone, and their height is one hundred fifty feet excluding the foundations, and their width is sixty feet; and these are one hundred seventy feet apart from each other, and they are linked together by arches. How could anyone fail to marvel (θαυμάζειν) at the expense made on them? (68.13.1–2)

Thus the difficulty of understanding the role of fiscal concerns in military decisions is only partly a result of the inadequacy of the ancient sources. These concerns seem to be inseparable from political and moral issues, questions of imperial image and posturing, and so forth. Clearly, to view Trajan's Danube bridge simply as a means of transporting troops and supplies across a river is to miss the point. Money was important, but what Trajan is buying here is not logistical support for his army but the awe and respect of his countrymen, and perhaps, from barbarians, terror.

We might wonder how he paid for it. It is possible that the money came out of the revenues from one of the only really lucrative military enterprises in the imperial period, the Dacian wars.

2.2. THE REWARDS OF CONQUEST

The forum of Trajan, dedicated in 112, was as large as the fora of Caesar, Augustus, and Nerva put together.[114] The fourth-century historian Ammianus Marcellinus represents it as the most impressive of all the spectacular sights that greeted Constantius II on his visit to Rome:

When he came to the forum of Trajan, a structure unique under the sun in our opinion, and marvelous even by acknowledgment of the gods, he

---

113. Richmond 1982, 35–37; O'Connor 1993, 142–144; and Galliazzo 1994, 1:74–75 and vol. 2, no. 646, on the bridge. It was not in fact made of stone, as Dio thought, but of brick and wood.

114. On Trajan's forum, see Packer 1997; La Regina 1988, 36–44; L. Richardson 1992, 175–178, s.v. "Forum Traiani."

stood frozen in astonishment, his mind taking in the gigantic constructions around, which are neither describable in words, nor ever to be attempted again by mortals. Thus abandoning all hope of trying anything on
this scale, he declared that he desired and was able to imitate the horse of
Trajan only, which stood in the middle of the atrium, bearing the princeps
himself. (16.10.12)

The forum had apparently required a massive excavation of the Qui-
rinal Hill, the depth of which was commemorated on a hundred-foot
column in the center, which also served as Trajan's tomb. On the column an extraordinary narrative sculpture, fashioned like a winding scroll,
depicts in detail the events of both Dacian wars.[115] The forum itself
was laid out like a military camp; the colonnades were decorated with
sculpted images of trophies, arms, and colossal Dacian prisoners in ethnic costume. The complex also featured some half dozen major sculpted
representations of the emperor himself, emphasizing his role as military
victor, four of them in triumphal chariots plus the equestrian figure that
so impressed Constantius II and the colossus atop the column. An inscription on the colonnade proclaimed *ex manubiis,* indicating that this
grandiose project was paid for "out of plunder" (Aul. Gell. 25.1).

The plunder referred to is unquestionably the booty of the same
Dacian wars commemorated on the column. The legend of this booty
survived into the sixth century in the treatise *De magistratibus* of John
Lydus; comparing Byzantine successes in the north ("Scythia") to the
glorious achievements of the past, he writes that "Trajan the Great was
the first to conquer [this land; sc., the land of the Scythians] along with
Decebalus chief of the Getae, and brought to Rome 500 myriad (= 5 million) pounds of gold, and twice as much of silver, apart from drinking
cups and equipment surpassing all limits of price, plus herds and weapons, and more than 50 myriads of warlike men with their arms" (2.22).[116]
Cassius Dio tells the strange story of the capture of Decebalus' treasury
in 106; it was hidden under the river Sargetia until a prisoner betrayed

115. On Trajan's column, see Lepper and Frere 1988; Packer 1997, 1:113–120. For
plates, see the recent edition of Settis et al. (1988).

116. The figures are obviously not realistic, despite the fact that Lydus names a source
here: Crito, Trajan's doctor, who accompanied him and wrote a commentary on the campaigns. Carcopino (1934) argues that Lydus inadvertently multiplied all numbers by ten,
but the numbers are extremely round and may rather be simply exaggerations of the type
that can be found in even the most sober historians of the Principate (see above, chap. 3,
pp. 105–106). However, the main point of Carcopino's argument—that this booty explains the apparent ease with which Trajan balanced his budget despite huge expenditures—is undoubtedly correct.

its whereabouts (68.14.4–5). The column depicts the plunder being loaded onto pack animals. It is perhaps with these proceeds that Trajan was able to finance his eastern campaign with its spectacular conquests, his lavish building program, and his many munificent domestic works, all without raising taxes in any form—thus buying himself the greatest reputation of any Roman emperor.[117]

Plunder, especially in the form of gold, silver, and slaves, was the most obvious and well-recognized economic benefit of war—not just for the state or the generals, but apparently for the common soldier as well.[118] Sometimes the amount of booty captured was substantial enough to have very significant economic effects: the defeat of Egypt was supposed to have caused the price of land to rise and interest rates to plummet (Suet. *Aug.* 41.1; Cass. Dio 51.21.5). The victory was a godsend to the emperor, who could now pay his troops and settle veterans.[119] Josephus records that the sack of Jerusalem caused the price of gold to drop by half in Syria.[120]

Josephus' *Jewish War* also contains a long description of the triumph of Titus, which featured among the masses of plunder the sacred objects from the temple of Jerusalem (7.123–150); the triumph appears on the arch of Titus too, where the menorah described by the historian is depicted prominently.[121] The pride that successful emperors took in displaying their plunder indicates that besides the obvious economic benefits, booty—which involved the humiliation of a barbarian enemy—car-

---

117. This is the convincing argument of Carcopino (1934); see previous note.

118. For a discussion of booty, see Isaac 1992, 380–382. For example, Cassius Dio writes that the Pannonian revolt was expensive because "a large number of legions were maintained for it, and only a little booty was taken" (56.16.4). Germanicus' campaigns generate "moderate plunder" (Tac. *Ann.* 2.7), although they are more for revenge than "worthwhile for the booty" (ibid., 1.3). The continuation of the above quotation from Zonaras (12.1) claims that Marcus received many times the cost of the war in plunder; and Maximinus' wars produced large amounts of booty according to Herodian (7.2.9). As Isaac also points out, Tacitus' generals seek to encourage troops with the prospect of booty; e.g., Suetonius Paulinus in Tac. *Ann.* 14.36 and Corbulo in ibid., 13.39; and Germanicus also rebukes mutinous troops: "comrades [of Tiberius] in so many battles, enriched by so much booty" (ibid., 1.42).

119. Cass. Dio 51.4.8, 51.17.7. In his eagerness to acquire the treasure, Cleopatra had tried to blackmail him by threatening to burn it (ibid., 51.8.6, 11.1); on the booty of Egypt, see Sidebotham 1986, 117–118.

120. *BJ* 6.317. See also Suet. *Jul.* 54.2 on the Gallic wars: "He [Caesar] destroyed cities more often for plunder than on account of some wrong; and so it happened that he had too much gold, and he sold it commercially for three thousand sesterces per pound in Italy and the provinces."

121. Hannestad 1988, 124–129 and fig. 78; Künzl 1988, 19–24, on Titus' arch.

ried immense prestige value. The spoils of war formed a regular part of any triumph; they were so important that Domitian is supposed to have faked the booty for his triumph over Decebalus.[122] Augustus dedicated parts of his Egyptian spoils in various temples (Cass. Dio 51.22) and is supposed to have ordered "those holding triumphs to create some work out of the spoils in memory of their deeds" (ibid., 54.18.2). That emperor's most eloquent expression of his public image, his forum with its temple of Mars the Avenger, was financed *ex manubiis* (*RGDA* 21.1); so were Tiberius' temples to Concord and to Castor and Pollux (Suet. *Tib.* 20). The booty of the Jewish war not only paid for Vespasian's "Forum of Peace" but was on display there for all to admire.[123]

However, Rome's really lucrative wars lay in the past, in the period of greatest expansion under the Republic. Some of these conflicts had been spectacularly profitable. Carthage, Rome's first truly rich enemy, was forced to pay an indemnity of 3,200 talents, later raised to 4,400 talents, or a total of over 100 million sesterces (Polybius 1.62, 3.27). Later, Antiochus III would pay an indemnity of 15,000 talents (Livy 38.38; Polybius 21.43.19). Also in this period, records were kept of the amounts of gold and silver carried in each triumph, which are sometimes reproduced in later sources; thus Plutarch tells us that in Aemilius Paullus' triumph over Macedon in 167 B.C. there were 250 chariots carrying statues and other artwork, 2,250 talents of coined silver as well as silver bowls and cups, and 231 talents of coined gold plus gold plate and a sacred vessel made from 10 gold talents.[124] Pliny's *Natural History* records that Scipio Aemilianus paraded 4,370 pounds of silver in his triumph over Carthage (33.141) and that Lucius Scipio displayed 1,400 pounds of silver and 1,500 pounds of gold in his triumph over Antiochus (ibid., 3.149); Livy adds to these figures 1,231 tusks of ivory, 234 gold crowns, 137,420

---

122. Triumph: Augustus' spoils from Egypt would have sufficed for all three parts of his triple triumph (Cass. Dio 51.21.7); Germanicus' triumph over the Germans included spoils (Tac. *Ann.* 2.41). Domitian: Cass. Dio 67.7.4: "he adorned the ceremony with much triumphal apparatus, not from what he had captured (much the reverse, for he also made expenditures in the peace treaty, since he paid a great deal of money immediately to Decebalus and gave craftsmen of every trade, of peace and of war, and he also promised to continue paying always)"; cf. Pliny *Pan.* 17.1. Note also Sen. *Clem.* 1.26.5, where no ornament becomes a prince like clemency: "not hostile arms taken from the conquered, not the chariots of barbarians dripping with blood, not the spoils captured in war"; and see Dio Chrys. *Or.* 2.34, where the only proper ornaments for a king are the spoils and arms of the enemy.

123. Joseph. *BJ* 7.158; L. Richardson 1992, 286–287, s.v. "Pax, Templum."

124. *Aemilius* 32–34; a collection of statistics, including those that follow, is available in Frank 1933–1940, 1:127–138.

pounds of miscellaneous silver, and, of coined money, 224,400 Attic tetradrachms, 321,000 cistophori, and 140,000 gold Philippics (37.59.2–4). Many other passages record equally impressive statistics, especially from Spain and the east.[125] The *tituli*, or labels, from Pompey's triumph announced that he had raised the annual tax revenue from 50 million to 85 million denarii and that his total in booty was 20,000 talents (Plut. *Pomp.* 45.3). In addition to moveable goods, tens of thousands of the enemy might be enslaved in a single campaign.[126] The total number of slaves in Italy, impossible to calculate with any accuracy, may have approached the free population by the end of the Republic.[127] Statistics on a similar scale are not forthcoming in the Principate, except for the legendary profits of the second Dacian war. It is also noteworthy that the Romans of all periods were obviously proud of the booty they captured from the enemy. Its value was not just economic, but social and psychological.

However, it was not considered ethical, though it sometimes happened, for a general to pursue warfare only for the plunder, though booty was perceived as a positive result of warfare. The most frequently invoked example of the power and danger of greed in Roman warfare is that of the Republican general Crassus, whose army was destroyed by the Parthians in the great debacle at Carrhae in 53 B.C.[128] Greed is also, though less frequently, attested in the imperial period as a powerful but not especially admirable motivation for war. Augustus himself is supposed to have been tempted to attack Arabia Felix by the legend of its wealth (Strab. 16.4.22), and similar considerations may have motivated Nero's Caspian expedition;[129] Nero is rumored to have rejoiced at the

125. Ibid.

126. Harris 1979, 80–82.

127. Brunt 1971, 121–125. On land, booty, and slaves as possible motives for Republican imperialism, see Harris 1979, chap. 2.

128. On Crassus' motives, see Vell. Pat. 2.46.2; Pliny *HN* 33.134: "nor would it be satisfied until he had usurped all the gold of the Parthians"; Sen. *Q Nat.* 5.18.10; see Plut. *Crass.* 1.2–2.8 on his greed or "φιλοπλουτία"; see also App. *B Civ.* 2.18, where Crassus is motivated by lust for glory and profit; Florus 1.46.2: "the greed (*cupiditas*) of the consul Crassus, who thirsted for Parthian gold, while both gods and men were opposed."

129. On Nero's expedition, see Braund 1986; for the idea that gold may be found beyond the Caucasus, Strab. 11.2.19, Pliny *HN* 6.30, App. *Mith.* 103. On Arabia Felix, see p. 78 above. Cf. Suetonius' comment on Caesar's motivation in the Gallic wars (*Jul.* 22) and attack on Britain (where he thought he would find pearls; ibid., 47). More general comments about the role of greed in warfare can be found, e.g., in Manilius 4.402–403: "we seek profit on the winds and follow Mars to booty"; see also Sen. *Helv.* 10.6, and Calgacus' famous speech in Tac. *Agr.* 30: "pillagers of the world [i.e., the Romans], when the earth is insufficient for their plundering, they search the sea; if the enemy is rich, they are

news of Vindex' revolt because "an opportunity had arisen to plunder very rich provinces [the Gallic provinces] by the right of war" (Suet. *Ner.* 40.4). Some expeditions that did not result in the occupation of new territory may have been worthwhile for the plunder alone: Ctesiphon was sacked twice after Trajan, but never occupied.[130]

There were other potential profits of war besides the spoils. As the sources perceive it, the natural resources of the conquered territory, and especially its mineral resources, became the property of the conquerors and subject to exploitation by them.[131] We sometimes encounter the idea that barbarians do not mine gold or silver until conquered by the Romans and forced to do so.[132] Mines were an important source of revenue for the state, as the passage cited above from Dio's speech of Maecenas (52.28.4) attests, as well as Statius' poem: the secretary *a rationibus* must keep track of "whatever Spain casts out of its gold-bearing trenches, what glitters on the Dalmatian mountain" (*Silv.* 3.3.89–90). According to Pliny certain gold mines in Dalmatia produced fifty pounds of gold per day (*HN* 33.67), and those of Spain, especially Asturia in the northwest, produced twenty thousand pounds per year (33.78). This figure is almost certainly exaggerated,[133] but it is true that the

---

greedy, if he is poor, they are ambitious. . . ." Menander Rhetor, discussing the benefits of Roman rule, points out that the army acquires slaves for everyone without their having to fight themselves (377 [= Russell and Wilson 1981, 93]).

130. By Verus' legate Cassius (Cass. Dio 71.2.3); and by Severus (ibid., 75[76].9.4, Herodian 3.9.10–11, SHA *Sev.* 16.5); see Isaac 1992, 381–382.

131. See Tac. *Agr.* 12: "Britain bears gold and silver, the reward of victory; the ocean produces pearls, too, but dark and bluish." Precious metals were by no means the only resources of interest to the Romans; for example, Balbus' triumph included a representation of Mount Gyrus, with a sign to indicate that gems were found there (Pliny *HN* 5.37), and Vespasian and Titus' triumph included balsam trees from Judaea (ibid., 12.111–112, and cf. 118); on timber (of Africa), see also Lucan 9.424–430.

132. See Tac. *Germ.* 5.3: "The gods—whether propitious or angry I do not know— have denied them gold and silver. However, I would not declare that there is no vein in Germany that produces gold and silver, for who has investigated?" Cf. Strab. 15.1.30 on the Indians, who, being inexperienced in mining, do not know what their resources are; and Florus 2.33.60 on the Astures of northwest Spain. After Augustus conquered them, "laboring in the depths they began to know their own resources and riches, seeking them for others"; see further ibid., 2.25, on the Dalmatians. Cf. Lucan 9.424–430: Africa has no mines, only timber that is not exploited by the inhabitants, only by Romans.

133. For scholarship on Roman mines, see Andreau (1989–1990); on the Dacian mines, see mainly Mrozek 1977 and Noeske 1977; on Spain, Domergue 1990; he attempts to describe the role of the Spanish mines in the Roman economy (ibid., 367–385). It is impossible to estimate their output, but what evidence exists suggests that Pliny's figure is exaggerated (ibid., 378). Records of the amounts of gold received from the mines must have existed, but Pliny's rather vague *quidam prodiderunt* suggests that these are not his source here. On Pliny's account of mining procedures as essentially accurate, however, see Bird 1984.

mines of Spain and especially the gold mines in the north of the peninsula were exploited with ferocious intensity until the early third century,[134] and this probably helps explain the substantial investment Rome was willing to make in retaining the area.[135] Trajan's annexation of Dacia was apparently followed by the transfer of large populations there, including miners from Dalmatia.[136]

The hope of acquiring new mines may have been an important factor in any decision about war, but we should note certain qualifications to this. The mines of northwest Spain probably were not worked before the Roman conquest, and it is unlikely that the Romans had reliable knowledge of the area's mineral resources before they conquered it.[137] These mines did not begin large-scale production until A.D. 15–20 — that is, thirty to thirty-five years after the last major revolt had been quelled.[138] Augustus may have been encouraged in a general way by the great mineral wealth of the rest of the peninsula, especially of the south, which had earned for Spain a reputation as a sort of El Dorado.[139] His information may not have been more specific than that. In the case of Dacia, it is also difficult to determine whether Trajan could have expected the lucrative results in the form either of booty or of mines before he conquered it. Neither Strabo nor Pliny the Elder describes the resources of the area in a way that reflects a reputation for wealth; Pliny the Younger, in his *Panegyric,* does not expect a parade of riches in Trajan's triumph but rather barbarian kings in chains (17). The first war of 102–103 did not end in annexation—thus, no mines—and the treasure of Decebalus was not captured until 106. It may have been as a result, rather than a cause, of the first campaign that the Romans became aware of the "Dacian gold." In the case of Britain, the reverse may have been true: Strabo believed it to be a rich source of gold and silver (4.5.2), and

134. Domergue 1990, 197–214, 219–223. The reasons for the abandonment of many mines in the early third century are mysterious, since the mines were not necessarily exhausted at this time (ibid., 221).

135. This is the thesis of R. F. J. Jones (1976).

136. Wilkes 1969, 173–174; Noeske 1977, 315–317; Mrozek 1977, 98–100. The first procurator of the mines dates to the reign of Trajan (ibid., 95). See also Tac. *Ann.* 11.20–21, where Curtius Rufus gets triumphal honors for digging a silver mine in Upper Germany.

137. Domergue (1990, 198) makes this point.

138. Ibid.; see Bird 1984, 349–350. This is very quickly, compared to the time lapses between conquest and exploitation common in the Republic, and probably reflects the state's need for bullion to balance its budget—very obvious in the early Principate (see above). However, such a delay seems inconsistent with the idea that the area was conquered specifically for its mines.

139. See Domergue 1990, 5–14, for a discussion of ancient references; note especially Strab. 3.2.8.

Tacitus repeats this idea (*Agr.* 12), though in fact very little gold was found there; and similarly little silver was produced, though the Romans extracted large quantities of lead.[140]

There were other methods of exploiting the provinces economically besides mining. Indebtedness and high interest rates were supposed to be the primary causes of the revolt of Sacrovir in Gaul (Tac. *Ann.* 3.40); and Cassius Dio claims that Seneca single-handedly provoked the revolt of Boudicca with forced loans in the province of Britain (Cass. Dio 62.2). Import and export taxes levied within the empire and at its borders were also substantial sources of income. Some Roman frontier structures may have had a tax-collecting function, as we have seen. The sources also reflect an interest both in promoting safe trade and in collecting taxes on it; and it is one of the empire's accomplishments that it assured an abundant supply of the world's products.[141] Caracalla is supposed to have made the point, in his proposal to marry the daughter of the Parthian king, that "the aromatics grown among [the Parthians] and their amazing fabrics, and, from the Romans, the products of their mines and the goods that are praised for their craftsmanship, would no longer be scarce and difficult to get" (Herodian 4.10.4). It was on the eastern trade that the Romans collected the highest taxes, a lucrative 25 percent.[142] While the Romans sometimes express concern about the disgraceful drain of bullion to the east, and in part the heavy tax may have been meant to correct this perceived imbalance,[143] nevertheless

140. On the disappointing level of gold and silver production in Britain, see Frere 1987, 275–278. The lead industry began within a few years of conquest (ibid., 276–277), which suggests that the Romans may have had high hopes of silver production when they conquered the island. On huge quantities of lead, see Pliny *HN* 34.164.

141. Taxes: e.g., Strabo's comments on the import taxes collected from Britain (2.5.8 and 4.5.3). On the *portoria,* the standard work is still Laet 1949. On safe trade and the blessings of commerce, see Strab. 16.2.20, Philo *Leg.* 47, Vell. Pat. 2.126.3: "When was grain more moderately priced, when was peace happier? . . . The Augustan peace keeps the corners of the whole world free from the fear of robbers." Also Pliny *Pan.* 29; Ael. Arist. *Or.* 26.11–13; cf. Nutton 1978, 21; and Pliny *HN* 14.2: "Indeed, who does not think that his life has profited by the commerce in goods and the community of blessed (*festa*) peace since the world has been unified by the majesty of the Roman empire?"

142. Some evidence indicates a 25 percent tax on the Red Sea trade (de Laet 1949, 306–311; Sidebotham 1986, 105–107). In *Periplus Maris Erythraei* 19 it is unclear whether the tax is being collected by the Romans or the Nabataeans; for the arguments, see Raschke 1978, n. 1350. It was customary for the Ptolemies to collect customs duties at high rates (Sidebotham, op. cit., 105), and the Romans may simply have retained this custom. On the well-attested 25 percent tax on goods crossing the border between Roman Syria and Parthia, see de Laet 1949, 335–336. Cf. Strab. 16.2.20, where it is reported that the trade with Arabia is safer now that the Romans have troops in Syria.

143. See n. 59 above; it is the argument of de Laet (1949, 309–310) that the tax was protectionist, to discourage the bullion drain.

Strabo also reports that considerable revenues were generated by the increased volume of the Red Sea trade with India after the Roman conquest (2.5.12, 17.1.13).[144] It is possible that Rome took a special interest in protecting this trade,[145] and it is possible that Trajan conquered and annexed Arabia partly in order to build a fortified road through it, which besides its obvious military function would have served to guard the transport of imported goods from the Red Sea.[146]

The resources of a conquered people would also flow to Rome through the tribute that Rome extracted from them. The annexation of a new province naturally made it liable to pay tax. Thus the annexations of Judaea, Cappadocia, and Dacia were all followed by a census, at which the Cappadocians revolted.[147] When Augustus seized Egypt, this also increased imperial revenues very considerably;[148] the income from Cappadocia allowed Tiberius to reduce the auction tax to 0.5 percent, no doubt a very popular gesture (Tac. *Ann.* 2.42).

In the early Republic the *tributum* was a tax on Roman citizens, to meet state expenses and especially the cost of war. But in 167 B.C., as a result of Aemilius Paullus' spectacularly profitable war with Perseus, the tax on citizens was abolished and tribute became something very different: money paid by the nations subjected to Rome for the benefit of Roman citizens.[149] It was partially punitive in character and might be raised after a revolt.[150] The Romans were proud of their ability to extract taxes from subject nations;[151] governors boast of making new ter-

144. Some have argued that Aelius Gallus' invasion, for which the main motive was profit, had the object of seizing control over the Red Sea trade, but this does not seem to be Strabo's impression, and it is difficult to prove (Sidebotham 1986, 121–122).

145. Sidebotham 1986, especially chap. 3. The evidence is rather scant. The army maintained and garrisoned roads in the Red Sea region, but the author also notes that mines were exploited there, which may have been one reason for this activity.

146. On this aspect of Trajan's road, see Sidebotham 1986, 74–76. The road ran to Bostra, the legionary headquarters and capital of the new province, and the author concedes that its purpose was primarily military. But note also Pliny *Pan.* 29.2: Trajan builds harbors and roads to facilitate trade.

147. Brunt 1981, 164; Tac. *Ann.* 6.41.

148. Vell. Pat. 2.39.2: "thus he contributed to the treasury nearly the same amount as his father did, from the Gauls."

149. See Nicolet 1988, 195–199, on the evolution of the term; cf. id. 1976 on the evolution of the tribute; Corbier 1988, 259–260, on the ideology of the tribute. See especially Cic. *Verr.* 2.3.12: *quasi victoriae praemium ac poena belli,* "a sort of reward of victory and punishment for war."

150. As in the case of Judaea (App. *Syr.* 50); see Isaac 1992, 283–284, for further discussion.

151. Pompey's triumph included signs indicating that he had raised the imperial revenues from 50 to 85 million denarii (see above); in Statius (*Silv.* 1.4.83–86) the glorious career of his subject includes a special tax mission to Africa: "Should I praise the astound-

ritory subject to tribute,[152] and we sometimes find in the sources the idea that empire in general makes Rome wealthy; and this wealth—the accumulation of the world's resources at Rome—is once again a source of pride.[153]

It is therefore not surprising that the purpose of the Roman army in the provinces is sometimes represented as that of forcibly collecting tribute.[154] If the army needed to retain the province was large and the province itself was poor, the Romans might lose money on the venture, as they well knew.[155] And ancient sources, especially Greek writers, sometimes express the idea that Rome disdained further conquests because of the unprofitability or "uselessness" of the territories that re-

---

ing obedience of the Libyan tribute and [sc., the booty of] a triumph sent to Rome in the middle of peace, and riches such as not even the one who appointed you had dared to expect?" Statius goes on in vv. 86–88 to say that the ghosts of Regulus and the fallen at Cannae exult in this revenge. See also *Silv.* 4.1.40–44: "Bactria and Babylonia remain to be reigned in with new tributes"; Vell. Pat. 2.39.3: "As he made these [provinces] [stipendiary] with arms, so by his authority he made Cappadocia stipendiary to the Roman people"; Pliny *Pan.* 31.3: "let Egypt learn and believe from experience, that she provides us not with sustenance [*alimenta*] but with tribute"; Tac. *Ann.* 15.6: Paetus boasts that "he would impose tribute and laws, and Roman rights (*ius*) on the conquered, instead of the shadow of a king".

152. The accomplishments of Ti. Plautius Silvanus include the fact that "he brought across more than 100,000 Transdanuviani *ad praestanda tributa*" (*ILS* 986); see also *ILS* 985 and Corbier 1988, 260.

153. This idea occurs in Cassius Dio as a rhetorical proposition. See Suetonius Paulinus' speech to his soldiers in 62.10.2, encouraging them to defeat the enemy and thus to choose "to rule, to be rich, and to be fortunate rather than the opposites of these" [ἄρχειν πλουτεῖν εὐδαιμονεῖν μᾶλλον ἢ τ᾿ἀναντία αὐτῶν]"; this is really a brief restatement of some of the main themes of Caesar's speech to his troops in 38.40. Cf. App. *Praef.* 7, where the city's revenue increases with empire. Resources: Ael. Arist. *Or.* 26.11–13 emphasizes the results of increased trade (cf. n. 141 above) and tribute—i.e., the produce of Egypt and Africa—and also mentions mines; see also Statius *Silv.* 3.3.89–95, proudly listing Rome's revenues (the Spanish and Dalmatian mines, the African and Egyptian harvests, pearls of the Red Sea, flocks from Lacedaemon, African wood, and even "the prestige of the Indian tooth" [*Indi dentis honos*]).

154. See Strab. 2.5.8 and 4.5.3 on Britain (and see below); Joseph. *BJ* 2.382–383 on Africa; on the actual role of the army in collecting taxes, see MacMullen 1963, 60–62; Isaac 1992, 283.

155. Strabo, locc. citt. (see previous note); App. *Praef.* 7: "though they lose money on some of their subject nations, nevertheless they are ashamed to set them aside though they are detrimental"; in Florus 1.47, it is "seemly and honorable" (*pulchrum ac decorum*) to have acquired the wealthy provinces of Gaul, Thrace, Cilicia, and Cappadocia, "and even" Armenia and Britain, "great names, if not in practical terms, at least as regards the appearance of the empire" (*ut non in usum, ita ad imperii speciem magna nomina*); Cassius Dio writes of Mesopotamia that "it brings in very little and costs very much" (75.3.3). See Isaac 1992, 388–389, on such economic rationalizing.

mained outside the empire.[156] Greed and its corollary, a cynical concern for the bottom line, played an important part in determining the ultimate shape of the empire. Wars could be lucrative in terms of booty, taxes, mines, and even, in some cases, improved trade routes. They could also be extremely expensive. But while there is no question that economic issues were important in military decisions, I have argued that a strictly economic model of Roman decision making does not fit the evidence. Moral and social concerns played an important part in budget constraints. And all of the economic benefits of warfare are closely linked to status issues—the glory and pride of empire, the subjection of foreign peoples to Roman rule.

One of the alternatives to war and conquest was economic, in a sense —the bought peace. Little evidence survives about the sums involved, but it is easy to imagine that they would in many cases have been less than the cost of a war or an army of occupation.[157] Cassius Dio seems to characterize Hadrian's combination of the bought peace with intensified military discipline as rational and praiseworthy;[158] and cash gifts to loyal allies, under certain conditions, were considered good policy. But as a strategic option, to prevent invasion—and nuances were important—the cash subsidy was a dangerous step. The prestige value attached to the extraction of tribute from subject peoples worked in reverse here: to buy peace was to compromise the majesty, the image, of Rome. Thus Domitian's treaty with Decebalus (Cass. Dio 67.7.4), which involved the payment of subsidies, is denounced in Pliny's *Panegyric* to Trajan and contrasted with that emperor's more glorious policy: "We receive hostages rather than buying them, nor by huge expenses and immense gifts (*munera*) do we reach an agreement that we have won" (12.2). When Pertinax became emperor, he renounced the poli-

156. App. *Praef.* 7: "Altogether, since they hold by good judgment the best parts of land and sea, they prefer to preserve them rather than to extend their rule boundlessly to barbarian tribes that are poor and unprofitable (πενιχρὰ καὶ ἀκερδῆ)"; Ael. Arist. *Or.* 26.28: "nothing escapes you, no city, no people, no harbor, no land, unless you despise the uselessness (ἀχρηστία) of some"; and cf. Strabo's comments on Britain (2.5.8 and 4.5.3), much cited in this chapter. See also Fronto *Principia historiae* 6 (Loeb 2:203) on an enemy who has escaped conquest because of his poverty, since subjecting this people would not be worthwhile; it is unclear which enemy the author is referring to.

157. The only references to specific amounts of money are Cass. Dio 78 [79].17.3, where Macrinus complains that Caracalla's subsidies burdened the state and were equal in amount to the pay of the soldiers, and 78[79].26.1, where Dio writes that Macrinus' total gifts to Artabanus amounted to 200 million sesterces. These figures are probably exaggerated by a hostile tradition, as subsidies were looked on unfavorably (see below).

158. 69.9; cf. Philostratus *VA* 2.26 on the policy attributed to the king of India.

cies of Commodus: "He [Laetus, the praetorian prefect] sent after some barbarians who had received a large amount of gold from him [Commodus] in return for peace (for they were still on the road), and demanded it back, saying to them, 'Tell those at home that Pertinax is emperor.'"[159]

It is difficult to separate the economic benefits of war—in tribute or in booty—from their symbolic status value, and the Romans probably did not separate these ideas. When they went to war with the Frisii over their tribute of ox hides, or when they annihilated the Nasamones in a tax revolt, the motivation was not strictly economic, though the wars were about money: the status issue explains the ferocity of the Romans' response and their willingness to wage expensive wars over what were probably trivial sums. The Romans were furthermore quite willing to undertake costly wars of conquest—like Domitian's German campaigns or Marcus' Danube wars—when they could have had little hope of lucrative results; the reputation of these regions as frost-bound and poverty-stricken would not have been encouraging.[160] We might speculate, however, that had these wars actually been profitable they might have been more successful, and that the relatively low profitability of war in the Principate may have been a reason for the much slower pace of conquest compared to the Republic.

The most notorious example of a new territory that proved a financial drain on the empire's resources, rather than an asset, was Britain. Cassius Dio tells us that when the chief Caratacus was captured and brought to Rome, "seeing its brilliance and its size, he said, 'Having acquired such things, and so many, do you really covet our little tents?'" (60[61].33.3). It was an apt observation; long before Claudius' campaigns, Strabo had concluded that despite the island's reputed mineral resources it would cost more to hold the province than could be extracted in tribute, and later sources confirm that he was correct.[161] Strabo's comment is interesting from several points of view and deserves quotation:

Though the Romans could have held Britain, they disdained it, seeing that there was not a single threat from them [the British tribes], for they are not strong enough to cross over and attack us, nor is there any advantage at all

159. Cass. Dio 73[74].6.1. Other examples: Caracalla's bought peace with German tribes is described in negative terms by Cassius Dio (77[78].14.1–2); Dio also ascribes Macrinus' bargain with Artabanus to Macrinus' own cowardice (δειλία) and his army's lack of discipline (78[79].27.1). In Herodian 6.7.9, Severus Alexander attempts to buy peace with the Germans, but the soldiers mutiny in protest.

160. Manilius 4.794–796; Tac. *Germ.* 2, 5; Cass. Dio 49.36.2; Herodian 1.6.1; etc.

161. Later sources: App. *Praef.* 5; Florus 1.47.1.

to occupying it. For it seems that more now is received from the customs duties than the tribute would be able to bring in, deducting the expense of the garrison to guard it and to collect the tribute from the island. And the unprofitability of the islands around it would be even greater. (2.5.8; cf. 4.5.3)

Strabo argues that Britain was neither a military threat nor economically lucrative; nor did his calculations on the latter issue prove false. Yet the Romans not only conquered Britain, they held it, as we have seen, with ferocious tenacity; as the ancient sources tell us, once conquered, it could not have been let go without disgrace.[162] Once again the question of image or face emerges as more compelling, more important, than the strictly economic issue. Conversely, the economic relationships between Rome and its subjects were a way of signaling status and thus establishing and maintaining image. The symbolic weight of these relationships was at least as important as their fiscal significance.

162. Disgrace: App. *Praef.* 7: "though they lose money on some of their subject nations, nevertheless they are ashamed to set them aside though they are detrimental"; Florus 1.47.1; cf. 30.1: better never to have conquered Germany than to have suffered the humiliation of losing it; note also Cass. Dio 62.9.1 (the speech of Suetonius Paulinus).

CHAPTER 5

Values

1. The Glory of Victory

The Romans were not ashamed to advertise their successes. Where the medium imposes constraints on the length of the advertisement—on an inscription, perhaps, or on a coin—the values of the society are thrown into relief: the patron must choose carefully what he wants to boast about. The well-known epitaph of the first-century governor of Moesia, Ti. Plautius Silvanus, has been discussed in various contexts, but not in the way that it was intended to be read—as a record of the governor's proudest achievements. These are, as they appear in order, after a list of his offices, the following: he brought 100,000 "Transdanuviani" across the river along with their wives, children, chiefs, and kings and made them tributary; he suppressed an "arising disturbance" (*motus oriens*) of the Sarmatians although he had sent part of his army to Armenia; he brought "kings previously unknown, or hostile to the Roman people, to the riverbank that he protected to adore Roman standards"; he returned relatives to the kings of the Bastarnae, Rhoxolani, and Dacians after capturing them from their enemies and received hostages from them, "by which means he confirmed and extended the peace of the province"; he rescued the "Chersonese that is beyond the Borysthenes [i.e., Crimean Peninsula or the Tauric Chersonese]" from

a siege by the king of the Scythians; and he was the first to send grain
to Rome from his province. For these achievements he received triumphal ornaments, and the emperor Vespasian himself made a speech in
his honor, from which he quotes.[1]

The epitaph emphasizes Plautius' dealings with foreign peoples, some
of them far away—the terrible Scythians, the remote Tauric Chersonese
—and some of them even "previously unknown." He has, in one way or
another, asserted Roman authority over all of them—interfering with
their military ventures, extracting tribute or hostages from them, convincing them to abase themselves by adoring the Roman standards. Plautius' epitaph attests that the assertion of Rome's superior status—and,
in connection with that, the humiliation of barbarian peoples—were
not only worthwhile but very important goals in themselves; thus the
symbolic nature of many of Plautius' achievements.[2] The image of Rome
is in itself a policy instrument.

Cornelius Gallus, the first prefect of Egypt, left a monument at Phy-
lae recording his achievements in that office.[3] In the inscription he boasts
that he put down a rebellion of the Thebaid in fifteen days, and reduced
five cities, which he lists; he took an army "beyond the cataract of the
Nile, to which place neither the Roman people nor the kings of Egypt
ever carried arms before"; he heard embassies from the Ethiopian king
and received him into protection; he established another ruler on his
throne. The Latin inscription is followed by a Greek translation and
surmounted by a relief showing a mounted cavalryman trampling a pros-
trate enemy. Gallus' achievements were more martial than those of Plautius, but his goals are essentially the same: the assertion Rome's superior status, whether by force or symbolically through the reception of
embassies; the humiliation of the enemy—especially enemies who were
far off, exotic, and strange.

The longest and most eloquent inscription of this sort that survives
is the epitaph of Augustus himself, which was inscribed on enormous
bronze doors in front of his mausoleum and which is known from pro-

1. *ILS* 986. A commentary is provided in Conole and Milns 1983, 183–184. The Scythian king was probably besieging the Greek city of Heraclea Chersonesus; the kingdom of
Bosporus was ruled at the time by Cotys, a Roman ally (ibid., 187–191).

2. Some of the elements of Plautius' epitaph are found also in *ILS* 985 (Tampius Fla-
vianus, a governor of Pannonia); e.g., *opsidibus a Tran[sdanuvianis acceptis, lim]itibus om-
nibus ex[ploratis,] [hostibus ad vectig]alia praestanda [adactis]* ("hostages received from
the Transdanuvians, all boundaries explored, enemies compelled to offer tribute").

3. *ILS* 8995; see Cass. Dio 53.23.5: "for he set up statues of himself in all of Egypt, so
to speak, and he also inscribed all the deeds he had done on the pyramids."

vincial copies, especially the copy on the wall of his temple at Ankara, which survives largely intact together with a Greek translation. The *Res Gestae* is divided into three sections (honors, expenses and munificence, and accomplishments proper), of which the last (chaps. 26–33) is important for this discussion.[4] Here Augustus presents his accomplishments in the area of foreign relations as he wished them to be remembered: "I extended the boundaries of all the provinces of the Roman people, on which there bordered tribes that did not obey our *imperium*" (26). This statement is followed by a lengthy catalogue of subjections, pacifications, hostages received, kings crowned, embassies heard, and remote regions explored.[5] The list contains a total of fifty-five geographical names. Many appeared in Latin for the first time under Augustus; some appear in Latin for the first time in this text.[6] Some are associated with the limits and most remote regions of the inhabited world: Ethiopia, Arabia, Meroë; the Cimbri, the Scythae, the Britanni; the river Tanais; India. The heading of the inscription is "Accomplishments of the divine Augustus, by which he subjected the world to the rule of the Roman people."[7]

One does not have to look very far, in the *Res Gestae* or in Latin sources generally, to get the impression that the Romans thought conquest was a good and glorious thing. To continue with one of the threads of our discussion so far: the Romans had a penchant for collecting and publicizing lists of the names of peoples or places that they had subjected to their authority; lists that should ideally include new, obscure, unheard-of names.[8] Augustus is able to name the farthest towns (*oppida*) reached by the expeditions of Petronius in Ethiopia ("Nabata, which is next to Meroë") and Aelius Gallus in Arabia (Mariba) because the commanders certainly kept records of the names of all the places they conquered (*RGDA* 26).[9] Pliny's *Natural History* confirms this: "Gallus destroyed [the following] towns, not named by authors who wrote before: Negrana, Nestum, Nesca, Magusum, Caminacum, Labaetia, and the aforementioned Mariba, 6 miles in circumference, and likewise

---

4. On the division, see Gagé 1977, 13–16.

5. Chaps. 26–33; for what follows, see Nicolet 1991, 15–27.

6. Ibid., 20–21.

7. See Gagé 1977, 72–73.

8. The *RGDA* has elements in common with several genres of inscriptions, including the *elogia* that adorned the statues of famous citizens, especially military heroes (Gagé 1977, 29–31). Nicolet (1991, 20) notices the resemblance to *tituli* carried in triumphs. On the following points, see also the discussion above, chap. 2, sec. 2.

9. Though "Nabata" is "Napata" in Pliny *HN* 6.181 and Caripeta is the farthest point reached by Gallus in ibid., 6.160 (see below).

Caripeta, the farthest point to which he progressed" (6.160). Pliny also provides a list of the towns captured by Petronius: "Pselchis, Primi, Bocchis, Forum Cambysis, Attenia, Stadissis; . . . and he sacked Napata as well."[10] Lists of this type sometimes adorned victory monuments; again, the *Natural History* preserves the text of the inscription on Augustus' monumental trophy in the Alps, which named fifty "tribes . . . reduced to the rule of the Roman people";[11] inscriptions and possibly personifications representing the new territories subjugated by him also adorned his forum.[12] After one of Germanicus' victories, his troops "saluted Tiberius as *imperator,* and built a mound, and in the manner of a trophy they placed arms on it, with the names of the conquered tribes inscribed underneath" (Tac. *Ann.* 2.18). Claudius' arch in Rome proclaimed that he had conquered eleven British tribes, though in this case they are not listed, and was "the first to reduce barbaric tribes across the ocean to the authority (*dicio*) of the Roman people."[13] Later, as we shall see, the imperial titulature came to resemble these lists somewhat. It is also possible that the letters and commentaries on wars composed by some emperors on campaign resembled the *Res Gestae* and the other sources discussed above in that they were basically lists of peoples conquered, received in protection, made tributary, and so forth; this is the impression conveyed by Appian's description of Augustus' commentaries on his Illyrian campaigns (*Ill.* 15), and passages from Suetonius and Velleius Paterculus on the career of Tiberius are similar.[14]

This habit of collecting place-names was not new to the imperial period. As far back as the evidence allows us to trace, Roman senators boasted—on epitaphs, for example—of two categories of achievement: political office and military victory. Often, in the latter category, place-names were included.[15] Aemilius Paullus reported that he had received the surrender of 250 towns in Farther Spain, which he governed from

10. 6.181; he adds that most no longer exist, though "Roman arms, however, did not create the desert in this case" (6.182).

11. *HN* 3.136–137, *CIL* 5.7817; see Picard 1957, 291–300.

12. Vell. Pat. 2.39.2. See Nicolet 1991, 42–43. It is possible that the caryatids that are known to have adorned the attics of the porticoes were personifications of subjected peoples, but this is speculative.

13. *CIL* 6.920 (= *ILS* 216); cf. Mela 3.49: "victor over tribes not only unconquered before him, but in truth even unknown."

14. Suet. *Tib.* 9; Vell. Pat. 2.106; or the historians may choose to present the available information in this form. Vell. Pat. 2.90 describes Augustus' achievements in terms very similar to the *Res Gestae;* in 2.89.5 he introduces the discussion, saying he will summarize "the wars waged under the emperor and the world pacified by his victories."

15. E.g., the Scipionic epitaphs (*ILS* 1, 3, 5); cf. Pliny *HN* 7.101–106. On these, see recently Flower 1996, 160–180.

190 to 189 B.C. (Plut. *Aem.* 4.2). Tiberius Gracchus, father of the famous tribune, also supposedly destroyed either 150 or 300 towns in Spain (Florus 1.33.9–10, Strab. 3.4.13). Pompey, of course, had the most impressive statistics of all; some are recorded by Pliny the Elder in his section on "extraordinary individuals." One inscription listed the lands and peoples of the east that he had conquered, received in protection, or subjected, in a manner similar to the *Res Gestae,* and ended with the claim that he had "made the boundaries of the empire equal to the boundaries of the earth, and safeguarded the revenues of the Romans and increased some of them. . . ." [16] His trophies in the Pyrenees announced the surrender of 856 towns in Gaul and Spain; his inscription on the Temple of Minerva at Rome, dedicated from his booty, declared that he had "routed, put to flight, killed, or received in surrender (*deditio*) 12,183,000 [people], sunk or captured 846 ships, received in *fides* 1,538 towns and forts, subjected the lands from Maeotis to the Red Sea." Pliny goes on to list fifteen lands and kings named in the *praefatio* of Pompey's triumph (*HN* 7.96–98).

For triumphs, a record of conquered places was especially important, because they formed a crucial part of the procession. In L. Scipio's Asian triumph, 134 "representations of towns" were carried (Livy 37.59.3). Sulla's triumph featured "many cities of Greece and Asia" but no Roman towns (from his civil wars; Val. Max. 2.8.7). Similarly, in the imperial period, Balbus' triumph in 19 B.C. included the "names and representations (*simulacra*)" of twenty-five towns, tribes, rivers, and mountains subjected by him. [17] During his eastern campaign, Trajan was voted the honor of triumphing over as many peoples as he wished, "for on account of the large number of them about whom he was continually writing to the senate, they [the senators] were not able either to understand some of them or to name them correctly" (Cass. Dio 68.29.2). The *simulacra,* representations, of conquered rivers, mountains, and cities were an important part of any triumph; these were probably personifications of the type familiar from other Greco-Roman iconography. [18] *Simulacra*

16. Diod. Sic. 40.4; Nicolet 1991, 32.

17. Pliny *HN* 5.36–37; cf. Propertius 3.4.16: "I shall read of the towns captured in the signs" (of an imagined triumph; *titulis oppida capta legam*).

18. On the *simulacra,* see Propertius 3.4.16; Ovid *Ars am.* 1.219–220; see Tac. *Ann.* 2.41 for the "representations of mountains, rivers, and battles" (*simulacra montium, fluminum, proeliorum*) carried in Germanicus' triumph; see also Brodersen 1995, 118–126; Ehlers 1939, 502–503. On personifications of rivers, see *LIMC* 4.1:139–148; Braund 1996. On the triumph in general, see also Campbell 1984, 133–142; McCormick 1986, 14–17; Künzl 1988, with a collection of literary testimonia (141–150). On the origins and early development of the triumph, see Versnel 1970.

of battles, apparently tableaux or reenactments, could also be included; in Titus' triumph, these were the most impressive element.[19]

Thus the imperialist aspect of Roman geography was very prominent. To take another example, the Romans perceived Germanicus' German war of A.D. 14–16 as the story of the reconquest of the geographical landmarks achieved by his father, Nero Drusus—from whom he also inherited his geographical, honorific title. Cassius Dio tells us that the farthest point Nero Drusus reached was the Elbe River; he did not cross over, but, warned by a dream, he set up trophies (τρόπαια) on its banks and withdrew, then died on the way back to the Rhine (55.1–2). Augustus boasts in the *Res Gestae* that his generals have conquered Germany to the Elbe (26.2), and Strabo tells us that Germany is unknown beyond that point (7.2.4). But after the disaster of Varus, the Rhine became the perceived boundary of the Roman empire: "because of this disaster it came about that the empire, which had not halted at the shore of the ocean, stopped at the bank of the Rhine River" (Florus 2.30.39). Tacitus writes that the Elbe was "once renowned and familiar, now only heard about."[20] The recapture of this boundary is an important theme in his account of Germanicus' campaigns; Arminius insists that the Germans will never tolerate the sight of the Roman rods and axes between the Rhine and the Elbe (*Ann.* 1.59); Germanicus encourages his troops by telling them that "already the Elbe is closer than the Rhine" (ibid., 2.14). Later, the general erects a monument with an inscription announcing that "the nations between the Rhine and Elbe" have been subdued (ibid., 2.22). Other geographical points, first conquered or discovered by Drusus, also come into play. Drusus, like Germanicus, had sailed the northern ocean (Dio 54.32.2). Dio tells us that in 11 B.C. Drusus bridged the Lippe and fortified the confluence of the Lippe and the Alme (Eliso) Rivers (54.33; 55.1.2–4). Florus emphasizes that he bridged the Rhine (2.30.22); and Germanicus, like his father, did the same (Tac. *Ann.* 1.49). He then followed "the footsteps of his father" (ibid., 1.56) and refortified the entire area up to "Fort Aliso" (2.7), by which the historian may mean the fort at the Lippe and Alme mentioned by Dio. At the same time, Germanicus rebuilt an altar to Drusus that had been demolished (ibid.). He sailed the "Drusian canal" constructed by his father, and then the ocean (2.8). And while we will never know where the Teutoburg Forest was, we know that it was the site of the terrible

---

19. "The greatest wonder of all was provided by the equipment of the moving floats" (Joseph. *BJ* 7.139); a description of the representations of the battles—very graphic, with lots of blood—follows (7.139–145).

20. *Flumen inclutum et notum olim, nunc tantum auditur* (*Germ.* 41.2).

disaster that turned the Elbe from a familiar landmark to a distant rumor, and that Germanicus returned there to bury the Roman dead
(*Ann.* 1.61).

The geographical aspect of victory, then, was a prominent one. There
were other important elements. Triumphs also included a lavish display
of the spoils of war; the important role of war booty in the Roman
imagination has been discussed in the previous chapter. Triumphal pro-
cessions also featured a parade of prisoners, which ideally included the
conquered barbarian king, in chains.[21] This aspect of the ceremony—
the humiliation of the enemy leader—was critical. Augustus was extremely disappointed by Cleopatra's suicide, for this reason (Cass. Dio
51.11.3, 51.14.6). King Mithridates of Bosporus begged Claudius not to
kill him by force or lead him in a triumph (Cass. Dio 60[61].32.4a; cf. Tac.
Ann. 12.21). Commodus' advisers point out, among their arguments as
to why he should continue the Danube campaigns, that it would be
splendid "to return home triumphing and leading bound barbarian
kings and satraps as prisoners" (Herodian 1.6.5).[22] Traditionally the enemy leaders were executed publicly in the forum at the end of the ceremony;[23] Claudius pardoned Caratacus, though, in an ostentatious display of clemency.[24] The triumph was one of the most jealously guarded
privileges of the emperor, and is perhaps the most eloquent expression
of the Roman glorification of conquest.

This theme in a general sense—the glory of victory—is so prevalent
in the literature, art, coins, and epigraphy of the Principate as almost to
defy coherent discussion. Over three hundred triumphal arches survive
or are known from coins or inscriptions.[25] "Victory" is the abstraction
most commonly personified on the coinage.[26] Augustus' imperialistic

21. Prisoners: Tac. *Ann.* 2.41, Joseph. *BJ* 7.138. On enemy kings, see Ovid *Ars am.* 1.215;
and see Vell. Pat. 2.121.3 on Tiberius' Pannonian triumph: "Who in truth would not marvel at the indulgence of fortune? For stories do not relate how all the most important enemy leaders were killed, but rather how the triumph displayed them, in chains." The floats
in the triumph of Vespasian and Titus included "the general of the captured city, in the
manner in which he was taken" (*BJ* 7.147); and see below.

22. On "satraps" see above, chap. 1, n. 7.

23. Augustus executes Adiatorix and his son after leading him and his family in a triumph (Strab. 12.3.35); Simon is executed in the forum after the Jewish triumph—a
"παλαιὸν πάτριον," ancestral custom (Joseph. *BJ* 7.153–154).

24. Tac. *Ann.* 12.36–37; the pardon included his wife and brothers too, so they expected to be executed as well; see Campbell 1984, 134–135.

25. I take the statistic from *Der kleine Pauly* 5:962, s.v. "Triumphbogen," where the
number given is 364; 53 in Rome. On triumphal monuments, see especially Picard 1957;
Hannestad 1988 is also a useful reference.

26. Wallace-Hadrill 1981, chart on p. 323, with commentary on p. 322; cf. Gagé 1933.

boasts in the *Res Gestae* are, as has often been noticed, faithfully echoed in the poetry of his reign.[27] One of the most famous examples is the passage from book 6 of Virgil's *Aeneid,* which predicts Augustus' accomplishments: "he advances the empire beyond the Garamantes and the Indians, the land that lies outside the stars, outside the paths of the year and the sun . . . at his approach even now the Caspian kingdoms tremble at the responses of the gods, and the land of Maeotis, and the mouths of the sevenfold Nile are stirred in alarm" (vv. 794–800); note again the emphasis on exotic geography. The campaigns of Germanicus and Trajan were celebrated in epic poems, now lost;[28] Lucian describes at length the profusion of histories, mostly panegyrical in tone, that followed Verus' successes in Parthia (*Hist. conscr.,* especially 7–13). Emphasis on his military accomplishments was an indispensable part of praise for any emperor, as, for example, in Statius' flattering verses about Domitian or in the *Panegyric* of Pliny the Younger.[29]

The glory associated with conquest can also be seen in the persistent idea that Rome had subjected the entire *orbis terrarum,* the world— an idea often symbolized by the imagery of the globe or sphere.[30] The ocean was the most suitable and most prestigious boundary for Rome's empire; Claudius had the distinction of going beyond even that, and the prestige associated everywhere with conquests in the world's most

27. On imperialism in Augustan poetry, see, e.g., Little 1982, 268–271, on Virgil; Gruen 1985, 55–59; id. 1996, 190–192; Nicolet 1991, 29–30; and Meyer 1961, arguing, however, that the ideology of the poets conflicted with Augustus' own policies. On victory propaganda in the art of Augustus' reign, see Gruen 1985, 59–63; id. 1996, 192–194; Zanker 1988, 185–192; Nicolet 1991, 41–47.

28. On Germanicus, see Sen. *Suas.* 1.15, with extensive quotation from the poem. On Trajan, see Pliny *Ep.* 8.4.

29. Pliny *Pan.* 14–17 makes up the military section; see McCormick 1986, 4 n. 11, for the later panegyrical tradition. Menander Rhetor tells us that the emperor's virtues should be divided for the purposes of flattery into the virtues of war and the virtues of peace; war should come first, with vivid descriptions of the battles; an interesting diversion might be to have the Ister, for example, complain about being crammed with corpses; the emperor's clemency should be praised, for not annihilating the enemy race (2.372–375). The theme is especially prominent in Statius and Martial (e.g., Sullivan 1985, 185, and id. 1991, 36–37; cf. ibid., 130–137; B. Jones 1992, 151; e.g., Statius *Silv.* 1.1, 1.4.154–159, etc.), perhaps because of Domitian's especially intense demands for flattery of all kinds (Williams 1978, 165–168). Statius normally addresses or designates Domitian by his victory title Germanicus (e.g., *Silv.* 1.1.5, 1.4.4, etc.); cf. Seneca's flattery of Claudius' military achievements in the notorious letter to the emperor's freedman Polybius (*Ad Polybium* 13.2).

30. On Roman ecumenism, see Vogt 1929; Nicolet 1991, chap. 2; see, e.g., Philo *Leg.* 8, where Rome rules over "the whole earth and sea"; Pliny *HN* 3.5, where Rome is "victor of the peoples of the world" (*victor orbis gentium*); Commodus is *Pacator orbis* (see below). Globe: Hölscher 1967, 41–47; Arnaud 1984; Nicolet 1991, 35–37, with n. 28 for bibliography; the globe begins to appear on coins of the Republic in the 70s B.C.

remote regions is clear.[31] It is also common to find in literature the contrast between foreign war and civil war—the former glorious, the latter destructive and disgraceful.[32] The ritual paraphernalia of conquest, carried over from the Republic and ever magnified in scale as it became the exclusive privilege of the emperor, is perhaps our most useful clue to the psychology involved—trophies, arches, public funerals, victory titles, triumphal statues with appropriate inscriptions, and of course the triumphal procession.[33] It is not surprising to find in the ancient sources

31. On the ocean as the most prestigious boundary, see Dion 1977 passim but especially 247–250, including many of the examples that follow; he notes milestones in Spain where the distance is given *ad oceanum* (249–250); see also Romm 1992, 141–148, on the ocean in the north. Augustus boasts of his fleets sailing on the ocean in the *Res Gestae* (26); see also Virgil *Aen.* 1.287 ("Caesar, who bounds his empire with the ocean and his fame with the stars"); Seneca *Q Nat.* 6.23.3 on the achievements of Alexander. Plutarch relates that Crassus is supposed to have been motivated by the ambition of conquering the east to the ocean (*Crass.* 16.2); Suetonius writes that Drusus had the distinction of being the first to sail on the northern ocean (*Claud.* 1.2). Florus laments that "the empire, which had not halted at the shore of the ocean, now stopped at the bank of the Rhine River" (2.30.39); Lucian claims that one overenthusiastic historian describes Verus' future campaigns in India and navigation of the ocean (*Hist. conscr.* 31). In Cassius Dio, Antony laments that if Caesar had not been forced to abandon his Gallic campaigns "we would no longer have as boundaries land and people, but air and the outer sea" (44.43.1); in Herodian, Commodus' advisers remind him how glorious it would be to extend Roman rule to the ocean (1.6.6). On Claudius, see his boast on his triumphal arch, above (*ILS* 216). On remote regions, see, e.g., Pompey's boasting in Lucan 2.583–595; and the boasts of Plautius, Cornelius Gallus, and Augustus, above; in Statius *Silv.* 3.2 Domitian seems to plan a glorious eastern expedition to "the unknown Indians and the Cimmerian chaos" (91–92).

32. A very common theme in Lucan is what Rome could have achieved if the civil wars had not happened—e.g., 1.10–32, 7.421–436; similarly, Plutarch laments that the civil wars kept Rome from conquering the rest of the world (*Pomp.* 70.3–5; C. P. Jones 1971, 125 n. 21); cf. Tac. *Hist.* 1.40: "the Roman soldiers, as though they were about to expel Vologeses or Pacorus from the ancestral throne of the Arsacids, and not on their way to cut down their own emperor, old and unarmed. . . ." See also Dio Chrys. *Or.* 2.75, where a bad ruler "does not direct his strength against the enemy, but against subjects and friends." On the different terminology for foreign and civil wars, see Rosenberger 1992, passim, especially 150–160. Civil wars were not supposed to bring triumphs or to be publicized (ibid., 156–158); Pliny notes that neither Julius Caesar nor Pompey publicized his civil victories (*HN* 7.92 and 7.96); see also Cass. Dio 51.19.1–5 on honors for Augustus' triumph over Cleopatra (not Antony); Mucianus is voted triumphal ornaments "for a civil war, but his expedition against the Sarmatians was alleged [as the reason]" (Tac. *Hist.* 4.4); Severus is ashamed to celebrate a civil war victory (Herodian 3.9.1). Note that provincial revolts are not normally considered civil wars, as the Jewish War propaganda amply attests and as the discussion of Rosenberger, cited above, makes clear. Tiberius celebrates a triumph for the Pannonian revolt (Vell. Pat. 2.121); Dolabella is denied triumphal honors for his bloody defeat of Tacfarinas, but his reputation soars nevertheless (Tac. *Ann.* 4.26); Poppaeus Sabinus wins triumphal ornaments for his defeat of the Thracians (ibid., 4.46).

33. The best example of honors for nonemperors comes early in our period; this is the case of Drusus. He died after reaching the Elbe River, where he set up trophies (Cass. Dio

praise and approval for emperors who pursued expansionist policies, and criticism for those who did not—though they sometimes voice concerns, especially fiscal ones, about annexing new territory.[34]

2. The Image of Rome

The glory associated with conquest and victory was two-fold, and in fact the Romans themselves made a distinction between the prestige that it brought to successful individuals—especially the emperor—and the honor and dignity that it brought to Rome as a state. They seem to have perceived foreign relations as a competition for honor and status between Rome and barbarian peoples; by proving its superior force through war and conquest, Rome extracts deference and reverence from other nations, who then remain submissive, refraining from revolt or attack. It is in this way that the empire is supposed to maintain security. Conversely, signs of weakness on Rome's part, such as a show of deference to a foreign people, or failure to avenge a defeat in war or to punish a revolt with sufficient ferocity, are considered invitations to disaster. For these reasons the Romans sometimes seem to react very aggressively to apparently minor breaches of treaty, to exaggerate the threat posed by rivals, and to respond to crises with conquest or even attempted genocide while insisting that their concerns are for their own security; they place a high value on victory, conquest, and the humiliation of the enemy. At the same time, although the superiority of the Romans is ultimately a superiority of military strength, the most essential element in this system is the state of mind of the enemy: Rome's empire depends on its ability to assert and enforce an image of itself as awe-

---

55.1.3; Picard 1957, 301–304); he received eulogies from Tiberius and Augustus, statues, an arch, burial in the Campus Martius, the title "Germanicus," and "a cenotaph on the Rhine itself" (Cass. Dio 55.2.2–3; Suet. *Claud.* 1.3).

34. See Tac. *Ann.* 4.32 on Tiberius: "the peace was unshaken or broken only slightly; the city's circumstances were doleful, and the emperor was indifferent to expanding the empire"; Florus 1 *praef.* 8 complains of the *inertia* of Trajan's predecessors. This was a topos associated with bad emperors (Telschow 1989). Tacitus also praises governors of Britain who added territory to the province and disparages those who did not (*Agr.* 14 and *Ann.* 14.29). Fronto is critical of Hadrian (*Principia historiae* 10 [Loeb 2:207]) and is admiring of Trajan (ibid., 4 [Loeb 2:201]). Cass. Dio writes that Marcus would have conquered "everything there" (i.e., north of the Danube) if he had not been poisoned by physicians bribed by Commodus (71[72].33.4); and Herodian criticizes Commodus' decision to abandon the Danube campaigns (1.6.7–9). See Millar 1982, 19–20. On economic concerns about imperialism, see above, chap. 4, n. 155.

some and terrifying. This image is defined in value terms, such as *decus* (honor), or *maiestas* (majesty), or equivalents. As a state, the Romans behave like Homeric heroes, Mafia gangsters, or individuals in any society based on violent competition for honor or respect.[35]

Symbols, which communicate image, are important in such a system. For example, the reception of embassies, sometimes from very far away, is perceived as an important "proof" of Rome's superior international status, and of the deference of foreign peoples.[36] The embassies should be sending gifts and seeking Roman friendship or arbitration (not, of course, the other way around).[37] Augustus boasts that "to me embassies of kings were often sent from India, never seen before this time by any Roman leader; the Bastarnae, the Scythians, and the kings of the Sarmatians that are on this side of the Tanais and of those beyond it, the kings of the Albanians and the Iberians and the Medes, sought our friendship through ambassadors" (*RGDA* 31). The Parthian king—"not conquered in war, but seeking our friendship through the pledge of his children"—sent hostages (ibid.).

Though here the enemy king was "not conquered in war," it is clear that the Romans saw their superior status as ultimately dependent on proofs of military prowess: Rome claimed respect based on a superiority of force. The feelings that the Romans hoped to inspire in the enemy

35. On Homeric heroes, see Adkins 1960; and van Wees 1992, especially 109–125. Van Wees cites literature on Chicago street gangs, soccer hooligans, and the Mafia in comparison (ibid., 61, 110, 164–165). On honor and vengeance in Roman society cf. Thomas 1984; see also Cohen 1995 on classical Athens. On honor in the Mediterranean world see Pitt-Rivers 1977 and the collection of Peristiany 1966. On the importance of the concept of honor in warfare, see also Kagan 1995.

36. On the protocol of Roman diplomacy as designed to create a "hierarchy of states" with Rome at the top, see Gagé 1959. Other studies of Roman diplomacy, including K. Ziegler 1964, Lemosse 1967, and Cimma 1976, are very legalistic in their emphasis and not as pertinent to this study.

37. The theme of barbarian embassies humbly seeking Roman friendship is a popular one. Suetonius echoes Augustus' boast (*RGDA* 32; see below) in *Aug.* 21.3; see also Hor. *Carm. saec.* 55–56: "now the Scythians seek responses, and the once-proud Indians." Florus writes that all those who were not "pacified" under Augustus, "who were independent from the empire, nevertheless felt its greatness and revered the Roman people, victor over nations. For both the Scythians and the Sarmatians sent legates, seeking friendship; and even the Seres, and those who live under the very sun, the Indians . . ." (2.34.61–62). The Indian embassy was a special point of pride; both Strabo and Cassius Dio emphasize that the Indian king sought Roman friendship and gave gifts (Strab. 15.1.73; Cass. Dio 54.9.8). After the victory over Tacfarinas, the Garamantes send an embassy, "rarely seen in the city" (Tac. *Ann.* 4.26). Seneca writes that good fortune for a non-Stoic would include a triumph, conquest, and kings humbly seeking arbitration (*De vita beata* 25.4); see also Stat. *Silv.* 3.4.62–63, flattering a favorite of Domitian, whose hand "the Getae seek to know, the Persians and Armenians and Indians seek to touch."

were awe and terror. Thus Roman diplomatic protocol was designed to impress; the general should be surrounded by a splendid and terrifying military entourage.[38] Peace was supposed to be requested by a defeated and frightened enemy, never by Rome.[39] Gaius was at first more successful with the Parthians than Tiberius, since King Artabanus, "who always made known his hatred and contempt for Tiberius, sought his [Gaius'] friendship of his own accord (*ultro*), and came to a meeting with the consular legate, and crossed the Euphrates and adored the eagles and the Roman standards and the images of the Caesars" (Suet. *Gaius* 14.3). Domitian's peace with Decebalus, perhaps the most notorious example of a disgraceful truce, is disgraceful partly because, "defeated by the Marcomanni and in flight, he sent hastily to Decebalus the king of the Dacians, and convinced him to make a treaty, which he had not granted him [Decebalus] before, though he had asked many times" (Cass. Dio 67.7). Herodian describes with contempt the first efforts of Severus Alexander to solve the crisis with the Persian monarch Ardashir; because of his love of luxury and of peace (Herodian writes that he had little experience with warfare), he responds to the Persian's aggression with diplomacy rather than force: "the course that first seemed best to him, when he had consulted with his friends, was to send an embassy and check the assault and the hopes of the barbarian with a letter" (6.2.3); Ardashir predictably ignores this overture (6.2.5). The proper procedure for the emperor would have been to reduce the enemy to a submissive state with a military defeat, then wait for him to offer peace. Thus Tacitus and Suetonius are both critical of Tiberius' penchant for solving problems through diplomacy rather than by force.[40] Suetonius also writes that in his retirement on the island of Capri, Tiberius allowed "Armenia to be occupied by the Parthians, Moesia by the Dacians and Sarmatians, the Gallic provinces to be devastated by the Germans, with great dishonor (*dedecore*) for the empire, and no less danger" (*Tib.* 41).

38. Onasander 10.13–14; cf. Campbell 1987, 13; and Herodian 6.4.4–6, where Ardashir follows the same principle in his embassy to Severus Alexander; also Dexippus *FGrH* 2, 100.6, quoted below.

39. The diplomatic ethos described here and below is essentially unchanged from that of the Republic as described by Rosenstein (1990, 133–138).

40. Tac. *Ann.* 6.32: "holding to his decision to conduct foreign affairs through counsel and cunning, and to keep war at a distance"; cf. 2.26; Suet. *Tib.* 37.4: "he repressed enemy attacks through his provincial governors (*legati*), undertaking no campaign afterward, and even through them only hesitantly and of necessity. Hostile or suspect kings he repressed by threats and complaints rather than force; some he drew to him with flattery and promises and did not let them go"; for similar charges against Caracalla, see Cass. Dio 77[78].12.1–2 and 77[78].20.22.

Here as elsewhere the word *decus* (or in this case its opposite, *dedecus*) is used to describe an intangible quality of "face" so crucial to Roman foreign relations; here as elsewhere this concept is closely connected with the idea of security. It is best translated as "honor," but in English this word is somewhat unsatisfactory, because it has outdated connotations of aristocrats slapping one another with gloves. Like most Latin value terms, the meaning of *decus* depended heavily on the context. It could be innocuous, meaning in some cases nothing more than "propriety." But it was also linked closely to other, more interesting words: *virtus* and the more terrifying *dignitas*. Like *virtus,* from the root meaning "man," *decus* had both a moral and a martial quality.[41] Many, many passages refer to the *decus belli,* the honor of warfare. Both individuals and the state could win *decus* in battle.[42]

It is thus not surprising that Augustus advertised his diplomatic success over the Parthians as a military victory, with the slogan "standards recaptured" on his coins and the boast that "I *forced* (*coegi*) the Parthians to return to me the spoils and standards of three Roman armies, and to seek the friendship of the Roman people as suppliants" (*RGDA* 29).[43] While Augustus gained considerable personal glory from his success, presumably with the urban population of Rome and with the army especially, nevertheless according to Roman ideas about international relations he had failed in a critical way: it is true that the Parthian king had shown deference to Rome, but he was not inspired by the feelings of terror and awe that could be produced only by a military defeat. Thus Tacitus writes that Phraates gave hostages to Augustus "although he had expelled Roman armies and generals," and adds that he acted "not so much out of fear of us as because he was suspicious of the loyalty of his people" (*Ann.* 2.1); Cassius Dio writes that "he [Augustus] received them [the standards] as if he had defeated the Parthian in some war" (54.8.2). The offense for which the Parthians were supposed to be punished and reduced to submission was the defeat of Crassus at Carrhae in 53 B.C.; we shall return to this point.

Cassius Dio records the commendable performance of the legate Vitellius, in the reign of Gaius (Caligula); he

41. For this and what follows, see Hellegouarc'h 1972, 413–415.

42. E.g., Val. Max. 2.8.1: "our ancestors believed that the *decus* of the city would be magnified by the glory of triumphs"; Livy 9.38.6: "fortune transferred the *decus* of war with the Romans from the Samnites to the Etruscans"; see also Pliny *HN* 7.95, where Pompey's victories add to the "*decus* of the Roman empire"; for a list of references, see Hellegouarc'h 1972, 414 nn. 6–10.

43. On this point, see Gruen 1990, 397–398.

governed brilliantly in many ways, but especially, when Artabanus was plotting against [Syria] because he had paid no penalty for Armenia, he overawed (κατέπληξε) him by encountering him suddenly when he was already
at the Euphrates, and reduced him to negotiations, and forced him to sacrifice to the images of Augustus and Gaius, and made peace with him
to the advantage of the Romans, and besides that even received his children
as hostages. (59.27.2–3)

Here we see what sort of situation was supposed to pose a threat to
the empire's security; Artabanus has grown arrogant because he has
been allowed to inflict a defeat on Rome on the issue of Armenia without suffering retaliation, and this has given him the confidence to challenge the empire directly by attacking Syria. The story behind the events
that Dio describes goes as follows: according to Tacitus, Artabanus had
been "faithful to the Romans" while the heroic general Germanicus was
alive. But after Germanicus' death

he soon assumed arrogance (*superbia*) against us and cruelty to his subjects
. . . despising the old age of Tiberius as unwarlike . . . he imposed Arsaces,
his oldest son [on the throne of Armenia], and added the insult (*contu-
melia*) of sending legates to demand the return of the treasure Vonones had
left in Syria and Cilicia; at the same time he was boasting with arrogant language and threats of the old boundaries of the Persians and Macedonians,
and that he would invade the territories possessed first by Cyrus and then
by Alexander. (*Ann.* 6.31)

Dio writes that "when no vengeance (τιμωρία) came about from Tiberius for this, he attacked Cappadocia and even treated the Parthians
rather arrogantly (ὑπερηφανώτερον)" (58.26.1).

Both Tacitus and Dio perceive Rome's relationship with Parthia as
one where a show of military weakness, usually on the issue of Armenia,
leads to *superbia* on the part of the enemy and ultimately to danger.
This word *superbia* is also used elsewhere to describe Rome's enemies,
as an argument for warfare; the most famous example is, however, from
the late Republic, in Caesar's account of his conflict with Ariovistus,
chief of the Suebi.[44] A vice characteristic of people of high status,[45] *superbia* was the opposite of deference and therefore exactly what one
wished to avoid in one's enemies. Thus Arminius, the leader of the revolt of the Cherusci against Varus in A.D. 9, "ridiculed the standards and
the eagles arrogantly" (*per superbiam;* Tac. *Ann.* 1.61). Pliny praises Tra-

44. *B Gall.* 1.33; Szidat 1970, 20; cf. Hellegouarc'h 1972, 440.
45. Hellegouarc'h 1972, 439–441; but it can also refer to people of low status acting
above their station, as Pallas in Tac. *Ann.* 13.23.

jan for controlling Parthian *superbia* by terror (*Pan.* 14.1). Conversely, what the Romans considered their *decus* would appear, from the barbarian point of view, like *superbia* (Tac. *Agr.* 30.4). It was important to suppress barbarian *superbia* with an appropriate show of force; thus Virgil writes that Rome's destiny is to "spare the conquered and to subdue the arrogant" (*superbos; Aen.* 6.851–853). Rome's failure to reduce the arrogant Artabanus to a state of terror and deference by vigorously exacting vengeance, in the passages cited above, is potentially disastrous. Vitellius restores the ideal relationship by "overawing" Artabanus with a show of arms and exacting a display of reverence for Rome. Suetonius tells us that, besides sacrificing to images of Augustus and Gaius as in the passage quoted from Dio, he was also required to worship the Roman military standards (*Gaius* 14.3), which also recalls Plautius Silvanus' boast that he forced foreign kings to adore the Roman standards.[46] This ritual of deference emphasized Rome's *military* superiority and contrasts with the *superbia* of Arminius regarding the standards, noted above.

Tacitus seems consistently to represent Rome and Parthia as engaged in this sort of competition for status with each other. When the Parthians request a king from among the hostages at Rome, "Caesar [Augustus] thought this reflected splendidly on himself" (*Ann.* 2.2), but the Parthians are overcome by "shame, that the Parthians had degenerated; that a king, infected with the habits of the enemy, had been sought from another world; now the throne of the Arsacids is received or given like a Roman province; where was that glory of the slaughterers of Crassus and the expellers of Antony . . . ?" (ibid.).[47] This passage demonstrates that military defeats inflicted back and forth are a way of keeping track of the status issue, and also that the conflict is framed in terms of honor and disgrace. The right or ability to appoint a king over another people is, obviously, an important symbol of superior status that if necessary will be defended by force. Romans and Parthians fought repeatedly over the right to appoint the king of Armenia; and while considerations of safety are important here, the conflict is described not in the modernizing language of "buffer zones" or "springboards for attack" but in terms of the *decus* of Rome, which must be maintained at all costs; and for the Parthians the concerns are supposed to be similar. In Claudius' reign, Pharasmanes (king of Iberia) placed his son on the throne of Armenia, murdering Rome's appointee; the governor of Syria and his advisers had to

---

46. On this ceremony, see also Tac. *Ann.* 15.29 (Tiridates) and Gagé 1959, 255–256.

47. Note that Suren, the victor over Crassus, was a Parthian epic hero; see Bivar 1983, 50–51; Wolski 1993, 89–90.

choose between a costly and dangerous war or the humiliation of the empire: "a few were concerned with the honor (*decus*) of the state, but most were talking about safety" (Tac. *Ann.* 12.47). Corbulo's first act, on assembling his army, was to demand that Vologeses "choose peace over war and, by giving hostages, continue the reverence for the Roman people that was customary for his predecessors" (*Ann.* 13.9). Later, Tacitus writes that "Corbulo considered it worthy of the greatness of the Roman people to regain what had been acquired by Lucullus and Pompey" (13.34). The Parthian king, on the other hand, wanted to "avenge the dignity (*fastigium*) of the Arsacids, scorned by the expulsion of his brother Tiridates" (15.1); and, like the Romans, Parthians were also motivated by a desire to recapture the traditional possessions of glorious ancestors.[48] In the story of Rome's conflict with Parthia, issues of honor, disgrace, and deference emerge repeatedly.

At one point in this conflict the general Caesennius Paetus—portrayed as weak and lax in contrast to the stern disciplinarian Corbulo—was forced to negotiate a truce with the Parthians. The loss of face involved in this situation is obvious. Pactus requested the peace himself, after a military defeat; he agreed to withdraw entirely from Armenia; a rumor circulated that his troops had been subjected to the ritual humiliation of the yoke; Armenian soldiers snatched back the spoils and slaves the Romans had captured.[49] All such treaties negotiated in the field had to be approved by the emperor. Thus Nero had to choose, once again, between "dangerous war" (*bellum anceps*) and "disgraceful peace" (*pax inhonesta;* Tac. *Ann.* 15.25); he chose war. The treaty ultimately negotiated by Corbulo, and approved by Nero, exacted signs of deference from the Parthians; Tiridates was forced to acknowledge the authority of Rome by going there as a suppliant; in the meantime, like Artabanus before him, he sacrificed before an array of Roman military standards, and a statue of the emperor, where he deposited his crown (Tac. *Ann.* 15.29; Cass. Dio 62.23.3–4). "Tiridates was on his way, practically a prisoner, to be a spectacle to the people" (Tac. *Ann.* 15.29).

Thus deference from the enemy is a critical goal in the conduct of Roman foreign relations; it was supposed to be won and maintained by force of arms and motivated by feelings of terror and awe on the en-

48. *Ann.* 15.2; cf. 6.31 and Cass. Dio 80.3.1–4 on the Persians. On this "policy" of the Arsacids, much discussed in modern literature, see Wolski 1966 and id. 1993, 119–121; Dabrowa 1984; Isaac 1992, 21–33.

49. *Ann.* 15.13–15; also see Cass. Dio 62.21.2 for Paetus' peace; on the "δύσκλεια," see 62.23.2; the rumor that the Romans had been led under the yoke is repeated in Suetonius (*Ner.* 39.1).

emy's part. In this respect Corbulo's success, like Augustus', left something to be desired: Corbulo had inflicted no military defeat on the Parthians to counterbalance or retaliate for the defeat of Paetus. Tacitus seems, cynically, to comment on this fact when he writes that spectators of Corbulo's successful negotiations were the more amazed because "the slaughter and siege of Roman armies [was] still printed on their eyes" (15.29). Thus Nero's spectacular ceremonial humiliation of Tiridates at Rome was not a complete propaganda success, at least not with his own class; Cassius Dio writes disparagingly that by the end of the visit the Parthian despised Nero's weakness but respected the more martial Corbulo. Nero also made the mistake of giving Tiridates huge amounts of money and—like Domitian to Decebalus later on—valuable artisans; the issue of money in diplomacy will be discussed below.[50] For now let us note some of the things that signal the deference of the enemy (and thus reflect or reinforce the *decus* of Rome) and some of those that, conversely, involve a loss of face and an appearance of weakness for the Romans. To be the first to offer peace communicated weakness and humiliation, as demonstrated above. The terms were also important; for example, any withdrawal from conquered territory was unacceptable. Florus records that it is *pulchrum ac decorum,* seemly and honorable, to have acquired new provinces, whether wealthy or poor (1.47.4), including Britain, "although divided from the whole world, still because it was pleasing to conquer them" (1.45.2). On the other hand, the shame of Germany's loss outweighs the glory of its conquest.[51] Nero thought about withdrawing from Britain; but he was prevented by "shame (*verecundia*), lest he should appear to detract from his father's glory" (Suet. *Ner.* 18).[52] Commodus' advisers warn him that to abandon the Danube wars will be both disgraceful (ἀπρεπές) and dangerous (ἐπισφαλές; Herodian 1.6.5). Here we see again the close link between Rome's dignity, or appearance of greatness, and its security.

Signs of deference that might be extracted from an enemy include, as in the case of Tiridates, Rome's right to crown their king.[53] Domi-

---

50. On the ceremony, see Cass. Dio 62.1–6 and Suet. *Ner.* 16; Tiridates despises Nero, Cass. Dio 62.6.4 and 6.

51. 2.30.21: *magis turpiter amissa est quam gloriose adquisita.*

52. Suetonius himself includes this passage among Nero's good acts (cf. *Ner.* 19.3) and in general seems to have opposed the expansion of the empire (see Brunt 1990, 465); but Nero's own motivation of shame is revealing.

53. *Rex datus* appears on coins of Augustus, Trajan, Antoninus Pius, and Lucius Verus, and the value attached to this is obvious; cf. Augustus' boast in *RGDA* 33; the king he gave to the Parthians was Vonones, son of Phraates, who had been a hostage in Rome (Tac. *Ann.* 2.1–2). On the giving of kings, see Gagé 1959, 252–255; on the coinage, Göbl 1961.

tian's right to crown the king of Dacia, which was not won by military force but negotiated after a defeat, is recognized as fraudulent: "Domitian placed the diadem on Diegis just as though he had truly conquered them (ὡς ἀληθῶς κεκρατηκώς) and could give any king to the Dacians" (Cass. Dio 67.7.3). We have seen that terms of peace might include an elaborate show of obeisance to Rome such as worshiping Roman standards or images of the emperor. The enemy should also give hostages as pledges of good faith; Augustus received hostages even from the Parthian king,[54] which he took pains to advertise (RGDA 32) and to show off (Suet. Aug. 43.4). The Romans, as noted above, demanded from Vologesis that "by giving hostages he should continue the reverence for the Roman people that was customary for his predecessors" (Tac. Ann. 13.9); Corbulo and Quadratus quibble over who should get credit for receiving them. But Tacitus comments cynically that Vologesis complies not out of terror of Roman arms (cf. 2.1) but "in order to prepare for war at his convenience, or that he might remove those whom he suspected of jealousy under the name of hostages"; thus Rome has not accomplished its main goal here. Conversely, it is dubious whether the Romans ever gave hostages in return in the Principate; if they did, the historical tradition has virtually suppressed all evidence of this diplomatic humiliation.[55]

Money payment was also a sign of deference, as argued in the previous chapter;[56] Severus Alexander, called to the Rhine frontier, made the terrible mistake of offering money to the Germans rather than demanding it, at which his army is supposed to have mutinied (Herodian 6.7.9–10). Cash gifts or support for foreign kings, when Rome was clearly in a position of superior status—when they rewarded loyalty or obedience, for example, or when they supported a king crowned or granted by Rome—were acceptable foreign-policy procedure. Thus Claudius' ap-

54. RGDA 32; Gagé (1977, 142–143) collects references; see also Brunt 1990, 462 with n. 61.

55. Only one example of the exchange of hostages (obsides, ὅμηροι) with barbarians—that is, in the sense of giving pledges or sureties rather than an exchange of prisoners (captivi, αἰχμάλωτοι)—in the literature of the Principate is known to me—namely, Cass. Dio 71[72].15, where Marcus grants some concessions to the Marcomanni in return for their grudging obedience to Roman demands, "τούς τε ὁμήρους ἠλλάξατο," "and he exchanged hostages," as though this were a usual occurrence. This passage, however, seems to be an anomaly, though a thorough investigation is needed. Cf. Aymard (1961, 136–137, with n. 3), who notes also a passage from Caesar (B Gall. 1.14.7) where the Helvetii insist that they are accustomed to receiving hostages, not to giving them. As often in the Gallic War, the arrogance of the enemy is indicated by his making boasts and claims that are appropriate only to Rome.

56. On subsidies and what follows, see especially Wolters 1990–1991, pt. 2, 116–121.

pointee Italicus of the Cherusci received money (Tac. *Ann.* 11.6); this was no doubt the spin that Domitian hoped to put on his payments to Decebalus.[57] That emperor also rewarded another loyal king of the Cherusci, who sent hostages and supplicated (ἱκετεύειν) him for aid; "he did not receive a military alliance (συμμαχία), but he did receive money" (Cass. Dio 67.5.1). That military support may have been the preferable alternative seems to be the implication of Tacitus' cynical comment on money paid to the Quadi and Marcomanni: "they are helped only rarely by our arms, more often by our money; nor are they the worse for it."[58] But Marcus Aurelius is adept at the correct usage of money in diplomacy: one tribe, approaching, we presume, humbly and offering an alliance, is supported with funds; they in turn help defeat another tribe, which is threatening war and demanding money; the emperor naturally rejects this demand (Cass. Dio 71[72].11.2). Cassius Dio writes that Marcus "received embassies from the nations, not all on the same terms, but according to whether each of them was *deserving* of receiving citizenship or immunity from taxes or relaxation of tribute, either permanently or for a specific time, or even perpetual subsidy" (71[72].19.1). This passage neatly illustrates not only the role of money in Roman foreign relations but also the ambiguity and blurring between the foreign and the domestic: the word ἔθνη here might mean either "provinces" or "tribes."

When the Romans handed over money without having achieved a position of superior status—when they asked for peace first, or when a wrong was insufficiently avenged—the gift then became a more or less disgraceful bribe to secure peace. This was how Domitian's treaty with Decebalus in fact appeared to his contemporaries; under Trajan, on the other hand, "now we receive hostages, we do not buy them; nor with huge expenditures and immense gifts do we come to an agreement that we have won" (Pliny *Pan.* 12.2). Commodus is criticized for paying money to end the Danube war on his accession;[59] Caracalla is supposed to have paid off the Cenni, who "accepted the name of defeat for a great deal of money, and allowed him to get safely back to [the province of] Germany" (Cass. Dio 77[78].14.2). Caracalla's disgraceful behavior was compounded by the allegation that he paid the barbarians in pure gold coin while pawning off debased coinage on the Romans (ibid., 77[78].14.4).

57. Ibid., 117–118.
58. *Germ.* 42.2, cf. 15.2; and Wolters 1990–1991, pt. 2, 119.
59. Herodian 1.6.6–8; with Whittaker 1969–1970, ad loc.

In general, it was important that Rome should be in a position of judgment and authority and should not appear to be negotiating with barbarians on equal terms.[60] Thus Maroboduus provokes the Romans with the behavior of his envoys, who "sometimes commended him [to the emperor] as a suppliant, but at other times spoke as though on behalf of an equal" (Vell. Pat. 2.109.2). But under Trajan, enemies "ask and supplicate, we grant or we deny—both from the majesty (*maiestas*) of the empire. They are grateful if they prevail; they do not dare complain when we deny them" (Pliny *Pan.* 12.2–3). Under Domitian, in contrast, Rome's enemies "would not even enter into a truce except on equal terms (*aequis condicionibus*), and would accept no laws unless they gave them" (ibid., 11.5). This is the meaning also of a seemingly odd episode from Tacitus, in which the Ampsivarii, a German tribe, seize and settle on land near the Rhine bank that is supposed to remain vacant; the tribe is homeless, and its king has distinguished himself by remaining loyal during the revolt of Arminius. The Roman legate, Avitus, is inclined to be sympathetic but in his response makes the point that "the commands of betters must be borne; it was pleasing to those gods to whom they prayed that judgment (*arbitrium*) should remain with the Romans, what to give and what to take away, and that they should allow no other judges but themselves" (*Ann.* 13.56).

It was also important that any prisoners, spoils, or other symbols of Roman military defeat—such as captured military standards—should be returned.[61] It is the short-lived emperor Macrinus' natural cowardice that induces him to come to terms with the king of Parthia after a defeat for the notorious price of, if we believe Cassius Dio, 200 million sesterces; to Tiridates, king of Armenia, he restored a hostage—the king's mother—and returned the spoils that his predecessor Caracalla had captured; Dio adds incredulously that he may have promised to restore parts of Cappadocia as well (78[79].27). The best surviving examples of the opposite case—the proper conduct of treaty negotiations—come both

60. On this point, see also Sen. *Clem.* 1.1.2–4 on the decisions within the emperor's power: "which nations should be eradicated, which should be resettled, to whom liberty should be given, and from whom it should be taken; which kings should become slaves and which heads it is fitting to encircle with the honor of kings . . ." See also Sen. *De vita beata* 25.4, cited in n. 37 above.

61. Augustus boasts in *Res Gestae* of securing the return of standards and spoils from the Parthians (*RGDA* 29; and see above); Petronius demands that the Ethiopians return the spoils captured in their attack (Strab. 17.1.54); Marcus grants peace to the Quadi when they offer him gifts of horses and cattle and promise to restore all captives and deserters (Cass. Dio 71[72].11.2); Severus attacks Parthian territories when they agree to return prisoners and spoils but not to accept a garrison (ibid., 75.1.1–2).

from before and after the time limits of this study and illustrate that the principles did not really change over the centuries. First, the diplomacy of Caesar, as described in his commentaries on the Gallic war, neatly illustrates all the points discussed above.[62] Like later commanders who eschew the diplomatic for the military alternative and force barbarians to ask for peace, Caesar sends envoys much more rarely than he receives them, and only when military action would otherwise be considered "unjust"—for example, against a "friend of Rome."[63] Conversely, it is obviously a sign of Ariovistus' *superbia* that, when Caesar invites him to a meeting, he replies that Caesar should come to him instead (*B Gall.* 1.36); likewise when the Helvetii inform him that they are accustomed to take hostages and not to give them (1.14). Caesar responds to Ariovistus not with a compromise but with an ultimatum; eventually Ariovistus is forced to offer what he had formerly refused (1.42). Sometimes foreign envoys are described as begging, weeping, or throwing themselves at Caesar's feet.[64] They may, in this situation, receive reasonable terms; thus when the Nervii humbly beg for peace after being nearly exterminated, Caesar allows them to keep their territory "so that he might be seen to show mercy to pathetic suppliants."[65] But when the Helvetii threaten him by reminding him of their military prowess, he makes no concessions (1.14). Of course, Caesar is hardly an impartial witness of his own actions and may not be recording events exactly as they happened; on the other hand, his account is good evidence for the values of his society for the same reason. And there seems to have been little that was unusual or nontraditional in his diplomacy except that he was, if anything, especially flexible for a Roman commander; thus his reputation for *clementia,* or mercy.[66]

Another excellent account of Roman diplomacy has survived in a substantial fragment of the history of Dexippus on the events of the year 270 A.D., in the reign of Aurelian. The emperor

defeated the Scythian Iuthungi by force, and destroyed many of them in flight at their crossing of the Ister; and the ones who were left came to terms and sent an embassy. But it seemed that the demand for peace was not being made with timidity and panic resulting from a defeat, so that the money that

---

62. For what follows, see Szidat 1970.
63. Ibid., 129–130.
64. *B Gall.* 1.20.1, 1.27, 1.31; Szidat 1970, 115–116.
65. *B Gall.* 2.28; *ut in miseros ac supplices usus misericordia videretur.*
66. Szidat 1970, 130–131.

had come to them from the Romans before might be restored to them. . . . The Roman emperor Aurelian, when he learned that the embassy from the Iuthungi had arrived, said that he would address on the following day the matters about which they had come; and he arranged his soldiers as if for battle, for the purpose of overawing the enemy. And when he was satisfied with the arrangement, he climbed up on a tribunal raised high off the ground, and putting on a purple robe he drew up the whole array around him in a crescent. And all of those in authority, who had been entrusted with office, he stationed around on horses. And behind the emperor were the standards of the elite army—these were gold eagles, and imperial images, and catalogs of troops revealed in gold letters. . . . And when all these things had been organized, he thought it suitable for the Iuthungi to pass by. And when they saw [these things] they were astonished and were silent for a long time. . . .[67]

Here we see that, for example, peace is requested by the enemy after a crushing military defeat; the terms of the treaty, especially the restoration of money subsidies, will depend on their submissive and terrified attitude. Aurelian, perceiving them to be insufficiently frightened and overawed, arranges an elaborate martial entourage to reduce them to this condition; he ultimately refuses their peace proposal and sends them away "awestruck." As argued in chapter 3 above, the barbarian must be terrified at all times; thus emperors like Tiberius or Commodus who are perceived as pursuing pacific policies are criticized for their weakness, which emboldens barbarians and endangers the empire; while more martial emperors like Trajan and Pertinax are praised for the opposite reason.[68] Domitian's defeat and notorious peace with the Dacians was perceived as disastrous for the empire's security; according to Pliny he is "that emperor who used to give the greatest evidence of his defeat and flight when he celebrated a triumph. Therefore they had raised up their spirits and shaken off the yoke, and were contending with us no longer for their own liberty but for our slavery" (Pan. 11.5). On the other hand, Trajan's military victories terrified the enemy and restored Rome to its superior international status (ibid., 12).

It was therefore important that any military defeat, breach of treaty, or revolt—which would involve a loss of face for Rome, thus inviting more of the same—should be repaid vigorously and aggressively, with invasion, conquest, and the humiliation, or even attempted annihila-

67. FGrH 2, 100.6; cf. Millar 1969, 25–26.
68. See above, chap. 3, p. 119.

tion, of the enemy. The Romans show extreme touchiness on such issues, so that sometimes even "planning" or "being about to" attack is
punishable by total conquest.[69] The role of revenge and retaliation in
Rome's foreign wars is very prominent. Conquests that are made in response to some provocation by the enemy—and that punish and avenge
a wrong—are perceived as "just" or "necessary"; thus Augustus' claim
that "I pacified the Alps from that region, which is next to the Adriatic
Sea, to the Tuscan [i.e., Tyrrhenian Sea], without making war on any
people unjustly" (*per iniuriam; RGDA* 26). His claim is echoed in Suetonius; after listing territories and tribes subdued, checked, slaughtered,
resettled, and reduced to servitude, the historian writes: "Nor did he
make war on any tribe without just and necessary causes, and he was
so far from the desire to increase the empire or his military reputation
by any means at hand that he forced the leaders of some barbarians to
swear in the temple of Mars the Avenger that they would honor the
promises and peace that they were seeking" (*Aug.* 21.2). The idea that
wars of conquest ought not to be simply plundering missions, land
grabs, or occasions for self-aggrandizement is very strongly attested,
although all these things were good and legitimate results of a "just"
war—of a war, that is, provoked by the enemy. Thus Pliny's praise of
Trajan: "raised on warlike glories, you love peace, nor . . . do you seek
triumphs at every opportunity; you neither fear war, nor provoke it"
(*Pan.* 16.1–2). Cassius Dio also distinguishes between most of Caracalla's campaigns, which are unprovoked and in which he behaves atro-
ciously, and his wars that are "ἀναγκαῖαι καὶ κατεπειγούσαι," necessary and urgent.[70] Severus Alexander encourages his troops with the
argument that "to begin unjust deeds does not hold the promise of a
wise challenge; but to shake off those who trouble us brings the confidence of a good conscience" (Herodian 6.3.4). In this he is acting in ac-
cordance with the advice of the tactician Onasander, who writes that

69. As in the case of Crassus and the Thracians; see Cass. Dio 51.25: "he was anxious
to retaliate against (ἀμύνασθαι) the Thracians, who had harassed him during his retreat
from Moesia; for at the time they were reported to be fortifying places and about to make
war"; and note the ferocity of Crassus' response. In Vell. Pat. 2.109 a major part of Maroboduus' offense seems to be that he is avoiding provoking Rome but will resist if provoked; Vespasian annexes Antiochus of Commagene's territory based on the (untrue) report that he is conspiring with Parthia (Joseph. *BJ* 7.7.1; and see Isaac 1992, 39–40);
Domitian declares war "to retaliate against (ἀμύνασθαι) the Quadi and Marcomanni because they had not helped him against the Dacians" (Cass. Dio 67.7.1); the second Dacian
war involved treaty violations but no direct aggression by Decebalus (Cass. Dio 68.10.3–
4); on this point, see Brunt 1978, 176, 181.
70. On unnecessary campaigns, see 77[78].12; necessary, 77[78].13.1.

soldiers will fight better if the causes of the war are clear and "they see that they are not starting [the conflict] but defending" (or "retaliating," ἀμύνονται).[71]

Nevertheless, these are not arguments for fighting wars with defensive goals only, and indeed the boast of Augustus, quoted above, is not comprehensible in this way. Rather, because the empire's security rests on its appearance of greatness, which in turn depends on demonstrations of superior military force, any defeat or breach of treaty signals arrogance and should be avenged vigorously and aggressively. The word Augustus uses to describe what he did not do—*iniuria*—was commonly used of the causes or provocations of warfare and is revealing about them. In the private sphere, Caesar uses the word to describe insults to his honor or *dignitas*. When Pompey retains the two legions he has borrowed; when he himself is required to return to Rome to run for the consulship—these are *iniuriae* for which Caesar waged world war.[72] Caesar also describes the offenses committed by the Helvetii and by Ariovistus as *iniuriae*, which justify his campaigns against them.[73] The important thing here is that an *iniuria* could be anything; the reference is not to the degree of harm suffered but the injustice of the act. Thus marching through Caesar's province against his will, harassing friends of Rome, or defeating a Roman army all might be called *iniuriae*; all of these were committed by the Helvetii, and all were justifications for war.[74] The other important aspect of *iniuriae*, in both the public and the private sphere, is that they were supposed to be avenged.[75]

71. 4.2; on the idea of the "just war" in the late Republic, see Brunt 1978, 175–183, including discussion of Caesar's commentaries; in the Republic generally, Albert 1980; on the idea of provocation, Mantovani 1990, 25–43. Conversely, in King Shapur's famous *Res Gestae* it is the Romans who always start the conflict (Dodgeon and Lieu 1991, 2.1.5, lines 6–8; 3.1.4, line 10).

72. Most strikingly in *B Civ.* 1.7, where he begins his address to his troops by relating "all the injuries of his enemies against him ever" and where he calls on them to defend his *laus, honos*, and *dignitas*. See also ibid., 1.9 and 1.31; and Raaflaub 1974, especially 125–152.

73. See *B Gall.* 1.12, 1.14, on the Helvetii; on Ariovistus, see 1.31 (Caesar is asked to "defend all of Gaul against injury from Ariovistus"), 1.33, 1.35; cf. 1.36, where Ariovistus accuses Caesar of *iniuria*, and 1.20, where Caesar forgives an *iniuria rei publicae*. In 3.10 Caesar refers to "the injury of detaining Roman knights" as being among the offenses of the rebellious Veneti. Cf. also 4.8, 5.1, 5.20, and 5.28, where Ambiorix encourages the Nervii to "take revenge on the Romans for the injuries they had received."

74. *B Gall.* 1.14. For *iniuria* as cause of war, see also Cic. *Fam.* 12.15.6 (*provinciam . . . ab iniuria defendere*), *Rep.* 2.38.10; Sall. *Cat.* 51.5; Val. Max. 5.1.1a; Livy 1.23.7, 2.6.3, 3.25.6, 31.31.2, 32.10.6; Tac. *Ann.* 12.45.

75. This was an essential element of *dignitas*; see MacMullen 1986, 515–519; see also Y. Thomas 1984, and Epstein 1987 passim. The close relationship between *iniuria* and *ulciscor/ultio* is attested in the very numerous passages where they occur together. A full

In Seneca's treatise *On Anger*, he imagines an objection to his philosophical argument about the need to control this emotion: "We shall be less despised," his imaginary interlocutor says, "if we avenge an injury" (2.33.1). The same, I would argue, was true in the public and international arenas: insult required vigorous retaliation if *decus* was to be maintained. Romans often respond to a raid on their territory or allied territory, a favorite cause for war, with total conquest.[76] Another common justification for war is a military defeat inflicted on Rome; here an example from the late Republic, that of Crassus, is perhaps the most striking. His campaign is universally represented in the literary tradition as motivated by greed and desire for personal glory; it was neither a "necessary" nor a "just" war.[77] Nevertheless, his defeat required retaliation; more than a century later Lucan still bewails the civil wars that Rome waged while "the ghost of Crassus wandered unavenged" (1.11–12). In the twenties B.C. Horace and Propertius look forward to victories in Parthia that will restore Rome to its pristine state of virtue after the demoralizing civil wars and avenge the defeat of Crassus;[78] by this time the Parthians had defeated Antony, too, though this had less effect on the Roman imagination. Horace seems wildly to exaggerate the dan-

---

analysis cannot be undertaken here, but I offer a few examples: Cicero uses the term *ultor iniuriae* or *iniuriarum* in *Div. Caec.* 11, 53, 54; *Mil.* 35; *Brut.* 268; and the verb *ulcisci iniuriam* or *iniurias* in *Div. Caec.* 60; *Part. or.* 96, 112, 131; *Phil.* 13.46; *Inv. rhet.* 2.81; *De or.* 3.116; *Red. pop.* 22; *Red. sen.* 23; *Scaur.* 23; *Verr.* 2.1.72, 2.2.9. On vengeance and litigation in the Republican period see David 1992, 171–176, and Epstein 1987, chap. 5. The words are very commonly used together in the philosophical works of Seneca (arguing, of course, that the philosopher should not desire *ultio* but nevertheless indicating that this desire was pervasive in his society): *Constant.* 12.3, 18.3; *De ira* 2.1.4, 2.3.5, 2.32.3–2.33.1, 3.5.8, 3.27.1; *Clem.* 1.21.1; *Ben.* 6.4.1. In a foreign-relations context, the words are used together in Cic. *Rep.* 2.38.10, *Phil.* 6.2, *Verr.* 2.1.84; Livy 7.30.12–14; Nepos *Conon* 5.1; Sall. *Iug.* 68.1.2; Tac. *Agr.* 16.2, *Hist.* 5.24, *Ann.* 12.45; SHA *Sev.* 3.7. *Iniuria* also commonly occurs with *vindico*.

76. Raids are very frequently named as reasons for conquest by Florus—e.g., the Cantabrians (2.33.47), the Pannonians (2.24.8), the Dalmatians (2.25.10). Crassus' aggression in Moesia was prompted when the Bastarnae attacked the territory of a Roman ally (Cass. Dio 51.23.4); the Raetians plunder "even Italy" in a raid described graphically in 54.22, leading to the conquests of Drusus and Tiberius; cf. Strab. 4.6.8–9; Marcus and Maximinus both respond to northern invasions with wars of conquest (see above, chap. 3).

77. See above, chap. 4, n. 128; and below, n. 123; see also Albert 1980, 112–114.

78. See Wisseman 1982 on the poetic tradition about the Parthians under Augustus, and especially 128–131, summarizing the years up to 20 B.C. See Hor. *Carm.* 1.2.21–24 for the civil war–foreign war theme; in vv. 50–52 he writes that Augustus will not allow the Medes to "ride about unpunished"; in 3.2.1–6 he emphasizes the need to return to ancient, warlike ways. In 3.5.1–12 he focuses on the humiliation of Crassus; see also 1.12.53–56 and 3.3.37–44 for more anticipation of Parthian victories. Propertius encourages Augustus to "expiate Crassus and his massacre" (4.1–10; cf. 3.5.47–48).

ger involved when he writes of the "Parthians, threatening Latium,"[79] but the "threat," of course, lay in the loss of face and appearance of weakness suffered by Rome as a result of these defeats. Augustus attempted to reverse the situation by retrieving the lost standards, prominent symbols of Rome's humiliation; this accomplishment he advertised very loudly, and was voted a triumphal arch; the image of the kneeling Parthian became a common theme in the iconography of his reign.[80] Indeed the retrieval of lost standards played an important part in many military campaigns, thus emphasizing the fact that their purpose was largely to restore face after a defeat; for example, the recapture of the standards lost with Varus is a key theme in Tacitus' narrative of Germanicus' campaigns,[81] and Germanicus' triumphal arch is voted "for the recapture of the standards lost with Varus" (*Ann.* 2.41). Florus still remembers the loss of these standards (2.30.31) and appears not to know that they have been recovered.

In the center of the cuirass of Augustus' famous Prima Porta statue, a bearded and trousered Parthian hands over the standards to a Roman amid symbols of world rule.[82] Ovid celebrates the victory at some length in the *Fasti:* "You [Parthian] no longer hold proofs of our shame" (5.580–594). The standards were dedicated in a new, hastily improvised temple to Mars the Avenger.[83] But as noted above, some perceived the emperor's policy here as insufficiently forceful; he had achieved the symbol without the substance. The only effective way to retaliate for an of-

79. *Carm.* 1.12.53; see Mantovani 1990, 38; and cf. Cass. Dio 56.23.1 (after the disaster of Varus, Augustus expects the Germans to attack Italy).

80. On Augustus' propaganda regarding the Parthian standards, see Gruen 1990, 397; Zanker 1988, 186–192; on the kneeling Parthian, ibid., 187.

81. In *Ann.* 1.59, Arminius boasts that "the Roman standards could still be seen in the groves of the Germans"; Germanicus retrieves one eagle (1.60); soldiers recall how Arminius ridiculed the standards and eagles (1.61); Germanicus attacks the Marsi on the information that they have one of the standards (2.25). The retrieval of the standards is also mentioned on the Tabula Siarensis, which records the honors voted to Germanicus on his death; coins also advertise "standards recaptured, Germans conquered" (*RIC* Tiberius 36). Augustus boasts, "By defeating enemies, I recovered a large number of standards lost by other generals, from Spain and Gaul, and from the Dalmatians" (*RGDA* 29); see the commentary of Gagé 1977, ad loc.; the emperor made a great display of retrieving the Dalmatian standards taken from Gabinius (App. *Ill.* 28); on Gabinius' defeat, see ibid., 12, and Gruen 1990, 401. Crassus attacks a fort to recapture standards taken by the Bastarnae (Cass. Dio 56.21.5); Claudius receives a well-deserved acclamation when his legates retrieve the last of the standards lost with Varus (Cass. Dio 60.8.7); Trajan retrieves the standards lost in Decebalus' defeat of Fuscus (ibid., 68.9.3).

82. See Zanker 1988, 188–192, on the Prima Porta statue; see also Hannestad 1988, 50–56.

83. Zanker 1988, 186–187; Cass. Dio 54.8.3.

fense was violently, and Augustus himself may have thought his success inadequate. The theme of Gaius' expedition to the east in 2 B.C. was, again, revenge: it was the year of the consecration of Augustus' new, more famous temple to Mars the Avenger, an event that was preceded by a mock naval battle re-creating the defeat of the Persians by the Greeks.[84] Ovid anticipates Gaius' triumph and writes: "Parthian, you will pay the penalty."[85]

In his commentaries on the Gallic war, Caesar—always in pursuit of self-justification and glory—repeatedly recalls the defeat of Lucius Cassius by the Helvetii nearly fifty years previously, to justify his own campaigns against that tribe (*B Gall.* 1.7, 1.12–14, 1.30). The Helvetii boasted of this victory, he writes, and "marveled that they had inflicted these *iniuriae* for so long without consequences" (1.14). Caesar, however, forces them to beg for peace after a campaign in which he claims to have slaughtered two-thirds of the *general* population (1.27–29). Thus revenge for an insult could be very violent and could come decades, even generations, later. Velleius Paterculus claims that the German conquests of Drusus and Tiberius were meant to avenge the defeat of the legate Lollius by certain German tribes in 16 B.C.—a standard had been captured—and Tacitus still remembers the *clades Lolliana*.[86] Cassius Dio does not make this connection; at first Augustus made peace with the Germans, and Drusus' campaigns came several years later;[87] but as noted above, the delay does not necessarily indicate that revenge was not a factor. The details of the situation—where the defeat occurred, for instance, and whether it was on Roman territory or enemy territory—sometimes do not seem to matter to the ancient sources and remain obscure to this day, partly for this reason. Suetonius writes that Domitian made war "unprovoked (*sponte*) against the Chatti, but of necessity (*necessario*) against the Sarmatians, who had destroyed a legion together with its legate" (*Dom.* 6.1). Apparently no further explanation is necessary. Cassius Dio writes that Verus' campaign against the Parthians was provoked when their king, Vologeses IV, destroyed a legion under the

---

84. Nicolet 1991, 44; Cass. Dio 55.10.7; Ovid *Ars am.* 1.171–172. On the Mars temple, see Cass. Dio 55.10.1–8; Suet. *Aug.* 29.1–2; Zanker 1988, 194–195; Nicolet 1991, 41–44.

85. *Ars am.* 1.177–228; the quotation is v. 179; see Syme 1978, 8–13, on Ovid and the expedition of Gaius; and Williams 1978, 77–80.

86. Vell. Pat. 2.97; Tac. *Ann.* 1.10.

87. See Cass. Dio 54.20.4–5 on Lollius' defeat; 54.32–33 on Drusus' campaigns. Florus writes that the Germans provoked Drusus by crucifying twenty Roman centurions (2.30.24). On the issue of whether a change to an aggressive policy in Germany can be perceived as an immediate result of the *clades,* see recently Wolters 1990, 153–157.

command of Sedatius Severianus, the Roman governor of Cappadocia, at Elegeia in Armenia in A.D. 161; what the legion was doing there is unclear.[88] In all of these cases, as in the famous case of Varus, Roman historiography emphasizes the injury to the Roman state as represented by the institution of the legion—not, for example, total numbers killed—and the death of its aristocratic commander.

One of the most striking examples of revenge for a military defeat is the case of Germanicus' campaigns, though here the element of "revolt" is also important; this subject will be discussed next. In any case, no *immediate* provocation for Germanicus' first invasion in the winter of A.D. 14 is obvious; the mutinous army wants to atone for its behavior with an attack on the enemy (Tac. *Ann.* 1.49). This first campaign involved a night massacre of unarmed, drunken Marsi (a motif that will recur in this discussion) and a slaughter of noncombatants (*Ann.* 1.50–51). The justification for the war occurred several years previously, in A.D. 9: at the beginning of his history, Tacitus tells us that it was fought "to abolish the infamy of the army lost with Quintilius Varus."[89] The eagles captured by the Germans were still in the possession of the enemy (1.59), and, as noted above, their retrieval is an important theme in the story of Germanicus' wars. Nor is it difficult to pick out the most memorable episode: Tacitus' baroque description of Germanicus' return to the grisly scene of Varus' slaughter in the Teutoburg Forest (1.61). Tiberius eventually recalls Germanicus, arguing that "Roman revenge (*ultio*) had been satisfied" (2.26), and Strabo writes that the Germans have paid the penalty for their acts in Germanicus' splendid triumph (7.1.4). But Tacitus does not agree; for him the war is not yet *confectum*, finished (2.41), and Germanicus himself, in the heat of battle, is made to declare that "only the destruction of the race would end the war."[90] But this was an extreme case.

The defeat of a Roman army was also, apparently, a prominent theme in the Dacian wars of Trajan, which are, however, less well attested. Sue-

88. Cass. Dio 71.2.1 and Fronto *Principia historiae* 16 (Loeb 2:215). Lucian *Alex.* 27 makes fun of Severianus' decision to invade Armenia. Vologeses also defeated the governor of Syria (SHA *Marcus* 8.6). On these events, see Angeli Bertinelli 1976, 25–26, with full references.

89. *Ann.* 1.3. On Germanicus' campaigns, see, e.g., Lehmann 1991, arguing for a continuous series of campaigns beginning with Tiberius' command of the Rhine legions in 12 B.C. Lehmann holds that the ultimate goal was the conquest of Germany until Tiberius' recall of Germanicus in A.D. 16–17.

90. 2.21. But note that in *Ann.* 2.26 Tacitus writes that the enemy was on the verge of asking for peace when Tiberius recalled Germanicus, implying that this (i.e., a suitably humiliating treaty requested by the enemy) would have been an acceptable outcome.

tonius writes that Domitian made two expeditions against the Dacians, "the first after the defeat of Oppius Sabinus, of consular rank; the second after [the defeat of] Cornelius Fuscus, prefect of the praetorian guard, to whom he had entrusted the command of the war" (*Dom.* 6.1). Other sources tell us that a legion was destroyed with Sabinus or Fuscus; and that the Dacians cut off Sabinus' head.[91] Thus these events follow the pattern of legendary military defeats described above, with emphasis on the slaughter of high-ranking commanders and the loss of a legion. Once again the details are obscure. The poet Martial, flattering Domitian, declares Fuscus avenged by the emperor's campaigns in Dacia and notorious treaty (6.76). But, as we have seen, aristocratic opinion was not satisfied, and years later Trajan's wars seem to have had the same object of retaliation for an old defeat and humiliation. This is what Cassius Dio means when he writes that the emperor first attacked the Dacians because "he considered the things they had done, and he was distressed by the money that they received every year" (68.6.1); that is, considering their injuries to Rome, vengeance and not subsidy was required. Pliny's *Panegyric* also emphasizes the disgrace that Rome suffered with Domitian's treaty (11.5).[92] Trajan's enormous monumental trophy at Adamklissi in Lower Moesia is dedicated to Mars the Avenger,[93] and one of the metopes seems to show a scene reminiscent of Germanicus' visit to the Teutoburg Forest.[94] Another metope perhaps shows the slaughter of noncombatants in wagons.[95] Cassius Dio

91. Eutropius 7.23.4: "He [Domitian] made a campaign . . . against the Sarmatians at the same time as the Scythians, and the Dacians at the same time as the Chatti. And he lost one legion together with the generals, and Sabinus the consular, and Fuscus the consular, fell with the whole army. But he celebrated a triumph over them [sc., the Dacians] shamelessly" (7.23.4). In Jordanes (*Get.* 76–77) the Goths (he equates Getae and Goths) begin the war by breaking their treaty with the Romans and devastating the bank of the Danube, expelling the garrison; they then defeat Sabinus and cut off his head; in response Domitian orders Fuscus to cross the Danube, where he is killed. Domitian puts Fuscus in charge of the war in Cass. Dio 67.6.5, but the surviving epitome does not record his defeat. On Domitian's Danube wars, see especially Strobel 1989.

92. Cf. Alexandrescu-Vianu 1979, 125.

93. Strobel 1984, 34–35; Rossi 1971, 55–56; on the inscription, see ibid., p. 49, and Picard 1957, 394–397. Mars Ultor also appears on Trajanic coins of A.D. 100 and 101–102 (ibid., 396–397; and Strack 1931, 90–91, 105–106).

94. Metope XXXIV. This is the suggestion of Rossi 1971, 62. The scene shows a Roman soldier, a headless corpse at his feet and a Dacian aiming an arrow at him. For a plate of the metope, see Florescu 1965, illust. 212, with commentary on p. 494; here the corpse is interpreted as a dead Dacian. I agree with Rossi that the corpse appears to be "mouldering."

95. Rossi 1971, 63–64, 150; metopes XL–XLII show a battle with wagons. In metope XL there is a dead woman, a dead child, and a male Dacian slumped but still alive. Perhaps he is supposed to have voluntarily killed his family (Florescu 1965, illust. 218, with commentary on p. 499).

writes that Trajan retrieved the lost standards in the course of the war
(68.9.3). Thus Romans not only perceived revenge as a cause for war but
celebrated it as a just and necessary cause. It is admirable that Marcus
Aurelius' aims in his war with the Quadi were "not to acquire their land
but to exact vengeance from [or punish, τιμωρήσασθαι] the people"
(Cass. Dio 71[72].20.2).

Just as a military defeat, regardless of circumstances, required a re-
assertion of Rome's military prowess, so any breach of faith by the conquered barbarian had to be punished with aggressive action. Peoples under treaty to the Romans, but not necessarily occupied by them, could
be harshly punished for failing to comply with terms, and some examples
of this have been noted: Claudius' invasion of Britain, which in one version was provoked when some tribes failed to return Roman deserters;[96]
and Trajan's second war with Decebalus, whose kingdom had not yet
been annexed (Cass. Dio 68.10.3). In the case of occupied territory, as
argued in chapter 3, armed revolt was not unusual. Here especially, or
in the case of repeated and persistent treaty violations, only the most extreme responses would suffice; anything less might be perceived as dangerously inadequate. It is especially in the context of revolt that ancient
sources express the idea that the annihilation of the offending tribe is
the only sufficient punishment, and indeed in spite of—or, we might
speculate, perhaps partly because of—brutally repressive measures, the
Romans sometimes faced repeated revolts in the same province.

In normal circumstances, to spare conquered barbarians, as opposed
to annihilating them, was considered an admirable show of clemency;
thus Augustus writes: "I preferred to preserve those foreign peoples
whom it was possible to forgive safely, rather than to extirpate them"
(RGDA 3). Statius could praise Domitian in similar terms: "not quick to
anger even against the frenzy of foreigners, you give peace to the Chatti
and the Dacians" (Silv. 1.1.26–27); in another passage he lauds the
emperor's "clemency, which grants merciful treaties to the conquered
Chatti, and to the Dacians their mountain" (Silv. 3.3.168–169). Menander Rhetor writes that it is nice to include in any panegyric some praise
of the emperor's φιλανθρωπία, philanthropy, in allowing part of the
justly conquered race to survive (2.374). However, as Augustus' comment quoted above suggests, it was not always considered safe or appropriate to grant peace at all[97]—for example, in the case of stubborn

96. Suet. *Claud.* 17.1; cf. Cass. Dio 60.19.1 for a different account.
97. In several cases the sources seem to indicate that to make any peace at all with
rebels might be dangerous or disgraceful; e.g., Tacitus criticizes Tiberius for calling off the
war with Tacfarinas "when some were left behind through whom the war might be re-

intransigence. This is the meaning of a passage from Cassius Dio, referring to the truce with Maroboduus and the events of A.D. 6: "they [the
Germans], being afraid of them [the Romans], made peace not only
once but twice. The reason for granting them peace again even though
they had broken the treaty in a short time was the situation of the Dalmatians and the Pannonians, which was greatly disturbed, and which demanded a sharp response." [98] The annihilation of foreign populations
could, in some circumstances, be something to boast about. [99] In the case
of a revolt, the most severe measures were warranted. The very prominent genocidal theme in Germanicus' campaigns has been noted; this
was a revolt, too, because the Romans had "conquered" Germany as far
as the Elbe; [100] so "the faithless and peace-breaking [Cherusci] must be
slaughtered for revenge and glory." [101] As in the case of Crassus, the fact
that tradition blamed Varus himself for the revolt seems unimportant. [102]
Tacitus criticizes Tiberius for his management of the very violent tax revolt of the Frisii: the governor of Lower Germany crossed the Rhine and
invaded, but he was defeated; and Tiberius, out of jealousy lest anyone
else win military glory, "disguised the losses. . . . Nor in this case did the
senate care if the outer reaches of the empire were disgraced (*deshones-
tarentur*)" (*Ann.* 4.74). For a similar offense Domitian's legate exterminated the Nasamones as they lay in a drunken sleep (Cass. Dio 67.4.6).
Other harsh measures short of extermination are attested. Suppressing
the Cantabri in Spain, Agrippa cut off the hands of prisoners and de-

---

newed" (*Ann.* 3.74). Marcus must make peace with the Iazyges because of the revolt of
Cassius; he would have preferred to exterminate them (Cass. Dio 71[72].16.2–71[72].17).
Cassius Dio attributes Commodus' peace with the Marcomanni to his laziness: "though
he could have destroyed (ἐχεϱγάσασθαι) them easily, because he hated hardship and was
hastening to the conveniences of the city, he made a truce with them" (72[73].2.2).

98. 55.28.6–7. Also see Brunt (1978, 183–185) on *clementia* in the late Republic; he also
concludes that it was considered best to spare a people the first time they were conquered,
but that once they had been conquered, revolt was punishable by the harshest measures.

99. Augustus boasts in a speech to the senate of exterminating certain Illyrian tribes,
with the explanation that they engaged in piracy (App. *Ill.* 16); Domitian boasts of annihilating the Nasamones (Cass. Dio 67.4.6); [Ael. Arist.] *Or.* 35.35 praises the unidentified
emperor for eradicating the Carpi.

100. Germany does not seem to have been considered an actual province, but sources
—including Augustus *RGDA* 26—represent territory west of the Elbe as conquered. On
this, see Wolters 1990, 199–201; see ibid., 201–208, on the nature of Rome's military occupation of Germany.

101. Tac. *Ann.* 2.13; cf. 2.21, quoted above; for slaughters of noncombatants, see 1.51,
1.56.

102. On Varus, see Vell. Pat. 2.117–118, Florus 2.30.31–34. Romans often blame the avarice, immorality, or incompetence of their own administrators for revolts; see, e.g., Cass.
Dio 54.5.1 on the Cantabri; Tac. *Ann.* 4.72 on the Frisii; ibid., 14.31, on Boudicca.

stroyed "nearly all those of military age" (Cass. Dio 53.29.2; 54.5.3). In the war against the Numidian rebel Tacfarinas, large numbers of the enemy are slaughtered unarmed in a night attack, and Tacfarinas himself is killed.[103] In the climactic battle against Boudicca, the Romans cut down women, pack animals, and an implausible eighty thousand of the enemy, according to Tacitus; "the glory (*laus*) acquired on that day was brilliant and equal to ancient victories" (*Ann.* 14.37). Later in the same province, the Ordovices revolted and annihilated their garrison; Agricola retaliated with near extermination (*prope universa gente caesa; Agr.* 18.3); and when Scottish tribes revolted after Severus conquered them, he is supposed to have instructed his troops to "invade their territory and kill everyone they met" (Cass. Dio 76[77].15.1).

Josephus' account to the Jewish war vividly illustrates the zeal with which Romans massacred rebellious populations.[104] The war's bloody nature was enthusiastically advertised in the very graphic battle scenes carried in Titus' triumph.[105] The spoils were displayed in Vespasian's new "Forum of Peace"—no irony was, of course, intended.[106] Later, when Judaea erupted again in the Bar-Kochba revolt, measures were equally severe or more so. Hadrian expelled the Jews from Jerusalem and refounded it as a Roman colony; and of the final repression, Cassius Dio tells us: "Indeed, few survived at all; and fifty of their most important forts and nine hundred eight-five of their most famous villages

103. *Ann.* 4.25–26; earlier he criticizes Tiberius for leaving the war unfinished (3.74). The theme of the night attack on unarmed and sometimes drunken barbarians recurs in Germanicus' assault on the Marsi (*Ann.* 1.50–51) and bears a close resemblance to the more mythical episodes of Camillus' slaughter of the Gauls (Livy 5.45) and Odysseus and Diomedes' slaughter of Thracians in *Iliad* X. These episodes therefore have a strong rhetorical element and obviously may not be true; nevertheless, the fact that the Romans are attracted to this story, especially in the context of a revolt, is revealing. The topos also illuminates Roman attitudes about their superior military discipline and the inferior discipline of barbarians; see below.

104. On the Jewish war, see Smallwood 1976, 293–330; Goodman 1987, especially chap. 10, "The Roman Reaction"; Millar 1993, 70–79; for the grisly details of the sack of Jerusalem, Joseph. *BJ* 6.403–434; in 6.420 he reports implausibly that 1.1 million died in the siege; see Smallwood, op. cit., 327 n. 152, for statistics in other sources. Note especially Joseph. *BJ* 6.414 on the treatment of survivors; and Titus uses prisoners in numerous gladiatorial games and wild beast shows (ibid., 7.23–24, 37–38).

105. *BJ* 7.142–145. The propaganda needs of the new regime and the fact that the ruling family had been responsible itself for putting down the revolt made for an exceptionally vigorous campaign of advertisement here; but other revolts were celebrated too, on a smaller scale, and not hushed up in embarrassment, as a civil war would be (see above, n. 32).

106. *Pax*, like *clementia*, seems to have meant different things depending on whether it was applied to foreign or civil war. See the article of Weinstock (1960) and the further discussion of Gruen (1985) on the idea under Augustus; cf. also Woolf 1993.

were completely destroyed, and five hundred eighty thousand men were slaughtered in the raids and battles, . . . so that nearly all of Judaea was made desert." [107]

Arminius and his Cherusci were the only tribe successfully to revolt against the Roman empire in the period under discussion. In every other case Rome was willing to do whatever it took to retain its territory, sometimes despite severe losses and often with very harsh reprisals. It is here more than anywhere, in the stories of violent revolt and brutal repression, that we get a sense of the prolonged struggle that was involved in forming the Roman empire. The Romans, in describing this struggle, do not frame their analyses mainly in "rationalizing" economic or geopolitical terms; these motivations alone—the desire to achieve defensible frontiers, for example, or to balance the budget through lucrative conquests or to retain the tax revenue of a rebellious province—are inadequate to explain the intensity and brutality of the Roman effort in many cases. Instead, the Romans perceived their struggle for empire in very different terms: crucial were issues of psychology, the emotions of terror and awe that they hoped to produce in the enemy; and moral and status issues, such as the need to repress *superbia,* avenge *iniuriae,* and maintain the honor or *decus* of the empire. It was on these things that, as they believed, their security depended; it was for these that they fought.

3. The Prestige of the Emperor

Just as Rome depended on repeated and vigorous proof of its military prowess to maintain its superior international status and, as the Romans saw it, the integrity and security of their empire, so the defeat and humiliation of barbarians was highly valued within Roman society and conferred immense *personal* prestige on anyone who could accomplish it. This is easily inferred from the extensive publicity that such success always received. The theme of the humiliated and submissive enemy—always easily recognizable by his long hair, beard, and characteristic ethnic clothing or, alternatively, nudity or partial nudity—is

107. 69.14.1; Hadrian probably took command himself during part of this war (Millar 1993, 106–108); on the Bar-Kochba revolt, see still Schürer 1973–1987, I:534–557; the plan for the colony at Jerusalem probably preceded the revolt and may have caused it (Cass. Dio 69.12; Schürer, op. cit., 535–543); on the refounding of Jerusalem as Aelia Capitolina, see ibid., 553–555.

extraordinarily popular in the iconography of the Principate; the kneeling barbarian and especially the bound barbarian prisoner were favorite themes on coins and monuments.[108] Colossal statues of bound Dacian prisoners decorated Trajan's forum; his gigantic *tropaeum* at Adamklissi was surmounted by a trophy with four prisoners at its foot.[109] Barbarians trampled under the foot of a victorious emperor, or under his horse in an equestrian representation, or being speared by the emperor on a horse, were also very popular; an extant statue of Hadrian shows the emperor in military uniform stepping on a barbarian; and the famous equestrian statue of Marcus Aurelius on the Capitoline hill may have originally crushed a barbarian[110] (the equestrian trampling theme was also popular on the tombstones of cavalrymen throughout the western empire).[111] The lower register of the Gemma Augustea, a large cameo, shows a bound barbarian prisoner, a kneeling, suppliant barbarian, and

108. For kneeling Parthian and Armenian kings on Augustus' coins of 18 B.C., see A. C. Levi 1952, 7–9; Brilliant 1963, 72; *RIC*[2] Augustus 287, 290. The theme appears also on famous silver cups from Boscoreale (Brilliant 1963, 73–74); see Zanker 1988, 187, for more kneeling barbarians under Augustus. On the coins of Domitian, who advertised his German victory in an extensive program, see Strobel 1987a, 435–436; Parthians kneel on coins of Trajan (Brilliant 1963, 109–110; see *RIC* Trajan 667–668); Dacians kneel (ibid., 214, 447, 448, 485–488, 499; nos. 510–512 show the goddess Pax with a kneeling Dacian). Prisoners are especially common—e.g., in Vespasian's famous *Judaea capta* series (*RIC* Vespasian 424–426; Hannestad 1988, 121; A. C. Levi 1952, 10–11). These coins were struck and distributed in Palestine, too, with Greek legends (Goodman 1987, 235–236). On the importance of costume in Strabo's ethnography, see van der Vliet 1984, 63–64; nude or seminude depictions of barbarians include, e.g., the metopes of the Adamklissi monument, the Gemma Augustea, and the "Ammendola" battle sarcophagus. Barbarians being crushed by horses on the tombstones of cavalrymen (see n. 111 below) are typically naked or partially clothed.

109. On Trajan's forum, see A. C. Levi 1952, 14–15; on the Adamklissi monument, Rossi 1971, 55–65; Florescu 1965; Strobel 1984, 34–40.

110. Coins show Trajan with his foot on a Dacian (*RIC* Trajan 210); on the statue of Hadrian, see A. C. Levi 1952, 16–18 with plate VI.1. Equestrian representations: Domitian's equestrian statue, described by Stat. *Silv.* 1.1, trampled the hair of the Rhine underfoot (vv. 50–51); that the barbarian is in this case the personification of a river hardly changes the gist of the message. For equestrian assaults depicted on Trajan's coins, see *RIC* Trajan 257, 284, 344, 361; and barbarians are trampled by the horse in ibid., 208, 534–545. For the theme in general, see Brilliant 1963, 96; see Hannestad 1988, 221, for a discussion of the original appearance of Marcus' statue. A twelfth-century guidebook indicates that the barbarian survived at least until then. Cf. also Suet. *Ner.* 41.2, where the emperor, on his way back to Rome during the revolt of Vindex, happens to notice "a Gallic soldier sculpted on a monument, being crushed by a Roman *eques* and dragged by the hair." Only a small number of examples have been gathered here; a full-length study of the portrayal of the barbarian on Roman coins and monuments is needed.

111. See Koepp 1924–1930, 3:9, with plates 6–10; Will 1955, 93–103; Collingwood and Wright 1965, nos. 108, 109, 121, 201.

a woman being dragged by the hair, while Roman soldiers erect a trophy; the upper register shows Augustus, naked to the waist and enthroned like Jupiter, being crowned by a personification of *oikoumene*— the inhabited world—amid symbols of world rule.[112]

Emperors advertised their military successes on triumphal arches and other victory monuments and in spectacular triumphal ceremonies, as well as on coins announcing territories "captured," "conquered," and "subjugated"; proclaiming victories *de Britannis, de Germanis, de Sarmatis;* or reading simply *Victoria Britannica, Parthica,* or *Germanica,* with a representation of the goddess; this last type becomes especially popular beginning with Commodus.[113] Poets and panegyrists praised the emperors' military victories at every opportunity,[114] and their victories were accumulated and celebrated in the imperial titulature itself. The martial element in this titulature was quite prominent. Augustus took the title *imperator*—traditionally voted to a victorious general by acclamation of the army—as his first name, and after Nero this became standard. It would appear again toward the end of the title, with a numeral to indicate the total number of acclamations.[115] All the Julio-Claudians were *Germanicus,* and Domitian took this title after his war with the Chatti; Trajan was the first to hold multiple victory titles (*Dacicus, Germanicus, Parthicus*), and after that, inflation seems to have set in. Marcus and Verus were *Parthici Maximi,* and after Severus, *Maximus*—greatest—became a standard part of any victory title.[116] Begin-

---

112. On the Gemma Augustea, see Zanker 1988, 230–232.

113. A search of the index of legends in *Roman Imperial Coinage* yields the following incomplete list: *Aegypt[o] capta* with crocodile (Augustus 275); *Armenia capta* (ibid., 513–515); the famous *Judaea capta* series (Vespasian 393, 424–427, 489–491, etc.); *Parthia capta* (Trajan 324–325); *Dacia capta* (ibid., 96, 585); *Germania capta* (Domitian 278a); *Judaea devicta* (Vespasian 148b, 289, 373); *Germania subacta* (Marcus Aurelius 1021, 1049, 1094); *De Britannis* (Claudius 30, 33, 44); *De Germanis* (ibid., 3, 35; Marcus Aurelius 629 [Commodus], 1179, etc.); *De Sarmatis* (ibid., 630, 632, 1185, etc.); *Victoria Britannica* (Commodus 440, 451–452, 459; Severus 247, 808; Caracalla 169, 172, 230, 483, 487; Geta 172, 178, etc.); *Victoria Germanica* (Marcus Aurelius 240, 256, 257, 1000, 1029, 1722; Caracalla 316; Maximinus 23, and on medallions, Maximinus 115, 121); *Victoria Parthica* (Marcus Aurelius 160; Verus 562, 571, 929, 1455; Severus 295–297; Caracalla 78, 144–145, 168a, 297, 299, etc.). Cf. Kneissl 1969, 25.

114. See n. 29 above.

115. On *Imperator* as praenomen, see Hammond 1957, 21–41; on Augustus, Syme 1958a; acclamations, Campbell 1984, 122–128; statistics, ibid., 124. The record holder was Claudius with twenty-seven.

116. On victory titles, see Kneissl 1969, with convenient appendices citing the inscriptions on which the titles can be found (pp. 186–241) and a list of the titles of each emperor (pp. 242–244); see also Rosenberger 1992, 168–170.

ning with Marcus and Verus, too, miscellaneous titles like "Extender of the Empire," "Invincible," or "Pacifier of the World" become popular.[117] An inscription from a milestone dedicated to Caracalla gives an idea of the cumulative effect; the title in the inscription reads: "To the Emperor Caesar Marcus Aurelius Severus Antoninus, Pious, Blessed, Augustus, victor of Arabia, victor of Adiabene, greatest victor of Parthia, greatest victor of Britain, chief priest, in the fifteenth year of his tribunician power, *imperator* twice, consul three times, father of his country."[118] It was usual for the emperor's full titulature to appear on milestones, and thus it was rather conspicuous; it would also appear on public monuments, on military *diplomata* (discharge documents granting citizenship) and other official documents, and parts of it (though obviously not all) would fit on coins. This raises the question of whom the emperor was trying to reach by publicizing his victories. For some publicity—including triumphal parades, the lavish ceremony of Tiridates' coronation, and perhaps monuments at Rome such as the imperial fora—the urban plebs may have been the chief audience. But another obvious candidate is the army, since not only *diplomata* but coins and milestones would all have been effective here, especially since their inscriptions were in Latin and not in Greek.[119] It is significant that ancient sources perceive a relationship between a martial, victorious image and the loyalty of the army.[120] We might well believe that such an image also

117. Marcus and Verus were *Propagatores imperii* (A. Birley 1987, 253–254), as was Septimius Severus (id. 1974). *Invictus* occurs first under Commodus as part of the formula *Pius Felix Invictus* but also occurs alone beginning with Severus (Storch 1968, 200–202). For *Pacator Orbis,* see Commodus' letters to the senate in Cass. Dio 72[73].15.5.

118. Imp. Caes. M. Aurelio Severo Antonino Pio Felici Aug. Arabico Adiabenico Parthico Max. Brit. Max. Pontif. Max. trib. pot. XV imp. II cos. III P. P. On milestones, see Chevallier 1976, 39–47; this inscription appears among the samples given on p. 42; it is *CIL* XIII.9129.

119. The point about milestones is made by Isaac (1992, 304–309). It is interesting that the literacy rate among legionaries was strikingly high, and even auxiliaries may have been more literate than the general population (Harris 1989, 253–255). There is some debate about the intelligibility of Roman coin types and the involvement of the emperor in choosing them; in favor of intelligibility, see mainly Sutherland 1959 and more recently id. 1983; against intelligibility, see mainly Crawford 1983, with bibliography in n. 2, arguing from the silence of ancient sources about *reverse* coin types, though substantial testimony on the obverse portrait of the emperor, which lent authority to the coin and was a mark of sovereignty, survives. Cf. also the argument of Levick (1982) that coin types were chosen not by the emperor but by sycophantic mint officials with a view to flattery; in either case the value attached to victory is obvious.

120. Campbell (1984, 383–387) argues that there is no clear-cut relationship between "martial" emperors and the loyalty of the army, which depended mainly on money; on the other hand, Germanicus tries to win over mutinous troops by reminding them of the

had a great deal of appeal for the emperor's own class—the senatorial aristocracy—as well, and that the emperors themselves must have shared these values, and been genuinely eager to defeat barbarians and genuinely proud of their successes. Certainly emperors with unwarlike images attracted sharp criticism from the literary sources, and a military background was considered a good qualification for the office.[121] And, while it is possible that Domitian could announce *Germania capta* on his coins to provincials and perhaps even to the army with impunity, the senatorial aristocracy could distinguish between honors and triumphs that reflected a "real" defeat of barbarians—one that met the criteria outlined in section 2 above—and undeserved honors voted in flattery.[122]

It is therefore not surprising that many emperors are supposed to have undertaken aggressive campaigns purely or mainly in order to enhance their own prestige. Understandably, the desire to acquire personal glory (i.e., *ambitio*, or φιλοτιμία), or a concern for *fama*, or δόξα, was considered an insufficiently "just" cause for waging unprovoked wars of conquest;[123] nevertheless, to the ancient sources the desire for a

victories and triumphs of Tiberius (Tac. *Ann.* 1.34), Tacitus writes that Suetonius Paulinus might have been nominated by the soldiers because of his military reputation (*Hist.* 2.37); and Marcus' speech to the troops in Cassius Dio also portrays the revolutionary Cassius' military reputation as his main attraction for them (71[72].25.3). Herodian also believes that a military reputation and image are important here; see, e.g., 2.2.8 (Pertinax), and see Campbell, op. cit., 385.

121. Criticism and contempt for unwarlike emperors: Suetonius records a couplet levied at Nero: "while our man plucks the cithara, the Parthian draws his bow; ours will be Paean, the other Hecabeletes" (*Ner.* 39.2); and the sentiment is expressed at greater length and with even greater scorn by Cassius Dio (63[62].8). Dio also criticizes Domitian for living luxuriously and decadently while sending others to conduct the war in Dacia (67.6.3). See Herodian 1.15.7, where Commodus should be proving himself fighting barbarians instead of in gladiatorial combat. Qualifications: on Vespasian, see Suet. *Vesp.* 4.1–2, Cass. Dio 65[64].8.3; on Titus, Suet. *Titus* 4.1; on Pertinax, Herodian 2.1.4.

122. Especially in the case of Domitian—e.g., Cass. Dio 67.7.3–4; in his case the celebration of triumphs was especially offensive (in Tac. *Germ.* 37.6, the Germans are "triumphed over rather than defeated"; Pliny *Pan.* 16.3–5 contrasts Trajan, as often, with Domitian); cf. Campbell 1984, 398. See also the case of Gaius, who is acclaimed *imperator* several times, "having won no battle nor killed any enemy" (Cass. Dio 59.22.2; cf. Suetonius *Gaius* 47). That the aristocracy was sensitive to the fine points of these issues is suggested by Dio's criticism of Claudius for accepting multiple salutations of *imperator* for the same war; strictly speaking, this should not happen (60.21.4–5). Cassius Dio also distinguishes between salutations that Claudius received deservedly, when his legates inflicted defeats on the Germans and retrieved the last of the standards lost with Varus, and triumphal ornaments for a campaign that preceded his accession, which he did not deserve (60.8.6–7). Macrinus misrepresents his achievements in the east but is ashamed to take a victory title after being defeated by the Parthians (ibid., 78[79].27.3).

123. "Ambition" is often coupled with greed as an unjust cause—e.g., in the case of Crassus (Plut. *Crass.* 14.4; App. *B Civ.* 2.18; Vell. Pat. 2.46.3) and of Caesar (Suet. *Jul.* 22.1,

title, a triumph, or a glorious reputation seemed a perfectly plausible explanation for war, including such a monumental effort as Trajan's Parthian war, or one with such important cultural consequences as the conquest of Britain.[124]

It is possible that the provincial aristocracy of the Greek east was less impressed with the emperor's military exploits than were his senatorial colleagues. It is possible to see something of a "language gap" on the foreign-relations issue: writers of Greek are more likely to describe the empire as surrounded by barriers and troops, thus emphasizing the defensive function of the army; they are more likely to protest the expense of new conquests and to deride the barbarians outside the empire as "useless" and "unprofitable."[125] Thus a martial emperor like Trajan might find himself listening to an extended parable by a Greek sophist on the follies of excessive militarism.[126] As ambassadors, doctors, secretaries *ab epistulis,* and hangers-on, Greek intellectuals were very prominent presences in the emperor's entourage.[127] It may have been this group that most influenced the philhellene Hadrian, whose foreign policy contrasts sharply with that of other emperors: he used no victory

---

where Gaul is rich and will furnish triumphs; see Mantovani 1990, 35–36, for further references). Domitian wages an unnecessary war for wealth and *dignitatio* in Suet. *Dom.* 2.1; and cf. Calgacus' famous speech in Tac. *Agr.* 30: "if the enemy is rich, they [the Romans] are greedy; if he is poor, they are ambitious (*ambitiosi*)." See also Florus 2.20.2 on Antony's *cupiditas titulorum*—desire for the titles of conquered peoples—engraved in the *elogium* under his statue; he attacks the Parthians "without cause or plan and without even the pretense of a declaration of war."

124. Claudius attacked Britain mainly to get a triumph (though a convenient provocation presented itself; Suet. *Claud.* 17.1); Severus' British wars are said to be motivated by his desire for a victory title (Herodian 3.14.2, 5); Caracalla desires the title "Parthicus," hence his eastern war (Herodian 4.10.1; indicating an "unjust" war). Trajan's Parthian war (Cass. Dio 68.17.1) and Severus' conquest of Mesopotamia (ibid., 75.1.1; Herodian 3.9.1) are motivated by a desire for δόξα. In other cases where literary evidence fails, the desire of a new emperor for an enhanced military reputation seems probable—e.g., Domitian's first war with the Chatti (Strobel 1987a, 427–428) and the advance beyond Hadrian's wall under Pius (Breeze 1988, 18). Cf. Cass. Dio 53.6.3, where Augustus says in a speech that many make war on account of τὸ εὐκλεές.

125. On defenses, see chap. 3, pp. 110–111; for "unprofitable," chap. 4, n. 156.

126. Dio Chrysostomus *Or.* 4, with Moles 1983. It is interesting that the imperialist boast at the head of the *RGDA* is missing from the Greek version (Gagé 1977, 72–73). See Nutton 1978, 210–211; and cf. Whittaker 1994, 36–37. On Greek attitudes to Rome generally, see recently Swain 1996.

127. See Bowersock 1969, chap. 4, for Greek intellectuals in the emperor's court. Ambassadors, e.g., Aelius Aristides (Bowersock, op. cit., 44–46); hangers-on, e.g., Dio Chrysostomus (ibid., 47–48). On sophists as secretaries *ab epistulis,* a prestigious post, see ibid., 50–58; on doctors, ibid., chap. 5 (on Galen); Trajan's doctor accompanied him on campaign in Dacia and wrote a commentary (ibid., 65).

titles, he took the controversial step of abandoning conquered territory, and Cassius Dio associates him with a policy of intensified military exercises, nonaggression, and money payments to barbarians—all of which the historian himself approves.[128]

It is an indication of the immense prestige that military victory could bring to an individual that by the middle of the first century A.D. all of its honors—triumphs, victory titles, monuments, acclamations of *imperator*—became the sole privilege of the emperor or his designated successor. Already early in the reign of Augustus, Cornelius Gallus was exiled for the publicity he gave his accomplishments in Egypt, and Licinius Crassus celebrated a triumph for his conquests in Moesia and Thrace but was denied the *spolia opima* for the defeat of an enemy commander in single combat.[129] The only military honors regularly offered to imperial legates were the *triumphalia,* or triumphal ornaments, which were often granted for nonmilitary reasons, and the ancient sources sometimes perceive them as hopelessly trivialized.[130] But other evidence indicates that senators were proud of this distinction nevertheless: Suetonius writes that Claudius granted them so frequently that "a joint

128. 69.9; note that, according to Cassius Dio, Hadrian succeeded in terrifying the barbarians with his ostentatious military exercises, so that they "used him as an arbitrator of their differences with each other," thus maintaining Roman dignity. On victory titles, see Kneissl 1969, 91–96; Hadrian initially used Trajan's titles on his coins, perhaps in connection with his questionable adoption, but took none of his own; also see Hannestad 1988, 190–192.

129. See Kneissl 1969, 24–25, and Campbell 1984, 348–362, on the control of victory honors. Suetonius notes that triumphs were still celebrated by nonemperors under Augustus (*Aug.* 38.1; cf. Cass. Dio 54.12.1); but the last such triumph was that of Cornelius Balbus in 19 B.C. (Campbell, op. cit., 358–359). Agrippa set the example in the same year by refusing a triumph for his exploits in Spain (Cass. Dio 54.11.6). Tiberius made a special exception and allowed Blaesus to be acclaimed *imperator* after his defeat of Tacfarinas (Tac. *Ann.* 3.7; Kneissl, op. cit., 24; Campbell, op. cit., 351). The last nonemperor to dedicate a trophy was L. Apronius Caesianus, for a defeat of Tacfarinas in A.D. 20 (Picard 1957, 247–248; cf. Tac. *Ann.* 3.21); and the last nonemperor to take a victory title (that of Chaucius) was P. Gabinius Secundus in A.D. 41 (Kneissl 1969, 24–25). On Gallus' boasting, exile, and suicide, see Cass. Dio 53.23.5–7; cf. Suet. *Aug.* 66.1–2; and see *PIR* II, C1369, and above, sec. 1. Crassus would have received *spolia opima* (Cass. Dio 51.24.4); on his triumph, see ibid., 51.25.2; for the argument that Augustus denied the *spolia opima* on the pretext that Crassus was not a consul, see Syme 1939, 308 n. 2; on Crassus and Gallus, ibid., 308–310.

130. On *triumphalia,* see Campbell 1984, 359–361. Tacitus ascribes a lull in activity on the Rhine to "the temperament of the generals, who, because the triumphal ornaments had become so debased, hoped for honor (*decus*) rather by having continued the peace" (*Ann.* 13.53). Nero is supposed to have granted *triumphalia* even to quaestors and *equites,* "and not always for military reasons" (Suet. *Ner.* 15.2); Tiberius is supposed to have granted them for informing (Cass. Dio 58.4.8).

letter in the name of the legions arose, asking that *triumphalia* should
be given to consular legates at the same time as their commands, so that
they would not seek every excuse for war";[131] and Plautius Silvanus
boasts of receiving the *triumphalia* in his epitaph (*ILS* 986). Thus legates
like Suetonius Paulinus might still be motivated to win glory through
victory; he is supposed to have invaded Mona "desiring to equal the
honor (*decus*) of the recapture of Armenia by conquering enemies"
(*Ann.* 14.29).

But it was not in the emperor's interest to allow too much of this.
It was dangerous to permit others of high rank to achieve military success.[132] Emperors are often supposed to be suspicious or jealous of
victorious subordinates, and successful commanders are described as
threats. On several occasions legates are supposedly recalled from potentially glorious conquests for this reason.[133] Verus entrusted the war
against Parthia to Avidius Cassius, who revolted with the army of Syria;
in Marcus' speech to the troops, it is apparently Cassius' fame "for his
deeds against the Parthians" that is his main attraction.[134] More and
more, emperors tended to assume command of campaigns themselves,
if the provincial army was insufficient (see chap. 1).

131. *ne causam belli quoquo modo quaererent* (Suet. *Claud.* 24.3); in Tac. *Ann.* 11.20
the petition circulates after soldiers are forced by their ambitious commander to dig gold
and silver mines.

132. Agrippa points out how dangerous it is, under a monarchy, to entrust military
commands to men of high rank (Cass. Dio 52.8.4); Maecenas gives similar advice (ibid.,
52.20.4); Pliny complains that when he served in the army under Domitian, "virtue was
suspected, inertia was prized . . . no authority for the generals, no respect in the soldiers"
(*Ep.* 8.14.7). See Campbell 1984, 337.

133. On imperial jealousy generally, see ibid., 334–337. Famous examples include Tiberius and Germanicus (Tac. *Ann.* 2.26); Claudius recalls Corbulo from exploits across the
Rhine; "learning of his ἀρετή (valor) and ἄσκησις (discipline), he would not allow him
to become too great (ἐπὶ πλέον αὐξηθῆναι)" (Cass. Dio 60[61].30.4–5; and see Tac.
Ann. 11.2 for the same story); Corbulo exclaims, "How fortunate the generals of yester-
year!" Later, Domitian hears of Agricola's success in Scotland "with a happy face but an
anxious heart . . . for within he was aware that his recent false triumph over the Germans
had been a source of scorn for him" (Tac. *Agr.* 39); for Agricola's recall, see ibid., 40, and
see Cass. Dio 66.20. The latter's contention that Domitian murdered Agricola out of jealousy is reflected in Tacitus' report of the rumor that Agricola was poisoned (*Agr.* 43).
Threats: Corbulo could have become emperor because he had "a great force and no small
reputation" (Cass. Dio 62.23.5); Suetonius Paulinus could have been nominated during the
civil wars because of his British campaigns (Tac. *Hist.* 2.37). Commodus entrusts Ulpius
Marcellus with the British war and then nearly executes him because of "his personal
ἀρετή" (Cass. Dio 72[73].8.2–6).

134. On Cassius being entrusted with the war, see Cass. Dio 71.2.3; on his revolt,
71[72].17, 22; Marcus' speech, 71[72].25.3.

All of this meant that, paradoxically, the very great prestige attached to military victory partially explains the slow pace of conquest under the Principate. Governors may have been relatively indifferent to new conquests for which they would receive minimal glory, or they may have feared the fate that too much success might bring—with good reason; emperors, also with good reason, would be suspicious of anyone who won glorious victories, and might well discourage this. Thus the ferocious competition for glory that fueled the conquests of the late Republic did not exist in the Principate. In addition, it was probably the need to prevent large armies from falling into the hands of rivals that accounts for the division of provinces like Moesia, Pannonia, and Germany; this was of strategic significance to the empire, because attacks that could not be handled by a provincial army required special commands and long delays (see chap. 3). Thus the emperor's need to control the prestige associated with victory contributed significantly to the general shape of foreign relations in the Principate. Finally, we should note that the goals of Roman foreign policy—domination and humiliation of the enemy, which did not necessarily, for example, involve the occupation of new territory—made it easier to substitute propaganda for more substantial achievement; and an emperor motivated mainly by prestige concerns, rather than more familiar, geopolitical strategic preoccupations, might well find it easier and cheaper to propagandize.[135] Nero's baroque ceremonial humiliation of Tiridates substituted for the more costly and difficult military effort that would have been necessary to achieve the reinstatement of Rome's nominee in Armenia—though as we have seen, emperors who chose this path risked criticism from their own class.

4. Discipline

So far this study has described a culture that placed immense value on the subjection of foreign peoples. This value system had, for example, a geographical element, as place-names figure prominently in the rhetoric of imperialism; and an economic element, as part of the glory of conquest lay in the acquisition of the material wealth of the conquered. It also had a social element, the prestige that accrued to suc-

135. Gruen (1990 and 1996) argues that this was the policy of Augustus.

cessful military commanders; and a moral and psychological element, more difficult to define, where foreign policy was perceived as a system of national honor, insult, and retribution that justified conquest and maintained security. The value attached to warfare also emerges in the very important Roman concept of discipline, which requires a brief separate treatment. If one were to ask the Romans to explain their success in building and maintaining their empire, it is unquestionable that a large part of the answer would be the discipline of the army. By this, Romans seem to have meant a certain sophistication of tactics and organization; but *disciplina,* or ἄσκησις, also had an important moral dimension; it is the opposite of decadence and luxury, and it is easily corrupted by money and peace.

At the beginning of a long digression on the training, organization, tactics, and equipment of the Roman army, Josephus writes that his discussion will show "that they hold such a great empire as a prize of valor (ἀϱετῆς κτῆμα), not as a gift of fortune." [136] Aelius Aristides includes an encomium of the Roman army's self-control and organization in his panegyric to Rome (86–88). Centuries later, Vegetius begins his treatise *On Military Matters* with the statement "It is evident that the Roman people have subjected the world by no other means than the exercise of arms, the discipline of the camps, and warlike practices." He adds, "What indeed could the small number of Romans have accomplished against the multitude of the Gauls? What could their shortness have dared against the tallness of the Germans?" (1.1).

As this passage suggests, the Romans often contrast their own superior discipline with the indiscipline of their barbarian enemies. Barbarians are often associated with a fighting style that is frenzied, sporadic, and disorganized. The stereotype can be found in Seneca's treatise *On Anger:* "What indeed is it that shatters the barbarians, so much more robust in body and so much more enduring of labors, if not anger, the quality most inimical to themselves?" If one were to give the Germans reason (*ratio*) and discipline, "it will certainly be necessary for us to return to Roman ways" (1.11.1–4). Barbarians, who tend to "rush into war," "disorganized, unafraid, reckless," are easily cut down by the Roman legions (3.2.6). Similar ideas can be found in Strabo, Tacitus, and elsewhere. Parthians, like other barbarians, cannot endure long cam-

---

136. *BJ* 3.71; the question of whether Romans owed their success to valor or fortune seems to have been a popular one; cf. Plut. *Mor.* 316–326 (*De fortuna Romanorum*), making the opposite case. On the subject of military discipline generally, see Davies 1968, especially for training and military exercises; Isaac 1992, 23–26; and Wheeler 1996.

paigns;[137] Germans, Gauls, and other northern barbarians are quick to attack and strong initially but lack perseverance and organization.[138] As we saw in chapter 2, this stereotype antedates the Principate and can be found, for example, in Polybius. Also in Polybius we discover a type of battle narrative that pervades the literature of the imperial period: the story of the triumph of Roman military virtues over barbarian vices. Again and again we read of the defeat of undisciplined barbarians by the superior hard work, organization, and self-control of the legions, sometimes against overwhelming odds.[139]

The topos of Roman military virtue contrasted with barbarian vice is especially prominent in Tacitus: Caecina escapes from near disaster when the Germans, ignoring Arminius' advice to wait until the Romans march out of their camp, instead follow the advice of Inguiomerus, "fiercer and pleasing to barbarians (*atrociora . . . et laeta barbaris*)," impatiently storming the camp (*Ann.* 1.68). Similarly, the defeat of Tacfarinas is accomplished in a night battle where "the Romans had drawn together the infantry, posted the cavalry in position, and prepared everything for battle; the enemy, on the other hand, ignorant of everything, had no arms, no order, no plan, but like beasts they were dragged, killed, and captured" (*Ann.* 4.25). Similar themes arise in the extended narrative sculpture on Trajan's column, which portrays the Roman army as con-

137. Trogus (Justin) 41.2; Tac. *Ann.* 11.10 ("the Parthians, though victors, rejected a distant campaign"); Cass. Dio 40.15.6. Also see Lucan 8.368–390: Parthians are invincible on their own territory because they have room for flight, but cannot endure hardship, have no military machines, and flee quickly.

138. Strabo, describing the Rhoxolani, comments of all barbarians: "against an organized and well-armed phalanx, all of the barbarian race is weak" (7.3.17). Tacitus presents the Chatti as especially organized and disciplined, for Germans (*Germ.* 30; "others go to battle, the Chatti go to war"); the traditional stereotype appears in 4.3: "large bodies strong only in assault; they have not the same tolerance of labor and work." Germanicus encourages his troops by reminding them of the weaknesses of the enemy's weapons; the Germans might look impressive and be "strong in a brief assault" but will turn and run after a setback (Tac. *Ann.* 2.14). Ariovistus' Germans are "not enduring of hardship in battles, nor do they employ reason or knowledge or anything except passion (θυμός), like beasts" (App. *Gall.* 3). On Gauls, see Strab. 4.4.2, Cass. Dio 38.45.4–5. Severus Alexander, encouraging his troops for the Persian war, tells them that in general barbarians are "daring in the face of withdrawal and hesitation, but against one who resists they [the barbarians] by no means stand their ground in the same way, since for them the fight at close quarters with rivals does not promise success, but they consider that it is by raiding and flight that they gain what they seize by plunder. To us belongs organization and good order (τὸ εὔτακτον ἅμα τῷ κοσμίῳ), and we have learned to defeat them always" (Herodian 6.3.7).

139. On Polybius, see Eckstein 1995, chap. 6.

stantly at work building forts, roads, and bridges; barbarians are notoriously lazy.[140]

Sometimes the barbarians' drunkenness—another typical trait—or
greed for plunder plays a role, as in Germanicus' slaughter of the Marsi,
who are lying in a stupor with no guards posted, thus displaying laziness
as well (*Ann.* 1.50–51). Tacitus' Sarmatian marauders in the invasion of
A.D. 69 are dispersed and weighted down in their greed for booty; but
"on the Roman side all was ready for battle," and the raid is easily repelled.[141] In Cassius Dio's account of the defeat of the Nasamones, the
barbarians have plundered the legionary camp and especially the wine
(67.4.6).[142] On the other hand, Suetonius Paulinus carefully chooses a
position and deploys his small force of ten thousand against Boudicca's
enormous army, which leaps about excitedly in all directions (*Ann.*
14.34); urging his soldiers to remain in formation and forget plunder,
he succeeds in killing eighty thousand of the enemy with only four hundred Roman losses (14.36–37).

It was therefore important to the Romans that their army should be
kept constantly in training either by warfare or by military drills and exercises. Josephus emphasizes that the Romans train even in peacetime
(*BJ* 3.72–75). In the speech composed for Maecenas by Cassius Dio,
he advises Augustus that the troops "should always be under arms and
should perform military exercises continually" (52.27.2). The Romans
sometimes, still in the Principate, show a deep suspicion of long peace
as a source of corruption and frequently express the idea that foreign
war is a positive thing from this point of view.[143] Horace looks forward
to war with the Parthians, which will restore Rome to its ancient military virtues (*Carm.* 3.2.1–6). Augustus is supposed to have undertaken
campaigns in Illyricum and Dalmatia "lest that thing most inimical to

140. The emphasis on the hard work of the Roman army is noticed by Rossi (1971,
99), Richmond (1982, 2–3), and Hannestad (1988, 158–159). For plates, see the recent edition of Settis et al. (1988). On laziness, see, e.g., Tac. *Germ.* 4.3 and 15.1.

141. *Hist.* 1.79. Cf. Dauge 1981, 752–753.

142. See also Tac. *Hist.* 4.29–30, contrasting Civilis' drunken, frenzied Germans with
the well-ordered, better-equipped legions. Very similar is Livy's account of Camillus' defeat of the sleeping, drunken, lazy Gauls (5.44–45). On the drunkenness of Germans, see
Tac. *Germ.* 22–23, *Ann.* 11.16; of Parthians, Pliny *HN* 14.144, 148; of Gauls, Polyb. 2.19.4,
Diod. Sic. 5.26.3; cf. Cass. Dio 51.24.2, where Crassus takes advantage of the notorious
drunkenness of the Scythians.

143. Most obvious in the still-popular idea that the destruction of Carthage marked
the beginning of Rome's decline. See Vell. Pat. 2.1.1; Pliny *HN* 33.150; Florus 1.47.2 ("the
overhanging fear of the Punic enemy preserved the old discipline"); Earl 1967, 18–19. On
the subject of discipline in the Republic, cf. Rosenstein 1990, chap. 3.

discipline, leisure, should corrupt the army" (Vell. Pat. 2.78.2); similarly, Cassius Dio writes that Severus "made a campaign against Britain, seeing that his sons were going astray and that the army was dissipated from idleness" (76[77].11.1; see Herodian 3.14.2). In Tacitus, the dangers of peace and lack of discipline can lead to mutiny.[144] During the suspension of duties at the death of Augustus, the soldiers "desired luxury and leisure, and scorned discipline and work"—thus the Pannonian mutiny (*Ann.* 1.16); it spreads to the Rhine army (1.31), where the cure is, naturally, foreign war—specifically, the campaigns of Germanicus.[145]

The ancient sources frequently criticize the perceived luxury and degeneration of the soldiers, and praise emperors and commanders who restore old-fashioned discipline. Corbulo stands out in this respect: in Tacitus' tangled account of his eastern campaigns, one image that emerges clearly is that of Corbulo walking around bareheaded in the Armenian winter, encouraging his frostbitten troops; he had found them "sluggish from long peace," but quickly rectified this situation.[146] Paetus, in contrast, fails properly to plan and organize his campaign (15.8), and grants leave to his troops liberally (15.9); thus his disastrous loss to the Parthians. Later, Hadrian compensates for a policy of nonaggression with increased discipline, constant visits to the troops, and the unusual legend *Disciplina Augusta* on the coinage.[147]

Emperors were themselves supposed to set an example of discipline for the soldiers, by sharing their hardships and their training,[148] and also to enforce it.[149] To Fronto, this means returning to a warlike policy after years of peace; he considers Hadrian's substitution of exercises and

144. On corruption and indolence due to peace, see *Hist.* 1.88, this time of the Roman aristocracy; cf. 2.17. Of the army in Britain under Trebellius Maximus (A.D. 69), Tacitus writes that "soldiers accustomed to campaigns became licentious in leisure" (*Agr.* 16.3; but cf. *Hist.* 1.60, where he blames Trebellius' greed and stinginess for the mutiny). See also *Hist.* 1.40–43 on the atrocious behavior of the army in the civil war.

145. *Ann.* 1.49: "The desire then entered their still-fierce minds to march against the enemy, in expiation of their frenzy; nor could the ghosts of their fellow soldiers be placated until they had received honorable wounds on their impious breasts."

146. *Ann.* 13.35; Corbulo had also brought harsh discipline to the Rhine (ibid., 11.18) and was famous for this quality (Walser 1951, 42–43).

147. On Hadrian's program, see Cass. Dio 69.9; and see Davies 1968 for detailed discussion. On virtues and personifications on Hadrian's coins, see Wallace-Hadrill 1981, 311–314; see also Hannestad 1988, 191.

148. A very common topos—e.g., Tac. *Hist.* 2.5 (Vespasian); Pliny *Pan.* 13 (Trajan); Fronto *Principia historiae* 13 (Loeb 2:209–211; Verus); Herodian 2.11.2, 3.6.10 (Severus); cf. Tac. *Ann.* 13.35 on Corbulo, above, and *Agr.* 20 on Agricola; also MacMullen 1976, 26, with n. 11; and Campbell 1984, 32–59.

149. Pliny *Pan.* 18; cf. Dio Chrys. *Or.* 1.29.

training maneuvers for real war a disaster.[150] Fronto tells us that the typical soldier whom Lucius Verus found when he arrived in the east was, once again, "reduced to idleness from long discontinuance of warfare" (*Principia historiae* 11 [Loeb 2:209]); it is Verus who, he writes, restored discipline in preparation for his Parthian war.[151]

But the most striking passage concerning the importance of military discipline in Rome's success comes at the very end of our period of discussion—almost at the very end, in fact, of the history of Cassius Dio. He has recently retired from his post as legate of the prestigious military province of Upper Pannonia; a man of wide experience, *amicus* of three emperors, he offers his own assessment of a new menace on the eastern horizon:

He [Ardashir, king of Persia] has become fearful to us, . . . not because he himself seems worthy of any note, but because our army is in such a condition that some are even going over to him, and others do not want to fight him off. For they enjoy such luxury, license, and irresponsibility that those in Mesopotamia have dared to kill their own commander, Flavius Heracleo, and the praetorian guard even accused me before Ulpianus because I governed the soldiers in Pannonia strictly. . . . (80.4.2–3)

The value the Romans ascribed to their superior tactics, engineering, and organization was inseparable from a broader moral background of discipline and degeneracy against which the Romans tend to project their ideas about the army and its maintenance, even as they tend to describe their foreign-relations goals in terms of honor or dignity, disgrace, and revenge.

Conclusion

Pillagers of the world, when the earth is insufficient for their plundering, they search the sea; if the enemy is rich, they are greedy; if he is poor, they are ambitious. Neither the east nor the west has satisfied them: they alone lust after wealth and poverty with equal passion. They call theft and slaughter and pillage by the false name of "empire," and when they have made a wasteland, they call it peace. (Tac. *Agr.* 30)

150. *Principia historiae* 10 (Loeb 2:207), with the article of Davies (1968, 75–84). On the idea of military discipline in the east, see recently Wheeler 1996, emphasizing that the literary topos arises from the Roman perception of the effete easterner and does not necessarily reflect a reality.

151. See Fronto's letter to Verus (Loeb 2:149–151) and *Principia historiae* 13 (Loeb 2:209–211). These passages are discussed extensively in Davies 1968 and Wheeler 1996.

The famous speech composed by Tacitus for the rebel Calgacus is of course a rhetorical exercise. It is easy to imagine the opposite argument: the Romans conquer not out of desire for money, land, or fame, but to retaliate for a wrong; they practice clemency when it is safe to do so, extermination in the face of stubborn arrogance and intransigence. In either case, this rare statement about Roman aims in the conduct of foreign relations reflects a reality. Greed and glory were plausible, though not necessarily respectable, causes for war. Still more plausible and respectable was the motivation of revenge, and of asserting or enhancing the honor and majesty of the Roman empire—provided, of course, that this could be done without causing invasion, revolt, civil war, or crippling expense. And if a tribe caused too much trouble, the Romans saw no moral or ethical argument against wiping it off the face of the earth. The relatively slow pace of conquest under the Principate should not be explained as the result of substituting a "defensive" strategy for the ideology of glory and conquest that prevailed in the Republic. The Romans at all times valued victory and conquest, as part of a system in which aggression, especially in retaliation for a perceived wrong, was crucial for maintaining honor and security. However, there were certain factors, mainly fiscal ones, that limited the size of the army; the Romans recognized manpower constraints as a limit on the growth of empire. And conquests that did not promise the immense profits of, for example, the acquisition of Egypt perhaps did not look as attractive as the lucrative ventures of an earlier era.

An extraordinary passage from Pliny's *Panegyric* praises the emperor Trajan for attacking the Dacians at the worst possible time: "at that time that is most favorable to them and most difficult for us, when the banks of the Danube are bridged with ice, and, frozen solid, it carries vast wars across on its back, when ferocious tribes are armed no less with their weather and their climate than with arrows" (12.3). As with the speech of Calgacus, one is at first tempted to dismiss this statement as mere rhetoric. Surely, we might argue, the terms the Romans used to frame their decisions about war and peace must have been quite different from those employed by Pliny here: the unscientific ethnic stereotype (ferocious tribes, grim climate); the idea that to demonstrate one's superior military prowess by attacking an enemy in midwinter was far more important than more practical considerations—in this case, of tactics.[152]

---

152. Very similar is Caesar's decision to construct a bridge over the Rhine, which he subsequently destroys, rather than cross by the usual method of lashing boats together; this would have been beneath Roman dignity (*B Gall.* 4.17–19).

But as this study has demonstrated, it is not necessary to make this assumption at all. Pliny the Younger came from precisely that small group of individuals that was entrusted with making Rome's most important decisions; and it was in rhetorical terms that this group was trained to think.

Pliny did not imagine Dacia as a territory of certain shape and extent, bounded by certain geographical features; such information, and such a picture, would be formed only after conquest, if at all. Dacia was a land beyond the Danube, a mighty river, which divided the Romans from the barbarians the way it had divided the king of Persia from the ferocious Scythians, in a half-mythical tale of conquest centuries ago. It was inhabited by a fierce, savage, warlike, barbarous people. In its icy and inhospitable climate it approached the earth's farthest, uninhabitable regions; it bordered on the frigid, sluggish ocean of the north. It was one of the remote corners of the earth—like Arabia, or India—still not subject to Roman domination. Such was the image that was most likely in Trajan's mind when he invaded it, proudly subjecting this wild and remote territory to land surveys, taxes, roads, a Roman colony. Trajan, like Darius, bridged the Danube.[153] No conquest in the imperial period brought any emperor greater glory; none was depicted on monuments so vast; none was commemorated in language so reverent.

To achieve this success, Trajan required approximately half of the Roman army and a vast amount of money. He was rewarded not only with fame and reputation but with immense sums in booty and ultimately from gold mines. But we must consider the likelihood that the Dacian wars, for all the immense effort that they required, would have happened even in the absence of greed. There were other considerations as well. Its king had humiliated Rome by inflicting defeats on the Roman army, and by wresting from Rome a treaty in which one clause especially— the financial subsidies paid to Decebalus—clearly conceded this defeat. Imagine, for example, some insignificant nation in Central America or the Middle East daring to behave in the same way toward, say, the United States!

The comparison is not totally inappropriate. Considering the disparity in size between Rome and the Dacian kingdom, one might well question whether the latter could ever have posed a "real" strategic threat to the empire. But for the Romans, their hegemony and their very security depended on universal recognition of their empire's *maiestas*, its

153. Cf. Hdt. 4.89, with Hartog 1988, 58–60. His footnote 107 is also appropriate for the Roman period: "Note that, nearly always, any engineering is Greek."

"greaterness." Their policy depended on perceived and acknowledged military superiority, on the terror and awe of the enemy; and if this image was challenged by invasion, defeat, or revolt, the Romans reasserted it with the maximum possible brutality and ferocity. Both of Trajan's Dacian wars were wars of punishment and revenge. Mainly for this, and for no other reason, the emperor was willing to commit military and financial resources of immense proportions. Modern superpowers occasionally behave in ways that are just as difficult to explain without invoking motivations similar to those that drove the Romans. Perhaps we can learn, from our study of the Roman mind, not only something about the forces that shaped the boundaries of one of the world's great empires, but something about ourselves as well.

Carthage Must Be Destroyed

Roman ideas and practices of warfare and empire are relatively well documented for the imperial period, and they changed relatively little over the centuries. The army remained about the same size,
or grew gradually; and so did the empire as a whole, after Augustus. And
it is especially in this period that we have, as evidence, the testimony of
the very class of people that made Rome's foreign-relations decisions.
That testimony does not exist for the Republic until the time of Caesar
and Cicero. But it is in the Republic that most of Rome's empire was
conquered.

In the beginning, we are told, there was a village on the Palatine composed of a few huts, such as the one preserved or reconstructed on the
hill in antiquity called the "hut of Romulus." Nothing extraordinary
distinguished this village from the other simple and apparently very
poor settlements in Latium, or the rest of Villanovan culture in northern Italy.[1] Nothing unusually impressive characterized its geographical
location: it was near a good crossing of a river; at the mouth of the river
could be found the valuable commodity of salt. The origins of the city
were indeed humble. But in the end, the Romans would go on to conquer the entire Mediterranean basin and all of western Europe. How

---

1. See recently Cornell 1995, 48–60; L. Richardson 1992, s.v. "*casa Romuli.*"

did this happen? Specifically, what forces motivated and drove Roman expansion? What was the nature and what were the rules of this competition in which Rome emerged as the ultimate victor? Anyone who has taught a course on Roman civilization knows how difficult it is to address this question. But it seems important to seek an answer—to see whether the conclusions from the study of the Principate, undertaken here, might shed light on the murkier, more shadowy period of the Republic.

Polybius is the first on record to assert that the Romans had achieved universal dominion over the *oikoumene,* the world. "For who among men is so ignorant or lazy," he writes in his famous introduction, "that he does not want to know how and by what sort of government almost everything in the world (σχεδὸν ἅπαντα τὰ κατὰ τὴν οἰκουμένην) was conquered and fell under the single rule of the Romans, in less than fifty-three years?" (1.1.5). Polybius perceives this conquest as a result of a deliberate plan or policy on the part of the Romans. At some point— perhaps after the first Punic war, or perhaps after the second, he writes —the Romans "not only boldly aimed at universal hegemony, but also attained their purpose."[2] He adds that this was neither the result of "fortune (τύχη), as some of the Greeks think," nor something that happened "accidentally (αὐτομάτως)." This last point is still a good one. The Roman empire is a phenomenon that demands explanation. I suggest that it is important, as mentioned, to establish the rules of the game before one can identify the qualities of the winner. Was the imperialism of the Republic governed by the same rules of honor and vengeance, insult and retaliation that were so prevalent in the Principate? Does the same mind-set we have described for the Principate apply to the Republic?

In this context Polybius' thesis, here greatly oversimplified,[3] has several interesting features. First, it is interesting that he believed that Rome had, by his time, more or less conquered the world. This raises the issue of what was meant by "world." We know something already about geographical ideas in the Roman period. The world of Polybius was substantially the world of Eratosthenes; that work had relied, for recent information, on the conquests of Alexander the Great and the

---

2. 1.63.9; cf. 3.2.6, 15.19.1; Harris 1979, 107–117; on this issue, see also Derow 1979, 1–4.

3. Thus despite Polybius' strong tendency to emphasize the importance of the intelligent individual over that of unpredictable fortune, "tyche" is also a vital force in his history, and in his interpretation of the rise of the empire (1.4.1, 15.20.6; Eckstein 1995, 254–271; Walbank 1994).

famous Hellenistic explorations that followed. Roman wars in Spain, Africa, and Cisalpine Gaul had also extended geographical knowledge; Polybius, friend of the Scipiones, had traveled in all of these places,[4] and had even navigated the western coast of Africa (Pliny *HN* 5.9). He incorporates the information available to him in geographical digressions, sometimes lengthy, in his work; and book 34, now lost, was devoted exclusively to geography. Like the authors of the Principate, Polybius saw geographical knowledge as a result of war and conquest (3.59.3). It may have seemed to the Greek historian that the main part of the "world" comprised, besides Rome, the empire of Carthage and especially the four great Hellenistic Greek empires.

Rome had not of course occupied or annexed all or even most of the territory of its rival empires. But I have argued that conquest in the imperial period was largely a status issue. It involved, most importantly, an attitude—deference based on fear; and just this definition of conquest has been ascribed to Polybius, too,[5] and can be found in other Republican sources. A famous story preserved in Livy, Polybius, and many other sources illustrates the point. Antiochus IV of Syria invaded Egypt, intending apparently to wrest Cyprus and the city of Pelusium from Ptolemy. The Roman senate passed a resolution ordering him to desist from the war, which was delivered to Antiochus by C. Popilius Laenas, who asked Antiochus to read it on the spot. Antiochus read the resolution and asked for time to deliberate with his friends. Popilius drew a circle in the dirt around Antiochus' feet and demanded an answer before he left the circle.

Polybius writes that this "seemed to be harsh and extremely arrogant"; the words βαρύ and ὑπερήφανον can also mean, though they do not here, something like "impressive." Either way, it is hard to imagine a more eloquent, though extreme, illustration of the basic principles of Roman diplomacy as we have described them for the imperial period. For the Romans, the scene with Antiochus was a symbolic assertion of their superior status. By extorting a show of deference with the threat of violence, they asserted an awesome and intimidating image. Astonished, Antiochus agreed to withdraw; the Romans then "took his hand and all together embraced him cheerfully" (Polybius 29.27.1–13).

4. 3.59.7, with the commentary of Walbank 1957–1979, 1:393–395; also see Aujac 1987a, 161–162, on Polybius.
5. Cf. Derow 1979, 4–6, arguing from 3.4.2–3 and other passages that obedience is the main proof of conquest in Polybius; on Polybius' view of the extent of the empire, see also J. Richardson 1979; and on the Roman definition of "empire," cf. Lintott 1981.

There was a more mundane aspect to Roman imperialism in this period as well. Even more than in the Principate, booty and indemnities were an important benefit of empire. At the time of Popilius' meeting with Antiochus—the year was 168 B.C.—Carthage was still paying off the indemnity from the second Punic war; the indemnities of Philip V and Antiochus III were by then paid up. In 167 Macedonia was made tributary. Sicily and Sardinia also paid tribute,[6] and in Spain there were vast and profitable mines.[7] All of Italy contributed to the army; by now huge tracts, impossible to estimate with accuracy, were *ager publicus,* Roman property.[8] An important element in the Romans' success was the price they exacted from the conquered. In the early period, this price was land and men, for the army; later, it was mainly money. Sometimes territory was annexed; if not at a rapid rate, this is understandable. The problems of occupying overseas territory without a professional army—or, as argued in chapter 3 above, even with one—are obvious.[9] But the deference of the vanquished took tangible form (money, land, manpower) in the Republican period just as it did later, and this was important. The Romans' insistence on these terms meant that each conquest added to their military and economic strength.

In modern times, the most problematic part of Polybius' account of Roman imperialism has been his theory of world conquest as the result of a deliberate and grandiose plan. Most modern historians reject this view. The theory of "defensive imperialism" is first associated with the great Theodor Mommsen in the later part of the nineteenth century.[10] Its most prominent proponent in English was Tenney Frank (1914), but its effects have been pervasive on much of modern scholarship, which sees here a reasonable if somewhat counterintuitive explanation for Roman actions. The Romans can rarely be seen attacking their neighbors without provocation; they conquered the world, it was argued, not from some grandiose drive to do this, but in order to secure their own safety. This theory has been out of fashion in recent years, but the present study suggests that it remains a valuable contribution toward the understand-

6. For a summary of Roman state income in this period, see Frank 1933–1940, 1:127–141.

7. Knapp (1977, 165–173) attempts to calculate the profitability of Republican Spain; by the late second century B.C. the province may have been only marginally profitable, considering the large occupying force it required.

8. Brunt 1971, 278–284.

9. See Sherwin-White 1980, 179.

10. On the cultural and intellectual context of this theory in the work of Mommsen and Holleaux, see Linderski 1984. A brief history of scholarship on imperialism can be found in Gruen 1984, 1:1–8.

ing of Roman imperialism, in the sense that the Romans themselves would not necessarily have disagreed with it. As we have seen, it was in fact important to them to fight only the "just"—that is, provoked—war. And safety, from their perspective, was potentially at stake after any breach of Roman dignity. I have argued that in the Principate safety was equated with honor, and honor with victory; ultimate victory in every conflict thus becomes a practical necessity, and security depended, in a fundamental sense, on "face." Thus the Romans might behave very aggressively while still insisting and even believing that they were concerned mainly for their own safety.

Another modern argument, also questioning Polybius' view of a "grand strategy" of world conquest, finds no long-term coherent plan behind Roman conquests; rather, expansion was a result of a series of ad hoc decisions, abounding with inconsistencies, not reflecting any far-reaching policy at all.[11] This thesis, also, is persuasive; indeed, we would not expect even the most sophisticated modern nation-states to pursue a single official foreign policy over a period of centuries or even generations. But if no long-term conscious plan can be found, then we must seek the result, the Roman empire, elsewhere—for example, in the values of the society.

In assessing the role of Roman values, another influential study (Harris 1979) has especially challenged the view that the Romans fought only defensive wars. Harris argues that the Romans were in fact profoundly aggressive, pointing to the rich rewards of conquest in glory, land, and wealth, and to the Roman tradition that perceived territorial expansion as a good thing. And again, this thesis is persuasive; all of these things—the economic rewards of warfare, the prestige of conquest—were important to the Romans of a later era as well. But can greed and ambition alone explain Roman actions? Certainly war could be lucrative for the peasant, if he was not killed and if the army was very successful. But no amount of wealth, glory, or territory could have been worth, from the peasants' point of view, the effort and suffering required in the exhausting first Punic war; nor, as we have seen, were greed, glory, and expansion considered "legitimate" causes for war. Harris has pointed out that, for most of the period of the Republic, the Romans went to war every year. Even after the exhausting devastation of the second Punic war, the average number of legions raised for the period from 203 to 168 did not decline; it remained at almost nine per year, which does not include the

11. Gruen 1984; Eckstein 1987. This is of course a much simplified version of the argument of these important works.

equal or greater number of troops provided by the Italian allies. In any given year, over 10 percent of Italy's adult male population was under arms.[12] This commitment to warfare and conquest is most comprehensible in the context of the ideas of national honor, vengeance, and terror that pervade the literature of the Principate, and of a tradition that valued military discipline as one of the most important and most "Roman" of virtues.

For the late Republic, substantial evidence exists to support the view that Roman foreign relations were governed by the same honor-based system of values that has been described for the imperial period. In a famous passage, Cicero lists the historical causes of Rome's wars, mostly in terms that need no translation into English: *honos, dignitas, imperium, fama,* and *caput,* "survival"; thus the ideas of honor and safety are closely connected for him (*De off.* 1.38). Caesar, as was argued in chapter 5, invokes ideas of honor, safety, and status (the "arrogance" of the enemy) in his war against Ariovistus; later, when he gives his reasons for crossing the Rhine, he writes of deterrence, terror, and vengeance.[13] When an African prince sought Roman aid against his enemies, he supposedly made the argument that the wrong (*iniuria*) done to him, a Roman ally, was an insult to Rome itself and that "it would befit the majesty of the Roman people to avert [my] injury" (Sall. *Iug.* 14.7–8). All of these passages depict issues such as arrogance and humiliation, honor and revenge, as the most important elements in Roman foreign policy. Perhaps it is not wise to project the evidence from the late Republic onto the great conquests of the previous two or three centuries; on the other hand, such ideas would persist, as we have seen, for centuries to come.

It is difficult to reconstruct Rome's very early past; the Romans did not start writing their own history until the late third century B.C., and the material from the first few centuries of its history often has the character of legend. But one might speculate that the image of the village on the Palatine should, in hindsight, inspire fear. The Romans were a terrifying people. Of their earliest institutions, little comes down to us; but historiography has preserved the memory of the ritual for declaring war—what the Romans called fetial law. With typical conservatism, they

---

12. For these figures, see Brunt 1971, 425–426; and Rich 1993, 45–46. Rich seeks mainly to modify Harris' views by pointing to fluctuations in the degree of Roman militarism over time, some social factors that opposed imperialism and expansion, and a strong defensive element in some wars. His article reminds us that a phenomenon as complex as Roman imperialism will never be adequately explained by a single cause or theory.

13. On the imperial views of Caesar and Cicero, see Brunt 1978.

continued to use this ritual sporadically in modified form until the second century A.D. It was characteristically Latin; that is, it was for the most part used only by Latin peoples; and it was very old, perhaps originating in the Neolithic period.[14] According to the ancient sources, the fetial priest went to the boundary of enemy territory with his head veiled, and demanded reparations for whatever wrong the enemy had committed. He called the gods to witness and heaped curses on himself if his demands were unjust. He then repeated the procedure to the first person he met inside enemy territory, and again at the city gates and in the forum. He then withdrew, and the enemy had thirty (or thirty-three) days to agree to Rome's demands. They could, of course, do just that—thus indicating deference and respect, and fear of Rome's military threat. If they refused, the Romans declared war.

The ritual is an illuminating one. Clearly, fetial law was not concerned with self-defense; it did not envision circumstances such as military invasion or anything else that could not wait thirty days for a response. It was a ritual of insult, deference, and retribution, suggesting that these were governing forces in Roman foreign relations from its earliest history. Causes, of course, can only be guessed at for the early period; but Livy sometimes mentions cattle raids, and this seems likely.[15] If a neighboring village raided Roman territory, a priest would soon arrive with an ultimatum; and the Romans would be back later, with an army.

Also very prominent in the diplomatic culture of Rome was the institution of *deditio*. Like fetial law, it probably arose very early; but unlike fetial law, it remained in frequent use until late antiquity. *Deditio* was unconditional surrender. There was an appropriate ceremony; Livy, telling the story of the surrender of Collatia in the reign of Tarquin I, tells us that the Roman priest was required to ask, "Do you surrender yourselves and the population of Collatia, the city, the fields, the water, the boundaries, the shrines, the equipment, and all things human and divine to the authority (*dicio*) of the Roman people?"[16] The conquered community might be granted reasonable terms after the surrender; the point was to avoid the horrific consequences of being taken by storm by the Romans. Thus *deditio* would be accepted only before the moment when the Roman siege engines touched the wall of the besieged city. But it was not customary to give any guarantees beforehand, even about

14. A. Watson 1993, 1–9.

15. Cf. Sherwin-White 1980, 177. On fetial law, see also the discussion of Harris 1979, 166–175. On early Roman warfare, see recently Raaflaub 1996.

16. Livy 1.38. On *deditio* in the Republic, including a discussion of the accuracy of Livy's description of the ritual, see recently Eckstein 1995a.

the survival of the tribe.[17] In the most famous *deditio* of all, the surrender of Carthage to the Roman ultimatum of 149 B.C., the Romans demanded the destruction of the city. Pompeius' treaty with Numantia in 139 B.C., which exacted hostages and a large indemnity, was repudiated as disgraceful by the senate because he had secretly given guarantees before the surrender (App. *Hisp.* 79). Again, the problem was one of image and attitude: the Romans must be perceived as relentless except where the enemy demonstrates sufficient terror and humility to accept any terms. The Romans could in fact be ruthless on these occasions and did not consider themselves ethically bound to spare a conquered people. Six years later, when Scipio Aemilianus reduced them to cannibalism in a protracted siege, the Numantines finally agreed to a *deditio;* Scipio sold all the survivors and destroyed the city (ibid., 97–98). The Romans did not always insist on this form of surrender, but usually they did. The great generals of the Republic, as we have seen, recorded immense lists of the *deditiones* they received; the prestige for the general who extracted this type of surrender was very great. But more than that, it was a form that served no other purpose than to establish firmly the superior status and dignity of Rome: to frighten the enemy, and then, when the tribe was spared, to inspire gratitude.

It may be significant that this last aspect of Roman foreign relations —the phenomenon of gratitude—seems better attested in the Republic than in the Principate.[18] In a typical pattern, Rome does a favor or *beneficium* for a foreign people, often by lending military aid; the ally then remains loyal not necessarily from fear but from more positive emotions. Rome, as benefactor, retains a position of superior status. The most famous, though somewhat atypical, example of this pattern is the tremendous outpouring of gratitude to Titus Flamininus after his defeat of Philip V of Macedon and "liberation of Greece" in 196 B.C. The shout that greeted his announcement of the withdrawal of Roman forces caused birds to drop dead from the sky.[19] Later, when Caesar reminded the Gauls of Rome's *beneficia* in order to secure their loyalty, he was using a traditional argument.[20] Sallust writes that Marius obliterated the city of Cispa partly because the people could be "compelled

17. Szidat 1970, 56–57, 138–139; Dahlheim 1968, 9–19.
18. Badian 1958; Gruen 1984, 1:172–184, emphasizing that the use of gratitude as an instrument of foreign policy is well attested in the Hellenistic world as well.
19. Plut. *Flam.* 10. On this event and its background, see Eckstein 1987, chap. 9, arguing that Flamininus himself was mainly responsible for the final form of this decision. As later in the case of Caesar and the Gauls, there was a substantial personal element here: the *beneficium* was granted by, and gratitude owed to, Flamininus personally as well as Rome.
20. Szidat 1970, 51–52, 124–126.

neither by *beneficium* nor by fear." These two emotions, then, were important policy instruments; but fear seems to have been perceived as the more effective of the two. This darker aspect is very prominent in Caesar's narrative: when the Veneti "rebel" after having offered *deditio* earlier, Caesar makes an example of them by selling the entire population into slavery (*B Gall.* 3.10, 16). The destruction of Numantia, mentioned above, was an earlier example of the same phenomenon. And Flamininus' famous gesture, of course, did not ultimately work, as the devastation wreaked by the Romans on the Greek peninsula fifty years later attests. When Roman envoys were insulted in Corinth, the city was destroyed and the Achaean League eviscerated, though not, apparently, annexed at this time.[21] The Romans did not insist by decree on gratitude or fear. They sought to inspire these feelings with their actions. This was an important, vital aim that would be brutally enforced if necessary.

The actions described above—like the fetial ritual itself—illustrate that the role of vengeance in Roman warfare was prominent from very early times. Cicero wrote that "just" wars were fought for vengeance or to repel an enemy;[22] note again the close connection between retribution and self-defense. Thus the idea of the great military defeat as a cause and justification for war, in the Republic as later, played an important part in the Roman imagination. For it was of course possible for Rome's enemies to enjoy success against them; and occasionally they might extract from a defeated commander terms humiliating to the Romans. In 321 B.C., the Samnites won a legendary victory at the Caudine Forks; the Romans were forced to cede territory and to give hostages; the army was subjected to the symbolic humiliation of going "under the yoke," naked, like oxen. Later, historians invented a face-saving sequel: the Roman senate and people, when informed about the treaty, repudiated it. The consuls who had made the peace were sent back to the enemy, naked and in chains; a better-attested example of this practice occurred later, in 137 B.C., when C. Hostilius Mancinus was handed over to the Numantines in Spain.[23] So lightly, we are supposed to conclude, did Rome hold the lives of its individual citizens compared to the dignity of its name.

Livy's highly rhetorical description of the shame felt by the Roman

21. Polyb. 38.12; Kallet-Marx 1995, 42–56.
22. Isidorus *Etymol.* 18.1.2: *illa iniusta bella sunt, quae sunt sine causa suscepta. Nam extra ulciscendi aut propulsandorum hostium causam bellum geri iustum nullum potest.*
23. See Rosenstein 1990, 148–149; for sources, ibid., app. 1.1.41. The main problem here was that Mancinus had requested peace after a defeat.

army and people after the disaster of the Caudine Forks fills seven or eight modern pages (9.4–9.7). It may not be true, as he says, that the war resumed immediately, with a succession of Roman victories—but the Romans did, sooner or later, resume the war, which continued off and on for seventeen years until the Samnite army was wiped out, twenty-six of their military standards were captured, and they were forced to beg for peace (9.44). This, then, was an early and legendary example of a humiliating military defeat avenged by brutal conquest—a pattern that was very important in the Principate, as argued in chapter 5.

The first such story was, of course, that of the sack of Rome by the Gauls in 390 B.C. Again, a face-saving sequel was invented: Rome was rescued, at the last minute, from having to pay cash ransom to the enemy, either because the hero Camillus defeated the Gauls on their way home from the city and recovered the money, or because he arrived to the rescue just as the ransom was being paid.[24] The "true" details of what happened are hopelessly lost—and the story of the sack of Rome is legendary in character. But it is just this type of understanding of events—legendary, "poetic"—that drove much of Roman policy in the Principate, and may have been even more important in the Republic. The story of the Gallic assault goes further. Livy recounts that the name of the tribe that sacked Rome was the Senones (5.3). A little more than a century later, they assaulted the Roman town of Arretium and defeated a Roman army and killed its commander—either that, or their leader executed some Roman envoys; the ancient sources disagree. In any case the Romans retaliated with measures apparently intended to obliterate the tribe. "He [the Roman consul] sold the women and children, and killed absolutely all the men of military age, and he destroyed the land in many ways and made it uninhabitable for the future" (App. *Celt.* 11). Florus adds that "Dolabella destroyed all the remnants of them in Etruria . . . so that no one should remain from the tribe who could boast that the city of Rome had been burnt by him" (1.8.21). The Romans planted a colony on the coast, but they did not settle the rest of the *ager Gallicus,* which supposedly remained a wasteland until a bill of 232 B.C. proposed colonies there, provoking more violent conflict. But the message is clear: all insults will be avenged, with extermination if necessary. And this vengeance was more important than the acquisition of territory.

The conflict that featured the defeat at the Caudine Forks was nei-

24. Livy 5.48–50; see the commentary of Ogilvie 1965 ad loc. for the alternate versions.

ther the first nor the last of the Samnite wars. Most of Rome's enemies in this period, as later, had to be defeated several times; thus the four Macedonian wars, the endless wars in Spain, and especially the three wars with Carthage. As later, ultimate victory required a more or less continual commitment of manpower over a long period of time. The first Punic war lasted for twenty-three years; for this conflict the Romans built a huge fleet, which was wrecked and rebuilt three times. In the end, Polybius writes, they lost some seven hundred quinqueremes; the Carthaginians lost five hundred—figures that become even more impressive when we recall that each quinquereme carried a crew of three hundred, plus marines. Polybius' figures are possibly somewhat exaggerated.[25] But they make an interesting point: the Romans did not prevail here because of their superior military or, still less, naval skill; they were patently inferior at seamanship and suffered more casualties than the Carthaginians. But in the end, Carthage ceded Sicily to the Romans; they agreed to pay a huge indemnity and to give hostages; that is, they lost. In the game of honor, insult, terror, and revenge the Romans were the most successful because the most ruthlessly determined; the most "believing," it is tempting to say—locating the crucial factor somewhere in the Roman mentality.

The importance of this psychological element in warfare seemed more clear to ancient historians than it sometimes does to modern ones, who, in hindsight, may be tempted to see the Roman conquest as easier or more inevitable than it in fact was. In the end, it seemed to ancient historians that the best illustration of what was unique—and, to them, admirable—about the Romans was the story of their perseverance in the face of their greatest defeat. The battle of Cannae in 216 B.C. was the third and worst of Hannibal's three crushing victories at the beginning of the second Punic war; the number killed on the Roman side is reported, not reliably, as 48,200 or 75,630;[26] Capua and other important allies in southern Italy defected. It seemed extraordinary that the Romans did not surrender. Instead, they undertook a ruthless and bloody campaign in their own territory, reconquering the Italian allies one by one.[27] Reprisals were very brutal even against allies who had surrendered to Hannibal under dire necessity. Tens of thousands were enslaved or killed—which might seem, to a modern observer, counter-

---

25. 1.63. Walbank (1957–1979, vol. 1, ad loc.) argues that they are only moderately exaggerated.

26. Livy 22.49; Polyb. 3.117; Toynbee 1965, 2:67–68.

27. This fascinating and horrifying tale is best told by Toynbee (1965, 2:20–33).

productive at a time when Rome, badly weakened, was fighting for its survival. But nothing could better illustrate the principles at work in Roman warfare: in this case, the crucial necessity of vengeance, even— or especially—in the case of one's closest allies. Rome won the war by reasserting its awesome and terrifying image—an image that could not have been maintained in the face of a surrender to the Carthaginians. These were the rules of the game, and victory did not necessarily depend on superior resources of whatever kind—technology, money, or manpower—though all of these things would of course help. Victory depended more on the willingness to expend these resources based on a commitment to a certain set of values we have described as a sense of national honor.[28]

In the end, it strikes me as misleading to describe Roman actions and policies as simply "aggressive" or "defensive." In fact, these terms may only rarely reflect with accuracy the policies of any nation. But especially with the Romans, we find a system that is not describable in terms of aggression and defense as easily as it is described in terms of insult and revenge, terror and deference. It is on these issues that we find subtlety and complexity in Roman thinking. But I do not claim here to offer an overall analysis of Republican imperialism—for which no single explanation can ever be adequate. Based mainly on famous stories and examples, the argument presented here is sure to strike many as simplistic. But legends are legends for a reason: because they reflect a larger truth. And perhaps the truth about Roman imperialism is not, after all, hidden from view, shrouded in rhetoric and myth. Perhaps the rhetoric, the myth, is the reality.

28. Cf. Polyb. 6.58; and Eckstein 1995, 56–70, especially 62–68, pointing out that Polybius admires both Carthage and Rome for their determination in preferring dangerous war to disgraceful peace at different points, and arguing that he attributes Roman success against Carthage and others in large part to this type of moral virtue.

References

Adams, J. P. 1976. The logistics of the Roman imperial army. Ph.D. diss., Yale University.

Adkins, A. W. H. 1960. *Merit and responsibility: A study in Greek values.* Oxford: Clarendon Press.

Albert, S. 1980. *Bellum iustum: Die Theorie des "gerechten Krieges" und ihre praktische Bedeutung für die auswärtigen Auseinandersetzungen Roms in republikanischer Zeit.* Kallmünz, Germany: Lassleben.

Alexandrescu-Vianu, M. 1979. Le programme iconographique du monument triomphal d'Adamklissi. *Dacia,* n.s., 23:123–129.

Alföldi, A. 1952. The moral barrier on Rhine and Danube. In *First congress of Roman frontier studies,* ed. E. Birley, 1–16. Durham, England: Durham University Press. First published as Die ethische Grenzscheide am römischen Limes, *Schweizer Beiträge zur allgemeinen Geschichte* 8 (1950): 37–50.

Alföldy, G. 1971. Der Friedensschluss des Kaisers Commodus. *Historia* 20:84–109.

———. 1976. Consuls and consulars under the Antonines. *Ancient Society* 7:263–299.

———. 1977. *Konsulat und Senatorenstand unter den Antoninen: Prosopographische Untersuchungen zur senatorischen Führungsschicht.* Bonn: Habelt.

Alföldy, G., and H. Halfmann. 1979. Iunius Maximus und die Victoria Parthica. *Zeitschrift für Papyrologie und Epigraphik* 35:195–212.

Alston, R. 1994. Roman military pay from Caesar to Diocletian. *Journal of Roman Studies* 84:113–123.

———. 1995. *Soldier and society in Roman Egypt: A social history.* London: Routledge.

Amit, M. 1965. Les moyens de communication et la défense de l'empire romain. *La parola del passato* 20:207–222.

Anderson, J. C. G. 1938. *De origine et situ Germanorum,* by Cornelius Tacitus. Oxford: Clarendon Press.

223

Andreau, J. 1989–1990. Recherches récentes sur les mines à l'époque romaine. 2 parts. *Revue numismatique* 6.31:86–112; 6.32:85–108.

Angeli Bertinelli, M. G. 1976. I Romani oltre l'Eufrate nel II secolo d.C. (le province di Assiria, di Mesopotamia, e di Osroene). *Aufstieg und Niedergang der römischen Welt* II.9.1:3–45.

————. 1979. *Roma e l'Oriente: Strategia, economia, società, e cultura nelle relazioni politiche fra Roma, la Giudea, e l'Iran.* Rome: L'Erma di Bretschneider.

Arnaud, P. 1983. L'affaire Mettius Pompusianus ou le crime de cartographie. *Mélanges de l'École française de Rome: Antiquité* 95:677–699.

————. 1984. L'image du globe dans le monde romain: Science, iconographie, symbolique. *Mélanges de l'École française de Rome: Antiquité* 96:53–116.

————. 1989. Une deuxième lecture du "bouclier" de Doura-Europus. *Comptes rendus de l'Académie des Inscriptions et Belles-Lettres,* 373–389.

Aujac, G. 1966. *Strabon et la science de son temps.* Paris: Les Belles Lettres.

————. 1987. The growth of an empirical cartography in Hellenistic Greece. In *The history of cartography,* ed. J. B. Harley and D. Woodward, vol. 1, *Cartography in prehistoric, ancient, and medieval Europe and the Mediterranean,* 148–160. Chicago: University of Chicago Press.

————. 1987a. Greek cartography in the early Roman world. In *The history of cartography,* ed. J. B. Harley and D. Woodward, vol. 1, *Cartography in prehistoric, ancient, and medieval Europe and the Mediterranean,* 161–176. Chicago: University of Chicago Press.

————. 1993. *Claude Ptolémée, astronome, astrologue, géographe: Connaissance et représentation du monde habité.* Paris: Éditions du CTHS.

Austin, N. J. E., and N. Rankov. 1995. *Exploratio: Military and political intelligence in the Roman world.* London: Routledge.

Aymard, A. 1961. Les otages barbares au début de l'empire. *Journal of Roman Studies* 51:136–142.

Badian, E. 1958. *Foreign clientelae, 264–70 B.C.* Oxford: Clarendon Press. Reprint, 1984.

————. 1968. *Roman imperialism in the late Republic.* 2d ed. Ithaca, N.Y.: Cornell University Press.

Balsdon, J. P. V. D. 1979. *Romans and aliens.* London: Duckworth; Chapel Hill: University of North Carolina Press.

Bardon, H. 1940. *Les empereurs et les lettres latines d'Auguste à Hadrien.* Paris: Les Belles Lettres. Reprint, 1968.

Barzanò, A. 1985. Roma e i Parti tra pace e guerra fredda nel I secolo dell'impero. In *La pace nel mondo antico,* ed. M. Sordi, 211–222. Milan: Vita e Pensiero.

Bekker-Neilsen, T. 1988. Terra incognita: The subjective geography of the Roman empire. In *Studies in ancient history and numismatics presented to Rudi Thomsen,* 148–161. Aarhus: Aarhus University Press.

Bell, B. M. 1995. The contribution of Julius Caesar to the vocabulary of ethnography. *Latomus* 54:753–767.

Bérard, F. 1984. La carrière de Plotius Grypus et le ravitaillement de l'armée impériale en campagne. *Mélanges de l'École française de Rome: Antiquité* 96:259–324.

Berthelot, A. 1930. *L'Asie ancienne centrale et sud-orientale d'après Ptolémée*. Paris: Payot.

Bird, D. G. 1984. Pliny and the gold-mines of the north-west of the Iberian peninsula. In *Papers in Iberian archaeology*, ed. T. F. C. Blagg, R. F. J. Jones and S. J. Keay, 341–363. Oxford: British Archaeological Reports.

Birley, A. R. 1974. Septimius Severus, *propagator imperii*. In *Actes du IXe congrès international d'études sur les frontières romaines*, ed. D. M. Pippidi, 297–299. Bucharest: Editura Academiei.

———. 1979. Die Aussen- und Grenzpolitik unter der Regierung Marc Aurels. In *Marc Aurel*, ed. R. Klein, 473–502. Darmstadt: Wissenschaftliche Buchgesellschaft.

———. 1981. The senatorial career under the Principate. In *The fasti of Roman Britain*, 4–35. Oxford: Clarendon Press.

———. 1981a. The economic effects of Roman frontier policy. In *The Roman West in the third century*, ed. A. King and M. Henic, 1:39–53. Oxford: British Archaeological Reports.

———. 1987. *Marcus Aurelius: A biography*. 2d ed. New Haven: Yale University Press.

———. 1988. *Septimius Severus: The African emperor*. 2d ed. New Haven: Yale University Press.

———. 1992. Locus virtutibus patefactus? Zum Beförderungssystem in der Hohen Kaiserzeit. Rheinisch-Westfälischen Akademie der Wissenschaften: Geisteswissenschaften. Vorträge G 318. Opladen, Germany: Westdeutscher Verlag.

Birley, E. 1954. Senators in the emperors' service. *Proceedings of the British Academy* 39:197–214. Later published in *The Roman army: Papers, 1929–1986* (Amsterdam: J. C. Gieben, 1988), 75–92.

———. 1957. Beförderungen und Versetzungen im römischen Heer. *Carnuntum-Jahrbuch*, 3–20. Later published as Promotions and transfers in the Roman army: Senatorial and equestrian officers, in *The Roman army: Papers, 1929–1986* (Amsterdam: J. C. Gieben, 1988), 93–113.

Bivar, A. D. H. 1983. The political history of Iran under the Arsacids. In *The Cambridge history of Iran*, vol. 3, *The Seleucid, Parthian, and Sasanian periods*, ed. E. Yarshater, i:21–99. Cambridge: Cambridge University Press.

Bogdan Cataniciu, I. 1981. *The evolution of the system of defence works in Roman Dacia*. Oxford: British Archaeological Reports.

———. 1990. Ptolémée et la province de Dacie. *Dacia*, n.s., 34:223–234.

Bolin, S. 1958. *State and currency in the Roman empire to 300 A.D.* Stockholm: Almquist & Wiksell.

Bonner, S. F. 1977. *Education in ancient Rome: From the Elder Cato to the Younger Pliny*. Berkeley: University of California Press; London: Methuen.

Bosworth, A. B. 1976. Vespasian's reorganization of the north-east frontier. *Antichthon* 10:63–78.

———. 1977. Arrian and the Alani. *Harvard Studies in Classical Philology* 81:217–255.

Bowersock, G. W. 1969. *Greek sophists in the Roman empire*. Oxford: Clarendon Press.

———. 1983. *Roman Arabia*. Cambridge: Harvard University Press.

———. 1987. The mechanics of subversion in the Roman provinces. In *Opposition et résistances à l'empire d'Auguste à Trajan,* Entretiens sur l'antiquité classique, no. 33, 291–317. Geneva: Fondation Hardt.

Braccesi, L. 1991. Alessandro e la Germania: Riflessioni sulla geografia romana di conquista. Rome: L'Erma di Bretschneider.

Braund, D. 1984. *Rome and the friendly king: The character of the client kingship.* London: Croom Helm; New York: St. Martin's Press.

———. 1986. The Caucasian frontier: Myth, exploration, and the dynamics of imperialism. In *The defence of the Roman and Byzantine East,* ed. P. Freeman and D. Kennedy, 1:31–49. Oxford: British Archaeological Reports.

———. 1994. *Georgia in antiquity: A history of Colchis and transcaucasian Iberia.* Oxford: Clarendon Press.

———. 1996. River frontiers in the environmental psychology of the Roman world. In *The Roman army in the East,* ed. D. L. Kennedy, 43–48. Ann Arbor, Mich.: Journal of Roman Archaeology.

Breeze, D. J. 1984. Demand and supply on the northern frontier. In *Between and beyond the walls: Essays on the prehistory and history of north Britain in honour of George Jobey,* ed. R. Miket and C. Burgess, 264–286. Edinburgh: J. Donald Publishers.

———. 1987–1988. The logistics of Agricola's final campaign. *Talanta* 18–19:7–28.

———. 1988. Why did the Romans fail to conquer Scotland? *Proceedings of the Society of Antiquaries of Scotland* 118:3–22.

Breeze, D. J., and B. Dobson. 1987. *Hadrian's wall.* 3d ed. London: Penguin.

Brilliant, R. 1963. *Gesture and rank in Roman art.* Memoirs of the Connecticut Academy of Arts and Sciences, no. 14. New Haven: The Academy.

Brodersen, K. 1995. *Terra cognita: Studien zur römischen Raumerfassung.* Hildesheim, Germany: Olms.

Brunt, P. A. 1950. Pay and superannuation in the Roman army. *Papers of the British School at Rome* 18 (= n.s., 5): 50–71.

———. 1963. Review of *Die Aussenpolitik des Augustus und die augusteische Dichtung,* by H. D. Meyer. *Journal of Roman Studies* 53:170–176. Later published as Augustan imperialism, in *Roman imperial themes* (Oxford: Clarendon Press, 1990), 96–109.

———. 1971. *Italian manpower, 225 B.C.–A.D. 14.* London: Oxford University Press.

———. 1974. Conscription and volunteering in the Roman imperial army. *Scripta classica israelica* 1:90–115. Later published in *Roman imperial themes* (Oxford: Clarendon Press, 1990), 188–214.

———. 1975. The administrators of Roman Egypt. *Journal of Roman Studies* 65:124–147. Later published in *Roman imperial themes* (Oxford: Clarendon Press, 1990), 215–254.

———. 1976–1983. *History of Alexander and Indica,* by Arrian. 2 vols. Cambridge: Harvard University Press.

———. 1978. Laus imperii. In *Imperialism in the ancient world,* ed. P. D. A. Garnsey and C. R. Whittaker, 159–191. Cambridge: Cambridge University Press. Later published in *Roman imperial themes* (Oxford: Clarendon Press, 1990), 288–323.

———. 1981. The revenues of Rome. Review of *Untersuchungen zu den direkten Staatsabgaben der römischen Kaiserzeit,* by L. Neesen. *Journal of Roman Studies* 71:161–172. Later published in *Roman imperial themes* (Oxford: Clarendon Press, 1990), 324–346.

———. 1983. Princeps and equites. *Journal of Roman Studies* 73:42–75.

———. 1990. Roman imperial illusions. In *Roman imperial themes,* 433–480. Oxford: Clarendon Press.

Callu, J. P. 1969. *La politique monétaire des empereurs romains de 238 à 311.* Paris: E. de Boccard.

Campbell, J. B. 1975. Who were the *viri militares? Journal of Roman Studies* 65:11–31.

———. 1984. *The emperor and the Roman army, 31 B.C.–A.D. 235.* Oxford: Clarendon Press.

———. 1987. Teach yourself how to be a general. *Journal of Roman Studies* 77:13–29.

———. 1993. War and diplomacy: Rome and Parthia, 31 B.C.–A.D. 235. In *War and society in the Roman world,* ed. J. Rich and G. Shipley, 213–240. London: Routledge.

Carandini, A. 1983. Columella's vinyard and the rationality of the Roman economy. *Opus* (Rome) 2:177–204.

Carcopino, J. 1934. Un retour à l'impérialisme de conquête: L'or des Daces. In *Points de vue sur l'impérialisme romain,* 71–86. Paris: Le Divan.

Carradice, I. 1983. *Coinage and finances in the reign of Domitian, A.D. 81–96.* Oxford: British Archaeological Reports.

Casson, L. 1989. *The Periplus Maris Erythraei: Text with introduction, translation, and commentary.* Princeton: Princeton University Press.

Champlin, E. 1980. *Fronto and Antonine Rome.* Cambridge: Harvard University Press.

Chaumont, M. L. 1976. L'Arménie entre Rome et l'Iran I: De l'avènement d'Auguste à l'avènement de Dioclétien. *Aufstieg und Niedergang der römischen Welt* II.9.1:71–194.

———. 1987. Un document méconnu concernant l'envoi d'un ambassadeur parthe vers Septime Sévère (P. Dura 60B). *Historia* 36:423–447.

Chevallier, R. 1976. *Roman roads.* Trans. N. H. Field. Berkeley: University of California Press. Originally published as *Les voies romaines* (Paris: A. Colin, 1972).

Cimma, M. R. 1976. *Reges socii et amici populi romani.* Milan: A. Giuffre.

Cohen, D. 1995. *Law, violence, and community in classical Athens.* Cambridge: Cambridge University Press.

Colledge, M. A. R. 1967. *The Parthians.* New York: Praeger.

Collingwood, R. G., and R. P. Wright. 1965. *The Roman inscriptions of Britain.* Vol. 1, *Inscriptions on stone.* Oxford: Clarendon Press.

Conole, P., and R. D. Milns. 1983. Neronian frontier policy in the Balkans: The career of Ti. Plautius Silvanus. *Historia* 32:183–200.

Corbier, M. 1977. L'*aerarium militare.* In *Armées et fiscalité dans le monde antique,* 197–234. Paris: Éditions du CNRS.

———. 1978. Dévaluations et fiscalité (161–235). In *Les "dévaluations" à Rome: Époque républicaine et impériale,* 1:273–301. Rome: École Française de Rome.

————. 1988. L'impôt dans l'empire romain: Résistences et refus (Ier–IIIe siècles). In *Forms of control and subordination in antiquity,* ed. T. Yuge and M. Doi, 259–274. Tokyo: Society for Studies on Resistance Movements in Antiquity; Leiden: Brill.

Cornell, T. 1995. *The beginnings of Rome: Italy and Rome from the Bronze Age to the Punic Wars (c. 1000–264 B.C.).* London: Routledge.

Coulston, J. C. 1986. Roman, Parthian, and Sassanid tactical developments. In *The defence of the Roman and Byzantine East,* ed. P. Freeman and D. Kennedy, 1:59–75. Oxford: British Archaeological Reports.

Crawford, M. 1975. Finance, coinage, and money from the Severans to Constantine. *Aufstieg und Niedergang der römischen Welt* II.2:560–593.

————. 1983. Roman imperial coin types and the formation of public opinion. In *Studies in numismatic method presented to Philip Grierson,* ed. C. N. L. Brooke, 47–64. Cambridge: Cambridge University Press.

Crook, J. 1955. *Consilium principis: Imperial councils and counsellors from Augustus to Diocletian.* Cambridge: Cambridge University Press.

Crow, J. 1986. A review of the physical remains of the frontier in Cappadocia. In *The defence of the Roman and Byzantine East,* ed. P. Freeman and D. Kennedy, 1:77–91. Oxford: British Archaeological Reports.

Crowther, N. B. 1983. Cornelius Gallus: His importance in the development of Roman poetry. *Aufstieg und Niedergang der römischen Welt* II.30.3: 1622–1648.

Cuntz, O. 1929. *Itineraria romana.* Vol. 1, *Itineraria Antonini Augusti et Burdigalense.* Leipzig: B. G. Teubner.

Dabrowa, E. 1981. Les rapports entre Rome et les Parthes sous Vespasien. *Syria* 58:187–204.

————. 1984. Le programme de la politique parthe en Occident des derniers Arsacides. *Iranica Antiqua* 19:149–165.

————. 1986. The frontier in Syria in the first century A.D. In *The defence of the Roman and Byzantine East,* ed. P. Freeman and D. Kennedy, 1:93–108. Oxford: British Archaeological Reports.

Dahlheim, W. 1968. *Struktur und Entwicklung des römischen Volkerrechts im dritten und zweiten Jahrhundert v. Chr.* Munich: C. H. Beck.

Daniels, C. 1991. The Antonine abandonment of Scotland. In *Roman frontier studies, 1989,* ed. V. Maxfield and M. J. Dobson, 48–51. Exeter, England: University of Exeter Press.

D'Arms, J. H. 1981. *Commerce and social standing in ancient Rome.* Cambridge: Harvard University Press.

Dauge, Y. A. 1981. *Le barbare: Recherches sur la conception de la barbarie et de la civilisation.* Collection Latomus, vol. 176. Brussels: Latomus.

David, J. M. 1992. *Le patronat judiciaire au dernier siècle de la république romaine.* Rome: École Française de Rome

Davies, R. W. 1968. Fronto, Hadrian, and the Roman army. *Latomus* 27:75–95.

————. 1969. The supply of animals to the Roman army and the remount systems. *Latomus* 28:429–459.

Debevoise, N. 1938. *A political history of Parthia.* Chicago: University of Chicago Press.

de Laet, S. J. 1949. *Portorium: Étude sur l'organisation douanière chez les romains.* Bruges: De Tempel.

de Neeve, P. W. 1985. The price of agricultural land in Roman Italy and the problem of economic rationality. *Opus* (Rome) 4:77–109.

Derow, P. S. 1979. Polybius, Rome, and the East. *Journal of Roman Studies* 69:1–15.

Desanges, J. 1978. *Recherches sur l'activité des méditerranéens aux confins de l'Afrique, VIe siècle avant J.-C.–IVe siècle après J.-C.* Rome: École Française de Rome.

———. 1980. *Histoire naturelle, livre V, 1–46,* by Pliny the Elder. Paris: Les Belles Lettres.

Destombes, M. 1964. *Mappemondes, A.D. 1200–1500.* Imago mundi: A review of early cartography, suppl. 4. Monumenta cartographica vestutioris aevi, vol. I. Amsterdam: N. Israel.

Develin, R. 1971. The army pay rises under Severus and Caracalla and the question of *annona militaris. Latomus* 30:687–695.

Dihle, A. 1964. The conception of India in Hellenistic and Roman literature. *Proceedings of the Cambridge Philological Society* 190 (n.s., 10): 15–23.

———. 1980. Plinius und die geographische Wissenschaft. In *Tecnologia, economia, e società nel mondo romano,* 127–137. Como: Banca Popolare Commercio e Industria.

Dilke, O. 1985. *Greek and Roman maps.* Ithaca, N.Y.: Cornell University Press.

———. 1987. The culmination of Greek cartography in Ptolemy. In *The history of cartography,* ed. J. B. Harley and D. Woodward, vol. 1, *Cartography in prehistoric, ancient, and medieval Europe and the Mediterranean,* 177–200. Chicago: University of Chicago Press.

———. 1987a. Itineraries and geographical maps in the early and late Roman empires. In *The history of cartography,* ed. J. B. Harley and D. Woodward, vol. 1, *Cartography in prehistoric, ancient, and medieval Europe and the Mediterranean,* 234–257. Chicago: University of Chicago Press.

———. 1987b. Cartography in the Byzantine empire. In *The history of cartography,* ed. J. B. Harley and D. Woodward, vol. 1, *Cartography in prehistoric, ancient, and medieval Europe and the Mediterranean,* 258–275. Chicago: University of Chicago Press.

Dion, R. 1977. *Aspects politiques de la géographie antique.* Paris: Les Belles Lettres.

Dobson, B. 1986. The function of Hadrian's wall. *Archaeologia Aeliana,* 5th ser., 14:1–30.

Dodgeon, M. H., and S. N. C. Lieu. 1991. *The Roman eastern frontier and the Persian wars (A.D. 226–363): A documentary history.* London: Routledge.

Domergue, C. 1990. *Les mines de la péninsule ibérique dans l'antiquité romaine.* Rome: École Française de Rome.

Duncan-Jones, R. 1974. *The economy of the Roman empire: Quantitative studies.* Cambridge: Cambridge University Press.

———. 1990. *Structure and scale in the Roman economy.* Cambridge: Cambridge University Press.

————. 1994. *Money and government in the Roman empire*. Cambridge: Cambridge University Press.

Dunn, T. J. 1996. *The militarization of the U.S.-Mexico border, 1978–1992: Low-intensity conflict doctrine comes home*. Austin: CMAS Books, University of Texas at Austin.

Dyson, S. L. 1971. Native revolts in the Roman empire. *Historia* 20:239–274.

————. 1975. Native revolt patterns in the Roman empire. *Aufstieg und Niedergang der römischen Welt* II.3:138–175.

Earl, D. 1967. *The moral and political tradition of Rome*. Ithaca, N.Y.: Cornell University Press; London: Thames & Hudson.

Eck, W. 1974. Beförderungskriterien innerhalb der senatorischen Laufbahn, dargestellt an der Zeit von 69 bis 138 n. Chr. *Aufstieg und Niedergang der römischen Welt* II.1:158–228.

————. 1984. Zum konsularen Status von Judaea im frühen 2. Jh. *Bulletin of the American Society of Papyrologists* 21:55–67.

Eckstein, A. 1987. *Senate and general: Individual decision-making and Roman foreign relations, 264–194 B.C.* Berkeley: University of California Press.

————. 1995. *Moral vision in the histories of Polybius*. Berkeley: University of California Press.

————. 1995a. Glabrio and the Aetolians: A note on *deditio. Transactions of the American Philological Association* 125:271–289.

Edelstein, E., and I. G. Kidd. 1988. *Posidonius*. Vol. 1, *The fragments*. 2d ed. Cambridge: Cambridge University Press.

Ehlers, W. 1939. Triumphus. *Real-Encyclopädie der klassischen Altertumswissenschaft*, ed. A. Pauly, G. Wissowa, and W. Kroll, II.7 (Hb. 13): 493–511.

Engels, D. 1978. *Alexander the Great and the logistics of the Macedonian army*. Berkeley: University of California Press.

————. 1985. The length of Eratosthenes' stade. *American Journal of Philology* 106:298–311.

Epstein, D. F. 1987. *Personal enmity in Roman politics, 218–43 B.C.* London: Croom Helm.

Fentress, E. W. B. 1979. *Numidia and the Roman army: Social, military, and economic aspects of the frontier zone*. Oxford: British Archaeological Reports.

Ferguson, J. 1978. China and Rome. *Aufstieg und Niedergang der römischen Welt* II.9.ii:581–603.

Ferrill, A. 1991. The grand strategy of the Roman empire. In *Grand strategies in war and peace*, ed. P. Kennedy, 71–85. New Haven: Yale University Press.

Fink, R. 1971. *Roman military records on papyrus*. Cleveland: Press of the Case Western Reserve University.

Finley, M. I. 1985. *The ancient economy*. 2d ed. Berkeley: University of California Press.

Florescu, F. B. 1965. *Das Siegesdenkmal von Adamklissi: Tropaeum Traiani*. Bucharest: Verlag der Akademie der Rumänischen Volksrepublik; Bonn: Habelt.

Flower, H. I. 1996. *Ancestor-masks and aristocratic power in Roman culture*. Oxford: Clarendon Press.

Forni, G. 1953. *Il reclutamento delle legioni da Augusto a Diocleziano*. Rome: Bocca.

Frank, T. 1914. *Roman imperialism.* New York: Macmillan.

———, ed. 1933–1940. *An economic survey of ancient Rome.* 6 vols. Baltimore: Johns Hopkins University Press.

Frere, S. 1987. *Britannia: A history of Roman Britain.* 3d ed. London: Routledge.

Frézouls, E. 1981. Les fluctuations de la frontière orientale de l'empire romain. In *La géographie administrative et politique d'Alexandre à Mahomet,* 177–225. Leiden: E. J. Brill.

Gabba, E. 1966. Sulle influenze reciproce degli ordinamenti militari dei parti e dei romani. In *La Persia e il mondo greco-romano,* 51–73. Rome: Accademia Nazionale dei Lincei.

Gagé, J. 1933. La théologie de la victoire impériale. *Revue historique* 171:1–43.

———. 1959. L'empereur romain et les rois: Politique et protocol. *Revue historique* 221:221–260.

———. 1977. *Res gestae divi Augusti.* 3d ed. Paris: Les Belles Lettres.

Galliazzo, V. 1994. *I ponti romani.* 2 vols. Treviso: Canova.

Gelzer, M. 1968. *Caesar: Politician and statesman.* Trans. P. Needham. Cambridge: Harvard University Press; Oxford: B. Blackwell. Originally published as *Caesar, der Politiker und Staatsmann,* 6th ed. (Wiesbaden: F. Steiner, 1960).

Göbl, R. 1961. "'Rex . . . datus': Ein Kapitel von der Interpretation numismatischer Zeugnisse und ihren Grundlagen." *Rheinisches Museum* 104:70–80.

Goldsmith, R. W. 1984. An estimate of the size and structure of the gross national product of the early empire. *Review of Income and Wealth* 30:263–288.

———. 1987. *Premodern financial systems: A historical comparative study.* Cambridge: Cambridge University Press.

Goodman, M. 1987. *The ruling class of Judaea: The origins of the Jewish revolt against Rome, A.D. 66–70.* Cambridge: Cambridge University Press.

Graf, D. 1989. Rome and the Saracens: Reassessing the nomadic menace. In *L'Arabie préislamique et son environment historique et culturel,* ed. T. Fahd, 341–400. Strasbourg: Université des Sciences Humaines de Strasbourg.

Graham, A. J. 1978. The numbers at Lugdunum. *Historia* 27:625–630.

Griffin, M. T. 1976. *Seneca: A philosopher in politics.* Oxford: Clarendon.

———. 1984. *Nero: The end of a dynasty.* London: B. T. Batsford; New Haven: Yale University Press, 1985.

Gruen, E. S. 1984. *The Hellenistic world and the coming of Rome.* 2 vols. Berkeley: University of California Press.

———. 1985. Augustus and the ideology of war and peace. In *The age of Augustus,* ed. R. Winkes, 51–72. Providence, R.I.: Center for Old World Archaeology and Art, Brown University.

———. 1990. The imperial policy of Augustus. In *Between Republic and empire: Interpretations of Augustus and his principate,* ed. K. A. Raaflaub and M. Toher, 395–416. Berkeley: University of California Press.

———. 1993. *Culture and national identity in Republican Rome.* Ithaca, N.Y.: Cornell University Press.

———. 1996. The expansion of the empire under Augustus. In *Cambridge ancient history,* 2d ed., vol. 10, *The Augustan empire, 43 B.C.–A.D. 69,* 188–194. Cambridge: Cambridge University Press.

232   REFERENCES

Gudea, N. 1979. The defensive system of Roman Dacia. *Britannia* 10:63–87.

Guey, J. 1966. De "L'or des Daces" (1924) au livre de Sture Bolin (1958): Guerre et or, or et monnaie. In *Mélanges d'archéologie, d'epigraphie, et d'histoire offerts à Jérôme Carcopino,* 445–475. Paris: Hachette.

Haase, W. 1977. "Si vis pacem, para bellum": Zur Bedeutung militärischer Stärker in der römischen Kaiserzeit. In *Limes: Akten des XI. internationalen Limeskongresses,* ed. J. Fitz, 721–756. Budapest: Akadémiai Kiadó.

Halfmann, H. 1986. *Itinera principum: Geschichte und Typologie der Kaiserreisen im römischen Reich.* Stuttgart: F. Steiner.

Hall, E. 1989. *Inventing the barbarian: Greek self-definition through tragedy.* Oxford: Clarendon Press.

Hammond, M. 1957. Imperial elements in the formula of the Roman emperors during the first two and a half centuries of the empire. *Memoirs of the American Academy in Rome* 25:17–64.

Hannestad, N. 1988. *Roman art and imperial policy.* Aarhus: Aarhus University Press.

Hanson, W. S. 1987. *Agricola and the conquest of the North.* Totowa, N.J.: Barnes & Noble.

Hanson, W. S., and G. S. Maxwell. 1983. *Rome's north west frontier: The Antonine wall.* Edinburgh: Edinburgh University Press.

Harl, K. W. 1996. *Coinage in the Roman economy, 300 B.C. to A.D. 700.* Baltimore: Johns Hopkins University Press.

Harris, W. V. 1979. *War and imperialism in Republican Rome, 320–70 B.C.* Oxford: Clarendon Press.

———. 1989. *Ancient literacy.* Cambridge: Harvard University Press.

Hartog, F. 1988. *The mirror of Herodotus: The representation of the other in the writing of history.* Trans. J. Lloyd. Berkeley: University of California Press. Originally published as *Le miroir d'Hérodote: Essai sur la représentation de l'autre* (Paris: Gallimard, 1980).

Hellegouarc'h, J. 1972. *Le vocabulaire latin des relations et des partis politiques sous la république.* Paris: Les Belles Lettres.

Holder, P. A. 1980. *Studies in the auxilia of the Roman army from Augustus to Trajan.* Oxford: British Archaeological Reports.

———. 1982. *The Roman army in Britain.* New York: St. Martin's Press; London: B. T. Batsford.

Hölscher, T. 1967. *Victoria romana.* Mainz: P. von Zabern.

Hopkins, K. 1980. Taxes and trade in the Roman empire (200 B.C.–A.D. 400). *Journal of Roman Studies* 70:101–125.

Howgego, C. 1990. Why did ancient states strike coins? *Numismatic Chronicle* 150:1–25.

———. 1992. The supply and use of money in the Roman world, 200 B.C.–A.D. 300. *Journal of Roman Studies* 82:1–31.

Instinsky, H. U. 1972. Cassius Dio, Mark Aurel, und die Jazygen. *Chiron* 2:475–482.

Isaac, B. 1984. Bandits in Judaea and Arabia. *Harvard Studies in Classical Philology* 88:171–203.

———. 1988. The meaning of 'limes' and 'limitanei' in ancient sources. *Journal of Roman Studies* 78:125–147.

————. 1992. *The limits of empire: The Roman imperial army in the East.* 2d ed. Oxford: Clarendon Press.

Jacob, C. 1990. *La description de la terre habitée de Denys d'Alexandrie.* Paris: Albin Michel.

Janni, P. 1984. *La mappa e il periplo: Cartografia antica e spazio odologico.* Rome: L'Erma di Bretschneider.

Jones, A. H. M. 1974. *The Roman economy: Studies in ancient economic and administrative history,* ed. P. A. Brunt. Oxford: B. Blackwell; Totowa, N.J.: Rowman & Littlefield.

Jones, B. 1992. *The emperor Domitian.* London: Routledge.

Jones, C. P. 1971. *Plutarch and Rome.* Oxford: Clarendon Press.

Jones, R. F. J. 1976. The military occupation of north-west Spain. *Journal of Roman Studies* 66:45–66.

Kagan, D. 1995. *On the origins of war and the preservation of peace.* New York: Doubleday.

Kallet-Marx, R. M. 1995. *Hegemony to empire: The development of Roman imperium in the East from 148 to 62 B.C.* Berkeley: University of California Press.

Keay, S. J. 1988. *Roman Spain.* Berkeley: University of California Press; London: British Museum.

Kennedy, D. 1980. The frontier policy of Septimius Severus: New evidence from Arabia. In *Roman frontier studies 1979,* ed. W. S. Hanson and L. J. F. Keppie, 3:879–887. Oxford: British Archaeological Reports.

————. 1987. The garrisoning of Mesopotamia in the late Antonine and early Severan periods. *Antichthon* 21:57–66.

Kennedy, D., and D. Riley. 1990. *Rome's desert frontier from the air.* London: B. T. Batsford; Austin: University of Texas Press.

Kennedy, P. 1991. Grand strategy in war and peace: Toward a broader definition. In *Grand strategies in war and peace,* ed. P. Kennedy, 1–7. New Haven: Yale University Press.

Keppie, L. J. F. 1983. *Colonisation and veteran settlement in Italy, 47–14 B.C.* London: British School at Rome.

————. 1986. Legions in the East from Augustus to Trajan. In *The defence of the Roman and Byzantine East,* ed. P. Freeman and D. Kennedy, 2:411–429. Oxford: British Archaeological Reports.

Kerr, W. G. 1991. Economic warfare on the northern *limes: Portoria* and the Germans. In *Roman frontier studies, 1989,* ed. V. A. Maxfield and M. J. Dobson, 442–445. Exeter, England: University of Exeter Press.

Kidd, I. G. 1988–1989. *Posidonius.* Vol. 2, pts.1–2, *The commentary.* 2d ed. Cambridge: Cambridge University Press.

Kirwan, L. P. 1978. Rome beyond the southern Egyptian frontier. *Proceedings of the British Academy* 63:13–31.

Kloft, H. 1970. *Liberalitas Principis: Herrkunft und Bedeutung.* Cologne: Böhlau Verlag.

Knapp, R. C. 1977. *Aspects of the Roman experience in Iberia, 206–100 B.C.* Valladolid, Spain: Universidad, D. L.

Kneissl, P. 1969. *Die Siegestitulatur der römischen Kaiser.* Göttingen: Vandenhoeck & Ruprecht.

Koepp, F. 1924–1930. *Germania romana: Ein Bilder-Atlas.* 2d ed. 5 vols. (in 2). Bamberg: C. C. Buchner.

Koeppel, G. M. 1980. A military itinerarium on the column of Trajan: Scene L. *Mitteilungen des deutschen archäologischen Instituts, römische Abteilung* 87:301–306.

Kolendo, J. 1981. *À la recherche de l'ambre baltique: L'expedition d'un chevalier romain sous Neron.* Warsaw: Wydawnictwa Uniwersytetu Warszawskiego.

Krentz, P., and E. L. Wheeler, eds. and trans. 1994. *Stratagems of war,* by Polyaenus. 2 vols. Chicago: Ares.

Kubitschek, W. 1916. Itinerarien. *Real-Encyclopädie der klassischen Altertumswissenschaft,* ed. A. Pauly, G. Wissowa, and W. Kroll, 9:2308–2368.

Künzl, E. 1988. *Der römische Triumph: Siegesfeiern im antiken Rom.* Munich: C. H. Beck.

Lachmann, K., F. Blume, and A. Rudorff, eds. 1848–1852. *Die Schriften der römischen Feldmesser.* 2 vols. Berlin: G. Reimer. Reprint, Hildesheim: Olms, 1967.

La Regina, A. 1988. La Roma di Traiano. In *La colonna Traiana,* by S. Settis et al., 17–44. Turin: G. Einaudi.

Lee, A. D. 1993. *Information and frontiers: Roman foreign relations in late antiquity.* Cambridge: Cambridge University Press.

Lehmann, G. A. 1991. Das Ende der römischen Herrschaft über das westelbische Germanien: Von der Varus-Katastrophe zur Aberrufung des Germanicus Caesar, 16/7 n. Chr. *Zeitschrift für Papyrologie und Epigraphik* 86:79–96.

Lemosse, M. 1967. *Le régime des relations internationales dans le Haut-Empire romain.* Paris: Sirey.

Lendon, J. E. 1990. The face on the coins and inflation in Roman Egypt. *Klio* 72:106–134.

———. 1997. *Empire of honour: The art of government in the Roman world.* Oxford: Clarendon Press.

Lepper, F. A. 1948. *Trajan's Parthian war.* London: Oxford University Press.

Lepper, F. A., and S. Frere. 1988. *Trajan's column: A new edition of the Cichorius plates.* Gloucester, England: Alan Sutton.

Le Roux, P. 1982. *L'armée romaine et l'organisation des provinces ibériques d'Auguste à l'invasion de 409.* Paris: Boccard.

Levi, A., and M. Levi. 1967. *Itineraria picta: Contributo allo studio della Tabula Peutingeriana.* Rome: L'Erma di Bretschneider.

———. 1978. *La Tabula Peutingeriana.* Bologna: Edison.

———. 1981. Map projection and the Peutinger Table. In *Coins, culture, and history in the ancient world: Numismatic and other studies in honor of Bluma L. Trell,* ed. L. Casson and M. Price, 139–148. Detroit: Wayne State University Press.

Levi, A. C. 1952. *Barbarians on Roman imperial coins and sculpture.* Numismatic notes and monographs, no. 123. New York: American Numismatic Society.

Levick, B. 1982. Propaganda and the imperial coinage. *Antichthon* 16:104–116.

Lewis, A. M. 1992. The popularity of the "Phaenomena" of Aratus: A reevaluation. In *Studies in Latin literature and Roman history*, ed. C. Deroux, vol. 6 (= Collection Latomus, vol. 217), 94–118. Brussels: Latomus.

Lewis, N. 1981. Literati in the service of Roman emperors: Politics before culture. In *Coins, culture, and history in the ancient world: Numismatic and other studies in honor of Bluma L. Trell*, 149–165. Detroit: Wayne State University Press.

Lindersky, J. 1984. Si vis pacem, para bellum: Concepts of defensive imperialism. In *The imperialism of mid-Republican Rome*, ed. W. V. Harris, 133–164. Rome: American Academy in Rome.

Lintott, A. 1981. What was the "imperium romanum"? *Greece and Rome* 28: 53–67.

Little, D. 1982. Politics in Augustan poetry. *Aufstieg und Niedergang der römischen Welt* II.30.1:254–370.

Lo Cascio, E. 1981. State and coinage in the late Republic and early empire. *Journal of Roman Studies* 71:76–86.

Lund, A. 1988. *Germania*, by Cornelius Tacitus. Heidelberg: C. Winter.

———. 1990. *Zum Germanenbild der Römer: Eine Einführung in die antike Ethnographie.* Heidelberg: C. Winter.

———. 1991. Versuch einer Gesamtinterpretation der "Germania" des Tacitus. *Aufstieg und Niedergang der römischen Welt* II.33.3:1858–1988.

———. 1991a. Kritischer Forschungsbericht zur "Germania" des Tacitus. *Aufstieg und Niedergang der römischen Welt* II.33.3:1989–2222, 2341–2344.

Luttwak, E. N. 1976. *The grand strategy of the Roman empire.* Baltimore: Johns Hopkins University Press.

MacMullen, R. 1960. Inscriptions on armor and the supply of arms in the Roman empire. *American Journal of Archaeology* 64:23–40.

———. 1963. *Soldier and civilian in the later Roman empire.* Cambridge: Harvard University Press.

———. 1976. *The Roman government's response to crisis, A.D. 235–337.* New Haven: Yale University Press.

———. 1976a. Two notes on imperial properties. *Athenaeum* 54:19–36.

———. 1980. How big was the Roman imperial army? *Klio* 62:451–460.

———. 1984. The Roman emperors' army costs. *Latomus* 43:571–580.

———. 1986. Personal power in the Roman empire. *American Journal of Philology* 107:512–524.

———. 1987. Tax-pressure in the Roman empire. *Latomus* 46:737–754.

———. 1988. *Corruption and the decline of Rome.* New Haven: Yale University Press.

Macve, R. 1985. Some glosses on Ste. Croix's "Greek and Roman accounting." In *Crux: Essays presented to G. E. M. de Ste. Croix on his 75th birthday*, ed. P. Cartledge and F. D. Harvey (= History of Political Thought 6), 233–264. London: Imprint Academic.

Mann, J. C. 1963. The raising of new legions during the Principate. *Hermes* 91:483–489.

———. 1974. The frontiers of the Principate. *Aufstieg und Niedergang der römischen Welt* II.1:508–533.

———. 1979. Power, force, and the frontiers of empire. Review of *The grand strategy of the Roman empire,* by E. N. Luttwak. *Journal of Roman Studies* 69:175–183.

———. 1983. *Legionary recruitment and veteran settlement during the Principate.* London: Institute of Archaeology, University of London.

Mantovani, M. 1990. *Bellum iustum: Die Idee des gerechten Krieges in der römischen Kaiserzeit.* Bern: P. Lang.

Marrou, H. 1956. *History of education in antiquity.* Trans. G. Lamb. Madison: University of Wisconsin Press. Originally published as *L'histoire de l'éducation dans l'antiquité,* 3d ed. (Paris: Éditions du Seuil, 1948).

McCormick, M. 1986. *Eternal victory: Triumphal rulership in late antiquity, Byzantium, and the early medieval West.* Cambridge: Cambridge University Press; Paris: Éditions de la Maison des Sciences de l'Homme.

Meyer, H. D. 1961. *Die Aussenpolitik des Augustus und die augusteische Dichtung.* Cologne: Böhlau Verlag.

Mickwitz, G. 1932. *Geld und Wirtschaft im römischen Reich.* Helsinki: Central-tryckeri och bokbinderi aktiebolag.

Millar, F. 1964. *A study of Cassius Dio.* Oxford: Clarendon Press.

———. 1969. P. Herennius Dexippus: The Greek world and the third-century invasions. *Journal of Roman Studies* 59:12–29.

———. 1977. *The emperor in the Roman world, 31 B.C.–A.D. 337.* Ithaca, N.Y.: Cornell University Press; London: Duckworth.

———. 1982. Emperors, frontiers, and Roman foreign relations, 31 B.C. to A.D. 378. *Britannia* 13:1–23.

———. 1988. Government and diplomacy in the Roman empire during the first three centuries. *International History Review* 10:345–377.

———. 1993. *The Roman Near East, 31 B.C.–A.D. 337.* Cambridge: Harvard University Press.

Miller, K. 1916. *Die Peutingersche Tafel oder Weltkarte des Castorius.* Stuttgart: Strecker & Schröder. Reprint, Stuttgart: Brockhaus/Antiquarium, 1962.

———. 1916a. *Itineraria romana: Römische Reisewege an der Hand der Tabula Peutingeriana.* Stuttgart: Strecker & Schröder.

Mitchell, S. 1976. Requistioned transport in the Roman empire: A new inscription from Pisidia. *Journal of Roman Studies* 66:106–131.

———. 1983. The Balkans, Anatolia, and Roman armies across Asia Minor. In *Armies and frontiers in Roman and Byzantine Anatolia,* 131–150. Oxford: British Archaeological Reports.

———. 1993. *Anatolia: Land, men and gods in Asia Minor.* 2 vols. Oxford: Clarendon Press.

Mitford, T. B. 1980. Cappadocia and Armenia Minor: Historical setting of the *limes. Aufstieg und Niedergang der römischen Welt* II.7.2:1169–1228.

Mócsy, A. 1974. *Pannonia and Upper Moesia: A history of the middle Danube provinces of the Roman empire.* London: Routledge & K. Paul.

———. 1978. Zur Entstehung und Eigenart der Nordgrenzen Roms. Rheinisch-Westfälischen Akademie der Wissenschaften: Geisteswissenschaften. Vorträge G 229. Opladen, Germany: Westdeutscher Verlag.

Moles, J. J. 1983. The date and purpose of the fourth kingship oration of Dio Chrysostom. *Classical Antiquity* 2:251–278.

Moynihan, R. 1986. Geographical mythology and Roman imperial ideology.

In *The age of Augustus,* ed. R. Winkes, 149–162. Providence, R.I.: Center for Old World Archaeology and Art, Brown University.

Mrozek, S. 1977. Die Goldbergwerke im römischen Dazien. *Aufstieg und Niedergang der römischen Welt* II.6:95–109.

Müller, Karl. 1882. *Geographi graeci minores.* 2 vols. Paris: Firmin-Didot.

———. 1883–1901. *Geographia,* by Claudius Ptolemy. 3 vols. Paris: Firmin-Didot.

Müller, Klaus. 1972–1980. *Geschichte der antiken Ethnographie und ethnologischen Theoriebildung.* 2 vols. Wiesbaden: F. Steiner.

Musurillo, A. 1954. *The acts of the pagan martyrs: Acta Alexandrinorum.* Oxford: Clarendon Press.

Mynors, R. A. B., ed. 1964. *XII Panegyrici latini.* Oxford: Clarendon Press.

Neesen, L. 1980. *Untersuchungen zu den direkten Staatsabgaben der römischen Kaiserzeit.* Bonn: Habelt.

Nicolet, C. 1971. Les variations de prix, et la théorie quantitative de la monnaie. *Annales (Économie, sociétés, civilisations)* 26:1203–1227.

———. 1976. *Tributum: Recherches sur la fiscalité directe sous la république romaine.* Bonn: Habelt.

———. 1984. Pline, Paul, et la théorie de la monnaie. *Athenaeum,* n.s., 62:105–135.

———. 1988. *Rendre à César: Économie et société dans la Rome antique.* Paris: Gallimard.

———. 1991. *Space, geography, and politics in the early Roman empire.* Ann Arbor: University of Michigan Press. Originally published as *L'inventaire du monde: Géographie et politique aux origines de l'empire romain* (Paris: Fayard, 1988).

Noeske, H. C. 1977. Studien zur Verwaltung und Bevölkerung der dakischen Goldbergwerke in römischer Zeit. *Bonner Jahrbücher* 177:271–416.

Nutton, V. 1978. The beneficial ideology. In *Imperialism in the ancient world,* ed. P. D. A. Garnsey and C. R. Whittaker, 209–221. Cambridge: Cambridge University Press.

Ober, J. 1982. Tiberius and the political testament of Augustus. *Historia* 31:306–328.

O'Connor, C. 1993. *Roman bridges.* Cambridge: Cambridge University Press.

Ogilvie, R. M. 1965. *A commentary on Livy, books 1–5.* Oxford: Clarendon Press.

Ogilvie, R. M., and I. Richmond, eds. 1967. *De vita Agricolae,* by Cornelius Tacitus. Oxford: Clarendon Press.

Packer, J. E. 1997. *The forum of Trajan in Rome: A study of the monuments.* 3 vols. Berkeley: University of California Press.

Paratore, E. 1966. La Persia nella letteratura latina. In *La Persia e il mondo greco-romano,* 505–558. Rome: Accademia Nazionale dei Lincei.

Parker, H. M. D. 1958. *The Roman legions.* 2d ed. New York: Barnes & Noble.

Parker, S. T. 1991. The nature of Rome's Arabian frontier. In *Roman frontier studies, 1989,* ed. V. A. Maxfield and M. J. Dobson, 498–504. Exeter, England: University of Exeter Press.

Pearson, L. 1954–1955. The diary and letters of Alexander the Great. *Historia* 3:429–455.

————. 1960. *The lost histories of Alexander the Great.* New York: American Philological Association.

Pédech, P. 1964. *La méthode historique de Polybe.* Paris: Les Belles Lettres.

————. 1984. *Historiens, compagnons d'Alexandre: Callisthène, Onésicrite, Néarque, Ptolémée, Aristobule.* Paris: Les Belles Lettres.

Pekáry, T. 1959. Studien zur römischen Währungs- und Finanzgeschichte von 161 bis 235 n. Chr. *Historia* 8:443–489.

————. 1968. *Untersuchungen zu den römischen Reichsstrassen.* Bonn: Habelt.

————. 1987. Seditio: Unruhen und Revolten im römischen Reich von Augustus bis Commodus. *Ancient Society* 18:133–150.

Peristiany, J. G., ed. 1966. *Honour and shame: The values of Mediterranean society.* Chicago: University of Chicago Press.

Pflaum, H. G. 1950. *Les procurateurs équestres sous le Haut-Empire romain.* Paris: A. Maisonneuve.

————. 1960–1961. *Les carrières procuratoriennes équestres sous le Haut-Empire romain.* 4 vols. Paris: P. Geuthner.

Picard, G. C. 1957. *Les trophées romains: Contribution à l'histoire de la religion et de l'art triomphal de Rome.* Paris: de Boccard.

Pitt-Rivers, J. 1977. *The fate of Shechem or the politics of sex.* Cambridge: Cambridge University Press.

Pitts, L. F. 1989. Relations between Rome and the German "kings" on the middle Danube in the first to fourth centuries A.D. *Journal of Roman Studies* 79:45–58.

Potter, D. S. 1991. The inscriptions on the bronze Herakles from Mesene: Vologeses IV's war with Rome and the date of Tacitus' *Annales. Zeitschrift für Papyrologie und Epigraphik* 88:277–290.

————. 1996. Emperors, their borders, and their neighbors: The scope of imperial mandata. In *The Roman army in the East,* ed. D. L. Kennedy, 49–68. Ann Arbor, Mich.: Journal of Roman Archaeology.

Purcell, N. 1990. The creation of provincial landscape: The Roman impact on Cisalpine Gaul. In *The early Roman empire in the West,* ed. T. Blagg and M. Millett, 6–29. Oxford: Oxbow.

————. 1990a. Maps, lists, money, order, and power. Review of *L'inventaire du monde,* by C. Nicolet. *Journal of Roman Studies* 80:178–182.

Quass, F. 1993. *Die Honoratiorenschicht in den Städten des griechischen Ostens.* Stuttgart: F. Steiner.

Raaflaub, K. 1974. *Dignitatis contentio: Studien zur Motivation und politischen Taktik im Bürgerkrieg zwischen Caesar und Pompeius.* Vestigia 20. Munich: C. H. Beck.

————. 1996. Born to be wolves? The origins of Roman imperialism. In *Transitions to empire: Essays in Greco-Roman history, 360–146 B.C., in honor of E. Badian,* ed. R. W. Wallace and E. M. Harris, 273–314. Norman: University of Oklahoma Press.

Rambaud, M. 1966. *L'art de la déformation historique dans les commentaires de César.* 2d ed. Paris: Les Belles Lettres.

Ramsay, A. M. 1925. The speed of the Roman imperial post. *Journal of Roman Studies* 15:60–74.

Raschke, M. G. 1978. New studies in Roman commerce with the East. *Aufstieg und Niedergang der römischen Welt* II.9.2:604–1378.

Rathbone, D. 1991. *Economic rationalism and rural society in third-century A.D. Egypt: The Heroninos archive and the Appianus estate.* Cambridge: Cambridge University Press.

Rawson, E. 1985. *Intellectual life in the late Roman Republic.* Baltimore: Johns Hopkins University Press.

Rebuffat, R. 1967. Les erreurs de Pline et la position de Baba Iulia Campestris. *Antiquités africaines* 1:31–57.

———. 1986. Le bouclier de Doura. *Syria* 63:85–103.

Reed, N. 1978. Pattern and purpose in the Antonine itinerary. *American Journal of Philology* 99:228–254.

Rich, J. 1993. Fear, greed, and glory: The causes of Roman war-making in the middle Republic. In *War and society in the Roman world,* ed. J. Rich and G. Shipley, 38–68. London: Routledge.

Richardson, J. S. 1979. Polybius' view of the Roman empire. *Papers of the British School at Rome* 47:1–11.

Richardson, L. 1992. *A new topographical dictionary of ancient Rome.* Baltimore: Johns Hopkins University Press.

Richmond, I. 1982. *Trajan's army on Trajan's column.* London: British School at Rome.

Ritterling, E. 1924–1925. Legio. *Real-Encyclopädie der klassischen Altertumswissenschaft,* ed. A. Pauly, G. Wissowa, and W. Kroll, 12 (Hb. 23–24): 1211–1829.

Rives, J. 1995. Human sacrifice among pagans and Christians. *Journal of Roman Studies* 85:65–85.

Rivet, A. L. F. 1977. Ptolemy's geography and the Flavian invasion of Scotland. In *Studien zu den Militärgrenzen Roms II,* ed. D. Haupt and H. G. Horn, 45–64. Cologne: Rheinland-Verlag.

Rivet, A. L. F., and C. Smith. 1979. *The place-names of Roman Britain.* Princeton: Princeton University Press; London: B. T. Batsford.

Romer, F. E. 1979. Gaius Caesar's military diplomacy in the East. *Transactions of the American Philological Association* 109:199–214.

Romm, J. S. 1992. *The edges of the earth in ancient thought: Geography, exploration, and fiction.* Princeton: Princeton University Press.

Rosenberger, V. 1992. *Bella et expeditiones: Die antike Terminologie der Kriege Roms.* Stuttgart: F. Steiner.

Rosenstein, N. S. 1990. *Imperatores victi: Military defeat and aristocratic competition in the middle and late Republic.* Berkeley: University of California Press.

Rossi, L. 1971. *Trajan's column and the Dacian wars.* London: Thames & Hudson; Ithaca, N.Y.: Cornell University Press.

Rostovtzeff, M. 1957. *A social and economic history of the Roman empire.* 2d ed. 2 vols. Oxford: Clarendon Press.

Roth, J. 1990. The logistics of the Roman army in the Jewish war. Ph.D. diss., Columbia University.

Russell, D. A., and N. G. Wilson. 1981. *Menander Rhetor.* Oxford: Clarendon Press.

Saddington, D. B. 1982. *The development of the Roman auxiliary forces from Caesar to Vespasian (49 B.C.–A.D. 79)*. Harare: University of Zimbabwe.

Saller, R. P. 1982. *Personal patronage under the early empire*. Cambridge: Cambridge University Press.

Sallmann, K. 1971. *Die Geographie des älteren Plinius in ihrem Verhältnis zu Varro*. Berlin: Walter de Gruyter.

———. 1987. Reserved for eternal punishment: The elder Pliny's view of Free Germania (*HN* 16.1–6). *American Journal of Philology* 108:108–128.

Schoff, W. H. 1914. *Parthian stations*, by Isidore of Charax. Philadelphia: Commerical Museum. Reprint, Chicago: Ares, 1976.

Schönberger, H. 1969. The Roman frontier in Germany: An archaeological survey. *Journal of Roman Studies* 59:144–197.

Schürer, E. 1973–1987. *The history of the Jewish people in the age of Jesus Christ*. Rev. and ed. G. Vermes and F. Millar. 4 vols. Edinburgh: Clark.

Settis, S., et al. 1988. *La colonna Traiana*. Turin: G. Einaudi.

Shaw, B. 1982. Fear and loathing: The nomad menace and Roman Africa. In *L'Afrique romaine*, ed. C. M. Wells, 29–50. Ottawa: Éditions de l'Université d'Ottawa.

———. 1982a. "Eaters of flesh, drinkers of milk": The ancient Mediterranean ideology of the pastoral nomad. *Ancient Society* 13:5–31.

———. 1986. Autonomy and tribute: Mountain and plain in Mauretania Tingitana. *Revue de l'occident musulman et de la méditerranée* 41–42:66–89.

Sherk, R. 1971. Specialization in the provinces of Germany. *Historia* 20:110–121.

———. 1974. Roman geographical information and military maps. *Aufstieg und Niedergang der römischen Welt* II.1:534–561.

Sherwin-White, A. N. 1967. *Racial prejudice in imperial Rome*. Cambridge: Cambridge University Press.

———. 1968. *The letters of Pliny: A historical and social commentary*. Oxford: Clarendon Press.

———. 1980. Rome the agressor? Review of *War and imperialism in Republican Rome, 320–70 B.C.*, by W. V. Harris. *Journal of Roman Studies* 70:177–181.

———. 1984. *Roman foreign policy in the East, 168 B.C. to A.D. 1*. Norman: University of Oklahoma Press; London: Duckworth.

Sidebotham, S. E. 1986. *Roman economic policy in the Erythra Thalassa, 30 B.C.–A.D. 217*. Leiden: E. J. Brill.

Silberman, A. 1988. *Chorographie*, by Pomponius Mela. Paris: Les Belles Lettres.

———. 1995. *Périple du Pont-Euxin,* by Arrian. Paris: Les Belles Lettres.

Smallwood, E. M. 1976. *The Jews under Roman rule: From Pompey to Diocletian*. Leiden: E. J. Brill.

Smith, R. E. 1972. The army reforms of Septimius Severus. *Historia* 21:481–500.

Speidel, M. A. 1992. Roman army pay scales. *Journal of Roman Studies* 82:87–106.

Speidel, M. P. 1975. The rise of ethnic units in the Roman imperial army. *Aufstieg und Niedergang der römischen Welt* II.3:202–231.

Sperber, D. 1974. *Roman Palestine, 200–400: Money and prices*. Ramat Gan, Israel: Bar-Ilan University Press.

Stadter, P. A. 1980. *Arrian of Nicomedia*. Chapel Hill: University of North Carolina Press.

Stahl, W. H. 1952. *Commentary on the Dream of Scipio,* by Macrobius. New York: Columbia University Press.

Ste. Croix, G. E. M. de. 1956. Greek and Roman accounting. In *Studies in the history of accounting,* ed. A. C. Littleton and B. S. Yamey, 14–74. London: Sweet & Maxwell.

Storch, R. H. 1968. The "absolutist" theology of victory: Its place in the late empire. *Classica et medievalia* 29:197–206.

Strack, P. 1931. *Untersuchungen zur römischen Reichsprägung des zweiten Jahrhunderts.* Vol. 1, *Die Reichsprägung zur Zeit des Trajan.* Stuttgart: W. Kohlhammer.

Strobel, K. 1984. *Untersuchungen zu den Dakerkriegen Trajans.* Bonn: Habelt.

———. 1987. Nochmals zur Datierung der Schlacht am *Mons Graupius. Historia* 36:198–212.

———. 1987a. Der Chattenkrieg Domitians: Historische und politische Aspekte. *Germania* 65:423–452.

———. 1989. *Die Donaukriege Domitians.* Bonn: Habelt.

Sullivan, J. P. 1985. *Literature and politics in the age of Nero.* Ithaca, N.Y.: Cornell University Press.

———. 1991. *Martial: The unexpected classic.* Cambridge: Cambridge University Press.

Sutherland, C. H. V. 1959. The intelligibility of Roman imperial coin types. *Journal of Roman Studies* 49:46–55.

———. 1983. The purpose of Roman imperial coin types. *Revue numismatique* 6.25:73–82.

Swain, S. 1996. *Hellenism and empire: Language, classicism, and power in the Greek world,* A.D. 50–250. Oxford: Clarendon Press.

Syme, R. 1933. Some notes on the legions under Augustus. *Journal of Roman Studies* 23:14–33.

———. 1939. *The Roman revolution.* Oxford: Clarendon Press.

———. 1958. *Tacitus.* 2 vols. Oxford: Clarendon Press.

———. 1958a. Imperator Caesar: A study in nomenclature. *Historia* 7:172–188. Later published in *Roman papers,* vol. 1 (Oxford: Clarendon Press, 1979), 361–377.

———. 1970. The conquest of north-west Spain. In *Legio VII Gemina,* 79–108. Leon: Diputación Provincial.

———. 1978. *History in Ovid.* Oxford: Clarendon Press.

Szidat, J. 1970. *Caesars diplomatische Tätigkeit im gallischen Krieg.* Wiesbaden: F. Steiner.

Szilágyi, J. 1954. Les variations des centres de prépondérance militaire dans les provinces frontières de l'empire romain. *Acta antiqua Academiae Scientiarum Hungaricae* 2:117–219.

Talbert, R. J. A. 1984. *The senate of imperial Rome.* Princeton: Princeton University Press.

———. 1987. Review of *Greek and Roman maps,* by O. Dilke. *Journal of Roman Studies* 77:210–212.

———. 1988. Commodus as diplomat in an extract from the *Acta senatus.* *Zeitschrift für Papyrologie und Epigraphik* 71:137–147.

———. 1991. Rome's empire and beyond: The spatial aspect. In *Gouvernants et gouvernés dans l'imperium romanum,* ed. E. Hermon, 215–223. Quebec: Université du Québec à Trois-Rivières.

———. 1992. Mapping the classical world: Major atlases and map series, 1872–1990. *Journal of Roman Archaeology* 5:5–38.

Tarn, W. W. 1984. *The Greeks in Bactria and India.* 3d ed. Chicago: Ares.

Telschow, K. 1989. Der princeps proferendi imperii incuriosus (Tac. *Ann.* 4.32): Ein Topos in den ersten beiden Jahrhunderten der römischen Kaiserzeit. In *Migratio et commutatio: Studien zur alten Geschichte und deren Nachleben,* ed. H. J. Drexhage and J. Sunskes, 299–317. St. Katharinen, Germany: Scripta Mercaturae Verlag.

Thollard, P. 1987. *Barbarie et civilisation chez Strabon: Étude critique des livres III et IV de la Géographie.* Paris: Les Belles Lettres.

Thomas, J. D., and R. W. Davies. 1977. A new military strength report on papyrus. *Journal of Roman Studies* 67:50–61.

Thomas, Y. 1984. Se venger au Forum: Solidarité familiale et procès criminel à Rome. In *La vengeance: Étude d'ethnologie, d'histoire, et de philosophie,* ed. R. Verdier and J. P. Poly, vol. 3, *La vengeance: Vengeance, pouvoirs, et idéologies dans quelques civilisations de l'antiquité,* 65–100. Paris: Cujas.

Thomson, J. O. 1948. *History of ancient geography.* Cambridge: Cambridge University Press.

Tierney, J. J. 1963. The map of Agrippa. *Proceedings of the Royal Irish Academy* 63:151–163.

Timpe, D. 1962. Die Bedeutung der Schlacht von Carrhae. *Museum Helveticum* 19:104–129.

Todd, M. 1987. *The northern barbarians, 100 B.C.–A.D. 300.* 2d ed. Oxford: B. Blackwell.

Toynbee, A. J. 1965. *Hannibal's legacy.* 2 vols. London: Oxford University Press.

van Berchem, D. 1937. L'annone militaire dans l'empire romain au IIIe siècle. *Mémoires de la Société Nationale des Antiquaires de France* 24 (= 8th ser., 10): 117–202.

———. 1973. L'itinéraire antonin et le voyage en Orient de Caracalla (214–215). *Comptes rendus de l'Académie des Inscriptions et Belles-Lettres,* 123–126.

———. 1977. L'annone militaire est-elle un mythe? In *Armées et fiscalité dans le monde antique.* Paris: Éditions du Centre Nationale de la Recherche Scientifique.

van der Vliet, E. C. L. 1984. L'ethnographie de Strabon: Ideologie ou tradition? In *Strabone: Contributi allo studio della personalità e dell'opera,* ed. F. Prontera, 1:27–86. Perugia: Università degli Studi.

van Wees, H. 1992. *Status warriors: War, violence, and society in Homer and history.* Amsterdam: J. C. Gieben.

Versnel, H. S. 1970. *Triumphus: An inquiry into the origin, development, and meaning of the Roman triumph.* Leiden: E. J. Brill.

Veyne, P. 1976. *Le pain et le cirque: Sociologie historique d'un pluralisme politique.* Paris: Seuil.

———. 1979. Rome devant la prétendue fuite de l'or: Mercantilisme ou politique disciplinaire? *Annales (Économie, sociétés, civilisations)* 34:211–244.

Vogt, J. 1929. *Orbis romanus: Zur Terminologie des römischen Imperialismus.* Tübingen: J. C. B. Mohr.

Walbank, F. W. 1957–1979. *A historical commentary on Polybius.* 3 vols. Oxford: Clarendon Press.

———. 1994. Supernatural paraphernalia in Polybius. In *Ventures into Greek history,* ed. I. Worthington, 28–42. Oxford: Clarendon Press.

Walker, D. R. 1976–1978. *The metrology of the Roman silver coinage.* 3 vols. Oxford: British Archaeological Reports.

Wallace-Hadrill, A. 1981. The emperor and his virtues. *Historia* 30:298–323.

Walser, G. 1951. *Rom, das Reich, und die fremden Völker in der Geschichtsschreibung der frühen Kaiserzeit.* Baden-Baden: Verlag für Kunst und Wissenschaft.

———. 1956. *Caesar und die Germanen: Studien zur politischen Tendenz römischer Feldzugsberichte.* Wiesbaden: F. Steiner.

———. 1995. Zu Caesars Tendenz in der geographischen Beschreibung Galliens. *Klio* 77:217–223.

Watson, A. 1993. *International law in archaic Rome: War and religion.* Baltimore: Johns Hopkins University Press.

Watson, G. R. 1956. The pay of the Roman army: Suetonius, Dio, and the *quartum stipendium. Historia* 5:332–340.

———. 1969. *The Roman soldier.* Ithaca, N.Y.: Cornell University Press; London: Thames & Hudson.

Weber, E. 1976. *Tabula Peutingeriana: Codex Vindobensis 324. Vollständige Faksimile-Ausgabe im Originalformat.* Graz: Akadem. Druck- und Verlagsanstalt.

Webster, G. 1985. *The Roman imperial army of the first and second centuries A.D.* 3d ed. Totowa, N.J.: Barnes & Noble.

Weinstock, S. 1960. Pax and the "Ara Pacis." *Journal of Roman Studies* 50: 44–52.

Weissbach, 1916. Isidoros (20). *Real-Encyclopädie der klassischen Altertumswissenschaft,* ed. A. Pauly, G. Wissowa, and W. Kroll, 9:2064–2068.

Wells, C. M. 1972. *The German policy of Augustus: An examination of the archaeological evidence.* Oxford: Clarendon Press.

———. 1991. The problems of desert frontiers: Chairman's comments on the session. In *Roman frontier studies, 1989,* ed. V. A. Maxfield and M. J. Dobson, 498–504. Exeter, England: University of Exeter Press.

Wheeler, E. L. 1991. Rethinking the upper Euphrates frontier. In *Roman frontier studies, 1989,* ed. V. A. Maxfield and M. J. Dobson, 505–511. Exeter, England: University of Exeter Press.

———. 1993. Methodological limits and the mirage of Roman strategy. 2 parts. *Journal of Military History* 57:7–41, 215–240.

———. 1996. The laxity of the Syrian legions. In *The Roman army in the East,* ed. D. L. Kennedy, 229–276. Ann Arbor, Mich.: Journal of Roman Archaeology.

Whittaker, C. R. 1985. Trade and the aristocracy in the Roman empire. *Opus* (Rome) 4:49–76.

———. 1994. *Frontiers of the Roman empire: A social and economic study.* Baltimore: Johns Hopkins University Press.

———. 1996. Where are the frontiers now? In *The Roman army in the East,* ed. D. L. Kennedy, 25–41. Ann Arbor, Mich.: Journal of Roman Archaeology.

———, ed. and trans. 1969–1970. *Herodian.* 2 vols. Cambridge: Harvard University Press.

Wilkes, J. J. 1969. *Dalmatia.* London: Routledge & K. Paul.

———. 1983. Romans, Dacians, and Sarmatians in the first and early second centuries. In *Rome and her northern provinces,* ed. B. Hartley and J. Wacher, 255–289. Gloucester, England: A. Sutton.

Will, E. 1955. *Le relief cultuel gréco-romain: Contribution à l'histoire de l'art de l'empire romain.* Paris: de Boccard.

Williams, G. W. 1978. *Change and decline: Roman literature in the early empire.* Berkeley: University of California Press.

Wissemann, M. 1982. *Die Parther in der augusteischen Dichtung.* Frankfurt am Main: P. Lang.

Wolski, J. 1966. Les Achémenides et les Arsacides: Contribution à l'histoire de la formation des traditions iraniennes. *Syria* 43:65–89.

———. 1983. Les relations de Justin et de Plutarque sur les esclaves et la population dépendante dans l'empire parthe. *Iranica Antiqua* 18:145–157.

———. 1993. *L'empire des Arsacides.* Louvain: Peeters.

Wolters, R. 1990. *Römische Eroberung und Herrschaftsorganisation in Gallien und Germanien.* Bochum, Germany: N. Brockmeyer.

———. 1990–1991. Zum Waren- und Dienstleistungsaustauch zwischen dem römischen Reich und dem Freien Germanien in der Zeit des Principats: Eine Bestandaufnahme. 2 parts. *Münstersche Beiträge zur antiken Handelsgeschichte* 9.1:14–44; 10.1:78–131.

Woodward, D. 1987. Medieval *mappaemundi.* In *The history of cartography,* ed. J. B. Harley and D. Woodward, vol. 1, *Cartography in prehistoric, ancient, and medieval Europe and the Mediterranean,* 286–370. Chicago: University of Chicago Press.

Woolf, G. 1993. Roman peace. In *War and society in the Roman world,* ed. J. Rich and G. Shipley, 171–194. London: Routledge.

Zanker, P. 1988. *The power of images in the age of Augustus.* Trans. A. Shapiro. Ann Arbor: University of Michigan Press. Originally published as *Augustus und die Macht der Bilder* (Munich: C. H. Beck, 1987).

Zehnacker, H. 1983. *Histoire naturelle, livre XXXIII,* by Pliny the Younger. Paris: Les Belles Lettres.

Ziegler, K. H. 1964. *Die Beziehungen zwischen Rom und dem Partherreich.* Wiesbaden: F. Steiner.

Ziegler, R. 1996. Civic coins and imperial campaigns. In *The Roman army in the East,* ed. D. L. Kennedy, 119–134. Ann Arbor, Mich.: Journal of Roman Archaeology.

Ziolkowski, A. 1993. *Urbs direpta,* or how the Romans sacked cities. In *War and society in the Roman world,* ed. J. Rich and G. Shipley, 19–91. London: Routledge.

Index

Page numbers in *italic* type refer to illustrations.

a rationibus (office), 128–29

ab epistulis (office), 6

accounts: agricultural, 123–24; imperial, 126, 128–29

Acta triumphorum, 30

Actium, battle of, 5, 84

Adamklissi, 190, *195*

Adiabeni, revolt of, 118

advisers, of emperor. *See* council; friends

Aelius Aristides, P. (d. after A.D. 181): on the defense of the empire, 111; on the *oikoumene,* 46; on the Roman army, 207

Aelius Catus, Sex., 10

Aelius Gallus, M. (prefect of Egypt), 30–31, 38, 78, 164

Aelius Sejanus, L. *See* Sejanus

Aemilius Paullus, L. (d. 160 B.C.), 152, 165–66

Afranius Burrus, Sex. *See* Burrus

Africa: exploration of, 27, 30, 31–32, 55–56, 64–65, 212; frontier in, 111; geography of, 30, 31–32, 39, 44, 51, 55–56; trade routes to, 36

ager Gallicus, 220

Agisymba (location in Africa), 31

Agricola, Cn. Iulius (d. A.D. 93): campaigns of in Scotland, 92, 115; career of, 19; dispatches of to senate, 32; explo-ration of Britain, 29, 39; invasion of Mona, 120; planned invasion of Ireland, 53, 104, 112; suppression of Ordovices, 120, 193

agriculture, 123–26; treatises on, 123, 125

Agrippa, M. Vipsanius (d. 12 B.C.): geo-graphical work of, 49–51, *50;* on the ge-ography of Africa, 30, 55; on the geog-raphy of Asia, 55; on the geography of Germany, 51; on the geography of India, 57; on the geography of Parthia, 59; on the geography of Spain, 39; suppression of Cantabrian revolt, 100n, 192–93

Agrippina the Younger, 7

Alani, 2, 11, 112

Albania (in Caucasus), 118

Albis (river). *See* Elbe River

Alexander the Great (of Macedon, d. 323 B.C.), 35, 56, 68, 175

Alexander the Pseudoprophet, 14

Alme River, 167

Amazons, 54

amber, 35

ambitio. See glory

amici. See friends

Ammianus Marcellinus (historian), 3; on the Forum of Trajan, 149–50

Ampsivarii, 181

Amyntas (author of *Stations of Asia*), 35

Anglesey (island). *See* Mona

Ankara, 164

Annaeus Lucanus, M. *See* Lucan

Annaeus Seneca, L. *See* Seneca; Seneca the Elder

annexation, in Roman policy, 120, 214

annona militaris, 134, 144. *See also* army, supply of

Antiochus III (king of Syria, d. 187 B.C.), 152, 214

Antiochus IV (king of Commagene, A.D. 41–72), 67

Antiochus IV (king of Syria, 175–164 B.C.), 231

Antonine itinerary, 28, 39, 146

Antonine wall, 113

antoninianus (coin), 137

Antoninus Pius (emperor), 12–13, 115

Antony (M. Antonius.), 38, 107, 176

Apollodorus (architect, reign of Trajan), 149

Apollodorus of Artemita (historian), 58

Appian (historian, second century A.D.): on Augustus' Illyrian commentaries, 33; on the defense of the empire, 111; on the geography of Britain, 52; on the geography of Spain, 39; on the Roman army and finances, 104, 129; on Roman diplomacy, 117

Apronius, L., 11

Arabia: annexed, 157; campaign of Aelius Gallus in, 30–31, 38, 78, 153, 164; ethnography of, 30–31, 74; frontier in, 114; geography and exploration of, 27, 30–31, 36, 38; nomad threat in, 113; reputation for wealth of, 78–79. See also *via nova Traiana*

Aratus (poet), 3, 15

archaeology: and ethnography, 76, 77; of frontiers, 20–21, 109

arches, triumphal, 165, 168, 170, 187

Ardashir (king of Persia, d. A.D. 241), 7, 13, 173

Ariovistus (king of Suebi, mid–first century B.C.), 175, 182, 185, 216

aristocracy, 1–22; confiscation of property from by emperor, 134; education of, 14–6; as landlords, 123–25; literary production of, 2–3, 15–16, 18

Armenia, Armenians: agreement with Vespasian, 96; annexed by Trajan, 94, 104; imposition of king on by Artabanus II, 68, 175; Corbulo's campaigns in, 29, 95,

179; crisis of A.D. 54 in, 6–7, 12, 112; defeat of Severianus in, 189; geography and exploration of, 27, 34, 40; and restoration of hostages to Macrinus, 181; Mithridates deposed in, 68–69; raided by Alani, 11; relations under Marcus Aurelius, 120; restored by Hadrian, 94; Roman policy in, 121, 176–77

Arminius (chief of Cherusci), 67, 78, 90, 167, 175, 204.

army: as army of occupation, 101–4, 214; barbarian units in, 87; in Britain, 102–3; command of, 8, 14, 15, 17–18; composition of, 85; cost of, 126–32, 138; 131; and defense of empire, 109–22; desertion in, 87–88; distribution of, 101–2, 104; on frontier, 112; function of, 21; and geographical exploration, 25, 26–35, 37–41; and intelligence gathering, 68; as labor force, 144, 145; length of service in, 84–85, 126, 128; loyalty of, 19, 84, 139–41, 197; mutiny of in A.D. 14, 127–28; pay of, 127–28, 130–32, 138, 139–41, 143; praetorian guard in, 85, 141n; records, 105; recruitment, 82, 84–88, 105; in revolt of Illyricum, 88–89; size of, 5, 82–84; in Spain, 100; speed of travel of, 99; supply of, 29, 134, 143–48; as tax collectors, 157; in wars of conquest, 91–95. *See also* auxiliaries; discipline; legates, imperial; legions; war

Arretium, 220

Arrian: career of, 2; on the circumnavigation of Arabia, 36; history of Parthia, 27, 58; military exploits, 11; *Periplus of the Euxine,* 38; as threat to Sanni, 120, 135–36; treatise of on India, 26, 57, 65; works of, 2, 18

arrogance. See *superbia*

Artabanus II (Parthian king, A.D. 10/11–38): as despiser of Tiberius, 175; imposition of king on Armenia, 68, 175; and negotiations with Vitellius, 174–75; as raised by Scythians, 71; as seeker of Gaius' friendship, 173; as threat to invade Syria, 68, 119, 175; worship standards of, 175

Artaxata, 40

Asia, geography and exploration of, 34–36, 40, 56

Assyria, province under Trajan, 104

astronomy, 15, 30

auction: "auction of empire," 141; of
    imperial property, 136, 141, 143
Augustus (emperor): Alpine trophy of,
    165; and appointment of budget-cutting
    committee, 133–34; and army at Actium,
    84; and army at Philippi, 84; and bound-
    aries of empire, 111; campaign against
    Getae, 30; clemency of, 191; and Cleo-
    patra's suicide, 168; conquest of Britain,
    plans for, 100; conquest of Spain, 100;
    council of, 8; and creation of inheritance
    tax, 126; and Danube frontier, 118; and
    discharge of civil wars veterans, 83–84,
    126; as donative giver, 140; and Egyptian
    spoils, 151; embassies to, 6n, 10, 57, 117,
    172; and expansionism, 60, 89–90; and
    Gaius Caesar's eastern expedition, 8, 34,
    60, 107, 188; on Gemma Augustea, 196;
    as giver of king to Parthians, 176; Illyrian
    commentaries of, 33; and pacification of
    Alps, boasts of, 184; and Parthian hos-
    tages, 172, 179; and poets' anticipation
    of Parthian war, 186–87; Prima Porta
    statue of, 187; *princeps*, 5; reasons for
    war in Illyricum, 205; recovery of stan-
    dards from Parthia, 60, 107, 174, 187;
    relations with Parthia, 107, 108; *Res Ges-
    tae*, 163–64; 111; as Temple of Mars
    builder, 152; testament of, 90–91, 128
Aurelian (emperor), negotiations with
    Iuthungi, 182–83
Aurelius, Marcus (emperor): auction of
    possessions of, 143; Capitoline statue of,
    195; conscription of gladiators, 87; coun-
    cil of, 19; and Danube wars, 93, 97–98,
    109, 116; education of, 15–16; imperial
    finances under, 136; and negotiations
    with Danube tribes, 13, 180; and pay-
    ment of subsidies to Danube tribes, 121;
    and peace with Iazyges, 87; plans to ex-
    terminate Iazyges, 98, 116, 121; plans of
    new provinces, 61, 93, 103, 116; preven-
    tion of migration of Quadi, 120, 191;
    refusal to pay donative, 141; regulation
    of trade across Danube, 113; works of, 3
auxiliaries: location of, 105; number of,
    82–83; pay of, 127, 130; recruitment, 86;
    special units, 87
Avidius Cassius, C. *See* Cassius, C. Avidius

Balbus (land surveyor), 28
Baltic sea, geography and exploration of,
    29, 35

barbarians: atrocities of, 78; clothing of,
    71, 72, 73, 194; cowardliness of, 74;
    drunkeness of, 71, 74, 75, 205; plunder-
    ing of, 74; food, 72–75, 77; in iconogra-
    phy, 187, 194–96; and lack of military
    discipline, 74, 203–5; and money, 75, 76;
    nomadic, 72–75; origin of term, 70, 73;
    polygamous, 71; religion of, 73, 74, 75;
    untrustworthiness of, 71, 74; warlike
    nature of, 72–75. *See also* ethnography
Bar-Kochba revolt, 102, 193–94
Bastarnae, 120, 162, 172
Batavians: revolt of Civilis, 86, 97; special
    units of, 87
Bedriacum, battle of, 87
bematists, 35
birth, as qualification for office, 16, 17n,
    19–20
Black Sea. *See* Euxine Sea
booty. *See* plunder
Borysthenes River (Dniepr), 10
Bosporus, kingdom, 118
Boudicca (queen of Iceni): cruelty of, 78;
    defeat of, 193, 205; reasons for revolt of,
    86, 135, 156; revolt of, 102–3, 105–6
bought peace. *See* subsidies
boundaries, of empire, 4, 40, 110, 118. *See
    also* frontiers
Britain: Agricola's campaigns, 92–93, 115;
    Antoninus Pius' war in, 115; army in,
    102–3; Augustus' plans to conquer, 60;
    circumnavigation of, 29, 86, 93; con-
    quest of, 40–41, 91–92; ethnography
    of, 72; as financially unprofitable, 160–
    61; Forth-Clyde isthmus of, 115; geogra-
    phy and exploration of, 27, 29–30, 36,
    39, 40, 52–53; Hadrian's wall in, 114, 115;
    imperial policies of governors in, 11;
    mineral resources of, 155; mystique of,
    40–41, 115; Nero's contemplattion of
    withdrawal from, 178; reasons for Clau-
    dius' war in, 9, 191, 199; reasons for
    Severus' war in, 206; revolt of Boudicca
    in, 86, 102–3, 105–6; revolt of Ordo-
    vices in, 120, 193; Severus' war in, 94,
    106, 116–17, 121, 193; subsidies paid to
    Scottish tribes, 98, 121; size of, 52; troops
    withdrawn from by Albinus, 98; troops
    withdrawn from Scotland, 93, 97, 98,
    103, 117; walls in, 110, 111, 113
budget, imperial, 123–42. *See also* rev-
    enues; accounts
Burrus, Sex. Afranius (d. A.D. 62), 7

Caesar, C. Iulius: on the arrogance of
Ariovistus, 175; and collection of intelligence from Gauls, 67; conquest of Dacia, plans for, 90; diplomacy of in Gaul,
182, 218; ethnography of Gaul, 74; ethnography of Germany, 75, 76; on the
geography of Britain, 30, 36, 52; on the
geography of Gaul, 51; reasons for war
with Germans, 216; Rhine, crossing of,
119, 216; suppression of Veneti, 219; and
war with Ariovistus, 185; and war with
Helvetii, 185, 188; and war with Pompey,
185; works of, 3; world conquest, plans
for, 59–60, 90
Caesennius Paetus, L. (legate of Syria),
10, 12, 67, 95, 177–78, 206
Caledonii, 121
Calgacus, 207–8
Caligula (emperor). See Gaius
Candace (queen of Ethiopia), 37
Cannae, battle of, 221
Cantabri, 100, 192
Cappadocia: annexation of, 91, 118, 157;
combined with Galatia, 112; invasion of
Alani, 11; revolt of, 157
Capua, 221
Caracalla (emperor): army, expenditures
on, 139; antoninianus, introduction of,
137; eastern conquests, boasts of, 33;
and military pay increase, 130–31; and
new taxes, 133; Parthia, informing senate
about, 67; peace with Cenni, purchase
of, 180; peace with Germans, purchase
of, 121; proposal of marriage to Parthian
princess, 156; war in Germany, 94; and
war in Parthia, 28, 94, 108; withdrawal
from Scotland, 94, 117
Caratacus, 102, 160, 168
careers. See office
Carpathian Mountains, 61
Carrhae, battle of, 66, 107, 153. See also
Crassus
Carthage: deditio, Roman demand for,
218; first Punic war, 221; indemnities,
payment of, 152, 214; second Punic war,
214, 215, 221–22; third Punic war, 218
cartography. See maps
Caspian Sea, 51, 54–55, 58
Cassius Dio (historian): on the "auction
of the empire", 141; on Augustus' retrieval of standards, 174; on the Bar-
Kochba revolt, 193–94; on Boudicca's

revolt, 106, 135, 156; on Caracalla's just
and unjust wars, 184; career and works
of, 2; on the causes of Trajan's first Dacian war, 190; on the causes of Trajan's
second Dacian war, 191; on the causes of
Verus' Parthian war, 188; on Claudius'
British expedition, 41; on Commodus'
departure for the Danube frontier, 13;
on the cost of the army under Caracalla,
131; on Crassus in Thrace, 120; on Domitian's German wars, 92; on Domitian's pay raise, 139; on the geography
of Britain, 52; on Hadrian's imperial
strategy, 159; on the imperial budget,
129; on Marcus Aurelius' aims in the
Danube region, 93; on Marcus Aurelius'
diplomacy, 180; on Marcus Aurelius'
education, 15–16; on military discipline
and desertion, 87–88, 207; on Nero and
Tiridates, 178; on the Pannonians, 77–
78; on the reasons for Severus' British
war, 205; on Severus' war in Britain, 106;
on taxes, 134; on Tiberius' truce with
Maroboduus, 192; on Trajan's Danube
bridge, 149; on tribes of Scotland, 72;
on Vitellius' negotiations with Artabanus, 174–75
Cassius Longinus, L. (cos. 107 B.C.), 188
Cassius, C. Avidius, 98, 101, 201
casualty statistics, 105–6
Caucasus Mountains: geography and exploration of, 29, 37, 39, 54–55, 59; Nero's
plans of campaign to, 92, 95, 153; possible Roman presence in, 112, 118
Caudine Forks, battle of, 219–20
causes of war, 208; desire for glory, 186,
198; discipline of army, 205–6; great
military defeat, 186–89, 219; greed, 153–
54, 186; iniuria, 185; "just war," 184–85,
219; raids, 186, 217. See also fetial law
Celts, 74
Cenni, 180
census, 105, 157
Charax (city on Persian Gulf), 34
Chatti, Domitian's war with, 92, 109, 188
Chauci, 12, 77, 110
Cherusci, 90, 179–80, 192. See also Arminius; Quintilius Varus
China, 36, 56
Cicero, M. Tullius, 68; on the causes of
war, 216; on the just war, 219
Cicero, Q. Tullius, 3

Cimbric peninsula, 29, 54
circumnavigation: of Britain, 29, 86, 93; of *oikoumene,* 51
Cispa, 218
civil wars: of late Republic, 84; of A.D. 69, 87, 95–97; of 193/7, 98; versus foreign, 170
Civilis, C. Iulius, 86, 97
Claudius (emperor): arch of in Rome, 165; and army for British conquest, 91–92; collection of gold crown tax, 134; conquest of Britain, 9, 41–42, 91–92, 169, 191, 199; order of Corbulo's withdrawal from Free Germany, 12, 110; pardon of Caratacus, 168; payment of donative, 140; payment of subsidies to Cherusci, 179–80; relations with Parthia, 107, 108; and Suebi, 9; trivialization of *triumphalia,* 200; works of, 3
Claudius Drusus, Nero. *See* Drusus, Nero Claudius
Claudius Ptolemaeus. *See* Ptolemy
clementia, 182
Cleopatra (VII, of Egypt), 84, 168
climatology, 44, 47, 73
clothing, of barbarians, 71, 72, 73, 194
coinage, 136; barbarians on reverse of, 195; devaluation of, 137–39, 141, 142, 147–48; drain to east, 136; emperor's face on, 138, 139; imperial titulature on, 197; imperialist slogans on reverse of, 196; theories about, 138–39; *Victoria* on reverse of, 168
Collatia, 217
Cologne, 113
Columella, L. Iunius Moderatus, on the profitability of viticulture, 125
Column of Trajan, 28, 78, 150, 151, 204–5
comites. See companions
Commagene, 10, 91, 118
commentaries, military, as geographical sources, 27, 32–33
Commodus (emperor): advisers to, 1–2, 3–4, 8; and fortification of Danube, 113; and new taxes, 133; payment of subsidies to Danube tribes, 180; and peace with Marcomanni and Quadi, 87; withdrawal of from Danube war, 1–2, 3–4, 13, 93, 119, 178
companions, of emperor, 6
consilium. See council
consulship (office), 8, 14, 16

continents, in Greco-Roman geography, 44, 47, 51. *See also* Europe; Africa; Asia.
Corbulo, Cn. Domitius: in Armenia, 10, 12, 29, 67, 95; demand of hostages from Vologeses, 177, 179; discipline of, 206; and geography of Armenia, 28, 29, 30; in Germany, 12, 110; and peace with Parthians, 177–78; and reinforcements on Euphrates, 112; and road repair in eastern provinces, 145
Corinth, 219
Cornelius Balbus, L.: exploration of Africa, 56; triumph of, 9–10, 30, 166
Cornelius Fronto, M. *See* Fronto
Cornelius Fuscus, 92, 190
Cornelius Gallus, C. (prefect of Egypt): career and works of, 3; death of, 9; military exploits of, 9, 109, 163, 200
Cornelius Scipio Aemilianus, P. *See* Scipio Aemilianus
Cornelius Scipio, L. *See* Scipio, Lucius
Cornelius Tacitus, P.(?). *See* Tacitus
council, advisory: of aristocrats in Republic, 8; of emperor, 2–8, 19; of governors, 12; social status of members of, 14
Crassus, M. Licinius (d. 53 B.C.): desire for glory of, 198n; greed of, 153; and Parthian war, 38, 66; retaliation for defeat of, 186–87
Cremona, battle of, 96
Crimaea. *See* Tauric Chersonese
Crispina (wife of Commodus), 13
Ctesiphon, 40, 98, 107, 108, 120

Dacia, Dacians: as annexed, 120; Augustus' plans for conquest of, 60; Caesar's plans for conquest of, 60, 90; as causes of wars with Domitian and Trajan, 189–90; dealings with Plautius Silvanus, 162; Domitian's wars in, 92, 116, 189–90; ethnography of, 30; geography and exploration of, 27–8, 40, 60–61, 110, 115; invasion of Moesia in A.D. 69, 96, 116; mines in, 155; and plunder from Trajan's wars, 150–51; Trajan's wars in, 27–28, 60, 67, 93, 103. *See also* Decebalus; Domitian; Trajan
Dalmatia, 101, 154
Danube frontier, 111; under Augustus, 118; under Domitian, 92; fortified by Commodus, 113; under Marcus Aurelius, 109, 121; regulation of trade across, 113;

Danube frontier (*continued*)
  reinforced by Rubrius Gallus, 97, 112;
  under Trajan, 114. *See also,* Aurelius,
  Marcus; Commodus; Dacia; Domitian;
  Moesia; Trajan
Danube River, 10; as boundary, 40, 110; as
  bridged by Trajan, 148–49, 209; exploration of, 29
Darius (Persian king, 522–486 B.C.), 209
Decebalus (king of Dacia), 9, 67, 120;
  Domitian payment of subsidies to, 121,
  159; and peace with Domitian, 92, 118,
  121, 173; and peace with Trajan, 87–88;
  treasure of, 150, 155
deditio, 217–18
defense: role of frontiers in, 109–15; role
  of terror in, 115–22
defensive imperialism, 214–15
deference, as goal in foreign policy, 22,
  171–83, 213
Denmark. *See* Cimbric Peninsula
desert frontiers, 113, 114
desertion, in army, 87–88
deterrence. *See* terror
devaluation, of coinage, 137–39, 141, 142,
  147–48
Dexippus (historian), on Aurelian's negotiations with the Iuthungi, 182–3
Didius Julianus (emperor), 141
Diegis, crowned by Domitian, 118, 179
Dionysius Periegetes (geographer), 25, 65;
  on the geography of Africa, 55; on the
  oikoumene, 46; reception of, 64
diplomacy, 13, 117–18, 121, 172–83; Severus
  Alexander's attempts at, 13, 98, 173. *See
  also* embassies, peace treaties
diplomata, 197
discipline, of army, 139–40, 202–7
dishonor. *See* honor
dispatches. *See* letters
doctors, 6
Domitian (emperor): advisers to, 8; criticism of in Pliny's *Panegyric,* 181, 183;
  and crowning of Diegis, 118, 179; Dacian
  triumph of, 152; in Dacian wars, 116,
  189–90; execution of man for possession of map, 42; extermination of Nasamones, 101, 120, 135, 192; military pay,
  increase of, 130, 131, 139; payment of
  subsidies to Cherusci, 180; payment of
  subsidies to Decebalus, 121, 159; and
  peace with Decebalus, 92, 118, 121, 173;

  and reasons for wars, 188; taxes of, 139;
  and war with Chatti, 92, 109, 188; and
  wars in Danube region, 92–93
Domitius Corbulo, Cn. *See* Corbulo
Don River. *See* Tanais
donatives, 131, 140–41, 148
draft. *See* army, recruitment
Druids, 74
drunkenness, of barbarians, 71, 74, 75, 205
Drusus, Iulius Caesar (d. A.D. 23), 8
Drusus, Nero Claudius (d. 9 B.C.), 167,
  188
Duncan-Jones, Richard, 137

Ecbatana, 40
economic factors in foreign relations, 123–
  61, 215; and expense of war, 142–49;
  imperial budget, 123–42; in Aelius
  Gallus' campaign, 78–79; indemnities,
  152, 214; mines, 154–56, 214; as payment
  for peace (*see* subsidies); plunder, 150–
  54, 214; slaves, 153; spoils of Egypt, 84–
  85, 126, 151; tax on luxury trade, 114,
  156–57; trade restrictions on Rhine/
  Danube, 113; tribute, 132–36, 157–58,
  214. *See also* coinage; inflation; revenues; taxes
education, of aristocracy, 14–16, 25
Egypt: army in, 101; geography of, 55;
  spoils of, 126, 151, 152
Elbe River, 60, 88, 167
Elegeia, 189
elite. *See* aristocracy
embassies, general, 6n, 8–9, 19, 69, 117–
  18; to Augustus, 57, 117, 172; to Augustus from Ethiopia, 10; to Aurelian from
  Iuthungi, 182–83; to Claudius from
  Taprobane, 58; from India, 57; to Marcus Aurelius, 180; to Nero from Parthia,
  69; from Parthia, 58; to Petronius from
  Ethiopia, 10; to Plautius Silvanius, 117;
  to Tiberius from Parthia, 67–68; symbolic value of, 172. *See also* diplomacy;
  peace treaties
emperors: and balanced budgets, 133–34;
  and control of military glory, 200–202;
  and enforcement of military discipline,
  206–7; faces of on coinage, 138–39; imperial accounts of, 126; list of, xvii–xviii;
  personal property, auction of, 136, 141,
  143; role of in foreign relations decisions, 1–14; titulature, 196–97; tram-

pling of barbarians on coins, 195. *See also individual entries*

Ems River, 143

equestrians, 14. *See also* aristocracy; office, equestrian.

Eratosthenes (geographer), 46, 47, 58

Ethiopia: geography and exploration of, 28, 31, 37, 44; Nero's plans of expedition to, 60, 95; Petronius' campaigns in, 10, 28, 164

ethnography, 21–22, 70–80; of Britain, 72; of Celts, 74; of Gauls, 74; as genre, 78; of Germans, 72; origins of, 73; of Parthia, 70–71, 107; of Persians, 73. *See also* barbarians

Euphrates frontier, 111, 112

Euphrates River: as boundary, 40, 110; geography and exploration of, 29, 34; meeting of Artabanus and Vitellius on, 110, 175; meeting of Gaius Caesar and Phraataces on, 110

Europe, geography and exploration of, 29, 35, 51–52, 54, 59

Euxine Sea (Black Sea), 38, 54, 77

experience, as qualification for office, 16–19

exploration, geographical, 26–41, 51, 53, 55–56

fama. See glory

fetial law, 216–17

Flaccus, Septimius. *See* Septimius Flaccus

Flamininus, T. Quinctius, 218

Flavius Arrianus, L. *See* Arrian

Flavius Josephus. *See* Josephus

fora, imperial, 149

Forth-Clyde isthmus, 115

fortune (*tyche*), 212

Forum of Peace, 152, 193

Forum of Trajan, 149–50, 195

fossatum Africae, 111, 113

Frank, Tenney, 214

freedmen, conscription on into army, 86, 89

friends (*amici, philoi*), of emperors, 2–8, 14, 20

Frisii, 11, 12, 118, 135, 192

frontiers, general, 20–21, 109–15; archaeology of, 20–21; defensive function of, 21, 109–15; desert, 113, 114; fuzzy, 118. *See also* boundaries; Danube frontier; Euphrates frontier; Rhine frontier

Frontinus, Sex. Iulius, 18

Fronto, M. Cornelius: on Antoninus Pius' British war, 12–13; on the discipline of the army, 206–7; as tutor of emperors, 2, 16; on Verus' letter to the senate, 32–33

frumentum emptum, 144

Fuscus, Cornelius. *See* Cornelius Fuscus

Gaius (emperor): German war of, 91; rapacity of, 134; and restoration of Commagene, 91; as squanderer of money, 136; successful diplomacy with Parthians, 173

Gaius Caesar (C. Iulius Caesar, grandson of Augustus): eastern campaigns of, 8, 34, 60, 107, 188; discovery of Spanish ships in Red Sea, 51; meeting with Phraataces, 107, 110

Galatia, 112

Galba (emperor), 140

Gallus, M. Aelius. *See* Aelius Gallus

Garamantes, 30, 31, 169

garrisons: in foreign territory, 69–70, 118; of provinces, 101–4

Gaul, Gauls: Caesar's wars in (*see* Caesar); ethnography of, 74; revolt of Civilis, 86, 97; revolt of Sacrovir, 101, 156; revolt of Vindex, 95, 154; and sack of Rome, 219; as suppliers of materials for Germanicus' war, 143–44

Gellius, Aulus, 15

Geminus (mathematical writer), on drawing maps, 46

Gemma Augustea, 195

genocide, 120–21, 189, 191–92, 220

geography, general, 24–66; cartographic vs. "odological," 39–40; in education, 25; errors in, 38; and historiography, 25–25, 65–66; and itineraries, 27–29; letters and commentaries as sources for, 32–33; and longitude and latitude, 30; merchants as sources for, 35–37; military and strategic use of, 26, 34, 43, 60–61, 115; place-names in *Res Gestae*, 165; place-names in triumphs, 30, 166; place-names on victory monuments, 165–66; and problem of Britain, 52–53. *See also* maps; oikoumene; *individual regions*

Germanicus, Nero Claudius Drusus (nephew of Tiberius): aims of for Elbe River, 167; as avenger of Varus' defeat,

Germanicus, Nero Claudius Drusus
(nephew of Tiberius) (*continued*)
189, 192; and bridgement of the Rhine,
167; epic poem about, 169; recapture of
standards of Varus, 187, 189; as respected
by Artabanus, 175; sailing of North Sea,
53, 143, 167; slaughter of noncombatants,
120; monument of in Germany, 165, 167;
and war in Germany, 67, 90, 143–44,
167–68, 189; works of, 3
Germany, Germans: Caesar's war with (*see*
Caesar); Caracalla buys peace with, 121;
Caracalla's wars in, 94; Corbulo in, 12,
110; Domitian's wars in, 92; ethnography of, 72, 75–77; Gaius' war in, 91;
geography and exploration of, 27, 29,
51; Germanicus' war in, 67, 90, 143–44,
167–68, 189; Maximinus' war in, 94, 116;
Nero Drusus' campaigns in, 167, 188;
peace with Commodus, 87; receipt of
subsidies from Claudius and Domitian,
179–80; revolt of, in A.D. 9, 90, 189, 192;
Severus Alexander's offer of money to,
98, 121, 179; Tiberius' campaigns in, 90,
188; as untrustworthy, 71; Vitellius withdrawal of troops from, 96; wars with
Rome under Augustus, 89. *See also* Arminius; Chatti; Cherusci; Frisii; Rhine
frontier
Getae, 10, 30
gladiators, conscription into army, 87
globe, as symbol, 169
glory (*fama, doxa*), general, 162–71, 194–
202; as motivation for war, 4, 186, 198–
99, 200–201; control of, by emperor,
9–10, 14, 200–202
governors, provincial: role of in foreign
relations decisions, 9–14; qualifications
of for office, 16–20
Gracchus, Ti. Sempronius (cos. 177,
163 B.C.), 166
grand strategy, defined, 81
gratitude, role in foreign relations, 218–19
greed, as motive for war, 153–54, 186
Greek intellectuals, 6, 199

Hadrian (emperor): and army discipline,
206; and Bar-Kochba revolt, 102, 193;
contemplation of abandoning Dacia, 7;
destruction of Trajan's Danube bridge,
149; foreign policy of, 121, 159, 199–200;
statue of, trampling barbarian, 195; and

taxes, 133; and withdrawal from eastern
provinces, 94
Hadrian's wall, 40, 111, 113, 114, 115
Hanno the Carthaginian (explorer, ca.
480 B.C.), 51, 55
Harris, W. V., 215
Helvetii, 182, 185
Herodian (historian): on Commodus'
withdrawal from Danube war, 1; on the
defense of the empire, 111; on the Parthian army, 70; on Severus Alexander's
negotiations with Ardashir, 173; social
status, 3
Herodotus (historian), 18, 26, 57, 61, 73
Hippocratic corpus, 73
Historia Augusta, on Severus Alexander's
published itineraries, 28, 146
historiography, statistics in, 105–6
Homer, 26, 65, 172
honor (*decus*): defined, 174; role of in
foreign relations, 4, 22, 107–8, 171–94,
208–10, 215–17, 221
Horace (poet), 3, 186–87, 205
hostages, general, 70, 159, 180; Augustus'
Parthian, 58, 68, 172, 174, 179; Corbulo's
demands from Vologeses, 177; given by
Artabanus, 175; given by Romans to
Samnites, 219; in Caesar's Gallic wars,
182; Macrinus restoration to Armenia,
181; from Numantia, 218; taken by Plautius Silvanus, 10, 163
Hostilius Mancinus, C. *See* Mancinus
Hyginus (land surveyor), on the assessment of tribute, 133n
Hyperboreans, 54

Iazyges: agreement of with Vespasian's
generals, 96; Marcus Aurelius' plans
to exterminate, 98, 116, 121; required to
furnish cavalry, 87; trade with, regulated
by Marcus Aurelius, 113
Iberia (kingdom), 11, 118, 176
Iceni, revolt of. *See* revolt, of Boudicca.
Illyricum: Augustus' conquest of, 33, 89;
revolt of, 88–89, 135
imperator (title), 5, 9, 196
imperium, 14
Inchtuthil, 97n
India: embassies to Rome, 57, 172; geography of, 26, 40, 56; trade routes
to, 35
Indus River, 56, 57n, 59

inflation, 131–32, 137–39
information. *See* ethnography; geography; intelligence, strategic
Inguiomerus, 204
inhabited world. *See* oikoumene
iniuria, 185
intelligence, strategic, 66–70
Ireland: Agricola's plans for conquest of, 104; geography and exploration of, 35, 44, 53
Isaac, Benjamin, 21
Isidore of Seville (d. A.D. 636), round maps of, 47
Isidorus of Charax (geographer), 34
Italicus (king of Cherusci), 180
itineraries, general, 27–29, 39–40, 43, 146; of Alexander's march, 35; Antonine, 28, 39, 146; *Parthian Stations,* 34–35; Peutinger Table, 39–40, 42–43. See also *periploi*
Iulius Agricola, Cn. *See* Agricola
Iulius Caesar Drusus. *See* Drusus
Iulius Caesar, C. *See* Caesar, C. Iulius; Gaius Caesar
Iulius Civilis, C. *See* Civilis
Iulius Sacrovir. *See* Sacrovir
Iulius Solinus, C. *See* Solinus
Iulius Vindex, C. *See* Vindex
Iuthungi, negotiations with Aurelian, 182–83

Jerusalem, 151, 152, 193
Jews. *See* Judaea
John Lydus (d. ca. A.D. 560), on Trajan's Dacian War, 150
Josephus, Flavius (historian): on the fall of Jotapata, 106; on the function of the army, 101; role in revolt of Judaea, 102; on the Roman army, 207; on the sack of Jerusalem, 151; on the triumph of Titus, 151
Jotapata, 106
Juba II (king of Mauretania), 34, 55
Judaea, Jews: army in, 102; nomad threat in, 113; revolt of, 95, 96, 101–2; tax on , 139. *See also* Bar-Kochba revolt; Jerusalem; Josephus; Titus, triumph.
Julian (emperor), 3
Julius Maternus, exploration of Africa, 31, 64
just war, 184–85, 219. *See also* fetial law

kings, given by Augustus to Parthians, 176; given by Domitian to Dacians, 118, 179; given by Rome in general, 117, 177–79; given by Tiberius to Parthians, 67–68
knights. *See* equestrians

latitude, measuring, 30
legates: imperial, 9–14, 16–20; legionary, 17
legions: command of, 17; demobilized by Vespasian, 87; lost in battle, 14, 82, 90, 188–89, 190; new, 86, 87, 88, 91, 92, 94, 103; number of, 82–84, 215; size of, 82; transfer of, in wartime, 95–96. *See also* army
letters to the senate: casualty figures in, 106; as geographical sources, 32–33
Licinius Crassus, M. (cos. 30 B.C.), 9, 120, 200
Licinius Mucianus, C. *See* Mucianus
Lippe River, 167
Livy (historian), 18; on the battle of the Caudine Forks, 219–20
Lollius, M. (d. A.D. 2), 188
longitude, established by eclipses, 30
love poetry, 3
Lucan (epic poet), 2; on the *oikoumene,* 46; on the Parthians, 73–74; round maps illustrating, 47, *48*
Lucian (satirist): on historiography, 32, 106, 169; on Severianus' invasion of Armenia, 13–14
Lucius Verus, emperor. *See* Verus, Lucius
Lydus, John. *See* John Lydus

Macrinus (emperor): military pay cuts by, 140; peace with Parthians, purchase of, 121, 181; tax cuts by, 140
Macrobius, 47, 64
Maeatae, 121
Maecenas, C., 7
Mancinus, C. Hostilius (cos. 137 B.C.), 219
mandata, 10
Manilius, M. (poet), 56
manpower. *See* army, size of
maps, general, 4, 24–25, 41–66; of Agrippa, 49–51, *50;* of Armenia, 28; cartographic projection, 47–49; of Ethiopia, 28, 37; *mappaemundi,* 47, *48;* and military strategy, 60–61; rare in antiquity, 41–43; round vs. oblong, 46–47. *See also* geography

Marcomanni: Marcus Aurelius' occupation of, 120; Marcus Aurelius' war with, 109; peace with Commodus, 87; receipt of subsidies, 180; Tiberius' war with, 88; trade with, regulated by Marcus Aurelius, 113

Marcus Aurelius, emperor. *See* Aurelius, Marcus

Marinus (geographer): on the exploration of Africa, 31; on the geography of Asia, 36; on the geography of Ireland, 35, 36

Marius, C., 218

Maroboduus (king of Marcomanni, d. A.D. 37), 88, 181, 192

Mars Ultor (the Avenger); Adamklissi monument dedicated to, 190; temple of, 152, 184, 187, 188

Marsi, 205

Martial (poet), on Domitian's victory in Dacia, 190

Martianus Capella, 64

Massagetae, 73

Maternus, Iulius. *See* Julius Maternus

Mauretania Tingitana, army in, 101

Maximinus Thrax (emperor): conquest to ocean, plans of, 61; raising of military pay by, 131; war in Germany, 94, 99, 116

Megasthenes, 56, 57

Mela, Pomponius. *See* Pomponius Mela

Menander Rhetor, 191

merchants, as geographical sources, 35–37

merit, as qualification for office, 19–20

Meroë (city in Ethiopia), 37, 56, 164

Mesopotamia: annexed by Trajan, 94; conquered by Severus, 94, 103, 115, 118; frontier, 111; geography of, 115; recaptured by Parthians under Severus, 98; restored by Hadrian, 94

milestones, 39, 148, 197

military tribunate, 17

mines, 129, 136–37, 144, 154–56, 214

Mithridates (king of Armenia), 68–69

Mithridates VIII (king of Bosporus), 168

Moesia (provinces), 88, 96

Mommsen, Theodor, 214

Mona (Anglesey), 11, 97, 120

money, barbarians' attitude toward, 75, 76. *See also* coinage; economic factors in foreign relations; subsidies

morality, as qualification for office, 20

Mucianus, C. Licinius, 29, 96, 116

mutiny, of A.D. 14, 127–28

Nabata, 164

Nasamones, 101, 120, 135, 192, 205

Nearchus, 56

Nero (emperor): advisers to, 2, 6–7, 8; and Armenian crisis of A.D. 54, 6, 112; and Armenian war, 69, 92 (*see also* Corbulo); contemplation of withdrawal from Britain, 178; devaluation of coinage, 138n, 147–48; exploratory missions under, 37; false Neros, 101; Ethiopian and Caspian campaigns, plans for, 60, 92, 95, 153; rapacity of, 134, 153–54; recruiting of new legion, 87; and Tiridates, 177–78; squandering of money, 136

Nerva (emperor), 133–34, 136

Nervii, 182

New Carthage, 119

Nile River, 44

Nisibis, 118

nomads: barbarians described as, 72–75; as military threat, 113

Numantia, 218, 219

Numidia, 113. *See also* Tacfarinas

ocean, 44, 53, 55, 65; as boundary, 4, 110, 115, 169; as goal of conquest, 60, 61, 93, 98, 169; navigation of, 51, 60, 143, 167

Octavian (C. Iulius Caesar Octavianus). *See* Augustus

office: senatorial, 14; equestrian, 14, 17n, 20; qualifications for holding, 16–20

oikoumene: general concept of, 44–47, 51, 55, 56; personified on *Gemma Augustea*, 196; Roman conquest of, 169, 212

Onasander (tactician): on choosing a general, 19–20; on the just war, 184–85

Onesicritus, 56

Oppius Sabinus, killed in Dacia, 92, 190

orbis terrarum. See oikoumene

Ordovices, 32, 120, 193

Orkney islands, 29

Osroeni, revolt of, 118

Otho (emperor), 87, 96

Ovid: on the climate of Tomis, 77; on Gaius' eastern expedition, 188; on the retrieval of standards from Parthia, 187

Paetus, L. Caesennius. *See* Caesennius Paetus

Palatine hill, 211

Palus Maeotis, 38, 44, 54

Parthia, Parthians: in Augustan iconography, 187; Augustan poets anticipation of war with, 186–87, 205; Augustus' receipt of hostages from, 172, 179; Augustus' retrieval of standards from, 60, 107, 174, 187; crisis of A.D. 54, 6–7, 12, 112; ethnography of, 66–67, 70–71, 73–74; geography of, 34–35, 40, 58–59; lack of military discipline, 203–4; Macrinus, purchase of peace with, 121; Mesopotamia, recapture of under Severus, 98; negotiations with Vitellius, 10, 110, 174–75; perceived as rival of Rome, 107; relations with Julio-Claudian emperors, 106–7; Roman relations with, 107–8, 177; seeking of king from Augustus, 176; seeking of king from Tiberius, 67–68; Trajan, relations under, 119; Verus, war with 116, 118, 188–89; Vespasian, agreement with, 96; Vespasian, relations under, 112; war of Caracalla, 94. See also Artabanus; Phraataces; Phraates; Vologeses; Vonones.

Patrocles (explorer, 3rd century B.C.), 51, 53

patronage, 16, 19

Paullus, L. Aemilius. See Aemilius Paullus

peace: and corruption of discipline, 205–6; Forum of Peace, 152, 193

peace treaties, general, 12, 173–83; of Corbulo with Parthians, 177–78; of Domitian with Decebalus, 92, 121, 173; of Macrinus with Parthians, 121; of Marcus Aurelius with Iazyges, 87; of Tiberius with Maroboduus, 88, 192; truce of Paetus with Parthians, 177–78. See also diplomacy; subsidies

periploi, 36, 37–38, 39, 43

Periplus Maris Erythraei, 36–37, 46; on Arabia's wealth, 78–79

Persia, Persians, 98, 116. See also Ardashir; Severus Alexander

Pertinax (emperor): property, auction of, 136, 141; economic measures of, 140–41; subsidies, ends payment of, 159–60

Petronius, P. (prefect of Egypt), 10, 28, 164

Peutinger Table, 39–40, 42–43

Pharasmanes (king of Iberia), 68–69, 176

Philip V (king of Macedon, 221–179 B.C.), 214, 218–19

philosophy, and aristocratic education, 15–16

Phraataces (Phraates V, Parthian king 3/2 B.C.–A.D. 2), 107, 110

Phraates IV (king of Parthia, ca. 38–3/2 B.C.), 58, 174

Plautius Silvanus Aelianus, Ti. (governor of Moesia), 10, 95, 110, 117, 162–63

Plautius, Aulus, 9, 102

Pliny the Elder: on Arabia's wealth, 79; on the Chauci, 77; on the circumnavigation of oikoumene, 51; as friend of Vespasian, 2, 20; on geographical exploration, 26–27; on geographies of Isidorus and Juba, 34; on the geography of Africa, 39, 55–56; on the geography of Arabia, 30; on the geography of Britain, 52; on the geography of Europe, 59; on the geography of India, 56–57; on the geography of Parthia, 58–59; on the geography of Scandinavia, 54; history of German wars, 27; on the map of Agrippa, 49; on the mines of Spain, 136–37; on the oikoumene, 46; sources for, 26, 65; on spoils in triumphal ceremonies, 152; on towns captured in Arabia and Ethiopia, 164–65; works of, 2, 20

Pliny the Younger: critique of Domitian's foreign policy, 181, 183; letters of recommendation, 20; as member of Trajan's council, 2; Panegyric, 169; praise of Trajan's attack on Dacia, 208–9; praise of Trajan's foreign policy, 184, 159; wealth of, 123, 125

plunder: and barbarians, 74; as benefit of war, 22, 150–54, 214; return of, in peace treaties, 181

Plutarch: on inadequate maps, 47; on the triumph of Aemilius Paullus, 152

Polyaenus (tactician), 18

Polybius (historian): on barbarians, inferior discipline of, 204; on Celts, 71, 74; exploration of African coast, 55; geography in, 212; on Popilius' circle, 213; on Roman imperialism, 212; on the sack of New Carthage, 119

polygamy, among barbarians, 71

Pompeius Trogus. See Trogus

Pompeius, Q. (cos. 141 B.C.), 218

Pompey (Cn. Pompeius Magnus): campaign in Caucasus region, 39; as cause of war with Caesar, 185; eastern triumph of, 153, 166; inscriptions of recording

Pompey (Cn. Pompeius Magnus) (*cont'd*)
    eastern conquests of, 166; trophies of in
    Pyrenees, 166
Pomponius Mela (geographer): on Brit-
    ain, 27, 40, 65; on Germans, 72; on the
    oikoumene, 46, 51; sources of, 26
Pontus, revolt of, 101
Popilius Laenas, C., 213
portoria, 156–57
Posidonius (d. ca. 51 B.C.), on the geogra-
    phy of the Caucasus region, 39
praemia, 126–27
praepositi annonae (office), 146
praetorian guard, 85, 141n
praetorian prefect (office), 6
praetorship (office), 14, 16–17
prefect of Egypt (office), 14
prestige. *See* glory; honor
Prima Porta statue, 187
Principate, defined, 5
prisoners: depicted on coins and monu-
    ments, 195; mutilation of, 192; paraded
    in triumph, 168; return of, in peace
    treaties, 181
Propertius, Sex. (poet), 186
Ptolemy (Claudius Ptolemaeus, astrono-
    mer, geographer): on cartographic pro-
    jection, 48; geography of Asia, 36; ge-
    ography of Britain, 39, 115; geography
    of Dacia, 61, 110; geography of Europe,
    51–52; geography of Scotland, 28–29,
    52–53; on inadequate maps, 47; influ-
    ence of, 61, 64; manuscript tradition,
    48n; world map, 61–64, *62–63;* on the
    width of Africa, 31–32
Punic wars: first, 221; second, 214, 215,
    221–22; third, 218
Pytheas (explorer), 52, 53

Quadi: Marcus Aurelius occupation of,
    120; peace with Commodus, 87; receipt
    of subsidies, 180; trade with, regulated
    by Marcus Aurelius, 113
Quadratus, Ummidius (legate of Syria),
    12, 69, 179
Quinctius Flamininus, T. *See* Flamininus
quinqueremes, 221
Quintilius Varus, P., 67, 82, 90, 167, 189

rationality: of Roman agriculture, 123–26;
    of Roman foreign relations, 22, 108–9

reconnaissance, 34–8
records: agricultural accounts, 123–24;
    military, 105; triumphal, 30, 152, 165–6
Republic, defined, 5
reputation. *See* glory
Res Gestae Divi Augusti, 163–64
revenge, in foreign policy, 22–23, 69, 119,
    120–21, 184–94
revenues, imperial, 132; *annona militaris,*
    144–45; from auction of imperial prop-
    erty, 134, 136, 141, 143; from auction
    tax, 157; from confiscation, 134; from
    gold crown tax, 134; from indemnities,
    152; from indictions, 134–35, 144; from
    mines, 129, 136, 154–56; from plunder,
    150–54; from *portoria,* 156–57; from
    taxes, 132–36, 139–40; from tribute,
    132–36, 157–58
revolt, general, 86, 95, 100–104, 120–21,
    183, 191–94; of Adiabeni, 118; of Armi-
    nius and Cherusci, 90, 192; of Avidius
    Cassius, 98, 101, 201; Bar-Kochba, 102,
    193; of Boudicca, 86, 97, 102–3, 105–6,
    156, 193; of Cantabri, 100, 192; of Cap-
    padocia, 157; of Civilis, 86, 97; of Frisii,
    118, 135, 192; of Illyricum (Dalmatia,
    Pannonia), 5, 88–89, 135, 192; of Judaea
    or Jews, 5, 95, 96, 101–2; of Nasamones,
    101, 120, 135, 192; of Ordovices in Wales,
    120, 193; of Osroeni, 118; of Pontus, 101;
    of Sacrovir, 101, 156; of Scottish tribes
    under Severus, 193; of Tacfarinas, 193;
    tax, 135–36, 139, 157; of Trajan's eastern
    provinces, 104; of Thracians, 86, 118; of
    Vindex, 95, 154
Rhapta, 36
rhetoric, and education of aristocracy, 3,
    15–16
Rhine frontier, 111; Domitian's wars, 109;
    fortified by Germanicus, 143; invasions
    under Severus Alexander, 13, 98–99;
    regulation of trade across, 113
Rhine River: as boundary, 40, 110, 167;
    bridged by Caesar, 119, 216; bridged by
    Germanicus, 167; in Caesar, 75
rhinoceroses, 31–32, 37
Rhipaean Mountains, 54
Rhoxolani: invasion of Moesia, 96; and
    Plautius Silvanus, 162; receipt of subsi-
    dies from Trajan, 121
rivers, as boundaries, 110
roads, 114, 144, 145, 148, 157

Romulus, hut of, 211
Rubrius Gallus (governor of Moesia), 97, 112

Sabaeans, 30
Sabinus, Oppius. *See* Oppius Sabinus
Sacrovir, Iulius (led revolt of Gaul in A.D. 21), 101, 156
Sallust (historian): on the destruction of Cispa, 218; round map illustration, 47
Samnites, 219–20
Sanni, 121, 135–36
Sarmatians: embassador to Augustus, 172; invasion of Moesia in A.D. 69, 96, 112; repressed by Plautius Silvanus, 10, 95, 162. *See also* Iazyges, Rhoxolani
satraps, 4
Scandinavia, geography of, 54
Scipio Aemilianus, P. Cornelius (d. 129 B.C.), 152
Scipio Africanus, P. Cornelius (d. 183 B.C.), 119
Scipio, Lucius Cornelius (cos. 190 B.C.), triumph, 152
Scotland. *See* Britain
Scythia, Scythians, 10, 13; ancestors of Parthians, 71; embassador to Augustus, 172; in Herodotus, 73
Sea of Azov. *See* Palus Maeotis
Sebastopolis (in Pontus), 38
Second Sophistic, 18
Segestes, 67
Sejanus, L. Aelius, 8
self-sufficiency, as agricultural principle, 125–26
senate: letters to, 32–33, 106; role of in foreign relations, 5–6, 8, 12; senatorial order, 14. *See also* aristocracy; office, senatorial.
Seneca, L. Annaeus (philosopher): as adviser to Nero, 2, 7; on barbarians' lack of discipline, 203; ethnography and geography in, 79–80; on Germans, 72; on the *oikoumene*, 46; on revenge, 186; and revolt of Boudicca, 156; treatise on India, 57, 79
Seneca the Elder, L. Annaeus, 15
Senones, 220
Septimius Flaccus, exploration of Africa, 31, 64
Septimius Severus, L. (emperor). *See* Severus

Severianus, Sedatius (governor of Cappadocia), 189
Severus (emperor): annexation of Mesopotamia, 94; and army, 139; confiscation of property, 134; conquest of Mesopotamia, 29, 94, 103, 115, 118; devaluation of coinage, 137, 139; exploration of Britain, 30; and increase of military pay, 130–31; and military spending, 148; reasons for British war, 206; sack of Ctesiphon, 108; and supply of eastern wars, 29, 146; suppression of revolt in Scotland, 121, 193; war in Britain, 94, 106, 116, 117, 121
Severus Alexander (emperor), 5; advisers, 7, 8; and diplomacy with Persia and Germans, 13, 173; encouragement of troops, 184; itineraries, publication of, 146; and march to the Rhine, 98–99; and money to Germans, 179; and Persian crisis, 7, 13, 98, 116; and Rhine invasions, 7, 13, 98–99, 121
Siculus Flaccus (land surveyor), on military supply, 146
Silures, 102
Sirmium, 88
slaves, 153
Solinus, C. Iulius (geographer), 64
Spain: army in, 100, 101; geography of, 39, 52; mines in, 136–37, 154–55, 214; revolt of, 100, 192
spolia opima, 200
Sri Lanka. *See* Taprobane
stade, length of, 31n
standards, military: Augustus' retrieval of from Parthia, 107, 174, 187; captured from Lollius, 188; ceremonial adoration of, 163, 173, 175, 177; Germanicus' retrieval of from Germany, 187, 189; ridiculed by Arminius, 175; Trajan's retrieval of from Dacia, 191
statistics, in ancient sources, 105–6
Statius, P. Papinius (poet): on the *a rationibus*, 129; on Domitian's clemency, 191; flattery of Domitian, 169; on military supply, 146
stereotypes. *See* ethnography
Strabo (geographer), 3; on Aelius Gallus' motives in Arabia, 78; on Britain, 102, 104, 155, 160–61; on cartographic projection, 48; on geographical exploration, 26; on the geography of Africa, 55; on

Strabo (geographer) (*continued*)
the geography of Arabia, 30; on the geography of Britain, 52; on the geography of Europe, 51; on the geography of India, 57; on the geography of Ireland, 44; on geography and warfare, 26; on Germans, 72; on Homer, 65; on the *oikoumene,* 44; on Parthia, 58–59; reception of, 44; sources of, 26
subsidies, to barbarian tribes or kingdoms, 98, 121, 159, 178, 179–80, 182–83
Suetonius Paulinus, C., 96; in Britain, 11; defeat of Boudicca, 102–3, 106, 205; exploration of Africa, 55; invasion of Mona, 97, 102, 201
Suetonius Tranquillus, C. (biographer): on Augustus' conquests, 184; on Augustus' testament, 128; on Claudius' donative, 140; on Domitian's pay raise, 139; on Domitian's wars, 188; on Tiberius' foreign policy of, 91, 173
superbia, 175–76
supply, of army, 134, 143–48
Syene (city in Egypt), 28, 37

Tabula Peutingeriana. *See* Peutinger Table
Tacfarinas, 193, 204
Tacitus, Cornelius (historian): on Artabanus' threats, 175; on Augustus' testament, 128; on Boudicca's revolt, 105–6; on Britain's mineral resources, 156; career and works of, 2; on Corbulo's army in Armenia, 95; on the dangers of peace, 206; on the distribution of the army, 104; on Domitian's German wars, 92; on the Elbe River, 167; on the foreign policy of Tiberius, 91, 173; on the Forth-Clyde isthmus, 115; on the function of the army, 101; on Galba's unpaid donative, 140; geography in, 65; on the geography of Britain, 27, 52; on Germanicus' German war, 167–68; on Germans, 73, 75; on imperialism in Britain, 11; on the mutiny of A.D. 14, 127–28; on Nero's advisers, 6–7; on the Parthian hostages, 174; on Roman-Parthian relations, 176–78; on speech of Calgacus, 207–8; on subsidies paid to Germans, 180; on trade across the Rhine frontier, 113; on the tribute, 129
tactical treatises, 18, 19–20
Tanais river, 44, 164, 172

Taprobane (Sri Lanka), geography of, 37, 57–58
Tauric Chersonese, 10, 38, 162
Taurus Mountains, 44, 51
taxes, general, 132–36; auction tax, 157; cut by Macrinus, 140; Domitian rapacious collection of, 139; emancipation from, 140; gold crown, 134; indictions, 144; on inheritance, 126, 140; on luxury trade, 114; *portoria,* 114, 156–57; remissions, 132–33; revolt over, 135–36, 139, 157; tribute, 132–36, 157–58
Templum Pacis. See Forum of Peace
Tencteri, 113
terra incognita, 24, 61
terror, in foreign policy, 22, 115–17, 119–22, 221–22
Teutoburg Forest, 167, 189
Themistius (orator), on the empire's frontiers, 115
Thrace, Thracians, 11, 67; Crassus in, 120; ethnography of, 74; revolt of, in A.D. 26, 86, 118; special units of, 87
Thucydides (historian), 18
Thule, 53, 93
Tiberius (emperor): campaign against Marcomanni, 88; council of, 8; as despised by Artabanus, 175; donation of king to Parthians, 67–68; and donative, 140; erection of temples from spoils, 152; and Frisian revolt, 192; nonexpansionist policy of, 91; relations with Parthia, 107, 173; Rhine campaigns of, 90; reduction of auction tax, 157; and Vitellius, 10; as "weak" emperor, 91, 119, 173
Tigranocerta, 65
Tigris River, 110
Tiridates (king of Armenia, reign of Nero), 95, 177
Tiridates (king of Armenia in A.D. 217), 181
titulature, of emperors, 196–97
Titus (emperor), triumph of, 151, 167, 193
Tomis, 77
trade: as benefit of empire, 156–57; luxury, 114, 136, 156–57; regulations on Rhine / Danube, 113; routes, to India, 35; routes, to Africa, 36; taxes on, 156–57
tragedy, 3, 74
Trajan (emperor): annexation of Dacia, 120; and causes of first Dacian war, 189–90; and causes of second Dacian war, 191; and Dacian wars, 27–28, 60, 67, 93,

103; Danube bridge, as builder of, 148–49; eastern conquests of, 104, 107, 93, 94; epic poem about, 169; foreign policy of, praise for, 159, 180, 183, 184; as militaristic, 119; military spending of, 148; and plunder from Dacian war, 150–51; retrieval of standards from Dacia, 191; road building, at Iron Gates of Orsova, 114, 148; road building, in east and Italy, 145; self-comparison to Alexander, 33; and subsidization of Rhoxolani, 121; and supply for Parthian war, 146; as unrapacious, 144; *via nova Traiana* in Arabia, as builder of, 114, 157

Trajan's column. *See* Column of Trajan
Trajan's forum. *See* Forum of Trajan
travel time, 11, 99
treaties. *See* peace treaties
tribute, general, 132–36, 157–58; assessments raised by Vespasian, 133; as levied in grain, 144, 214
triumph (ceremony), 4, 9–10; of Balbus, 30, 166; eastern, of Pompey, 153; geographical elements in, 30, 166–67; parade of prisoners, 168; parade of spoils, 151–53; privilege of emperor, 168; of Sulla, 166; of Titus, 151, 167, 193
triumphal arches. *See* arches
triumphalia (triumphal ornaments), 200–201
Trogus, Pompeius (historian), on Parthians, 71
trophies, 165, 166, 167, 170, 190, 195
Tullius Cicero, M. *See* Cicero, M. Tullius
Tullius Cicero, Q. *See* Cicero, Q. Tullius

Ulpian (lawyer), 129, 207
Ummidius Quadratus. *See* Quadratus

Varus, P. Quintilius. *See* Quintilius Varus
Vegetius: on the discipline of the army, 207; on itineraries, 28
Velleius Paterculus (historian; praetor A.D. 15), on the *clades Lolliana,* 188
Veneti, 219

vengeance. *See* revenge
Vercingetorix, 78
Verus, Lucius (emperor): and Avidius Cassius, 201; and causes of Parthian war, 188–89; Parthian war, 32–33, 97, 108, 116, 118; as restorer of discipline in eastern army, 207; and roads for Parthian war, 145; and supply of Parthian war, 146
Vespasian (emperor): advisers to, 2, 8; as dealer with eastern kings, 96; demobilization of legions, 87; Forum of Peace, as builder of, 152, 193; imperial finances under, 136; as reorganizer of eastern frontier, 112; tax increases by, 133
via nova Traiana, in Arabia, 114, 145, 148, 157
Victoria, on coins, 168
vigintiviri (office), 16
Vindex, C. Iulius, 95, 154
Vipsanius Agrippa, M. *See* Agrippa
Virgil (poet), on Augustus' conquests, 169
viri militares, 17n
Vitellius (emperor), 87, 96
Vitellius, L. (cos. A.D. 34), 10, 12, 110, 174–5
Vitruvius (architectural writer), on chorography, 42
Vologeses I (Parthian king, A.D. 51/2–79/80), 67, 69, 177, 179
Vologeses IV (Parthian king, A.D. 147/8–191/2), 120, 188
Vonones (king of Parthia, A.D. 6–12, and of Armenia), 71, 175

war: authorization for, 10, 12; causes (*see* causes, of war); civil, 84, 87, 95–97, 98; expense of, 142–49; foreign vs. civil, 170; intelligence, 66–70; just war, 184–85, 219; plunder, 150–54; reconnaissance, 34–38. *See also* army; auxiliaries; fetial law; legions; revolt; *individual regions and emperors*
Whittaker, C. R., 21
women, 6, 7; barbarian, 71, 73

Compositor: G&S Typesetters, Inc.
Printer: Haddon Craftsmen
Text: 10/13 Galliard
Display: Galliard